The Jews of Europe
in the Modern Era

The Jews of Europe in the Modern Era

A Socio-historical Outline

by

Victor Karady

CEU PRESS

Central European University Press
Budapest   New York

© 2004 by Victor Karady
English translation © Tim Wilkinson 2004

First published in Hungarian as *Zsidóság Európában a modern korban. Társadalomtörténeti vázlat* by Új Mandátum Könyvkiadó, Budapest in 2000, pp. 87–392 and 415–464.

English edition published in 2004 by
Central European University Press

An imprint of the

Central European University Share Company
Nádor utca 11, H–1051 Budapest, Hungary
Tel: +36–1–327–3138 or 327–3000
Fax: +36–1–327–3183
E-mail: *ceupress@ceu.hu*
Website: *www.ceupress.com*

400 West 59th Street, New York NY 10019, USA
Tel: +1–212–547–6932
Fax: +1–212–548–4607
E-mail: *mgreenwald@sorosny.org*

Translated by Tim Wilkinson

ISBN 963 9241 52 0 Cloth

Library of Congress Cataloging-in-Publication Data

Karady, Victor.
[Zsidóság Európában a modern korban. English]
The Jews of Europe in the modern era: a socio-historical outline /
  by Victor Karady.p. cm.
Includes bibliographical references and index.
ISBN 9639241520 (hardbound)
1. Jews--Europe--History--19th century. 2. Jews--Europe--History--20th
  century. I. Title.
DS135.E83.K3713 2004
940'.04924--dc22

2004002565

Printed in Hungary by
Akadémiai Nyomda

In memoriam

Mihály Szamek (1854–1933)
József Grünbaum (1903–1945)

Contents

Chapter 4   **The Road to the Shoah. From Christian Anti-Judaism to Radical Anti-Semitism**

List of Tables

Preface

This book attempts to outline some of the long term processes and structural transformations considered as essential for the interpretation of major changes seen in the European Jewish populations during, approximately, the last two centuries. The focus is laid here on Ashkenazi Jewry, though occasional references are also made to the destinies of Sephardi groups in the Balkans and other Mediterranean countries. Topically, my investigations are marked in chronological order by the beginnings of the decisive diversification of Jewish identity options following the 'Berlin *Haskalah*' (Jewish Enlightenment), the various reactions to the challenges of civil emancipation and chances of integration in emerging nation-states or multi-national empires since the French Revolution, the crises of assimilationism due to the age of political anti-Semitism in the outgoing 19th century, the rise of Nazism and the Shoah, new conditions of social accomodation of survivors since 1945.

The organization of the study, though historical by nature, ignores the criteria of a strictly chronological narrative and responds rather to the needs of an analytical discussion of developments, occurrences and events affecting sizable Jewish clusters and modifying their collective attitudes, their relations with given Gentile environments, particularly their chances of professional self-assertion, mobility and creativity.

Thus the first chapter presents the demographic specificities of modern Jewry (notably its very early engagement in the 'demographic transition'), as well as striking aspects of the professional and economic restratification of a proto-bourgeois cluster into a largely middle class social formation. This gave rise, since the late 19th century, to the spectacularly high share of Jews in entrepreneurial and modernizing economic, professional as well as intellectual elites in Berlin, Paris, Vienna or Budapest, but also to the 'abnormal' social structure of contemporary Jewry (close to the reverse of gentile societies)— much deplored by 'enlightened' Jewish reformists and Zionists alike.

The second chapter is entirely dedicated to the three signal models of modern 'Jewish policies' in Europe leading ultimately to legal emancipation. This was carried out by and large unconditionally in the West, inspired by the recognition of civil equality as a basic human right following social philosophies of the Enlightenment. Emancipation was much more controversial, conflictual and protracted in Central Europe where the post feudal powers that be in Germany and the Habsburg Empire tended to link it to certified assimilationist achievements of those concerned. In Eastern Europe full civil emancipation was denied to Jews till the end of the first World War (1919 in Romania, the February 1917 Revolution in Russia).

The third chapter deals with the complex issues connected to the new collective identity options opening up following agendas of social integration and cultural assimilation inaugurated by Moses Mendelssohn's *Haskalah* movement in Berlin and the first emancipation decrees of the revolutionary National Assembly in France. The crises of assimilationism staged by the emergence of political anti-Semitism in the late 1870s and the 1880s provoked the partial reorientation of modern Jewish identity strategies towards universalistic salvation ideologies (like socialism) on the one hand, Jewish nationalism (Zionism, autonomism, *Bund*) on the other hand.

The fourth chapter is dedicated to the development and historical transmutations of anti-Judaism, cumulating by the outgoing 19th century in fateful formulations of the infamous modern 'Aryan myth' and racist political anti-Semitism. Based on social Darwinist references this served as the direct harbinger of the Brown Plague under the Third Reich. The devastating consequences of the genocide in various countries under Nazi rule or influence, though an utterly external factor in Jewish social history and thus not a central concern of this book, are summarily evoked here.

The last chapter sums up the new social conditions of Jewish existence in post-Shoah Europe, including the ambiguities of liberation in the sovietized part of the continent, the difficult return and reception of survivors in their home countries, the impact of the State of Israel on the exodus of eastern Jewry. The importance of the reference to Israel, the genocide ('people of the Shoah'), further secularization as well as religious revivalism in the reconstruction of new Jewish identities is discussed in special sub-chapters. The implications and reasons of the attraction exerted by the Communist mirage, the opposition of Soviet type and Western anti-Semitism as well as renovated patterns and new chances of social integration in European societies offer the main topical perspectives for a conclusion that warns against too far fetched optimism as to the secure future of Jews in contemporary Europe.

The idea of this book was born from a triple source, my experience of research and teaching, as well as a previous short version of the topic published by Fischer Taschenbuchverlag (Frankfurt).

Since the 1970s I have been indeed committed to the study of social inequalities of education and professional mobility within processes of post-feudal modernization in Western and Central European nation-states (notably in France and in Hungary) as fellow of the French CNRS (*Centre National de la Recherche Scientifique*). This was how I first met the problem of Jews as preeminent 'modernizers' in the European scene of the 19th and 20th century. The main results of these investigations pertaining to empirically grounded historical sociology were published in the *Actes de la Recherche en Sciences Sociales* edited by the late Pierre Bourdieu, my unforgettable mentor.

At the same time I was offered the chance to conduct regular yearly research seminars at the *Ecole des Hautes Etudes en Sciences Sociales* in Paris, where I could test some of the working hypotheses to interpret the trials and tribulations of Jewish populations in contemporary European societies. Since 1993 I am also teaching annual courses on the social history of contemporary Jewry at the Central European University in Budapest. The reactions and questions of my students have vastly helped me in the elaboration of the conceptual framework and foci of the present book. I am also grateful to the CEU for the support granted to further my research on unexplored problem areas of Central European Jewry (like 'over-schooling', conversion patterns, mixed marriages, 'nationalization' of surnames, linguistic shifts, pre- and post-Shoah identity choices). I am also happy to acknowledge the debt I owe for their subsidies to the Hungarian State Support Scheme for Scientific Research (OTKA) and the Hungarian Support Agency for Advanced Research Projects (OKTK). The outcome of my studies partially sponsored by these organizations have been published mostly in Hungarian in a number of recent books[1] and articles.

Finally the present work is much indebted to the *Fischer Taschenbuchverlag* for its initial short version commanded to complete the collection under the serial title *Europaische Geschichte*.[2] The text of this book, translated from French by Judith Klein, has been thoroughly modified, enlarged, corrected and rewritten to be published in Hungarian as a new essay with the permission of the *Fischer Verlag*[3]. The latter publication has served as a basis of the present edition, though I have considerably reorganized the presentation of its chapters, and once again revised and completed the whole study ingeniously translated by Tom Wilkinson - to whom I am equally grateful for some relevant corrections he was kind enough to suggest.

---

[1] See particularly: *Zsidóság, asszimiláció és polgárosodás* /Jewry, assimilation and embourgeoisement/, Budapest, Cserépfalvi 1997; *Felekezeti egyenlőtlenségek és iskolarendszer. Történeti-szociológiai tanulmányok* /Denominational inequalities and school system. Studies in historical sociology/, Budapest, Replika-könyvek, 1997; *Juden in Ungarn : Identitätsmuster und Identitätsstrategien*, Leipzig, Simon Dubnow Institut für jüdische Geschichte und Kultur der Universität Leipzig; *Zsidóság és társadalmi egyenlőtlenségek (1867–1945). Történeti-szociológiai tanulmányok.* /Jewry and social inequalities. Studies in historical sociology/, Budapest, Replika könyvek, 2000; *Önazonosítás és sorsválasztás. A zsidó csoportazonosság történelmi alakváltozásai Magyarországon* /Self-identification and choice of destiny. Historical transformations of Jewish identity in Hungary/, Budapest, Új Mandátum, 2001; (with István Kozma), *Családnév és nemzet. Névpolitika, névváltoztatási mozgalom és nemzetiségi erőviszonyok Magyarországon a reformkortól a kommunizmusig,* /Surnames and nation. Politics of nomination, movement to change names, relation of forces between national clusters in Hungary since the *Vormärz* to Communism/, Budapest, Osiris, 2002; *Túlélők és újrakezdők. Fejezetek a magyar zsidóság szociológiájából 1945 után.* /Survivors and those who start again. Chapters of the sociology of Hungarian Jewry after 1945/, Budapest, Múlt és jövő, 2002; *A túlélés traumái. Újabb fejezetek a magyar zsidóság szociológiájából 1944 előtt és után.* /The trauma of survival. New chapters of the sociology of Hungarian Jewry before and after 1944/, Budapest, Múlt és jövő (forthcoming).

[2] *Gewalterfahrung und Utopie. Juden in der europaischen Moderne.* Frankfurt am Main, 1999. 302 pages.

[3] See *Zsidóság Európában a modern korban. Társadalomtörténeti vázlat.* /Jewry in Europe in the modern age. An outline of social history/, Budapest, Új Mandátum, 2000. 503 pages.

The book is dedicated to the memory of my grandfather on my cherished mother's side and of my would-have-been father-in-law. Both had lived in the 8th district of Budapest. Mihály Szamek was a blacksmith and a Jewish convert into Lutheranism with a German-Hungarian family. József Grünbaum, a victim of the Shoah, was a Magyar-Jewish taxidriver of Orthodox background from Eastern Hungary. His remains are buried in a nameless tomb somewhere in Austria, similarly to over fifty relatives from the same extended family.

Let their souvenir remind us of the tragic diversity in this part of the world of contemporary Jewish destinies. Social history may, possibly, bring us closer to an understanding of their life trajectories or, failing that, help to fulfill the obligation of remembering.

Chapter 1

Demography and Social (Re)Stratification

The Diaspora in Europe and the world in numbers

Before we embark on any historical survey, it is worthwhile outlining the demographic evolution of the population that forms the subject of our study.

It is immediately clear from Table 1 (see p. 44–45) that the world's total Jewish population at the dawn of the modern era, in the late eighteenth century, was considerably less than 2 million. Close to ninety per cent—the vast majority Ashkenazim—lived in Europe, though this continent comprised barely one-sixth of the world's total population. It should be noted that by far the biggest proportion of all the Jews of Europe were to be found within the borders of a single state, Russia, as this is where the great bulk of the Jews of Polish–Lithuanian origin ended up through the successive partitionings of Poland between 1772 and 1795. These overall ratios persisted substantially throughout the nineteenth century. Around 1900 Europe was still home to four-fifths of the world's Jews, who then numbered 10 million (with Russia alone accounting for almost one half), whilst no more than one quarter of all humanity then lived in Europe. Although a shift in the center of gravity of world Jewry to outside Europe was already under way at the end of the nineteenth century, a good part of that development occurred in the twentieth century, and during two periods.

The first of these took place roughly during the thirty years leading up to the First World War, with the main flow of the emigration heading for the United States of America—indeed, with such vigor that by 1920 America's Jews had already grown to become the second greatest concentration within any states of the world (still behind Russia). In 1877, before this big wave of departure got under way, the Jewish community to be found in America still amounted to no more than a rather modest 226,000 in total. The growth in that number was to pick up spectacularly thereafter: by 1918 there were more than 3 million Jews living there, with half of them settling in New York or its immediate environs. The majority of the new arrivals originated from territories that were under Russian sovereignty (with over 2 million emigrants between 1881 and 1914) whilst smaller contingents had come from Austrian Galicia (whence 236,000 set out between 1881 and 1910) or Romania (more than 70,000 started off from there over the same period, though many of those were to stay in Europe).

This rapid, continual influx was reduced to a trickle by strict regulation of immigration (with the US introducing a quota system by national groups under the Immigration Acts of 1921 and 1924). Henceforth growth was more and more due to merely natural reproduction amongst the relatively young immigrant population, so that the numbers of overseas Jews had increased to almost 5 million by the eve of the Second World War. From the inter-war period on, the USA moved to the top of the list of countries comprising the largest Jewish populations, well ahead of Poland and the Soviet Union, in a dead heat for second place with around 3 million each. If we also take into account the half million Jewish immigrants who had meanwhile settled in Canada and Latin America, it would be fair to say that, from then onwards, at least one-third of the world's Jewish population was living overseas, and Europe's Jewish population was not even 57 per cent of a total which, in 1939, amounted to not less than 16.7 million. Thus, the evening-up of the Diaspora's continental distribution in favor of the Americas began well before the Shoah.

The second big world-wide wave of geographical rearrangement of the Jewish population–and at one and the same time probably also the definitive end of its preponderance in Europe–was, directly or indirectly, a consequence of the Nazi reign of terror. The 'final solution' in countries that fell under the dominion of the Third Reich disposed of close to 6 million souls. In 1948 the world's Jewish population had plunged back to 11.3 million, that is, a mere two-thirds of the pre-war total, or in other words, back to the level it had reached by the end of the nineteenth century. This appalling destruction also completely redrew the map of the territorial distribution of the survivors. The majority of those involved in the mass migrations that developed following the Second World War headed for Palestine which, on the 14th of May, 1948, officially became the state of Israel. During the twenty years after its foundation, Israel's population more than trebled, largely through net immigration of Jews. The other main destination remained the United States, which in the decades after the Allied victory was to be home for some 43–44 per cent of world Jewry, with Argentina and Canada as the most popular of the other host countries. Henceforth at least half of the world's Jews would be living on the other side of the Atlantic.

The geographical composition of world Jewry thereby underwent rapid change after the Second World War: the earlier bipolar distribution, with the Ashkenazi Jews of Eastern Europe predominating, was replaced by a quadripolar pattern, with America, Israel, the Soviet Union and Western Europe as its (new or old) territorial centers. One not insignificant concomitant of this rearrangement was that North Africa and the Near East outside Palestine—ancient localities of Jewish civilization—and most Eastern European countries outside the Soviet Union (with Hungary, in population terms, as the only significant, even if not particularly sizeable exception) were gradually to vanish from the Diaspora's spectrum, primarily to the benefit of Israel and Western Europe. A further consequence of the post–1945 situation was that several hitherto secondary centers of settlement were boosted. That concerns historically 'young' population zones of the Diaspora that were settled only late by Europeans: primarily South America, South Africa and Australia. Amongst these secondary drifts, the Arab–Israeli conflict and the East–West Cold War played an instrumental role in the departure of the overwhelming majority of Jews still living in Islamic countries and in the Communist camp (outside the Soviet Union itself) for countries within the democratic West. After around seventeen centuries of virtually absolute European predominance, the total Jewish population in Europe (including the Soviet Union) fell to under a mere one-third of the Diaspora.

The broad thrust of this major geographical restratification, including the population shifts that were directly prompted by the Nazi horrors, is fairly unequivocal. The movement is always directed away from regions marked by intense anti-Jewish pressure towards countries that display less pressure. In this respect too the establishment of Israel was, of course, a new factor of decisive importance since for committed Zionists the Jewish state signified an end to the Diaspora predicament and the beginnings of the historical 'normalization' of the Jewish people, insofar as every Jew could again (at least potentially) expect to find a definitive home on the land of remote ancestors with which the Diaspora, until then, could only maintain connections that, however cherished, were mostly rather symbolic. Seen from that perspective, the Jewish people were therefore 'returning to their own land,' and Israel had regained its place amongst the community of nations. The rocketing growth of the Israeli population, over and above its role in the spiritual and political representation of world Jewry, would now, for the foreseeable future, adumbrate a new, tripolar distribution of ethnic groups claiming their Jewish identity, with two main centers—the Jewish state and America—and a secondary one in Western Europe, as a veritable exodus from the Soviet Union and its successor states got under way already since the early 1970s, a process that has continued, with greater or lesser interruptions, to the present day and in the course of which the vast bulk of Jews living there have by now chosen to depart.

Beginnings of 'strategic' migrations in the modern era and the immigration into Hungary

We cannot touch here on every detail of these often highly complex international trends of migrations. We shall have to make do with sketching the broad thrusts of the population movements that occurred within Europe itself. The return to the West of certain Sephardic groups (descendents of those expelled from Spain and Portugal at the turn of the fifteenth–sixteenth century), particularly Marranos ('hidden Jews' in Christian Mediterranean countries) but also Ashkenazim from Eastern Europe had already started during the Enlightenment period (indeed, even earlier in the Netherlands and England). The displacements that would take place during the modern era were far larger in scale. These affected the former territories of Poland and Lithuania above all, though without ending the numerical preponderance of Jews in these countries within the European Diaspora. For an outline of the most relevant movements in this field, it is best to start with the state of geographical dispersal of Jews in Europe at the beginning of the modern era.

As can be seen from Table 1, the core of the Jewish population around the turn of the eighteenth into the nineteenth century was still entirely located in Eastern Europe.

With the partitioning of Poland–Lithuania, the greater part of this population (approximately 59 per cent) was transferred to Russia. There they represented just 3.5 per cent of the total population of the Tsarist Empire, though a far higher proportion of the populace in the permitted (and also compulsory) 'Pale of Settlement.' Another 11 per cent of European Jewry at that time were living in what had, by then, become the Habsburg province of Galicia (where, progressing from the western to the more easterly areas, they made up between 3 and 8 per cent of the local population). Compared with these conglomerations, other clusters of Jews, whether old-established (as in Bohemia and Moravia) or newer (in the sense that the bulk of their numbers had arisen through settlement in the eighteenth century, including the Jews of Hungary and Moldavia), were much more modest, albeit not negligible. Germany around 1820 accounted for 8 per cent of the European total and thereby, after an interval of three centuries, was once more beginning to occupy a place amongst the more important Jewish centers of population, particularly when, under the terms of the last partition of Poland, a relatively large number of Jews were brought under the protectorate of the Kingdom of Prussia. The Jewish communities living in France, Great Britain, Holland, and other Western European countries were small. Even in aggregate they made up less than 5 per cent of the continent's Jewry. This under-representation of western Jews is startling, even when one also takes account of Amsterdam, which at that time had the biggest urban community of around 30,000–35,000 Jews, most of whom were of Ashkenazi descent. There were substantial Sephardic groups in Europe (outside Amsterdam, London and Bordeaux) only in the Balkans then still under Ottoman suzerainty: Greece, Wallachia, Serbia and Bosnia. Around 1800, for all practical purposes, no Jews had been living in Alpine and Danubian Austria proper (i.e. outside the other Habsburg territories like Bohemia, Moravia, Galicia and Bukovina) or in the states of the Iberian Peninsula al-

ready for some 130 and 300 years, respectively. Spain and Portugal
have in fact remained almost blank spots on the map of the Diaspora
till the twentieth century (though decreasingly so).

Three successive, relatively massive displacements were to take
place in this highly uneven dispersion of populations, heavily
weighted as it was to the eastern territories over the century and a half
between the partitions of Poland and the Shoah.

The first of these lasted from the 1740s up to 1848. A wave of migration originating from Galicia and Bukovina headed principally
towards Hungary, and from all the partitioned Polish territories towards Germany (especially from the region of Poznań [Posen], then
part of Prussia, to the capital, Berlin). During the decades around 1800
less brisk movements could also be observed from these same areas
(primarily from the border regions of the Russian province of Bessarabia) towards Moldavia. The peak of mass immigration into Hungary (at least according to the not fully reliable estimates of the time)
occurred during the two decades of that country's Reform Age, from
the early 1830s, and came to an end in the decade following the 1848–
49 War of Independence.

As to the dimensions of this migration, the figures speak for themselves. Whilst the Jewish population of Galicia, despite the vigorous
natural reproduction, merely doubled over seventy years (rising from
an estimated 212,000 to 449,000 between 1785 and 1857), Hungary's
Jewish population quintupled (from 81,000 to 408,000) in the same
period. By 1910, as a result of numerous other migratory trends
(though admittedly these too originated principally from Galicia,
heading for Vienna in the first place and later America) and an ever
more differential natural movement of populations, the total number
of Jews living in Hungary was already 911,000, and hence by then
considerably in excess of the number of their co-religionists in Galicia
(872,000).

The explanation for this extraordinary wave of migrations, during
which Hungary became the prime goal for Jewish population movements for close to half a century, is to be found in a whole complex of
historical, economic and socio–political reasons.

First of all, Hungary belonged to the Habsburg Empire, and thus
national borders presented no impediment to migration between
provinces. Although the chancellery and Hungary's feudal Diets dab-

bled with plans to curb immigration on more than one occasion, in practice no serious attempt was made to implement control to this effect. Quite the reverse. Living conditions and new legal dispositions could only encourage to settle in the kingdom all those prepared to leave Galicia and Bukovina, economically the most backward and rather stagnating provinces within the Habsburg Empire. Amongst others, the Hungarian Diet passed in 1840 an act of 'semi-emancipation' under which Jews were allowed to settle freely in towns (except in some 'mining cities' endowed with special feudal privileges) and all previous restrictions on their business entrepreneurship were lifted. It is no accident that Jewish immigration into Hungary seems to have peaked during the 1840s. The *shtetl* dwellers did not even have sufficient resources to provide for the basic necessities associated with their high rate of natural reproduction. Moreover, by the nineteenth century, the Polish gentry were showing themselves to be ever less reliable economic and political partners than their predecessors had been during the period of repopulating the Ukraine, to which East Galicia—part of Austria since the partition of Poland—belonged and which, at the same time, had become the most densely Jewish-populated area in the entire province. On the one hand here Jewish inhabitants, above all their elite, were often forced to make difficult political decisions as to whether to comply with the mutually contradictory demands of Polish nationalist policy, as represented by the local gentry, or the Austrian imperial program, as implemented by imperial officials, and the corresponding Polish or Germanic versions of linguistic–cultural acculturation. All this offered fairly consistent 'push' factors for Jewish emigration from Galicia. On the other hand, however, distinctly attractive 'pull' factors, springing from the development of liberal nationalism in Hungary contributed to the intensity of this movement.

Hungary at that time was still struggling with a serious dearth of population, a result of the devastations and emigrations caused by the wars against the Ottomans up to the outgoing seventeenth century, and the subsequent bids for independence. The chancellery and big landowners had been in virtually open competition with one another since the early eighteenth century in their efforts to repopulate the Great Plain of the historic kingdom. The overwhelming bulk of settlers pulled in as a result was of German and Slavic stock, but

Hungary's landowning aristocracy was ready to attract Jewish settlers as well to their properties. Many of them and among the most prestigious (to cite as just one example the country's most powerful landowning family, the princely house of Esterházy, proprietors of seven 'Jewish villages' in western Hungary) had long experience of the economic benefit to be derived from Jewish capital investments as well as organizational and commercial skills. For those concerned, it counted as a particular advantage that the country was unique in Europe for the complexity of its ethnic and religious composition, given the fact, for example, that neither the Magyars, the titular ethnic cluster, nor the Roman Catholics, adherents of the state religion, enjoyed numerical superiority. Both represented indeed less than half of the kingdom's population, the rest being made up of Slavic and German ethnic minorities or members of the Eastern Orthodox and Uniate (Greek Catholic) churches and various Protestant denominations. This may have been part of the reason why anti-Semitic intolerance rarely flared up in Hungary. The fact that large tracts of the territory had been left with few or no Jewish inhabitants after the Ottoman conquest may also have exercised an appeal, allowing for entire traditional congregations, or sizeable portions of them, to resettle and recreate their own communal superstructures without having to face limitations from those already established or competition from other Jewish persuasions.

This is well shown by the geographical map of this early Jewish Diaspora in Hungary. The north–west would become the zone of settlement for those who came from Bohemia and Moravia, whereas the counties in the north–east, nearest the Galician border, would be taken over by the Orthodox 'Poylish' (Galician) Jews, many of whom were supporters of *Hasidism*. This East–West split in Hungarian Jewry, between the more traditionalist and initially Yiddish-speaking 'Galicians,' and the groups of more modern inclination of mostly western origin, using a language closer to written High German, was to persist thereafter in large measure (albeit in not quite such a simplified structure), often even after substantial fractions of both branches of the immigrant population had moved on further into central Hungary (the Great Plain) and the southern parts of the Carpathian Basin.

The logic of the East–West migratory movements

The shift towards the Prussian capital likewise had a diversity of causes. One was the mobility imposed upon the Jewish populace living in the Polish territories annexed to Prussia in 1793 and 1795. As a result, Jews found themselves caught between the Germans and Poles, exposed as they were to the forceful Germanizing policy of the new ruling nation-state on the one hand whilst also pressured by local Polish élites, now thrust into an inferior role, to share its irredentist commitments. Many Jews, trapped between the jaws of this vice of nationalist forces, preferred to head for the center of the nascent new empire. That too was occasionally swept by anti-Jewish agitation and violence (well illustrated by the so-called 'Hep! Hep!' protest movement spreading throughout Germany in 1819), it is true, but then Prussia had already voluntarily followed the French example of bestowing equal civil rights on its Jewish citizens in 1812. Several smaller German states—notably Baden, Frankfurt, Hanseatic cities, Württemberg—had emancipated their own Jewish inhabitants still earlier.

Though Jewish emancipation was to be partially rescinded in many places later on, there were other reasons why the German cultural zone served as a powerful magnet for immigrants. Its dynamically developing territories, embarking upon the industrial revolution, offered new forms of urban lifestyle and chances of social mobility that economically backward countries like Hungary or Romania were unable to compete with. At the same time, the ideals of the Enlightenment significantly moderated the anti-Jewish prejudices nourished in leading circles, as attested by the reforms of the Prussian state initiated in 1808 and put subsequently into statutory effect. Moreover, the various dialects of the German-speaking territories all had more or less close affinities to the Yiddish–Deutsch of the eastern Jewish masses, which materially lowered the barriers to cultural assimilation. For many Ashkenazi immigrants German was not just another idiom, familiar as a quasi-mother tongue, but also an instrument to benefit from the highly developed German educational system and a more than symbolic direct means of leaving the cultural ghetto represented by the Yiddish 'jargon' and integrating into European civilization.

Last but not least, the emerging modern German federal state was now the rising intellectual great power of Europe. Its universities, speedily transforming themselves in the wake of Humboldt's reforms at the beginning of the nineteenth century, were objects of admiration for the entire 'developed' world. They turned out the *Bildungsbürgertum*—the educated bourgeoisie of civil servants, academics, professionals and Protestant pastors—that was to make Germany a country of high culture. The ideal of the new nation-state, sanctified by the social prestige of the educated middle classes, acted as a model to mobile élite groups of Eastern Europe, and upward-striving Jews in particular. It is not fortuitous that Moses Mendelssohn (1729–1786), the first Jewish philosopher to gain recognition in the German-speaking intellectual class, should usher in the Jewish Enlightenment, the 'Berlin *Haskalah,*' thereby setting in train a major trend of modernization in European Judaism, the impact of which is still being felt to the present day. Adherents of religious reforms and those attempting a redefinition of traditional Jewish identity would all establish tangible contact with Berlin as the intellectual center of modern Judaism, many to the extent of actually resettling there.

Jews arriving in Berlin from Galicia or Lithuania must have felt that a decisive phase was opening in their lives, on a path that was leading out of the ghetto towards collective salvation of sorts. At last they had been given a chance to escape from the effects of a protracted, oppressive social marginality and enter into a 'normal' and dynamic national civilization, the cultural import of which could increasingly be considered as universal. As a result, from the late eighteenth century onwards the entire Jewish elite of Central and Eastern Europe fell more and more under the spell of German culture. In the initial phase of modernizing mobility, after leaving the ghettos, Jewish elite groups throughout this area (Bohemia, Hungary, Bukovina, Poland, and even, later on, Russia as well) were to become more or less Germanized before a new start was made in individual cases—and usually in tandem with maintaining a demand for German high culture—on acculturating to the local (Czech, Hungarian, Polish, etc.) titular élites of would-be nation-states.

For these reasons, German cities, much more than the cities of other western states, however more liberally they were disposed, served initially (roughly up to the 1870s) as meeting places for Jews of eastern origin committed to modernity. Thus the numerical share of Germany in the total Jewish population of Western Europe (here including Italy and Belgium) rose from 61 to approximately 66 per cent between 1820 and 1860. Even in 1900 there were still more Jews in Germany (57 per cent) than elsewhere in the West, despite the fact that the bulk of the new large-scale East–West migration, under way since the 1880s, was now directed primarily to the more westerly democracies. At all events, the relatively more populous Jewish community of the German-speaking territories was to play the decisive role throughout the nineteenth century—and particularly for the Jews of Central and Eastern Europe—in working out paradigms of Jewish modernization and religious reform, above all in devising models of modern Jewish identity, public demeanor and creative activity (specifically in the field of economy, science and high culture as well as modern middle class manners and ways of life).

A trickle away from the eastern provinces of the Habsburg empire (principally Galicia and Bukovina, but also Bohemia and Hungary) and centered on Vienna that got under way within the framework of a similarly motivated drive, was to swell to mass proportions the moment that the imperial capital city opened it gates to Jewish settlement on the morrow of the 1848 revolution. In 1846 still only around 3,000 individuals were entitled, as 'tolerated' Jews, to live in Vienna, but their strength had risen to 15,000 by 1854. At the end of this process, in 1910, there were 176,000; indeed by 1923 (boosted by the arrival of tens of thousands of war refugees) Vienna's Jewish population exceeded 200,000, making it the third largest urban Jewish community in Europe, after Warsaw and Budapest.

The administrative, cultural and university center of the multinational empire, Vienna was also its biggest city and most important economic, industrial, financial and commercial market. In these respects it had no real rival or counterpart anywhere else within the empire and much beyond in the East up to the very end of the long nineteenth century. The distinguishing mark of Jewish immigration into Austria, literally to the very end (i.e. the dissolution of the Habsburg Empire in 1918), can be identified in its extreme concentration, directed as it was almost entirely towards the capital and its immediate environs (Lower Austria) and virtually not at all elsewhere further up the Danube or the Alpine provinces. The reasons for that lay, in part, on economic considerations, the domineering position of Vienna in business, but also on the securities provided by the proximity to the imperial court as well as, in part, on the survival of a far more virulent anti-Jewish inclination in Austrian provincial élites as compared to court circles, which proved to be guided by a more or less liberal outlook since the days of Metternich's chancellorship. It is hardly surprising, then, that over nine out of ten Jews in Austria lived in Vienna (91 per cent) or the surrounding region (5 per cent).

The educational background and social and occupational mobility of the immigrant masses was, to be sure, extraordinarily variable, which was given striking expression in their differentiation according to living quarters and districts in Vienna itself. New arrivals from Galicia and Bukovina, on the whole more traditionally-minded and poverty stricken Jews, settled primarily in the then fairly new lower class neighborhoods of Leopoldstadt (Second District) and Briggitenau (Twentieth District), on the far bank of the Danube Canal facing the city center. The better-educated Jews and those of higher social standing, mostly from Bohemia–Moravia and Hungary, ready to seek integration in the Gentile middle classes and élites, sought dwellings chiefly within the heart of the Old City, now demarcated by the Ringstrasse, in the vicinity of the imperial palace, the ministries, the universities and major gymnasiums, the opera house and the theatres. Jewish middle class neighborhoods of the central First District were extended over the north side of the Ring in the Ninth District (Alsergrund). Among others, Dr Sigmund Freud also lived there in the Bergstrasse.

The third large-scale migratory shift within Europe took place in the decades leading up to the First World War. This, too, got under way from the big collecting center of European Jewry in the East and led westwards, but it was much more dispersed in its direction than previously, and it mobilized even greater masses. Its beginnings may be dated to 1881–84, the time of the first big country-wide waves of pogroms in Russia. Whole strata of those who were more readily able and willing to move around (the young, university students, intellectuals) began to leave Russia *en masse*. The initial impetus was incontestably given by outbursts of anti-Jewish violence and the ensuing repressive legislation in the Empire of the tsars, but the flow quickly spread to other economically stagnant and, from a Jewish perspective, unpromising regions of Eastern Europe, including Galicia and Bukovina within Austria, as well as Romania and even the easternmost parts of Hungary (Sub-Carpathia). Most of the emigrants were heading for the United States to be sure, though a smaller, but still substantial tributary (principally from the Baltic region and Lithuania) branched off towards England, which, like North America, enjoyed a good reputation for its liberalism. Many others endeavored to reach France and Belgium, and smaller groups the Netherlands or, even less often, a Scandinavian country. The influx into Germany, on the other hand, slowed down, though it never completely halted, even with the outbreak of the First World War. These western countries in reality often served merely as temporary staging posts for the new arrivals, before they set off for one or other of the New World countries that offered a place for permanent settlement.

In the aftermath of the First World War, some South American states which had embarked on the European road to modernization (above all Argentina, Brazil, Chile and Uruguay) featured as destinations far more often than earlier.

There was also a technological dimension to this migratory flood, based on the build-up of international railway connections and the proliferation of modern, high-capacity intercontinental steamships. The railways between Vienna and Galicia, and eventually Bukovina, had no small part in the swarming of broad swathes of the Jewish populace in the economically vegetating eastern fringes of the Austro–Hungarian Monarchy to the imperial capital and westwards. From 1881 ships were sailing regularly, and at prices that many could afford, from Odessa, Fiume, Trieste and the Baltic ports to Marseilles, Hamburg or London and thence on to the New World.

The major outflow of Jewry from Eastern Europe, it is clear, fell largely on the periods prior to 1914, although it was to continue at a slower rate during the Great War and also in the inter-war decades. During and after the hostilities, fresh contingents of Jews arrived, this time round principally in Germany and Austria, from the East. These eastern Jews were initially compelled to flee from areas of military engagement (principally in Polish-inhabited territories), later on from pogroms of unprecedented scale (above all in the Ukraine) that were unleashed by the Russian civil war. The refugees from Bolshevik Russia were joined by émigrés from Romania, Hungary and the newly refounded Poland, who were hastening to leave state formations with régimes standing for more or less radically anti-Semitic programs. Shortly after January 1933, the first victims marked out by the triumphant Nazi party in the Third Reich were also to start appearing in the West.

Though they may often have flagged and come to a standstill, these migratory shifts, over a period of sixty years, never wavered in their overall direction towards the big (and sometimes the small) western-type democracies on both sides of the Atlantic. Since the majority of the Jews who had settled in Western Europe, by then in the demographic transition of modernization à la Malthus, were more and more expressly limiting the size of their families, natural growth of western-type Jewry was tending to slow down. After 1919 it actually tipped over into the negative, virtually everywhere. Further increases in the Jewish population in the West during this period are therefore explicable, first and foremost, by migratory influxes.

The number of Jews in Great Britain rose, accordingly, from 65,000 in 1880 to not less than 300,000 by 1914, and by the eve of the Second World War to around 400,000 (including the first refugees from Nazism), despite the fact that meanwhile huge numbers of immigrants had moved further on to the United States, Canada, Australia, South Africa, and other territories of the British empire open for settlers. Similarly, between 1900 and 1939 the Jewish population of France trebled from around 80,000 to 260,000 (though a big part of this growth was due to the re-annexation of Alsace-Lorraine in 1919, with its many Jewish inhabitants). Belgium's Jewish population during the same forty-year period may be estimated as having risen from 20,000 to 100,000 (also including refugees from Nazism). Similar, albeit smaller-scale flows of immigration substantially boosted the numbers of Jews living in the Netherlands and the Scandinavian countries.

The decisive shifts in European Jewish demography during the modern era were thus induced by migratory movements. The occupational–economic and cultural stratification of Eastern European Jewry also underwent a process of 'westernization' (modernization)—to be discussed later—in parallel with the departure of large segments for the West, representing the start of a process of demographic equalization to the detriment of what, up to the beginning of the nineteenth century, had still been an absolute preponderance in the East. *Landsmannschafts* (regional refugee associations) of *shtetl*-like neighborhoods sprang up in Paris, London and other western metropolises which, until then, had very little acquaintance with Jews other than the 'westernized' type.

'Overurbanization'

Migrations between the states of Europe strengthened the existing trend to urbanization, which has been one of the paradigmatic features of Jewish social history since the late Middle Ages.

However decisive it may have been, it should not be overlooked that from time to time, depending on the economic cycle or local conditions for settlement, there were also processes working in the opposite direction, even during the modern era. In East Galicia during the latter half of the nineteenth century, for example, many Jews left the towns and *shtetl*s for the villages. Jewish retailers whose livelihood was linked to the peasant economy found it necessary to relocate their residences to the villages. They could not compete with rivals and the proliferating cooperative (or mutual) savings banks otherwise than by offering their services (consumer credits, mortgages, speculative preemptive purchases of agricultural commodities that had yet to be harvested, a small tavern or a general store) in direct proximity to their customers. This distinctive (and probably not unparalleled) form of withdrawal from the town must nevertheless be considered only as an exception to the general rule of concentration in cities.

What Jewish 'overurbanization' denotes is that, other things being equal, Jews, when given the choice, were much readier than non-Jews to opt for an urban residence and lifestyle. It should be noted, however, that other things were never equal for Jews and non-Jews, and over time they were also highly variable from country to country. At the beginning of the modern age, in most European countries (with the partial exception of France, the Netherlands and Britain) self-governing cities, e.g. in Hungary, the 'royal free boroughs' (up to the Act of 1840) and 'mining towns' (up until 1867) still retained the right to accept or reject applications for residential permits from new arrivals (and thus Jews in particular). Generally speaking, these were old privileges that only disappeared after the complete dismantling of the legal heritage of feudalism. Before their official emancipation, free choice of place of settlement for Jews was made possible by progressively implemented equal-rights measures—an era that in Central Europe was broadly brought to a close only in the mid-nineteenth century with the revolutions of 1848 and the legislation of the ensuing 'modernizing' (if not necessarily liberal) reaction to these.

Up to this point, regulations for urban settlement of Jews were hugely diverse. Freedom of Jews to choose their place of residence or to migrate was only granted in Prussia, for instance, with the emancipation law of 1812. (Even then it was not uniformly implemented, to be partially rescinded later on.) In Hungary free settlement was established in 1840, whilst in Vienna only in 1849. In Russia settlement rights remained severely limited by various regulations, even within the permitted 'Pale of Settlement', before they were finally annulled as late as 1915. The right 'not to tolerate Jews' that had been held by the 'royal boroughs' of former Poland was abrogated in 1862 only. Within Russia's Jewish 'Pale of Settlement' there were cases where Jews were excluded from certain villages on perfectly legal grounds (e.g. following the repressive 'May Laws' of 1882). Much the same happened in Romania in 1867, within the framework of appropriate restrictive decrees. Taking into account this variability of residential legislations, it goes without saying that the trend to 'overurbanization'—as a distinctive Jewish behavioral paradigm—can only be validated insofar as there was a legal freedom as to the choice of one's place of residence.

The final outcome, in any event, was spectacular. By the end of the nineteenth century, Jews throughout Europe—and thus, for all practical purposes, the entire world—were much more often town-dwellers than the contemporary population as a whole and their social counterparts in professional or class terms. That means, for one thing, that the proportion of Jews was a good deal higher in towns than in rural areas, and second, that, as a general rule, an absolute majority of Jews were living in towns, most often in major or capital cities and the vicinity of the largest towns. A few examples will suffice for Western Europe to illustrate various patterns of overurbanization typical of modern-day Jewish populations.

London, for instance, has retained a central role in the settlement of Jews in England to the present day ever since, after an absence of over three centuries following their expulsion by Edward I in the thirteenth century, Jews were readmitted into the country by Oliver Cromwell in 1656. It is likely that at all times at least one half of all British Jews have lived within the Greater London area: around 1880, 45,000 out of 60,000; around 1914, 150,000 out of 300,000; and by around 1970 280,000 out of 450,000. There is good reason to deduce that more of them likewise chose to reside in the capital, rather than elsewhere, during the period of mass migrations.

The situation appears to be much the same in the Netherlands. Here Amsterdam was always the main center for Jews, but growing in relative importance with the passage of time. Up to the beginning of the nineteenth century it ranked as the biggest urban concentration of Jews in the world. In 1830, half of all Dutch Jews resided there, by 1909 some 61 per cent, and in 1945 it had 65 per cent of all Dutch survivors of the Shoah.

A similar observation applies to the Scandinavian countries. Since the eighteenth century more than three-quarters of Danish Jews have been concentrated in Copenhagen, whilst in Sweden the bulk of the country's Jewish populace has always been distributed between Stockholm and the next two largest cities (Göteborg and Malmö).

The situation evolved though quite differently in Paris, where measures to exclude Jews remained in force up to the very end of the *ancien régime*. The total Jewish population of France in 1798 can be put at about 40,000, but barely more than 500 lived in Paris. By 1869 French Jewry numbered some 80,000, with 30,000 residing in the capital. Following the loss of Alsace-Lorraine in 1871, a large-scale migration towards the center of the country got under way. By 1880 already some 40,000 of France's 80,000 to 100,000 Jews were based in Paris. Those who arrived with subsequent waves of immigration out of Eastern Europe (approximately 25,000 between 1881 and 1914) and, after 1908, immigrants from the south-easternmost parts of Europe (Salonika, Constantinople and Smyrna) likewise primarily boosted the Parisian numbers. That preponderance was also maintained after the mass resettlements from the former French colonies of North Africa after 1956 (Morocco, Tunisia) and in 1962 (Algeria), even though these newcomers increasingly chose to settle in cities of Mediterranean France as well, Marseilles in particular.

The evolutionary process observed in Berlin was in many respects similar to that in Paris, with the difference that a Jewish community had been resident in the Prussian capital since the seventeenth century. Though admittedly negligible in its size, this was to some extent counterbalanced by its considerable economic weight and intellectual cachet, which steadily grew over time. There may still have been a mere 6,400 Jews living in Berlin even in 1816, but under the impact of immigration from Eastern Europe and the territories of East Prussia, the community embarked on a path of such a rapid growth that a century later its size had already swollen to 150,000. In 1910 more than one quarter of the Jewish population of the entire German Empire was to be found in its capital city.

There were similar developments elsewhere in Central Europe. The case of Vienna has already been discussed. The pace and scale of growth there paralleled those of Berlin, though appreciable settlement started later and the absolute dominance of Vienna Jewry in the small Republic of Austria's total Jewish population was also incommensurate with the metropolitan concentration of Jews in actually any other European country.

Budapest, broadly speaking, followed a rather different pattern. While there had been a Jewish community in the aristocratic and later royal domain of Óbuda, the free royal borough of Buda did not admit Jews up to the end of the eighteenth century. The same restriction applied to the then separate city of Pest, but of the future capital's three constitutive parts it was Pest where the development of the Jewish community displayed the most dynamism in respect both of its total and its proportionate size. Around 1850, the total Jewish population of the still separate cities of Buda, Pest and Óbuda numbered around 11,000. By the end of the century, however, there were already 200,000 Jews living in the capital (unified since 1873), or close to one quarter both of Hungary's total Jewry and the population of Budapest. Following the country's dismemberment by the 1919 Treaty of Trianon, Budapest became home for as much as around half of all Jews remaining in the rump state or having moved there from former Hungarian territories.

Prague was another example of this type of Jewish 'overurbanization.' The size of the Jewish community was considerably smaller, it is true, since the restricted human reserves of Bohemia's Jewish population were never replenished by any major influxes of migrants from abroad in modern times. Quite the reverse, indeed, since there was no small measure of emigration away from here, primarily bound for Hungary during the eighteenth century and, after 1848, towards Vienna. None the less, from the early Middle Ages on, a substantial fraction of the Jewish population of the Czech provinces had always lived in this at times royal, at times imperial capital and quondam center of the Holy Roman Empire. In 1880 the 20,500 Jewish inhabitants of Prague represented 22 per cent of the Jews of Bohemia proper (excluding Moravia), but fifty years later, in 1930, they numbered 35,000 and had doubled their share in the province's total Jewish population (46 per cent).

Similar processes can be observed in the eastern parts of the continent, except that there the urban concentration of Jews was, if anything, even more marked in comparison to that of other ethnic groups, and as against the general underurbanization to which these regions were subject until the commencement of Soviet-style process of industrialization and centralization. Nevertheless, as a result of the relative economic backwardness of the Russian Empire and the restrictions imposed on Jewish settlement by the tsarist authorities, ratios of urbanized Jews relative to the total local Jewish population remained lower than those observed in the West or Central Europe. Thus, paradoxical as it seems, relative 'overurbanization' often co-existed here alongside a measure of 'underurbanization' in the absolute sense. The big urban concentrations of Jews could not be found in the two capitals of Moscow and St. Petersburg, of course, nor even in the various provincial centers, since under tsarist rule the vast bulk of the Jewish population was prohibited from settling in towns outside the designated 'Pale of Settlement' covering most of the Polish, Ukrainian and Belorussian inhabited territories. In pre-Soviet times, therefore, Jewish urbanization was almost exclusively concentrated within this zone, with its most important city centers as follows: Warsaw (with 219,000 Jewish inhabitants, or 34 per cent of the total population in 1900), Odessa (with 139,000 Jewish inhabitants, likewise 34 per cent of the total population in 1900), Lódz (100,000 and 31 per cent) and Vilna (64,000 and 41 per cent). Similar or even higher ratios were to be found not only in many smaller cities of the Russian 'Pale of Settlement' but also in many moderately sized towns of Austrian Galicia and Romanian Moldavia, as in the case, for example, of Minsk (48,000 Jews, making up 52 per cent of all inhabitants), Lemberg or Lvov (44,000 and 28 per cent), Vitebsk (32,000 and 53 per cent), Daugavpils (32,000 and 47 per cent), Jassy (30,000 and 39 per cent), Cracow (26,000 and 39 per cent), Mogilev (22,000 and 50 per cent), Pinsk (21,000 and 74 per cent), Bobruisk (21,000 and 61 per cent), Gomel' (20,000 and 55 per cent), etc.

This urban orientation, striking from the very outset, was to undergo drastic further evolution as a result of the political shake-up in Eastern Europe following the First World War. With the Jews of Russia finally being emancipated after the February Revolution in 1917, their surge into the towns under the Soviet régime was to assume huge proportions, but not in the customary direction. Henceforth the capital cities, that had previously been off-limits (or where a permit to settle could only be obtained by meeting special educational or economic qualifications) were now thrown open. That freedom to move into urban areas was asserted with explosive effect during the inter-war years in the Soviet Union. The total of 8,500 Jewish inhabitants that Moscow had in 1900 became 400,000 by 1939, which corresponded to a more than tenfold growth of their representation in the total population (from 0.8 to 11 per cent). The few thousand Jews that had been 'tolerated' in St. Petersburg in 1900 were joined by a further 270,000 over that same period. In Kiev their number jumped from 32,000 to 175,000, in Kharkov from 11,000 to 150,000.

Residential differentiation, segregation and urbanization

A typical concomitant of the pull into towns everywhere was the distinct conglomeration of Jewish inhabitants into certain specific city districts, usually in the center.

The example of Vienna has already been cited, but this was also mirrored by Berlin, Budapest, Prague and Warsaw, with the bulk of the local Jewish community in all cases remaining in the city center whilst the various inner-city districts underwent a distinct social stratification of their Jewish clusters. These processes of residential differentiation within the city in fact followed one of two divergent patterns. They either represent the expansion of the old historical ghettos, as in the case of Prague, or else the building up of new neighborhoods that fit in with the process of industrialization.

The best example of the latter type is Budapest. During the nineteenth century the focus of that conurbation's Jewish population shifted increasingly from its traditional center in Óbuda to the new industrial and commercial hub of Pest, and more specifically to four of its inner districts. The Fifth District (Lipótváros or Leopoldstadt) was where the upper middle-class entrepreneurs installed themselves, establishing their limited companies and bank headquarters, and also where the most successful of those in the liberal professions sought residences and offices; the Sixth District (Terézváros or Theresienstadt) became the residential area of the middle classes and other professionals, whilst the Seventh (Erzsébetváros or Elizabethstadt) and Eighth (Józsefváros or Josephstadt) Districts housed the petty bourgeois traders and artisans as well as the Jewish proletariat. These distinct features were also manifested in the system of religious institutions, with traditionalist Orthodox prayer houses put up in the narrow streets of the Sixth and Seventh Districts, whereas the modern synagogues of the 'Neologues' (liberal Judaism) were situated close to the residential districts of the upper classes.

There were cases where the role of the Jewish residential quarter was taken over by districts lying outside the inner-city centers, especially in places where the continuity of a Jewish presence had been interrupted historically. Thus, in London the rocketing growth of the Jewish population after 1880 did not allow an exclusive concentration in the old residential districts, so that new quarters sprang up, ranging from the suburbs in the north–west (with their residences for the middle and upper classes) across to those in the north–east (with dwellings for the lower social classes). In Cracow, from the time of their expulsion in 1495 onwards, the local Jewish population moved into the nearby Kazimierz suburb. In order to preserve their positions at the city's markets, Jews banned from the city simply resettled on the far bank of the Vistula (outside the sphere of the municipal authorities), building up a residential belt of their own, which persisted up until the Shoah.

The mainsprings for urbanization were to be substantially altered and renovated in the modern era, as compared with the previous centuries. For religious reasons (synagogues had to be near the dwelling place, to be in walking distance on the Sabbath and high holidays) and security considerations new factors were added, the forerunners of which had already been sporadically present prior to the modern era. In any case, security was not necessarily more dependable in city centers than in the countryside. At times of anti-Jewish disturbances, communal defense was no doubt easier to organize in an urban environment, but then one also had to reckon on more massive onslaughts when it came to drives to stage major pogroms. The other reasons for overurbanization derived more from new factors relating to the position of emancipated Jews in Europe.

Since preference for urban settlement rested on firmly established historical traditions, families which had already integrated in cities drew in others, who tended to congregate around the earlier settlers because the reassuring proximity, local knowledge and economic know-how of the latter contributed to the success of their own integration. At other times, cemeteries and synagogues, the symbolic sites of earlier Jewish presence, would have to be reconstructed or repossessed, but without exception these would lie in the old cities, the older parts of towns. Renewing their function not uncommonly required the entire local Jewish tradition to be recreated, for often Jews had not inhabited these places for several centuries since the time of their historical expulsion in the middle ages or after in countries like France, Britain and in many German states. The principal reason for 'overurbanization,' just as for concentration in city centers, was the concern for the closeness to markets. For tradesmen and financiers, whether large or small, this was an important, if not absolutely necessary, condition for their occupation, and yet they constitute the spine of the scattered communities at the opening of the modern age. With the differentiation of the economically active population, for those in professional or intellectual occupations, entrepreneurs and wholesale dealers, a domicile in the city signifies a tangible gain in odds, allows better market positions to be taken in the new middle classes, whose working circles usually continue to be concentrated in the old city centers.

The cities of industrial societies serve as lures for, above all, the socially mobile strata who have already set off down the path to embourgeoisement (*Verbürgerlichung*), in other words, every sort of economic 'freelancer,' or at least anyone with a chance of rising to the ranks of the employed middle classes. Urban environments offer almost exclusively basic conditions for adopting the style and quality of life of the modern middle classes. This includes access to schooling, the press and other cultural infrastructures and services (theatres, concert halls, exhibition galeries, museums, cinemas) as well as other institutionalized loci of social life and modern leisure-time culture (cafés, swimming pools, sports grounds, parks, salons), and various organized arrangements of asserting collective, especially political interests (clubs, parties, trade unions, initiatives of civil society). The recourse to such services are part and parcel of strategies of social integration and mobility, since participation in such agencies or the active demand for such supplies strengthen group specific chances of getting ahead in the competition for positions in social élites. We know from studies of Jewish micro-milieus that often the most tangible motive for decisions to 'move up' into the town, besides the search for better economic opportunities, was the desire of parents to secure for their children the best possible standard of education.

From the beginning of the nineteenth century, among growing sectors of Western and Central European Jewry one also comes across groups choosing an urban existence in order to free themselves from religious obligations liable to be much more strictly controlled in smaller rural communities. For them, cities offered real possibilities of leading an 'anonymous' private life, building up a network of personal contacts, making an individual choice of marriage partner, and redefining a 'looser' or individual relationship to traditional group identity. That is why representatives of 'modern,' secularly inclined Jewry are increasingly encountered in the towns, whereas the masses maintaining traditional patterns of faith continue to live in village communities, whenever they can.

'Demographic transition' and modernization

For clarity's sake, I have so far deliberately disregarded the effects of marriage, birth and mortality rates amongst factors bearing on the size and residential distribution of Jewish communities. 'Vital' as these rates are in multiple senses, however, these aspects of demographic evolution permit one of the differentiating characteristics of contemporary Jewish social history (namely 'demographic modernization') to be demonstrated, and they also contribute to explain some of the aforementioned geographical regroupings.

Our demonstration here should be limited to core elements of the 'demographic transition' as far as Jews were involved. This key concept refers to the historical process of modernization that occurred in the physical reproduction of population during the nineteenth and twentieth centuries and which, in most European Jewish communities, preceded and was also completed more rapidly than similar processes in the local populace as a whole. In this context a relatively early advent of drastic limitation of birth rates (hence decrease in family size), a generally low mortality, and—additionally—the rarity of illegitimate births must be stressed.

Up to the dawn of the modern era, fertility amongst Jews barely differed from that amongst other ethnic groups in Europe. This was the 'natural' fertility rate depending essentially on demographic variables like the age at marriage, the frequency of bachelorhood, and female (and especially peri- and postnatal) mortality, etc. and not on the behavior of married couples, who were no more able to influence the risks of mortality than the number of births. In traditional Jewish circles, the age of married couples at the time of formal espousal was ideally very young and generally not comparable to what was customary in other ethnic groups around them. There are no accurate statistics however on the actual frequency of early adolescent matrimonial bonds contracted by both genders on attaining puberty, from the age of 12–13 years onwards. At any event, the practice should certainly have increased the total number of children liable to be born, even if, as we know, such marriages were only consummated at a later age. In Orthodox Jewry very high crude birth rates of the order of 40 to 50 per thousand, corresponding to 'natural' (i.e. uncontrolled, unrestricted) rates of fertility, have often been recorded. It is common knowledge that such rates are always connected to a number of demographic factors (the probabilities of their occurrence calling for separate analysis). Amongst these are the age distribution and the age specific gender ratios of the population in question, the relative age of married spouses (big age differences—typical of patriarchal families—leading for instance to a reduction of fertility), the marriage rate (i.e. the proportion of unmarried women of childbearing age), the average age at marriage (which used to be always older than the above-mentioned young ideal age), the divorce and mortality rates, the frequency of remarriage by widows (which was usually high amongst Jews) and by divorcees (which was rather uncommon), the frequency of births outside marriage (and its social acceptability), etc. Above all, other things being equal, a young population would produce more progeny than a more aged one, especially if it experiences stable and socially consolidated livings conditions.

In the case of Europe's Jews this correlation, understandably, led to a large variability of fertility rates in the various Jewish aggregates, often because of migratory shifts having a profound impact, from one locality to another, on the age distribution, marital prospects and living conditions of the population concerned. Refugees, of course, might be of any age or gender, but those who set off abroad or moved into towns in the hope of improving their living standards and other 'strategic' emigrants were generally young and, for the most part, males. If such disturbing factors are disregarded, it is fair to say that for Jewish populations living in relatively stable conditions, the 'natural' birth rate prevailed throughout Europe up to the mid-nineteenth century and, in Eastern Europe, up to the early twentieth century (or even later, in some traditional niches).

Accordingly, as is shown in Table 2 (see page 46), birth rates observable among Jews and surrounding populations up to the late nineteenth century show no great disparities. In Bulgaria or Romania for example, following quantified evidence just prior to 1900, birth rates for Jews was identical to, or even (in Romania) higher than that of the general population. Elsewhere the indices for the Jews tended to be somewhat lower, though not appreciably. More striking are the changes that ensued *after* the turn of the century. Henceforth the fertility rates show everywhere a dramatically diverging tendency between Jews and the general population.

Population dynamics, however, do not depend on reproduction alone, the chief component of which being provided by birth rates, but on depletion, the main cause of which being death rates (leaving emigration or renunciation of faith aside). An essential distinctive feature of the evolution of Jewish populations up to the beginnings of 'modernization' in the twentieth century was linked to the fact that natural growth stayed at a high level for a long time (generally up to the end of the nineteenth century), while mortality started to decline steeply much earlier. The entire history of European Jewry in recent times has been accompanied by the incidence of a lower than average mortality, as it emerges from the sporadic data that can be collected in this matter from the eighteenth century on, just as from information related to the 'demographic transition' itself.

It is well established that four or five stages are ubiquitously distinguishable in the course of the demographic transition. In the initial (high stationary) phase, high fertility was accompanied by a high risk of mortality. In the second (early expanding) phase the birth rates remained high but death rates fell and therefore the overall growth rate of the population concerned surged. In the third (late expanding) phase birth rates started to fall back whilst the death rate continued to decline, which sustained a further natural increase for a while (through the preservation of differences between birth and death rates). In the fourth (low stationary)—and for some demographers final—phase, birth rates went on declining through the deliberate regulation (birth control), so that at some point it dropped to the level of the diminishing death rates. This could then tip into what some demographers would regard as the final phase when the decline in birth rates exceeded that of death rates, and the population thereby entered into a state of natural decrease. Now, it looks very much as if Jewish populations remained for a particularly prolonged period—much longer than other groups—in the second phase at a time when the majority of European populations were still stuck in the initial phase. Afterwards Jews appeared to switch faster than others into the third and then fourth (indeed fifth) phases of demographic transition.

At the start of the modern age—insofar as the available data can be relied on—it would appear then that amongst Jews mortality declined rapidly whilst fertility did so at a much slower pace (if it did so at all up to the late nineteenth century), although here too there are significant differences from country to country, and again a clear contrast between West and East. The overall mortality stayed at the same high level in Romania between 1881 and 1910, whereas the death rate for Romanian Jews declined by well over one-third. In Hungary the decline in mortality after 1890 can be regarded as general, but a disparity between Jews and non-Jews persisted up till the 1930s. The trend in Galicia and other parts of Poland was similar. In the West, by contrast, the discrepancy in mortality statistics between Jews and non-Jews was smaller even according to the oldest data, though over time this discrepancy also narrowed down and in some cases even reversed (as in Italy from the 1920s onwards, in Vienna from 1934, in Prussia from 1926). In all probability, unequal but still large-scale declines in birth rates themselves were the chief factor in this turning point, since a shortage of children has always a direct impact on the aging of a population. Now a rise in the proportion of the elderly in the age structure inevitably implied an increase in the global death rate, even when age-specific death coefficients continued to be more favorable (as may be assumed) for Jewish populations.

If we rely on the 'pure' mortality indices, such as the data for child mortality or age-specific deaths, it is easy to establish that in all places the risk of dying remained lower for Jews than for non-Jews. Those differences, however positive they could be, were generally insignificant in western countries, whereas in Eastern Europe they were sometimes very substantial. In Amsterdam, for example, the infant mortality rate (number of children dying before their first birthday) in the period from 1907 to 1909 was 75 per 1,000 live births for Jews and 90 for the population as a whole. Between 1919 and 1923 those rates fell to 41 and 51 per 1,000, respectively. Similar differences between Jews and the general population were considerably greater in Rome (72 and 138 for 1901–07), Florence (149 and 218 for 1838–47), Berlin (43 and 90 for 1924–26) or Budapest (159 and 271 in 1880; 63 and 114 in 1926). Such divergences open up even more markedly as we progress further eastwards, so it could happen that non-Jewish child mortality rates were several multiples of the losses recorded amongst Jews, as in the case of Poland between 1931 and 1936 where the corresponding figures were 139 and 49, or Latvia (89 and 38 in 1926–27), Lithuania (156 and 35 in 1927), and the Soviet Union (174 and 57 in 1926). (These data are from the same source as in Table 2.)

A reduction of average family size amongst general populations occurred everywhere a good deal later than amongst Jews, so the Jews were manifestly way ahead of other ethnic groups as to the speed and intensity of the 'demographic transition.' In Romania the birth rate of Jews moderated to under one half during about forty years (between 1881–86 and 1926–28) whilst the decline was barely perceptible in the general population (from 41 to 36), and a substantial part of even that is attributable to the marked change among Jews themselves counted with the general population (especially after 1919, when Romania's Jewish population had an increased demographic weight). The same process took place in Bulgaria. During the 1890s birth rates for Jews and the total Bulgarian population were still the same, but thirty odd years later the Jewish birth rate had already plummeted to half the earlier figure whilst there was barely any noticeable change for the general population (and there again the Jews themselves would have played a part in this). Similar trends could be observed in Hungary. Here too the birth rates amongst Jews and non-Jews during the 1890s still stood quite close to each other. Thereafter a fairly rapid decrease occurred in both aggregate figures, but this shift among Jews was so much sharper that the divergence between the two birth rates widened increasingly, to such an extent that forty years later the Jewish rate amounted to just half the rate for the rest of the population. Similarly diverging curves can be traced in Italy (where the rates went from parity to a twofold difference by 1931–35), Prussia (where the same divergence had occurred by 1933), or Czechoslovakia in 1930. In the latter case (not shown in Table 2) the birth rate for Jews was no more than 7 per 1,000 (a sign of a very serious demographic deficit), whereas that for the population as a whole was still running at 18 per 1,000 (which in itself was also low in absolute terms, but still around the simple replacement rate).

It is also apparent from Table 2 that as a result of the aforementioned disparities—and the relatively protracted second phase of the 'demographic transition,'—the natural growth of population in the initial period of modernization was everywhere higher amongst Jews than amongst non-Jews. In Hungary it was chiefly on this account that the number of Jews doubled over the fifty years after 1850–60, during a period when increasingly sporadic immigration was more than counterbalanced by emigration. The same natural increase of population explains the demographic saturation of the *shtetlah* of Galicia and russified Poland, which not even the ever-greater intensity of emigration could offset. The local Jewish overpopulation contributed there to a general impoverishment, to say nothing of the tensions it provoked with the surrounding general population.

The data in Table 2 also provide a measure of how quickly the switch to the small family model with merely 1–3 children was accomplished in most Jewish communities, especially in towns. In the period between the two world wars the natural growth of Jewish populations turned negative in Prussia and Italy just like in Hungary, and one can go so far as to speak of a genuine demographic depression in the metropolitan areas of Budapest, Vienna or Berlin alike. There can be little doubt that similar trends would be demonstrable in the countries of Western Europe—for instance France and Britain—had the early secularization of public records related to vital events (implemented since the 1860s or 1870s) not suspended the collection of denominationally linked demographic indices.

Social circumstances of rapid demographic modernization

The success with which Europe's Jewish populations managed to regulate their growth with such extraordinary rapidity, and at any event well before most other ethnic groups, was closely tied up with their social condition at that time. Obviously, standing on a higher footing than those around them in respect or urbanization, literacy (as will be discussed later), and other cultural or 'bourgeois' attainments in general (as attested by their distinctive level of education), Jews were more readily able to master the technical means of birth control. Yet the adoption of those techniques requires a conscious intention to do so; it was not sufficient merely to have a basic knowledge of how they worked. It was necessary, first and foremost, to abandon the principle of accepting 'natural fecundity.' A reduction in population increase will only be sought by groups which develop a basically individualist and voluntaristic way of thinking about the future, having shaken off the idea of the future being conceived as an inevitable 'destiny' in order to construct a positive (i.e. creative) relationship with the morrow. The disposition to regulate births is a product of much the same advance-planning decisions as building an economic or professional career or long-term strategies for social mobility projected over one's life span or, indeed, that of one's descendants.

All this presupposes basic forms of existential discipline. A similar discipline, however, is also at the foundation of traditional Jewish lifestyle and religious practice which impose strict rules both on the use of time (the separation of the mundane and festal ritual, compliance with religious prescriptions relating to the consumption of meat and dairy products, etc.) and of the family or communal living space (following requirements of a *kosher* household, prescriptions relating to synagogue attendance or cleanliness), with, incidentally, far-reaching regulatory impact on sexuality or other forms of private, everyday conduct. Although compliance with the stipulations of tradition does not embrace acts of individual planning for the future, the habitus developed through religious discipline must have provided an objective, if not sufficient, conditional frame for the provision of behavioral paradigms facilitating early 'demographic transition' for all those concerned, when they worked out their strategies for intellectual modernization, the corresponding patterns of professional mobility and rational life planning.

That sort of mentality calls for a positive view of the future, faith in a foreseeable and predictable future. This is more likely to evolve in groups whose collective career is on the rise and whose chances of upward mobility appear to be reasonable functions of strategic decisions. That was the position of growing sectors of European Jewry from the Enlightenment onwards: they were henceforth able to nurture increasingly real hopes of social elevation, with future prospects of equality of rights, social acceptance into modern nation-states, and professional mobility realized in a more and more free market economy. It is easy to see how, at this Promethean moment in history, the Jews were capable, precisely by virtue of their social status, of introducing new types of rational behavior and decision-making in the conduct of their private lives, and in matters related to their own family's reproduction in particular, all the more so as this directly affected the chances for the family's offspring to be successful. When a group is in such a socially rising situation, a smaller family size improves the odds not only for the parents but for their descendants (by increasing the available 'reproductive' investments on schooling, health, quality of home life, emotional support, etc. devoted to each child). The adoption of new techniques for birth control, as for other areas of organizing life, was thus linked to the experienced need for rational optimization of the future, planned for one's offspring.

In this context, it is low mortality, or the faster than average decline of group specific death rates that call attention to themselves, since these seem to precede historically the appearance of the other variables of 'modernity.' One may hazard a guess that cautious scrutiny may identify in this the impact of many collective features of Jewish community life already present during the early phases of modernization. Even though local analyses of the subject are exceedingly deficient, we may hypothetically recognize some objective circumstances that could favorably influence the early reduction of mortal risks among Jews. In this context one can mention the previously discussed pattern of early 'overurbanization,' high rates of literacy and more than average 'middle-class' social stratification of Jewish groups (at least inasmuch as that stratification was not burdened by the poverty stricken peasant masses—erstwhile serfs—who formed a majority of most non-Jewish populations in the modern era). An urban, 'middle-class' (or incipient middle-class) way of life almost always offered better chances of personal hygiene (at least outside the ghettos), and for obtaining information relating to this (in school lessons on hygiene if not elsewhere), of taking advantage of medical care (especially in a group with many doctors), of better nutrition, or less exhausting economic activity, of recuperating as a result of having more spare time, and—in some cases at least—of healthier housing conditions. These factors indeed also tend to reduce the mortality risk.

There are also several distinctive and, at the same time, basic cultural components of Jewish living conditions that should be equally taken into consideration here.

Cleansing, whether ritual or habitual (obligatory hand washing before meals, taking ritual bath via immersion of the whole body in running water at certain ceremonial occasions), and *kosher* dietary laws (prohibition of bloody or not absolutely fresh meat, separation of utensils for foods deemed as 'meat' and dairy products, etc.), drastic moderation in alcohol consumption (not a consequence of a religious prohibition proper but that of an effective moral control), the infrequency of sexually transmitted diseases following strict observance of communal moral police and traditional marital norms (i.e. early marriage), etc. would each have played a part in disease avoidance in nineteenth-century Europe, which was still very underdeveloped in respect of general medical attendance. The average rigor of moral control kept on young Jewish women, which in Europe (if not in overseas immigrant communities) also found expression in the conspicuously low rates of extramarital births and the rarity of prostitutes, also displays a not insignificant link with the reduced mortality risk in the early period of the 'demographic transition.' Illegitimate births were then still affected by a demonstrable added risk of death, both amongst the new-born babies who often came into the world and were kept amidst adverse hygienic conditions, and amongst their mothers. According to a number of studies, prostitution was connected to exceptionally high suicide rates, whilst the occurrence of sexually transmitted diseases represented substantial mortality risks in the days without effective prophylaxis and antibiotics. Statistics for causes of death by denominations in Central Europe (Hungary, Austria and Germany) clearly demonstrate that, from the late nineteenth century onwards, Jews enjoyed a significant degree of relative protection from the most devastating infectious diseases, endemic in those days, such as syphilis and tuberculosis. In the same regard, the fact that already then a high (and growing) proportion of doctors were themselves Jewish, may well have played an additional part in this, as even long before the earliest historical measures of emancipation (since 1782 within the Habsburg Empire) Jews were admitted to medical studies at certain European universities. At the very least, it must have been one reason why Jewish patients benefited more often than others from medical care (and, no doubt of better quality), as evidenced by data on the percentage of deaths occurring (from the late nineteenth century onwards) under medical assistance in territories of the Austro-Hungarian Monarchy. Finally, Jewish communities at all times maintained a well-endowed network of institutions to care for the physically frail (the sick, the handicapped, the blind or the deaf-mute) and those in direst economic need (widows and orphans). Such institutional support for the weak, could again have contributed to the limitation of social inequalities before death and, incidentally, to a certain reduction of mortality risks. Overall, this too would have been reflected in the better-than-average death rates generally recorded for Jewish populations. (It should not be forgotten that in the days when state provision of social welfare and medical care for the bulk of the population—especially those in socially marginal positions—were extremely primitive, if at all available, the degree of social inequality in mortality figures exceeded by far the extent of similar disparities observable today.)

Another aspect of Jewish demography, whilst perhaps not of primary importance, but nevertheless distinctive for most Jewish groups observed, appears to be the above-mentioned rarity of illegitimate births. Low extramarital fertility is generally connected to reductions both in numbers of children and mortality rates. Even without a detailed exposition of data, one can demonstrate essential aspects of the social background of these processes. At almost all times in the modern era, since any relevant data started to be collected, the proportions of Jewish children born outside wedlock were merely fractions of those for non-Jewish children in comparable environments. Clearly, a relatively high uptake of birth-control techniques will have played a part in the avoidance of extramarital births, but in the majority of Jewish communities, even the poorest, relatively few women were exposed to unwanted pregnancy simply because their maidenhood was spent under much closer family and communal supervision. The main reason for that is closely tied up with the stratification of European Jewish populations in recent history. This was marked by the fact that, among other things, relatively few Jewish women were left to take up domestic service in a period when chambermaids made up by far the largest segment of working women and remained in most cases totally beyond family control. Likewise, due to the absolute rarity of Jewish peasantry or (later) industrial proletariat, few Jewish women became day-laborers or engage in other manual occupations. This is why few turned to prostitution, the latter profession being always largely recruited from the above-cited strata.

One may also list amongst the reasons the ideal of early marriage and (at least in the Orthodox family milieu) stricter-than-average collective supervision of women. In the milieu of conservative reform Jewry, amongst 'liberated' young women, the technical know-how for preventing unwanted pregnancy may well have been also better than average. Collective moral domestication and control of young girls, of course, was aimed not only at the preservation of prenuptial virginity that (prior to the late-twentieth-century 'sexual revolution') was so highly prized throughout the Jewish–Christian world, but also at warding off the risk of 'mixed' liaisons, the chances of which increased in direct relation to the age augmenting, amongst other things, the danger of being 'left on the shelf.' The infrequency of illegitimate births, as has already been noted, in itself moderated the incidence of child mortality because medical provision, ineffective as it was anyway for long, was even less extended to unmarried women and their children who, as a result, had substantially lower chances of survival than other members of their age-group.

Demographic consequences of renouncing religious affiliation

In the contemporary world, affiliation to denominationally or ethnically defined 'particularistic' communities is increasingly based on the voluntary acceptance or refusal of inherited identity. Since the nineteenth century, in an era of growing secularization, where ethnic boundaries started to be to some extent neutralized, the optional nature of identity choices has also been gaining ever-growing weight in the historical trends, as shown by demographic indices as well. That applies especially to Jewish communities, continually subjected to social pressure and often directly endangered, or at least threatened, as they have been. The Jews therefore always had to take account of 'strategically' motivated individual withdrawals (but also, occasionally, conversions or 'reversions') and the attendant impact on their numbers. In Judaism, at any rate, individual identity choices most often entailed negative, loss-provoking consequences, though adoption of Judaism was also not quite unknown (especially in the twentieth century). Since alliance with non-Jews and formal renunciation of religious identity represented the most palpable techniques for the prevention of the danger to which Jews continued to be exposed, and they might also rescue one's descendants from the in-built risks of Jewish social identity in the Christian world, it is hardly surprising that baptism (conversion) and mixed marriage often assumed a significant role in social strategies of modern Jewry.

Conversion to the Christian faith or entering marriage with a non-Jew were, in effect, rather similar mechanisms of withdrawal, and in the life strategies of those concerned they were often closely interdependent, with the one frequently following the other. The logic of these actions, as demonstrated by statistical indicators, is nevertheless in part rather divergent. While the frequency of conversions was strongly connected to outside social and political circumstances (like, notably, anti-Jewish crises), mixed marriages followed long-term trends and appeared to depend much less on historical junctures.

Quitting a denominational community essentially always rests on individual decision. The circumstances of admission into a new religious community usually play only a secondary role in the success of the undertaking, though it did happen that the authorities of the host church would make the integration of converts conditional on certain criteria (obligatory study of doctrine, a probationary period, proof of 'sincerity' of conversion, etc.). Changing faith only makes any sense in a social environment in which a negative valuation of Jewish identity is tied to religious status (rather than to bloodline, for example, as with the Nazis who interpreted religious status as no more than confirmation of 'racial' affiliation) and when the host church is able to offer advantages to offset the losses and disadvantages tied to apostasy. The balance of advantages and disadvantages (which is, for those affected, generally subject to an explicit weighing-up) naturally hinges on the entire set of material, political, moral and cultural goods that come into account, but purely symbolic considerations may also play a part (e.g. shame at deserting a community in its hour of danger, the moral odium of 'betrayal').

For that reason, change of faith by Jews is more likely in societies that are less or not at all secularized, and above all where and when apostasy is a major factor for social success or for reducing the threat to which Jews are exposed. In those cases, conversions can have consequences that are also demographically demonstrable.

It is also necessary that conversion should be acceptable to those concerned. In other words, it should not represent too great a 'price' or too big a 'leap in the dark.' In societies where conditions of segregation and mutual exclusion of Jews and non-Jews prevail because both of them attribute great significance to their religious and ethnic affiliations—where for instance they are radically separated by an ideology of 'otherness' based on political or 'racial' difference—Christianization signifies a way of 'changing sides,' 'going over to the enemy' or 'to the other side of the barricade.' This is not so readily acceptable either to those contemplating baptism or to their milieu. The 'deserted' group, the community of Jewish descent, has therefore always punished apostates more or less severely by cutting ties of friendship, business or even kinship (to the extent that traditional

Jewish families would go into public mourning for the defector treated as dead from the community's point of view). Often the 'host' religious community would itself display reservations towards 'strategic neophytes,' to say nothing of the fact that when anti-Semitism was gaining political ground, it was easy and common to reclassify converts or their descendants as 'legally Jewish' (as was universally the case in nazified Europe, through passage of 'Jewish laws' following the Nürnberg model).

Nor did Christianization hold the same significance for the two genders. As Jewish women rarely had an economically active role in most societies in question before the Shoah, 'strategic conversion' could hardly do much to smooth out a woman's career. Thus, conversion to increase one's professional chances was much more of a temptation for active males, whereas in case of women the underlying impetus was mostly linked to marital plans, with the existentially motivated aim of avoiding formal involvement in a 'mixed' marriage in a non-secularized milieu.

For all these reasons, the more far-reaching demographic consequences of converting to Christianity were manifested chiefly among 'westernized' Jews during periods when there was a drive for 'assimilation' (often coupled with a drive to miscegenation) and, above all, at times when the historical conditions were either highly favorable or highly unfavorable for the social integration of Jews. Within a traditional Jewish setting the demographic impact of apostasy was therefore, at all times, slight as compared with countries that offered better circumstances for assimilation. In addition, the proportion of converts was always highly subject to the cyclical strength of general attractive or oppressive factors. The attractive factors coincided with the totality of social advantages that went with assimilation. The most important oppressive factor was always the level and the crudity of anti-Semitism. Paroxysms of anti-Jewish hysteria generally (but only as a function of the affected community's current level of assimilation) tended to unleash tidal waves of conversions.

These phenomena are readily discernible in Berlin, for instance, which was the principal center for assimilation of German Jews from the end of the eighteenth century onwards. For that city we possess highly detailed statistics on baptism and defections from Jewish congregations. (From 1873 indeed, the legislation of the German Reich permitted individuals to leave the Jewish faith without entering another religious denomination.) The almost two centuries of relevant Berlin data, from 1750 onwards, can be projected onto the corresponding units of Jewish population. During the eighteenth century apostasy still occurred in negligible numbers (between 0 and 40 per 10,000 population). Those proportions then showed a rising tendency, particularly in the early nineteenth century when, admittedly with fluctuations, the first distinct wave of conversions is detectable during the 1810s and 20s. This was the period of Prussia's first emancipation law hallmarked by the nationalistic fervor of Germanized Jewish circles, with the anti-Napoleonic 'war of national liberation' as its background. Many Jews sensed that the opportunity had arisen for identifying with Germaneness and complete assimilation into local society. This may explain the large numbers of conversions which in some years ran as high as 150–180 per 10,000. Later, with the partial rescinding of the emancipatory measures, the 'spontaneous' assimilatory fever abated, but the proportion of those seeking a refuge from pressures (the 'Hep! Hep!' disturbances of 1819, for instance) continued to rise. That accounts for why conversions persisted at a high level of around 150–170 per 10,000 over subsequent decades. Despite these efforts on the part of Jews to assimilate, a slump in the numbers of conversions set in around mid-century, almost certainly because the 'assimilees' came to realize that their hopes of complete integration clashed with the hostility of most parts of German society. From the middle of the nineteenth century until the revolutions following the First World War (up to the anti-Semitic riots of the early Weimar Republic, around 1919) the rate of conversions ran at a low level: under 15 per 10,000 on average. In 1919, however, the index bounced back to 40, then subsequently fell back slightly up until the next outbreak of anti-Semitic violence marking the Nazi accession to power. In 1933 the index reached 63, only soon to surpass 120 and then remained at this high level, with some fluctuations, throughout the entire period of National Socialist rule, and that despite the fact that changing one's religion no longer warranted an exemption from persecution.

Similar trends are observable in other less secularized countries with blatantly anti-Semitic régimes where social segregation within classes was widely governed by the principle of religious affiliation. A typical case was Hungary, and most notably Budapest (for which there are more accurate sets of data comparable over time). The two critical periods of anti-Semitic outbursts—that of 1919–20 (the 'White Terror' which bloodily put down the short-lived Soviet Republic and introduced a *Numerus Clausus* to limit university entry by Jews) and then the period stretching from the so-called 'First Jewish Law' of May 1938 to the country's occupation by the German *Wehrmacht* in March 1944—both sparked large-scale waves of conversion. In the Hungarian capital the mean annual number of Jews adopting Christianity per 10,000 was around 300 in 1919, 400 in 1938, and in the months after the German invasion in 1944 (according to survey estimates) approximately 600.

In Italy, during the two years preceding the *Manifesto della Razza* of July 1938 (the first ever anti-Semitic measures in the country since its unification), there were no more than around 10 conversions per 10,000 Jewish inhabitants, but in its immediate wake this shot up to not less than 620 on average for the years 1939–40.

The demographic effect of such conversions can be traced in the ratio of neophytes in the 'host' population, that is to say, amongst those of Jewish origin (or 'of Jewish blood', in the statistical terminology of the Nazi era). Indices of this sort are only available for those countries and periods where statisticians of National Socialist persuasion attempted, with misplaced obduracy, to differentiate between 'Aryans', Jews and 'those of mixed blood.' In Austria, it is estimated that 21 per cent of the population (among them 90 per cent Viennese) subjected to racial persecution under Nazism were not members of the Israelite community. In Hungary, the 1941 census recorded that 7.8 per cent of the entire population 'of Jewish blood' were nominally Christian (which is almost certainly an underestimate). In the rump territories, remaining after the Trianon peace treaty, that ratio was 12 per cent, whilst in Budapest it was not less than 17 per cent. In the Protectorate of Bohemia and Moravia, of the 118,000 individuals deemed by the Nazi authorities to be Jewish, about 27 per cent were not of Israelite faith. In the Netherlands where, historically, anti-Jewish tensions had possibly been less palpable than anywhere else in Europe during the modern era, some 10 per cent of those affected by the German imposed racial laws did not belong to the Jewish community. Even in Berlin, the 1939 Nazi census recorded that 8.5 per cent of the remaining population 'of Jewish race' were Christian. That index must have been much higher in the times before the National Socialists came to power, as selective emigration and flight had no doubt sorted out more of the better assimilated, Christianized elements from the ranks of the persecuted. The baptized were, indeed, more likely to belong to the middle and upper classes of the local Jewish community, with a greater proportion of them having contacts abroad or capable to get their capital out of the country in the hope of establishing a new existence.

It is futile looking for similar data in Eastern Europe. East of the Elbe, extraordinarily little information is available on the extent of conversion, apart from certain categories of those who were coerced into Christianizing. One such example is provided by the Jewish children who were forcibly conscripted into the tsarist army between 1827 and 1856 (the so-called 'cantonists'). This suggests that in the Orthodox world of Eastern Europe conversion was reckoned to be exceptional. The demographic effects of those leaving the faith was appreciable only in some (but not in all) 'western'-type Jewish communities, and even there mainly in the critical periods, like those immediately prior to the Shoah.

Heterogamy and de-Judaization

It was noted earlier that entering a mixed marriage, the second factor for deserting Judaism, was in part driven by a quite different rationale. This holds good in two particular respects.

For one thing, marriage is an alliance of two adults which, by nature, is also binding on any offspring and, indeed, to some extent on the collateral relatives of the spouses and sometimes even on ascendants. The very possibility of mixed marriage therefore usually presupposes some measure of prior easing of the social segregation of the Jews and non-Jews in question, that is to say, a certain predisposition to accommodation on the part of the majority (non-Jewish) society towards the Jewish partner. Generally, the extended family on both sides will be opposed to or at least raise reservations against a proposed marriage between a Jew and a Christian. Indeed, an alliance of this kind most often can only take place if the would-be couple is able to withstand pressures exerted against their union. In that sense (despite appearances), mixed marriages are usually based on firm, voluntary decisions of the interested parties, or in other words, on more personal motivations and a far stronger joint resolution on the whole, than other (endogamous) marriages. That is indeed why those committed to mixed marriages are able to overcome the hostility and prohibitions with which they are confronted, and which other, less committed partners would be unable to withstand. It emerges from certain studies (e.g. for the years preceding the rise of fascism in Hungary) that mixed marriages entered into by Jewish men were less fragile (that is, had a lower probability of ending in divorce) during these least propitious times for Jewish–gentile wedlock. The implication could be that a stronger personal commitment is manifested in mixed marriages, and the marital bond here has a greater emotional freight than in the average of homogamous matches. (That appears to be less true, however, of mixed marriages contracted by Jewish women.)

At all events, we know from relevant studies that mixed marriages took place more regularly, above all in circles that professed universal scales of values: within the educated middle classes or between working-class partners who had been influenced by secularized, generally left-wing salvation ideologies. Their statistical frequency can therefore also be regarded as a good index of assimilation, in the same way as that of Christianization, though with a rather divergent meaning: unlike the response to threat, which is the most common motive force for apostasy, mixed marriages are more representative of specific cases of 'spontaneous' or 'natural' assimilation (that is those not directly under duress).

This overall characterization of mixed marriages is barely altered if we know that at times of rising anti-Jewish tension (e.g. throughout Central Europe during the 1930s) the Jewish party to a mixed marriage (especially if that was the male) may have initiated it in the interests of promoting his social acceptance, with a view to a kind of self-applied strategic 'whitewashing.' Marriage to a non-Jew may have secured a partial gain in status for the Jewish spouse in an anti-Semitic milieu or historical juncture. Considerations of this kind might have been the basis for marriage, but it has no decisive influence on the broad statistical trends, since their chances of success would always be dependent on the number of potential Christian spouses and the existence of circles willing to admit them. That explains why (and, at the same time, this is the other characteristic feature of the drive to mixed marriage, in comparison with conversion) the number of mixed marriages does not display the same extreme swings or fluctuations over time as the number of Christianizations. On the contrary, it is easy to see why the number of mixed marriages generally decreased during flare-ups of anti-Semitism, whereas it tended to rise in normal periods and under more favorable circumstances. At the same time, however, those affected show a very similar distribution by occupational class (with a preponderance of the urban educated middle classes and the working class) in regard to the probability of both mixed marriage and conversion. There was an equally similar contrast between the predominantly Western and Central European Jewish communities disposed to assimilate and the more strongly traditionalist Eastern European communities.

Statistical examination of mixed marriages raises a string of complex issues which, although they cannot be detailed here, do at least deserve mention. Amongst these is the system of contrasting chances of Jewish men and women on the 'market' of matrimonial mixing which was generally much lower for women. It is also interesting to study the historical evolution of motives for entering into 'strategic' mixed marriages. The denominational distribution of non-Jewish partners, which in some periods shows an over-representation of Protestant faiths, even in predominantly Roman Catholic societies (as in Vienna, for example), offers a measure of the relative distance opposing Jews to the members of various Christian denominations. The ethnically linked probabilities of mixed marriages in multiethnic communities have the same functions as to inter-ethnic distance. Correlations between social mésalliance and denominationally mixed marriages (the practice of 'double Jewish heterogamy,' whereby Jewish men could choose to enter a strategic mixed marriage with a woman of 'lower class'), point to strategic uses of matrimony in anti-Semitic environments. The incidence of 'pseudo-mixed' (between two already 'converted' Jews) or 'covert mixed' (between an already 'converted' Jew and a Christian) marriages show the complexity and problematic nature of the statistical indicators or matrimonial mixing. One should also take into account historical metamorphoses of power relations between the spouses in mixed marriages. The frequency (usually uncommon) with which commitments are made prior to marriage regarding the faith of any progeny can be an indicator of secularization of those concerned: the statistical distribution of denominations actually chosen for the offspring affected can also demonstate the actual power relations within the couple, together with the more or less 'assimilationist' orientation of the Jewish partner. The observed risk of divorce (often higher than average) and the number of offspring (generally below the average) may serve for an assessment of the solidity and/or the individualized nature of the matches as compared to homogamous marriages.

We may cite a few examples of the phenomenon that carry significant demographic weight in this respect, without going into any extensive analyses.

Already by 1876–80 some 14 per cent of Jews who entered into marriage in Berlin, the big center of Jewish assimilation in Germany, wedded a non-Jew, and that proportion had more than doubled, elevated to 30 per cent by 1929. Taking Germany as a whole, during this same half century the proportion of Jews who married a Christian rose from 7 to around 24 per cent. A virtually identical process took place in Vienna. At the end of the nineteenth century 8 per cent of all marriages contracted by Jews were to Christian partners, and that had risen to 30 per cent by 1930. The picture is similar for Budapest, the main assimilatory melting pot in Hungary. There the frequency of mixed marriages shows a steady increase from the end of the nineteenth century (when these were first permitted at all under the legislation of 1894 on civil marriage), even during the 1919–20 anti-Semitic excesses and despite the 'Christian' political course pursued by Hungarian régimes of the inter-war era. It reached a first peak (approximately 20 per cent of Jewish men marrying in Budapest) on the eve of the First Anti-Jewish Law of 1938 and again in the months before the 'race-protectionist' Third Jewish Law came into effect on the 1st of November, 1941. In some provincial cities (Szeged, Pécs, Arad, Temesvár-Timişoara) the proportion of marriages that Jews entered into with Christians approached, and often surpassed, that for the capital. The trend in Czechoslovakia, albeit under sharply different socio–political circumstances, was similar. From a very modest base (less than 2 per cent of marriages entered into by Jews in 1910 were mixed), this proportion suddenly jumped: by around 1930 the rate of mixed marriages in Czechoslovakia—at that time the sole democracy in Central Europe—had reached 28 per cent. In Trieste, another major Central European center of socially well assimilated Jewry, this proportion was already 18 per cent by 1901–03, and in little more than twenty years such marriages were in a clear majority (56 per cent in 1927). A relatively high and (critical periods apart) steadily growing incidence of mixed marriages can also be picked up in those Western European countries for which such information is available at all (e.g. in the Netherlands and Italy).

In keeping with the lower degree of assimilation of the local Jewish population, a different course was taken by the marriage market in Eastern Europe where the available—in any case sporadic—data point to mixed marriages being stuck at a lower level. In Galicia, during the period of 1895–1909 there were just as few Jews marrying non-Jews as there had been in 1881–85, a statistically negligible 0.4 per cent in either period. Both then and later on, right up to the Shoah, the same can be found for the easternmost parts of Hungary (e.g. County Máramaros) and from 1918 in the eastern territories of Czechoslovakia, another major area of settlement for Jews of 'eastern type.' Only after the Shoah did the surviving contingents of the Jewish community start to attain a previously unknown degree of social integration (primarily through the aggressively assimilationist and anti-religious policies pursued by régimes drawn into the Soviet sphere of influence). The proportion of Jewish-Christian marriages rose there to many times the earlier rate since the 1950s, until these gradually lost their exceptional character (as will be discussed in the final chapter).

To sum up, we can conclude that only in 'western'-type Jewish communities did 'strategic' renunciation of Judaism play a role—but a growing role—in making them numerically weaker before the Shoah. For those eastern Jews who escaped the carnage and stayed there, Communist régimes would later create the conditions for mixed marriages to become the general rule, albeit at the price of more or less coerced surrender and loss of their Jewish identity.

Table 1: Numerical evolution of the Jewish population in the world (1780–1967)*

	1780	1820	1860	1900	1939	1948	1967
Austria				180	191 (2.8)	31 (0.4)	13 (0.1)
Belgium		2 (0.1)		20 (0.3)	70 (0.9)	45 (0.6)	40 (0.6)
Bulgaria					50 (0.7)	45 (0.6)	6 (0.4)
Czechoslovakia					357 (2.4)	42 (0.3)	15 (0.1)
Bohemia	39	60	90	93	76 (1.2)		
Moravia		28	43	44	41 (1.2)		
Slovakia					137 (4.1)		
Ruthenia					103 (14.1)		
Estonia					5 (0.5)		
France	40 (0.2)	50 (0.2)	70 (0.2)	80	260 (0.5)	235 (0.6)	540 (1.0)
Galicia	151	240	450 (9.7)	811 (11.1)			
Germany		223 (0.9)	450 (1.0)	587 (1.0)	240 (0.3)	153 (0.4)	30 (0.05)
Great Britain		20 (0.1)	60 (0.2)	200 (0.5)	340 (0.7)	345 (0.7)	450 (0.8)
Greece				10	73 (1.2)	9 (0.1)	7 (0.1)
Hungary	81 (0.9)	150 (1.5)	450 (3.3)	850 (5.0)	445 (5.0)	174 (1.9)	80 (0.8)
Italy	25	25 (0.1)	35 (0.1)	48 (0.1)	53 (0.1)	35 (0.1)	
Latvia					95 (4.9)		50 (2.0)
Lithuania			32	78 (5.5)	155 (7.6)		25 (0.1)
Netherlands		45 (1.8)	104 (2.0)	112 (1.4)	28 (0.3)	30 (0.3)	
Poland					3,250 (10.0)	88	21

Romania		80 (2.4)	267 (4.5)	850 (4.7)	380 (2.3)	110 (0.6)
Russia		1,600 (3.5)	5,190 (4.9)	2,825 (2.1)	2,600 (1.1)	2,600 (1.1)
Sweden		2		7 (0.1)	15 (0.2)	
Switzerland	2 (0.1)	13 (0.4)	18 (0.5)	35 (0.8)	25 (0.4)	13 (0.2)
Turkey¶				50 (4.0)	80 (0.4)	40 (3.3)
Yugoslavia				68 (0.5)	10 (0.08)	7 (0.05)
Serbia		2	6	20		
Croatia		9	18			
Bosnia	1.5		8	14		1.3
EUROPE		2,730	8,690	9,870	4,360	4,070
N. AMERICA	5	8 (0.15)	1,016 (1.3)	5,115 (3.6)	5,180 (3.5)	6,150 (2.8)
S. AMERICA			34 (0.09)	331 (0.5)	567 (0.5)	781 (0.3)
ASIA			420	1,047	1,030	2,544
Palestine (Israel)	45		78 (12.0)	475 (32.4)	750 (75)	2,436 (86)
N. AFRICA			298 (1.1)	452 (1.1)	563 (1.5)	63 (0.1)
W. AND S. AFRICA			40 (3.9)	91 (0.9)	154 (0.7)	132 (0.3)
OCEANIA	1		17 (0.3)	32 (0.3)	41 (0.4)	75 (0.4)
TOTAL†		3,280	10,600	16,940	11,900	13,840

* Figures in 1,000; percentage of the total population in parenthesis

¶ Including Asia Minor

† Including countries and areas not separately designated

Source: *Encyclopaedia Judaica*, based on the entries under 'Population' and 'Demography' as well as those for individual states. All figures are estimates, given that data in many cases vary from source to source.

Table 2: Birth and death rates per 1,000 inhabitants for some Jewish populations

		Births		Deaths		Natural increase	
		Jews	Total	Jews	Total	Jews	Total
Amsterdam	1899–1900	25	30	12	17	13	13
	1912–22	19	22	11	11	8	11
Bulgaria	1891–95	38	38	23	28	15	10
	1904–07	34	43	14	22	20	21
	1925–28	22	35	11	18	11	17
	1933–36	17	28	10	15	7	13
Galicia	1882	46	48	29	36	17	12
	1901–02	38	44	19	27	19	17
	1910	32	39	16	24	16	15
Hungary	1891–95	36	42	19	33	17	9
	1906–10	29	36	15	25	14	11
	1926–30	13	26	14	17	−1	9
	1931–35	11	22	14	16	−3	6
Budapest	1931–34	8	16	15	16	−7	0
Italy	1851–75	29	37	24	31	5	6
	1876–1900	23	36	20	26	3	10
	1901–10	18	33	17	22	1	11
	1921–30	16	28	17	17	−1	11
	1931–35	11	24	17	14	−6	10
Russian Poland	1906	29	39	16	23	13	16
Poland	1926–30	21	32	11	17	10	15
	1931–35	19	28	10	15	9	13
Warsaw	1930–36	13	14	10	12	3	2
Prussia	1822–40	36	40	22	30	14	10
	1876–80	32	39	18	24	14	15
	1906–10	17	32	14	17	3	15
	1921–25	14	23	13	14	1	9
	1933	7	15	16	11	−9	4
Berlin	1925	12	12	14	11	−2	1
Romania	1881–86	47	41	26	26	21	15
	1906–10	30	40	17	26	13	14
	1926–28	20	36	13	22	7	14
	1936–38	14	31	13	19	1	12
Vienna	1880	28	40	14	28	14	12
	1901–10	18	27	14	18	4	9
	1934	4	6	14	12	−10	−6

Source: *Encyclopædia Judaica.*

Dismantling of feudalism as a liberating process

The political modernization of European states and the attainment of Jewish emancipation were very much functions of the success in removing all the restrictive legal frameworks that rigidly and, in large part, immutably, fixed the positions assigned to various groups in the social hierarchy and in public spheres of activity, including economic life. For Jews, burdened by a multiplicity of occupational prohibitions, the break-up of feudalism, from the very start and at virtually all times, was associated with an alleviation and restriction of the constraints that had been applied against them. Economic emancipation of Jews in reality usually preceded, to a large extent, legal emancipation. Only the sway gained by totalitarian régimes inspired by right extremism, above all Nazism and the rise of Fascism in a majority of the states of Central Europe, was to buck the prevalence of this historical trend over the long term.

The process of liberation took place under basically three different disguises. First and foremost, there was a broadening of the range of occupations and economic activities open to Jews, Jews gaining progressively more or less free access to economic—and (above all in the West) sometimes even political—positions that had formerly been barred to them. Second, the possibility of making investments of an economic or status-symbolic nature was equally opened up for Jews, with the freedom of long-term capital investments to secure their status and promote the social reproduction of the group. These included the acquisition of property (land, home, money-making property), investments in capital equipment (businesses, machines, workshops), procurements of intellectual capital of a secular nature (public schooling, training in music, art and other intellectual domains, along with their material preconditions, such as access to libraries, theatres, etc.), and last of all, to assert that enhanced social status, the purchase of 'trophy' goods or those of social distinctions (country house, stable of horses, estate, luxury boat, car, sword collection, etc.) or investments of a purely symbolic kind (a 'good' address, family name with a 'national' ring, university qualifications, a patent of nobility, officially bestowed forms of address such as *Hofrat*, or privy councilor—all much-esteemed titles in Austria–Hungary and imperial Germany). Third, the fall of feudalism entailed a growing degree of legal security regarding the occupations that Jews could get engaged in and the investments that they effected. That legal security varied, of course, with the degree of emancipation: it remained weak (though far from inexistent, thanks to the partial independence of tribunals) in Russia and Romania, whilst becoming ever more complete, from the mid-nineteenth century onwards, elsewhere in Europe. Accordingly, they were no longer exposed to the risk of arbitrary expulsion from town, village or country (except of course precisely in Russia and Romania). Depending on local circumstances, Jews henceforth possessed legal remedies with which they could protect themselves from anti-Semitic violence or official abuses. Their economic investments were also protected by laws that were enforced with growing efficacy, in many cases even under régimes that were in cahoots with political anti-Semitism.

Helpful as it may be to emphasize the liberating nature of the process, however, it also has to be noted that nowhere did this achieve its final objectives. Full equality of opportunity between Jews and non-Jews, the complete neutralization of the special social status of Jews was never accomplished before the Shoah. The risk of discrimination did not disappear entirely, even in the western democracies, however reduced and marginal they could appear by the twentieth century. Indeed, new types of exclusion and corresponding forms of prejudicial treatment sprang up everywhere, even after the official granting of emancipation. Sanction was thus given to the practice of allotting to Jews—whilst still upholding official principles of equality – various forms of negatively distinctive lot within the prevailing social set-up. The sources of further rigidification of relations between Jews and non-Jews became, to be sure, more tangled than ever before. Criteria of attraction, preference and choice between groups, of the cohesion of the 'like-minded,' were augmented with additional factors. Amongst these, naturally enough, was the persistence of anti-Judaism, whereby the prospects for Jews to prosper in certain areas of activity or investment would happen to be sometimes dramatically reduced. Yet economic or occupational aptitudes and options that had been historically developed and become fixed as 'customary' within Jewry itself were likewise powerful channeling agencies of professional and economic orientations, to say nothing of the sometimes decisive role that continued to be played by old investments (for example within families of traders) that held heirs within the sphere of attraction of their economic inheritance. Some occupational choices were determined by the religious needs and commitments of active traditionalist Jewry.

For all these general reasons, during the period of social regeneration and the rise of nation-states in Europe the Jewish world also experienced substantial professional and economic transformations, though these might display extreme disparities according to the local socio–economic stratification and opportunities. Those variations can be categorized by three main features.

First and foremost, after the fall of feudalism, Jews were generally much more often and closely involved in building a free market economy, and exploiting chances for social mobility that this opened, than the majority of their Christian fellow-citizens. Taking into account the pace of *embourgeoisement* (*Verbürgerlichung* in the German historical terminology) Jews were usually (though not universally and in every historical juncture) considerably ahead of their milieu in terms of entrepreneurial creativity, intellectual innovations, professionalization or technological modernization of industry and trade. Jews were therefore (as compared to their demographic size) much more likely than non-Jews to be found in some of the new occupations created by the dynamics of economic modernization.

Consequently, almost everywhere in nineteenth and twentieth century Europe a 'time-lag'—sometimes quite marked—can be observed between Jews and non-Jews in favor of the former in matters of modernization. (That is not necessarily to imply that Jews surpassed non-Jews everywhere by their objectivated achievements in mobility and professional success, since the historical starting position and the social conditions for modernization were by far not the same for the two clusters.) If we examine the grounds for these disparities, it turns out that these are largely deriving from the positions that Jews occupied within the feudal structures.

Finally, certain mechanisms giving rise to the shifts and 'time-lags' cited continued to operate after legal emancipation of Jews (in some cases down to the present day), particularly in societies and phases of historical development marked by Judaeophobia. Occupational choices and patterns of professional behavior obey a certain historical logic, sometimes inherited from a long-gone past, often being passed on from one generation to the next—again to say nothing of the continuity of family investments—until they come to be seen, often enough, as 'natural' options sanctioned by custom (or even justified by religious needs, in some cases). As a net result, the occupational–economic stratification of Jews remained distinctive throughout Europe, and indeed elsewhere, even in the present age.

A lot of continuity has been preserved indeed across all the subsequent processes of restratifications of Jewry throughout the ages. In interpreting these one has to take into account, first of all, the relevant historical antecedents, especially the particular prerequisites that religious affiliations set for the array of economic and occupational choices among the Orthodox. We can then endeavor to present the concrete outcomes of major economic and professional transfers in modern times, and lastly, show the mechanisms by which 'overeducation,' the accumulation of high levels of intellectual capital, on the one hand, the assimilationist drive, on the other hand, exerted their effect.

Historical antecedents of economic modernization: exclusion and its compensation

To somewhat simplify matters, one may distinguish three historical dimensions of Jewry's traditional socio-economic status that would continue to exert an influence after the fall of feudalism: the occupational exclusions and prohibitions experienced under the feudal system together with distinctive patterns of compensatory capital accumulation that sprang from this; the collective propensities and competences of a proto-capitalist nature built up during the same era by Jews; and finally, a number of basic attitudes and dispositions attributable to religious particularism.

We can analyze here only some of the most general, and what should be judged as the most typical interconnections, so it is not possible to consider every local peculiarity of the socio–economic status that was reserved for Jews or that they succeeded in carving out for themselves. The discussion must be restricted, to boot, to Christian societies, which embraced the overwhelming bulk of European Jewry, but differed in their economic condition from the Balkan provinces under Ottoman suzerainty up the middle of the nineteenth century.

The feudal system of exclusion, as it related to Jews, was a dual one. In general, Jews were forbidden from pursuing occupations and activities in which they might come into direct and widespread competition with Christians. This meant, above all, exclusion from the agricultural and craft-industrial production that gave employment to the bulk of active majority in feudal societies. The only exemptions from this prohibition concerned small-scale crafts meeting the internal needs of the Jewish community and, in some cases, the cultivation of, or rather the employment of others to cultivate leased lands. Accordingly, apart from farming, Jews were usually also prohibited from acquiring mines and, most especially, landed property. They were likewise excluded from industrial production for the market, that is to say from craft guilds, with their local monopoly positions, but also from most services that had a handicraft character, except the very few occupations that were not subject to guild regulation. Similarly, they could not invest in income-bearing real estate or proprietary rights (e.g. fishing rights, vineyards, hunting-grounds, etc.); indeed, with occasional exceptions, they were not allowed to purchase building plots or private dwelling-houses either (not even, more often than not, for purposes of constructing a synagogue). Only exceptionally were they allowed, individually, to hold positions of power or public offices, in most cases only in the service of Jewish communities.

Observable more or less everywhere, this combination of legal prohibitions pushed the permitted sphere of activities for Jews to the periphery of pre-industrial Europe's economic structure. With the possible exception of certain lately colonized territories in 'New Russia,' nowhere was a single form of economic autonomy (above all the independence that could be secured through self-sufficient food production) accessible to Jews in relation to the big estates of the feudal social order: serfs, guild-organized merchant and artisan burghers, landowning gentry, and urban patricians (who often joined landed estates to its commercial and industrial capital). The only roles open to them, then, were essentially those outside the productive economy proper, yet highly dependent on it, such as certain occupations concerned with barter and middleman services between producers, consumers and investors. These narrow occupational niches—in international or interregional trade, pawnbroking, usury, dealing (in some goods only, like second-hand clothes, leather, feathers), peddling or hawking, for instance—were often, particularly in Eastern Europe, explicitly reserved for 'foreigners' anyhow, who had no independent legal status within the local feudal system. 'Jewish' economic functions, therefore, not infrequently overlapped the spheres of other ethnic and social outsiders—in Eastern Europe, for instance, the likes of the Armenians, 'Greeks' (including Romanians or Serbs often qualified as such following their Eastern Orthodox faith) or other 'Levantines' (usually citizens of the Ottoman Empire), and sometimes even Germans in particular.

Besides these 'intermediary' occupations, Jews might gain access to other specific markets, equally restricted but shared between 'natives' and 'outsiders,' the privileges for which were at the disposal of members of the feudal ruling class or (less often) which functioned as intellectual free markets. Amongst the former were the leaseholds on aristocratic or princely benefices (distilling, inn-keeping, collecting taxes and bridge or road tolls, etc.) and the management of estates (the two often going together in Eastern Europe), amongst the latter, certain emergent liberal professions, such as medicine, private teaching (e.g. music and languages) or branches of private scholarship (e.g. astrology). To those must be added activities connected to the ritual needs of Jewish communities, which, in the absence of an institutionalized clergy and due to the multiplicity of social functions they performed (additionally to ritual functions proper), mobilized probably a larger proportion of the active male population than was the case with Christian Churches.

The exclusions implemented in the feudal system can be interpreted, above all, as tight shackles on socio–economic mobility, yet also, at the same time, as factors whose effect could and indeed often tended to switch sign with the breakdown of feudal society.

The same restrictions and occupational choices that had been imposed on Jews prior to emancipation were subsequently to evolve into what was more or less a distinctive set of conditions for successful engagement in free markets of the early capitalist system. Already at the very outset of modernization, precisely due to their exclusion from the main branches of the feudal economy, Jews constituted a sort of proto-bourgeois stratum, inasmuch as they were already then driven to certain forms of rational economic behavior—including the principle of maximizing profitability, risk assessment, calculation of anticipated rates of return, entrepreneurial innovations, exploration of new (not forbidden) economic markets, minimization of consumption in order to maximize capital accumulation, etc.—that would later be characterized as emanating from the 'capitalist spirit.' All this was customary for most Jews, let it be emphasized, even before the conditions for a free market economy were in place. As a result, at the favorable historical juncture that followed the abolition of feudalism and the start of the process of industrialization, substantial proto-bourgeois sections of Jewry were able to assume rapidly certain essential market functions of the capitalist entrepreneurial stratum and professional intelligentsia, since they were often better prepared than their fellow-competitors (especially in lately industrialized Eastern Europe) to adopt not just the economic behavior but also the mentality and life strategies required by the emergent free markets. In short, the earlier disadvantages all at once turned into cyclical advantages. Whereas Jews, precisely due to the constraints they had endured, had always been obliged to seek market success, and had evolved a corresponding set of coping mechanisms, it was much harder for other agents in the feudal economy, on emerging from the closed and regulated structures of that economy, to adapt to the rules for free market success and exploit its opportunities.

What, specifically, did that mean in concrete historical terms?

First and foremost we must be reminded of the fact, that since Jews had not been permitted to tie up capital in land and other immovable property, they had always been obliged to accumulate more liquid assets. The depositing of cash in strong-boxes was also motivated by a need to have at one's disposal reserves that could easily be mobilized and concealed at times of uncertainty over collective existence, risk of expulsion, attacks or other danger. This gave them a head-start in the market for financial métiers and, at the same time, allowed them, when capitalist markets opened up and legal security started to be secured, to invest in the most lucrative-looking industrial, commercial and other markets. It is also likely that the very activities forced on them in feudal times, especially wholesale trading, 'money management' and other 'intermediary' services, proved to be more profitable—investments of time and labor being equal—than the occupations erstwhile closed to them. (Moreover, the balance of time taken up in pursuit of the 'Jewish' occupations permitted the preservation of a traditional religious culture, based as it was on individual and family ceremonies and the prominent cultic role for men, together with its requirement of an incomparably greater intellectual effort and time than in Christian worship.)

Second, when the medieval Church prohibited Christians from charging interest on loans of money (usury) it handed the Jews this highly lucrative business in a situation where lack of credit was a structural bane of the economy. In the end, the restrictions they endured necessarily also led to the development of certain competitive qualities and virtues that promised to compensate for socio–economic disadvantages, making those involved tenacious and disciplined, fostering self-restraint and a readiness to 'seize the moment,' disposing them to evolve a strict work ethic, enlarge their market intelligence, etc. Put in more general terms, through being compelled to remain alien from the scale of values prevailing in the feudal caste system, and thus not having cultivated the corresponding rules of behavior within their circles, Jews were subsequently able to turn far more easily to occupations that many of their potential fellow competitors— scions of the gentry, urban patricians of commoner descent, guild craftsmen—looked on as undignified and beneath their station (*nicht standesgemäss*). That is how in countries that entered late feudalism, in other words throughout Central and Eastern Europe, Jews were able to retain their key roles in the world of banking and most branches of wholesale trade, because the members of the Christian new middle classes continued to turn their noses up at the business of 'money-grubbing,' as also at certain occupations that called for a 'service' cast of mind (especially those involving a manual and not only intellectual element, such as human and veterinary medicine). Of course, one of the reasons why these métiers often enjoyed such a lowly prestige on the feudal and post-feudal hierarchy of professional values was precisely because they had traditionally been allotted to Jews or other 'inferior aliens.' The fact that Jews often proved more suited than non-Jews to thriving in the new capitalist markets can be, thus, traced back to their historically evolved collective skills and mental aptitudes, the characteristics of the fields of activity that they had taken up on the emergence of the free market economy.

In this connection, the objective social selection Jews underwent when they were authorized to settle in various countries of immigration deserves special attention. In many places, such as the cities and states of Germany before emancipation, Vienna up to 1848 for example, only those Jews in possession of a pre-fixed intellectual or financial capital (i.e. wealthy moneylenders and merchants, physicians and sometimes other scholars) received permits to settle down. In practice that applied to most western host countries in the modern and contemporary eras. From the seventeenth century onwards, the *Hoffaktors* and other privileged Jews accordingly formed locally tiny bourgeois and intellectual élites endowed with a high material status and often also a distinguished educational level. When feudal restrictions were abolished, they therefore had a head start in filling the role of a modern entrepreneurial class and professional intelligentsia. But, prior to emancipation, they numbered no more than a few hundreds or thousands in cities that had been otherwise closed to Jewish immigration (such as Vienna, Berlin or Paris). In even more general terms, the self-selection of immigrants was universally a function of age (preferentially the young) and gender (primarily males), in addition, of course, to expertise, professional adaptability and capital means. The same is also observable in the big 'strategic' migratory waves to Hungary (prior to the 1850s), Vienna and Germany (in the latter half of the nineteenth century) or America (out of Germany from the 1850s onwards, and out of other parts of Central and Eastern Europe after the 1880s). Such 'positive selection' can be regarded as instrumental in the fact that many of these immigrants found it easier than possible rivals to gain a footing in the emerging economic markets of host countries.

The exceptional capabilities linked to the vocational specialization earlier enforced on Jews were, in any event, strong contributory factors to their competitive ability in capitalist markets. Those advantages were brought to bear most directly in financial disciplines, the practitioners of which necessarily had to make constant assessments of risks and expected profits. This is a type of economic rationality the principles of which were certainly not readily applicable to other branches of pre-industrial activity (notably agriculture or mining). However, the position of exclusion from the feudal system also contributed in part to developing conducts of 'worldly asceticism,' to borrow Max Weber's expression which, of course, was not without moral support in the Judaic faith and obviously favored economic success. As noted

above, Jews had little chance to tie down their capital, before emancipation, over the long term, so that they either invested it in businesses
that promised the best return, or possibly accumulated it in cash form
as a safety reserve, or to await more profitable investment opportunities in the future. Purchase of a castle, manor, town mansion and the
like was totally out of the question, so they were unable to enter into
the feudal élite's consumer culture of acquiring patrimonial status
symbols. On the contrary, the anti-Judaism of their environment, and
the need to ward off its attendant risks, impelled them to avoid atten-
tion-seeking in any aspect of their outward appearance (dress, mode of
travel, place of domicile). They were thereby further constrained to
extreme moderation in relation to their income level. The Jews' customary (albeit often compulsory) uniformity of dress prior to emancipation concealed a similar self-discipline and self-restriction. Ghetto
life in itself, typical in western countries, forced them into systematic
'residential underconsumption,' if only because growth in the population enclosed within the walls was inversely related to the living space
at their disposal. In the ghetto there was no way of expanding the living space according to needs, of setting up in line with one's financial
standing.

Furthermore, even at the dawn of the modern age, the leaders of
their communities were still setting the authority of stern traditional
law against conspicuous consumption. The *Halakhah*'s legal rulings
against any kind of luxury, often delving into the minutest detail, were
first codified in Spain, in opposition to the Jewish élite of the time,
many of whom were living in considerable opulence. Subsequently,
between the sixteenth and eighteenth centuries, that code spread more
or less generally to other communities in Europe. The aim was partly
to moderate 'overconsumption' by wealthy Jews, but partly also—and
this is the odder feature—to set upper limits to what were acceptable
expenditures for any particular person in relation to his income. Such
regulations to limit consumption obviously served to boost the community cash-box as well, but also to institutionalize the moral com-
mandment to assist co-religionists in need. The logic of success in the
capitalist markets, however, equally demanded a degree of self-
restraint via the preference to be given to investments producing a
calculable return over unproductive expenditures, or in other words, to
reining back on consumption. Ingrained habits of 'inner worldly as-

ceticism' amongst affected Jews likewise became a precursor to their enhanced chances of success in the free market economy that opened up with the decline of feudal society.

Religious intellectualism and economic modernization

The demands of Judaic religious practice played an especially important part in cultivating the socio-economic virtues, capabilities and aptitudinal factors that were found across a broad spectrum of active Jewish men at the dawn of the modern age, and from at least three distinct viewpoints, namely, those of religious intellectualism, habitual discipline and self-control, and the sense of community.

Religious intellectualism denotes the whole system entailing the obligatory acquisition of the knowledge and abilities necessary for the practice of their religion by adult male Jews, making up the bulk of the economically active population. That means, primarily, a sufficient level of familiarity with the Hebrew language, enabling the study of Hebrew works—the Bible, the *Talmud*, etc.—constituting the essential religious and cultural heritage of Jewry (the only collective patrimony considered indeed as 'sacred' since the destruction of the Temple by the Romans). Thus, literacy and learning were, on the one hand, an indispensable practical requirement for taking an active part in public worship and for conducting the many rites carried out at home (for example, the family celebration of Pessah, or Passover), whilst, on the other hand, they fulfilled the basic cultural ideal of religious Jewry. From that simple fact alone it follows that in pre-modern Europe Jews constituted the sole ethnic group expecting from its adult male members to be both literate and bi- or multilingual. Indeed, besides the Jewish dialect(s) used in everyday life (Yiddish, Ladino, etc.) together with the practical knowledge of one or several language(s) of the country, anyone seeking to be a worthy member of his community also had to have some command of classical Hebrew.

The actual degree and depth of that literacy and multilingualism may have differed from case to case. These will certainly have covered wide disparities within the groups in question. Yet even so, Jewish religious intellectualism as characterized above was an unusual phenomenon on the cultural map of pre-modern Europe, especially in the Central and Eastern parts of the continent, where the overwhelming majority of world Jewry lived at that time and where substantial sections of even the titular feudal élites—let alone the rank and file indigenous population (for instance, the Greek Orthodox clergy or the petty nobility in Hungary, Poland, Russia, Ukraine, etc.)—remained partially or wholly illiterate up to the nineteenth century and, sometimes, beyond.

It should be emphasized that this Jewish 'cultural exception' was not purely a matter of ability to read and write. The scope of application of Jewish religious intellectualism spread much wider, at least for males. For a by no means negligible fraction of men, regular study of the *Pentateuch* and post-Biblical texts also held to be holy (*Talmud, Gemara, Kabbalah, Shulchan Arukh, Halakhah*), irrespective of their occupation, constituted an organic part of their religious obligations and often occupied a large portion of their free time throughout their life. Though similar prescriptions do also exist for certain Protestant sects, Judaism is at any rate the sole denomination in modern Europe that prescribes continual engagement with the literature forming the basis of the faith. This included, ideally, when opportunity arose, rote learning and interpretation of substantial chunks of text, and this from early childhood (4–5 years of age) on, throughout the entire life-cycle of males.

In most parts of Europe dominated by the Roman Catholic and Greek Orthodox Churches (though perhaps to a lesser extent in Protestant countries), the general level of instruction of the lower classes, even after the nineteenth century, displayed very serious shortcomings, even in urban environments, because of the lack or the weakness of the network of primary schools. Meanwhile, Jewish communities everywhere, even in the most impoverished parts of Eastern Europe, were committed to transmitting the written Judaic culture by maintaining elementary *chederim* and, in many places, also *yeshivot,* supplying higher levels of religious education. In traditionalist Jewish communities—even in the poorest ones—substantial proportions of young men actually attended the latter institutions too. The instruction handed down within their walls was conducted in two Jewish languages—first in Hebrew and second, in Yiddish (for purposes of explanation, translation and commentary) in the Ashkenazi world. Religious instruction thus demanded, as a matter of course, a high degree of intellectual effort and also a certain bilingualism, in principle, from most of the Jewish male population.

This intellectualism tied to the practice of religion had a manifold impact on the improvement of professional chances of all those concerned, especially during the first period of modernization. Here we shall only point to the most important connections.

Once the gates to institutions of middle and higher-level schools had been opened to Jews (e.g. following Joseph II's Tolerance Patent in Austria–Hungary), the conditions favoring religious culture and literacy facilitated success in every other intellectual occupation. A religious 'cultural capital' of this sort in the broader sense meant, to start with, that the furniture in homes would include writing-desks, shelves for books and other facilities for study. Furthermore Jews were used to handling familiarly books, reading them, reflecting upon their message, hence getting engaged in logical reasoning. Particularly for purposes of interpreting articles of faith and ritual laws, they also developed the habit of thinking in abstractions as well as a corresponding oral culture to verbalize that. These skills were readily convertible into applied and secular learning habits, in a common intellectual capital of sorts, obviously instrumental in the pursuit of occupations such as medicine, legal careers, journalism, teaching, etc. Certain crafts related to religious intellectualism, such as publishing and decorating holy texts, working precious metals in the applied arts, architecture that served ritual purposes, etc. could be transferred virtually immediately into secular intellectual occupations (in the book trade, publishing, printing, the press, the applied arts, and so on).

Thus, more generally, religious intellectualism became the basic historical paradigm for Jewish intellectual investments, also leading on to secular 'overeducation' (which will be discussed in detail later in this chapter). The secularization of religious learning habits opened up opportunities for a wide spectrum of career choices, for greater occupational mobility, but also for the progressive secularization and rationalization of lifestyles and life strategies, including in many cases the withdrawal from Orthodox religious traditions.

The relation to Judaism and to the religious tradition could, indeed, have a manifold concrete influence, positive or negative, on career preferences as well as on the chances of success in the chosen occupation.

Traditionalist Jews were always able (and doing their best) to reconcile religious needs and demands that were important to them with those of their occupation. This was the root of the requirement for economic independence and for the dwelling to be close to the prayer house, a necessary condition for unhindered compliance with the Sabbath and holiday ritual requirements (abstention from work, prohibition to travel or even to use vehicles, attendance by men at collective worship in the synagogue). Only pursuing certain kinds of commerce, financial services, and craftwork as a self-employed person (or as an employee of such) made that possible. Similarly, such occupations only permitted one's free time to be dedicated to initiating children into religious studies. That is one reason why trade, banking and other related occupations have always remained consistently overrepresented in the economic stratification of traditional Jewry. Religious intellectualism did also develop, incidentally, instrumental abilities that could be of direct use in certain branches of the economy: commerce in general and international trade in particular. In *chederim* and *yeshivot* young Jews learnt how to handle figures and certain abstract concepts, which was a training for developing in due course the set of habits required by rational market behavior.

Bilingualism practiced in religious studies constituted a linguistic competence that was likewise of material use in commerce, enabling Jewish traders to conduct correspondence and settlement of accounts amongst one another in Hebrew (which in practice also excluded the risk of indiscretion to outside competitors), whilst a rudimentary multilingualism assured the mental preparation invaluable to acquiring other useful foreign languages. Jews therefore found it easy to pick up local dialects, German above all, which, from the eighteenth century onwards, functioned as the language of communication between élites and the broad urban strata throughout Central and Eastern Europe. That, as well as its proximity to Yiddish itself, is how German would become the vehicle for the secular culture of virtually the entire Ashkenazi Jewry. At the same time, knowledge of German (and, occasionally, other western or local languages) made it possible for culturally mobile Jews of Central and Eastern Europe to adopt the fruits of contemporary western high culture and in many cases (especially in Vienna and Prague but also Czernowitz serving as centers of modern German–Jewish culture), as time went by, participate increasingly themselves in shaping, developing creatively and reproducing it. This also facilitated the establishment of relations by emancipated Jews with national élite groups that more or less everywhere east of the Rhine (in Bohemia and Poland just as much as in Hungary or Romania) either had become culturally Germanized, or at least fallen under the sway of an increasingly recognized German 'cultural ascendancy.' Thus, religiously motivated multilingualism could be naturally expanded, expediting geographical mobility in the sense that, in the event of emigration or for requirements of international commerce, it reduced the cost factors that always attend situations accompanied by linguistic alienation or including the need of getting accommodated to a new linguistic milieu.

Another effect, worth noting in this context, consists in the stimulus given to intellectual mobility, that is a readiness to innovate, a propensity to assimilate new information, a disposition to self-reflection, etc. All this belongs to an anthropological culture invested with a strong sense of verbalization that became implanted in broad strata of traditional Jewry—likewise a rather uncommon phenomenon in pre-modern Europe.

Collective dispositions and group identity as economic capital

The set of requirements imposed by the practice of Judaism had equally a hand in fostering other collective habits, behavioral and dispositional characteristics, the manifestations of which may have been less striking but exerted all the greater an impact on economic achievement. This concerns, above all, bodily and intellectual discipline, self-control and control over impulses and the material environs, all being directly conditioned by the system of domestic rituals.

In understanding this essential aspect of Judaism it is necessary to recall the extraordinary importance—incomparably greater than in Christianity – assigned to family rituals and domestic rules extending to all members of the family. A large part of the studying, praying, and observance of the Sabbath and holidays, associated with the practice of Judaism, take place at home. This weighs far more in the time budget of the faithful than amongst Christians, and from time to time calls for significant intellectual efforts as well. Domestic ritual requirements also affect the size and the lay-out of the dwelling, as the separation of various ritual functions makes a certain amount of space necessary, and thus influences the quality of housing. That is perhaps why, in those places for which data at all are available (Warsaw, Copenhagen and Budapest, for instance), Jews tended to live in better housing conditions than was typical for their respective social class in the rest of the population. Observance of the *kosher* dietary rules, the system of hygienic and ritual prohibitions, prescriptions and recommendations pertaining to eating and sexual activity, gender differences in the performance of religious roles, clothing and lifestyle, the arrangement of matrimony, etc.—each and all called for a perpetual discipline and a conscious planning and organization of action. The whole way of life of Orthodox Jewry is founded on compliance with this ordinance, which is only achievable at the cost of a high level of self-restraint. Moderation, the curbing of passions, a constant effort to spare time and energy, limited enjoyment of alcoholic beverages (since alcohol consumption reduces the capacity for self-control), and a number of similar demands are not merely important elements of the moral message of Jewish religion—they may occur in other denominations too—, but they also form an organic part of the everyday practice of faith.

This lifestyle had a manifold impact on chances of socio–economic advancement and restratification for those concerned, especially in the initial phase of free market economies. Let it suffice here to mention three specific examples related to the paucity of alcoholism, the renunciation of physical violence and 'productive asceticism.'

The avoidance or outright rejection of alcoholism (with moral arguments of self-distinction) is almost an extreme case of the assertion of Jewish religious discipline, drastically differentiating Jewish practice from the dietary customs widespread throughout Christian Europe. Indeed in both the Eastern Orthodox and the Roman Catholic world (with the partial exception of societies affected by Protestant morality) even the slightest celebration was an occasion and an excuse for the consumption of alcohol, often amounting to the deliberate search for or pursuance of drunkenness. For young men in most of Europe, almost regardless of social class and cultural or ethnic affiliation, heavy drinking was an almost universally established, indeed properly ritualized and codified mode of expression of virility. By contrast, in the initial stages of modernization in Eastern Europe, the absence of alcoholism became a significant factor in the social definition of Jewry: whereas 'normal' locals drank ostensibly, the Jews did not, though they did supply the means, since, in a vast geographical region stretching from the former territories of Poland to Eastern Hungary and Moldavia, for a long time they were effectively holding a quasi-monopoly on the production and distribution of alcohol. Yet alcoholism is always detrimental to economic productivity and efficiency. Conversely, since alcohol undermines work ethic and can generate irrational modes of professional behavior—if only by leading to a preponderance of unproductive consumption—, and indeed may directly inhibit the reproduction of working abilities, refraining from it will always confer a better overall chance of social elevation upon those concerned. Consistent antialcoholism, consequently, may be historically identified as a dual factor of professional success: both as a strategic constituent in the domination of certain specialist markets (particularly that for alcoholic beverages) falling within the zone of Jewish interests and as an elementary precondition for the generalization of rational market behavior. From the viewpoint of differential chances of economic success, this may have had a much greater significance in the early phases of industrialization than it did subsequently. Nevertheless, traces of Jewish temperance (together with its economic outcomes) may still be detected later on, right down to the present day, in even the most assimilated (or culturally de-Judaized) fragments of Jewry.

A similar analysis may be applied to the traditional taboo on physical violence, which is an integral part of Jewish religious ethic. Judaism, in matters of everyday behavior, is an essentially consensual, non-violent culture which gave ever less scope for displays of strength and the use of force the nearer we get to the modern age. Alongside that, of course, symbolic violence played a considerable part amongst the accepted Jewish cultural patterns and in its system of customs, taking a wide variety of forms, the classic components of which are the joke, irony, the anecdote with a punch line, the philosophically 'revelatory' cautionary tale, the disparagement and vocal pillorying of opponents, or—in extreme cases of gross breach of religious law (e.g. the public 'mourning' for those who enter mixed marriages or become baptized) – ostracism and excommunication proper of culprits. The external display of non-violence together with efficient internal moral police was also, with regard to dominant host societies, an essential element in the survival and integration strategies of Jewry, for obvious reasons. Deprived as they were of any kind of political and military power, given the unfavorable balance of forces, Jews could thus hope for the diminution of consequences of frictions and conflicts with the outside world. The principle of non-violence also acted to moderate conflictual relations in a more general sense, whilst in the event of disagreements of an economic character, it encouraged contractual anticipations, negotiated conciliation, the 'euphemization' and settlement of controversial issues. The respect for rules of market competition typical of Jews was, in itself, an expression of the primacy of symbolic displays of force as against other means of violent coercion.

At the same time, the taboo on physical violence in the moral economy of modern Jewry, the concrete manifestations of which can be perceived in many areas (such as a conspicuous scarcity of antipersonnel violence in Jewish criminal records), also meant that a primacy of intellectual over physical achievements evolved early on. If, for Jews, scrapping at school was unseemly, or less seemly than for non-Jews, excellence in physical training was less expected from and rarely achieved by them. This could lead to direct stereotyping of the 'weak' or 'cowardly' Jew (which was not necessarily intended to be anti-Semitic, since the same stereotypes also figured in the self-image of those concerned). Educational excellence was demanded all the more in Latin, mathematics and other 'serious' subjects for Jews. It is easy to imagine the sort of performance-oriented drive this scale of values must have represented in a modernizing economy and social life.

Their religious doctrine thus prepared Jews from the outset for the administration of business and market relations of capitalist societies, in which social or market success, in the final analysis, always predicates restraint of overtly aggressive impulses. This instrumental aspect of traditional Jewish morality, as it was put to application in modern economic life, gained particular socio–historical significance in comparison with what, in Central and Eastern Europe, were the all-too obviously obsolescent systems of values and conduct of the aristocracy and gentry on the one hand, the erstwhile servile peasantry and, later, the proletariat on the other. For a long time all these clusters maintained in male conduct certain ritualized versions of giving vent to physical violence in old-established forms, such as the cult of dueling, inter-group rivalries, and the disciplining or bullying of social inferiors (servants or children). In feudalism, the right to carry and use weapons (even for hunting) was a privilege reserved for non-Jews, primarily for the nobility. At this point, Jews were totally excluded from the armed forces, which was one of the opportunities for advancement for young men who signed up for, or were pressed into, service as mercenaries. Thus, even later on, 'martial virtues' could develop gradually and moderately only amongst Jews in the course of the assimilation process.

But there is yet another aspect in which religious doctrine links even more directly to economic rationality. Moderation in consumption, the self-restraint and disciplined life that are enjoined by *kosher* rules themselves, the behavioral manifestations of 'worldly asceticism,' may all have had a stimulatory effect, in the above-discussed sense, on profitable investment and productivity. The mandatory allocation of space within the Jewish household, like the strict organization of time in the daily, weekly and yearly rhythm of life (through periodic ceremonies as well as the observance of Sabbath, holidays and dietary rules) could serve as paradigms of rational economic behavior. Here too it is possible to pin down a link between Jewish religious doctrine and the 'bourgeois ethos' of nascent capitalism.

Finally, there is yet another connection in which Judaism can be classed as a primordial agency of economic success, namely, by the implementation of concomitants of the affiliation to a community. The network of bonds amongst those of the same faith including mutual assistance, mutual trust and obligatory solidarity (at least in the event of anti-Jewish threats) might in given circumstances also become a basis for professional collaboration, advancement and pooling of interests. From the moment they entered the modern economy, Jews often had to confront a hostile milieu. For that reason, they would in turn seek and find group-specific assets or trump-cards for achieving their goals with the help of economic allies and partners of their own faith. In the age of emergent capitalism, affiliation to the community represented a veritable economic security against bankruptcy, fraud, and unbridled competition for many individual entrepreneurs. The fund of trust, associated with collective identity, not infrequently functioned as a palpable business warranty, allowing in concrete terms, at times. the extension of credit lines among co-religionists. More generally, networks of Jewish entrepreneurs of early capitalism, not infrequently spanned large regions, and sometimes the entire continent, offering thus excellent opportunities for gaining professional training and practical experience abroad to novice entrepreneurs, private clerks and artisans of the same faith. For those in Eastern Europe, this involved the chance to acquire more developed western technologies and business management techniques. For active leaders in the economy, this same mechanism encompassed the possibility of economic collaboration with those of the same community who—rightly or wrongly—were judged to be more reliable than others. It was therefore not uncommon for marketing networks that had been built up and operated by Jewish capital (big department stores, chains of commercial outlets) to sell primarily the products of firms in which other Jews held interests (e.g. in the textile trade).

True, similar 'ethnic networks' were operated under feudalism and early capitalism (often even later) by other minorities as well in many places in the world. This was in particular the case of Greek, Serb, Armenian and other Balkan or Levantine merchants in Central and Eastern Europe during the seventeenth and eighteenth centuries. Jews actually took over some of their roles and positions in the nineteenth century, thanks to their competitive edge. At all events, with the benefit of hindsight, 'Jewish networks' proved to be often better than their rivals to grasp new opportunities in industrial and commercial markets. It is conceivable that the demon of 'Jewish solidarity,' as touted all too often in anti-Semitic discourses, showed up (and perhaps continues to show up) in the form of accords of economic interests among members of Jewish in-groups more often than elsewhere.

External socio–historical conditions of restratification

In certain, mainly western regions of Europe (Britain, Holland, Italy, southern France, and the cities of Germany, Bohemia and Moravia) the socio–economic modernization of Jewry had already got under way at the beginning of the modern era, and it had reached an advanced stage by the late eighteenth century. Jews in these places demonstrated a much more clear-cut 'proto-bourgeois' initiative than elsewhere, in part as a product of selective immigration (with only those importing economic or intellectual capital being permitted to settle), in part (and not unrelated to that former factor) because those concerned often became recognized and respected partners of local political and economic élites or even (as in the case of *Hoffaktors*) of ruling princes themselves. At the same time, thanks to the ready cash in hand that they held as capital, the early onset of industrialization opened up opportunities to plug into the modernization process. In some of the most advanced western countries (notably in Holland and Britain) the squeeze of occupational restrictions, economic prohibitions and over-taxation had already started to relax well before the formulation of any plans for legal emancipation. For the great masses of Jews living in Eastern Europe, however, the first manifestations of modernity only arrived with the French Revolution and, more particularly, the direct impact of the Napoleonic wars on host countries. The Napoleonic wars not only raised explicit hopes of legal emancipation (given that this had been achieved by then in France, Holland and, temporarily, Prussia) but for broad strata of Jewry also significantly modified the ingredients of their economic and socio–political situation. Through the partitions of Poland, a substantial new Jewish population came under the suzerainty of Central European powers (Prussia and Austria). Economic modernization and political reforms in these states gave Jews a direct opportunity to take part in ongoing transformation processes. The wars themselves created favorable circumstances for arms suppliers and those engaged in the interregional grain trade, many of whom were Jewish. This accelerated the accumulation of bigger and smaller cash fortunes, and the availability of this liquid capital, ready for investment, contributed to infiltrate the fruits of the western-initiated industrial revolution into Central and Eastern Europe. As the outcome of this European dynamism of industrialization, a major textile industry emerged in Bohemia and Moravia and the cities of Galicia and Russian Poland (Lemberg, Łodż, Cracow, etc.), food industry (most notably milling) in Hungary, and mining in the Ukraine, with Jewish capitalists playing a big part in all these developments.

Throughout Europe, then, Jews held from the very outset a share in modernizing enterpreneurship, and in the process their fields of activity and occupational structure also underwent a wholesale change, so as to substantially alter their positions in the socio–professional stratification of nascent nation-states. This development produced numerous parallels, albeit with certain temporal lags, in various parts of the continent, so that all indicators point to a distinctive—in some respects unique—mechanism of restratification of modernizing Jewry. In the same time one must remark that the pace of this development was very disparate from region to region by virtue of at least three kinds of external factors.

First of all, and regardless of the local variants of the phenomenon, Jewish economic modernization was more rapid and complete when it was preceded by emancipation or when restrictions on enterprise, urban settlement, and freedom of movement were lifted even much before any formal proclamation of equality before the law. That was still more the case where emancipation was preceded or accompanied by a significant degree of social integration of Jews. Overall, then, Jewish modernization was wider in scale in states that historically secured early emancipation. In other words, on the whole, it was most vigorous in Western, South-western and North-Western Europe, relatively vigorous in Central Europe (Austria–Hungary and Germany), and much weaker in Eastern Europe (Russia, Romania and the Balkans). Occupational restratification took place much more slowly in places where important middle-class activity remained out of bounds for Jews, as for example in the case of the legal professions in Romania up till the First World War or in Russia between 1889 and 1905. Instead, in the lack of opportunity to penetrate new branches and professional roles, Jews continued to seek success in occupational branches they had traditionally pursued.

Second, the restratification of Jewry was a function of the general developmental dynamics of host countries. In that respect, too, opportunities were more open in western and central regions of the continent than in the less industrialized East. That inequality, however, had a paradoxical outcome. Whilst modernization in the West may have been accomplished earlier and more completely, the role that Jews played in it proved to be relatively limited, indeed virtually minimal in most fields. That was due in part to their demographic weakness, in part to the competitive strength of local non-Jewish élites. The latter became similarly 'bourgeoisified' so as to be party to the tasks of modernization. Thus, everywhere in the West, non-Jews formed an absolute majority of the protagonists in that process. In Central and Eastern Europe, by contrast, even though the mass of Jewry remained much more traditionalist in economic as in other terms, Jewish economic élites made a much more powerful contribution to setting the post-feudal economic system in train—so much so, in fact, that in certain branches of activity, which amounted to developmental motors for entire countries, they could acquire dominant, if not outright monopoly economic positions, which were often preserved right up to the Shoah.

Third, the prevailing socio–economic structure of Jewry was profoundly determined, apart from the two above-mentioned vital circumstances, by the net balance of migratory waves, that is to say, the number and the social composition of newcomers and emigrants. During the era of industrialization and emancipation—in the course of the long nineteenth century, given that these processes took place at different points in time across Europe—almost all societies in Western and Central Europe (with the partial exception, for very divergent reasons, of Bohemia, Italy, Spain, Portugal and the Scandinavian states) accepted masses of Jews, most of them arriving from further east. At the same time though, in some cases, they were also losing part of their own previously settled Jewish population. For example, many Jews emigrated to America from the eastern counties of Hungary in the pre-First World War decades and, even prior to that, cases of wealthy Hungarian–Jewish bourgeois families moving to Vienna or elsewhere were far from rare. All this obviously had an impact on the social and occupational make-up of local Jewish populations. In Western Europe, the new arrivals from the East struck the long-established Jewish communities as a sort of historical 'retrogressive' force, in that they were bringing along with them obsolescent economic structures and conduct. The economic attitudes and competence of 'eastern Jews' (*Ostjuden* in the German terminology) were most of the time far too perceptibly old-fashioned as compared to westerners. There were cases, however, in particular places and at particular times, where precisely the reverse was true. At the turn of the nineteenth into the twentieth century, Jewish university students and young intellectuals left Russia and Romania *en masse* to escape discrimination or quotas at school, and the same happened in Hungary after 1920 and in the other parts of Central and Eastern Europe as Nazism took hold. German, Austrian, Hungarian and Czech Jews in particular, seeking a sanctuary from the Nazi threat in Western Europe or America, often came from the most modernized segments of the middle classes affected. Hence their countries of origin lost major clusters capable to share the burden of modernization, precisely because many who left depleted the thin ranks of the westernized bourgeoisie and intelligentsia.

With these strictures, we are now somewhat better placed to estimate the net effect of archaism or traditionalism and the early pre-modern disposition on the socio–economic transformation of the Jewish world in a regenerating Europe from the end of the eighteenth century. It is likely that we would, in principle, reach similar conclusions regarding many non-Jews as well. However, the situation of Jews was not com- mensurate with that of Christians, given the entirely different pattern of stratification among the latter at the start of the modernization process (specifically the absolute numerical preponderance of the peasant stra- tum), the legal conditions Jews were seeking to assert (in many places the abolition of feudal privileges and the removal of impediments to social mobility on individualistic principles only partially preceded emancipation), and the framework of their political existence (Christian élites everywhere retaining their hold on power, even when there were no explicitly 'anti-Semitic' barriers to mobility towards positions of political leadership). Consequently, following the current scholarly po- sition, it is impossible, in practice, to make an overall assessment of differences between Jews and non-Jews as to their 'pure' (that is, group specific) proclivities for social mobility. One cannot empirically discern the impact of their basically different initial situation and continuously contrasting conditions when comparing the socio–economic mobiliza- tion of Jews and non-Jews.

General features of economic modernization: self-sufficiency and urban concentration

Before surveying which branches of the economy Jews were most active in during modern and recent times, it will serve for readier comprehension to present first some general trends of development. Pride of place amongst these has to go to the striking degree of urbanization, the relative or absolute predominance of the self-employed in the Jewish work force, the preference for entrepreneurial, administrative or properly intellectual activities over manual ones. To these must be added the already mentioned uncommon market intelligence (or 'feel' for the market) whereby Jewish participants were often better prepared than others to exploit untapped economic opportunities, plug 'gaps' and win ground in free markets, left 'unprotected' by public authorities or Christian élites.

These characteristics conform, in part, with the same developmental logic. Cities always were focal points for the 'self-employed' and those in civil or professional service requiring intellectual competence. Conversely, self-employment necessitates, amongst other things, expertise and/or organizing ability, which can avert a decline to the status of manual laborer. That logic nevertheless has its own limits, because, taking the period between the two world wars as a basis for comparison across Europe, in most societies such high proportions of intellectual and self-employed workers as existed amongst Jews were not to be found amongst urbanized non-Jews. These occupational choices and endeavors, then, do allow us to place a finger on a form of 'Jewish singularity'—one that derives exclusively, or at least primarily, from the socio–economic constraints and interests typifying the position of Jewry. These may be analyzed under the headings of maximization of profit, a sense for security, the questioning of collective identity, and the exploitation of occupational continuities as well as of collective skills and flair.

There are two mutually contradictory historical explanations for the source of Jewry's characteristic, almost universally observable over-urbanization, and the historical conditions under which they gravitated so strongly to occupations that tied them to cities in modern times. In certain places prior to the modern age—Russia, Romania and, indeed, several Italian states—Jews were simply forbidden to settle in villages, to the extent that infringement of this proscription might sometimes result in expulsion from the country. Elsewhere, mostly in Sweden, Holland, France and many German territories up to beginning of the emancipation process Jews were only admitted (or historically readmitted) into certain cities specifically designated for the purpose. In many feudal societies during the period before emancipation (and this covers a highly disparate group ranging from pre-partition Poland, Hungary and some German states, such as Bavaria and Württemberg, to pre-Revolutionary Alsace-Lorraine), the cities generally laid claim to choose their citizens for themselves and thereby blocked settlement by Jews. To the extent that this ploy succeeded, Jews were obliged to seek a domicile in the villages, primarily under the protection of feudal landlords (and in return bound themselves to offer 'gifts,' pay special taxes, provide economic and other services). Thus, in some regions of Europe, Jews became town dwellers from the very outset, whereas elsewhere their drift to the towns only started or picked up with the abatement of feudal constraints. Often enough this went somewhat ahead of actual emancipation, as in the case of Vienna from 1848 (as well as many German cities that had long been *judenrein*), or Hungary following the semi-emancipatory law of 1840.

A marked overrepresentation of Jews in towns, and their further speedy urbanization as compared with the rest of the population, was in any event observable throughout Europe from at least the latter half of the nineteenth century onwards. (One of the few exceptions was Austrian Galicia at the end of that century, where a degree of 'ruralization' was also discernible amongst some segments of the Jewish populace, who were squeezed out of the towns by the limited opportunities of their stagnant, underdeveloped economies.) This general 'over-urbanization' had many causes, the components of which were in part independent of another. It is easy to understand why cities, and especially capital cities, the seats of princely and central authority, should attract groups that had set off on the road to embourgeoisement, as cities represented the biggest markets for their commercial, financial and, later, manufacturing activities. Jews entered these markets whenever a legal opportunity to do so presented itself, in most cases even before they had gained proper entrepreneurial freedom. It was all the easier for them to move to towns as in many places, prior to emancipation, they were rarely authorized to acquire property rights in their residence or purchase other real estate that embodied 'stock' or 'rootedness' and so, being overly invested with emotional values as a patrimony, might 'tie' them to a place. Generally speaking, that may be why Jews were less wedded to symbols of local affiliation which might have curbed their residential mobility, including mobility to towns. (At the same time, in their collective memory, many tended to preserve—in family legends, for instance—a trace of the migratory route taken by their ancestors, usually under duress. The notion of Diaspora has lived on particularly firmly in the historical consciousness of traditionalist Jewry, as exemplified by the ritual Passover invocation: 'Next year in Jerusalem!')

Urbanization was driven not just by sheer economic rationality, but also by a search for a better quality of life in the long term, and a concern for the optimization of the descendants' chances of social advancement. Cities were not just the seats of virtually every institutional agent in economic modernization (big industrial firms, banks, commercial and press agencies, stock exchange, etc.), in whose development Jews themselves usually had a hand, but also major markets for most intellectual and liberal professions. These, as will be seen, had a major role everywhere in success strategies of upwardly mobile Jews. The legal profession, medical practice, the political, scholarly and literary press, psychoanalysis, and most new services supplied by the intelligentsia represented more or less essentially or exclusively urban functions. Institutions of higher education and public hospitals were to be found in cities. Jews came to take advantage of these highly specialized public services far more intensively, in general, than other town dwellers, according to all the available data on the subject.

Urbanization also played an important, though extremely diverse, role in contemporary patterns of definition of collective identity. First and foremost, cities provided a residential setting for the largest Israelite communities, able to secure for their congregations an incomparably broader scale of ritual and social services than others. They also offered a richer range of options amongst congregations of various ritual obedience. That alone was an attraction for many in Central Europe, both in Austria–Hungary and in Germany, as tensions between Orthodoxy and Reform Judaism grew in the course of the nineteenth century. It was not uncommon that a move into the city was motivated by or served as a precipitating factor for the need to join the appropriate community of faith. More particularly, it might be that a single district or neighborhood would provide the desired religious microclimate and network of contacts. But the opposite could also happen, insofar as the anonymity of the urban social space offered the best chance for those bent on secularization to escape the undesirable controlling eye of religious authorities. It was therefore precisely in urban Jewish clusters that disinterest in religious observance tended to gain ground steadily. This can be unequivocally demonstrated by conspicuously high rates registered for political or identity options and strategies incompatible with religious observance, such as support for Socialist or Communist movements, baptism, nationalization of surnames, mixed marriages, and so on. All the evidence points to the cities as being foci of the first rank for assimilation, so it is hardly surprising that those intent on this should seek to settle in them.

Lastly, such factors as the hope of greater collective security from the proximity of state authorities and executive arms and a greater police presence and calculations related to better chances of self-defense in the event of an attack, as compared with isolated rural habitations, were likewise draws to the city for members of a group in whose historical experience physical threats to person and property had left deep scars. During the nineteenth century that history represented a spur to urbanization even in Western Europe, let alone Central or Eastern Europe, where pogroms or attempted pogroms occurred in the lifetime of practically every generation. It hardly needs to be underlined that the above factors for concentrating in cities applied almost exclusively to Jews alone.

Many circumstances were likewise instrumental in accounting for why the proportion of 'self-employed' outside the agricultural sector should have been so much higher in the Jewish workforce than amongst non-Jews. Comparing the socio–economic stratification of European Jewry directly prior to the Shoah with that in the nineteenth century, the surprise is that, despite all the intervening disturbances, the vast majority managed to avoid becoming proletarians or hired workers of other kinds, with the bulk of them being self-supporting as company directors, shopkeepers running small retail, artisan or handicraft businesses, freelances, private officials, proprietors, or those living on their own capital. Jewish and non-Jewish authors alike have described this phenomenon as a veritable Jewish 'trend' or 'preference' finding it particularly significant in relation to traditionalist Jewish communities. Undoubtedly, the fact that in the economic strategies of practicing Jews, as already discussed, 'self-sufficiency' offered greater scope than the status of a subordinate employee (especially in Christian businesses) for the unhindered practice of one's religion, played a part in this development. It stands to reason that for Jews, defined as they were by their cultural uniqueness and therefore frequently exposed to threats, humiliations and gross assaults, economic self-sufficiency made it easier to keep their distance from undesirable Christian milieus and to avoid situations of inescapable contact with them (in workshops, offices, canteens, rest areas, etc.). One can therefore see why even Jewish proletarians (in places such as the former Polish territories where they emerged at all in any substantial numbers) most often sought employment in small and medium-sized companies under Jewish direction. 'Independent small traders' (artisans and shopkeepers) indeed always represented the chief recruiting pool for Orthodox Jewry throughout Europe.

Free market propensities and entrepreneurial flair

At the same time, it should not be overlooked that in European countries the main social base for the constitution of proletariats and strata of employees in urban services was neither the guild craft industry nor shopkeeping (the numbers employed by these were tiny, due precisely to the low level of urbanization attained during the feudal era) but the former bonded peasantry. As previously discussed, Jews, on the whole, were stuck outside the agricultural economy that occupied 90 per cent of the labor force in feudal societies, with the bulk of them forming a prototypical petty bourgeoisie or middle class to provide services 'outside the system.' It was therefore natural that in the post-feudal era they should continue to furnish relatively populous categories of independent entrepreneurs active in non-agricultural sectors of the economy.

Through an extension of this socio–historical line of thinking, we come to an observation, so often inveighed against by anti-Semitic propaganda: Jews, whether as bosses, employees or even laborers, try hard to avoid dirty, tiring, manual jobs that involve heavy physical effort. In reality, career orientations and preferences of this kind follow primarily the logic of social mobility chances of a group that, even when it occupied the lowest rung of the urban social ladder, was still able to play its cultural trump cards (e.g. its literacy or the secular by-products of its 'religious intellectualism') and, as was often the case with young men of the Jewish petty bourgeoisie, take advantage of the protective and supportive functions, and possibly also training opportunities, provided by their inter-regional or even international community network in order to avoid the most onerous and vulnerable forms of proletarianization. That often made it possible, even for Jews coming from the humblest urban stratum (proletarians proper, artisan or craft employees), to find employment in some relatively highly skilled categories (as watchmakers, printers, workers in precious metals, etc.), or at least in less strenuous but still gainful branches of activity (typically tailoring, furriery, and jewelry), in which the dominance of Jewish entrepreneurs secured to employees a degree of economic protection. Numerous branches of the retail and wholesale trades became concentrated in the hands of Jews in many places where, during the feudal era, they had virtually no other opportunity to gain work. These, too, were among the less physically demanding manual occupations, predicated more on know-how that might be gained through the family or the subculture (knowledge of the market, a flair for assessment of risks, skill in calculating profits and losses, etc.). It was only logical that the staff of such enterprises, often from the lowest to the highest level, should be recruited primarily from Jewish milieus. Since the majority of European Jews were engaged in some form of trading activity at the start of modernization, that in itself played a big hand in determining the subsequent placement of less mobile but active Jews in the ranks of non-manual or 'light' manual commercial workers and employees.

The initial dominance of commerce at the same time provides an explanation for the last general feature typical of Jewish professional mobility. This is a question of their preferential engagement in competitive markets, as against the 'protected' markets of public (state, municipal, county, etc.) authorities. Along with an acceptance of competition went a greater receptivity to innovation, risk-taking, and exploitation of new economic opportunities opened up via modernization. Admittedly, that 'competitive streak' in most countries, and practically everywhere throughout Central and Eastern Europe, is merely the obverse of their continuous exclusion, right up till the Shoah, from state protected markets, reserved for Gentiles in general or to old élite groups in particular. In most countries, sometimes (even if rarely) in Western Europe as well, posts in the civil service, positions of political power and employment in public utilities (railways, water works, gas and electricity industries, public transportation, etc.) were either covertly or openly, but fairly consistently, the preserves of non-Jews. Under those circumstances, the competitive markets of private industry were the only openings left for Jews. That 'dual structure' of the set-up for social mobility—with the state as the province for non-Jews, the free markets for Jews—was still very palpable up to the Shoah in countries as divergent in their development and stratification as Germany, Congress Poland, the Habsburg Monarchy or inter-war Austria. The constrained duality, however, also produced major reactions, leading to still further ossification of the system. Since the 'protected' state sector did not impose the same demands as competitive markets for hard work or performance (slacker discipline, shorter working day, the habit of filling posts on formal educational or social criteria rather than 'fitness,' competence or actual achievement), the dualism of the markets often connoted qualitative differences between Jews and non-Jews in their average successfulness, preparedness, and readiness to work.

Wherever they may have stood in the social arena, in competitive markets Jews always had to hold their own, without any external safety net (disregarding possible community solidarity). They were therefore forced to be better than their rivals in developing their professional expertise, work ethic, the most rational patterns of behavior in matters economic, educational or political, as well as in strategies of consumption and physical reproduction (for instance, as discussed earlier, in the early adoption of birth control). This all fell in with the values and demands of the market. Historically, this epitome of 'bourgeois' behavior aimed at maximizing one's chances of success, in many places came up against, indeed palpably clashed with, the model of conduct in civil service professions. In a number of Central and Eastern European countries containing significant Jewish populations, the public services continued for long to bear the imprint of a 'gentroid' outlook. The reason was precisely the preferential recruiting from the nobility and from its clienteles, as well as through the long persistence (sometimes right up to the advent of the Socialist era) of the political hegemony of the aristocracy in public office and political power. This applied particularly to Poland and Hungary (and also, although it was of lesser significance from the viewpoint of a Jewish presence, Croatia), countries with nobility historically strong both numerically and in terms of prestige, authority and power. Under those circumstances, it is hardly surprising that, both amongst the data relating to stratification and in stereotypical self-images of the societies concerned, one often comes across the connection between Jewry and modernity, especially in more backward countries or those of belated industrialization, possessing a scanty indigenous bourgeoisie (in other words, virtually everywhere in Central and Eastern Europe). On the strength of positions occupied in economic, political, intellectual and artistic markets, Jews were often simply driven into fulfilling the roles of entrepreneurs, innovators or initiators, as well as (and in Central and Eastern Europe this amounted to one and the same) transmitting many western novelties in fields as various as agriculture, technology, academic science or high culture. This kind of creative 'flight to the fore,' by its very nature, was to some extent able to counterbalance their persistent social disadvantages and thereby vindicate the 'net social utility' that Jewish and non-Jewish reformers had claimed for Jewry since the eighteenth century.

We know that in places where this differentiating link of Jews with modernity proved most spectacular, that is to say, in certain belatedly but rapidly industrializing Central European countries (Austria and Hungary, for instance), it sometimes served to their advantage, as when they sought to accommodate to certain factions of the indigenous élite (whose class alliance they required in order to realize their modernization programs), but equally it was often to their detriment in that it furnished anti-Semitic agitation with an ideological weapon. The Jews as 'alien modernizers,' 'conspicuous beneficiaries' of modernization, agents of the 'wicked cities,' robbing the nation of its 'natural' ancestral endowments—hostile bombast of this ilk regularly turns up in the revived nightmare visions of the traditional Judaeophobia of circles that had lost out in the process of industrialization, above all in the latter half of the nineteenth century. In many places the most diverse strata—the descendants of *déclassé* gentry, proletarianized craftsmen, landless peasantry, and so on who had been forced to make a livelihood in the towns—were each able to portray themselves as victims of an economic modernization that had been cooked up by the Jews 'for their own profit.'

Reproduction of intermediary functions in commerce and finance

If the stratification of Jewry before the Shoah regularly appears to be more 'bourgeois,' or more modern as compared to host societies, that is first and foremost a consequence of the above-mentioned fact that in western Jewry peasantry was virtually always lacking, whereas in Eastern Europe the proportion of Jews in agriculture remained vanishingly small to the end. (Among the rare exceptions of any note there was Transcarpathian Ruthenia, where some 27 per cent of the economically active Jews tilled the soil, mostly as propertied farmers.) At the same time, in most European societies up to the Second World War, except in the most developed countries of the West, the agricultural sector alone continued to fix the quasi-majority of the active population. In truth, the socio–economic transformations through which the Jewish world passed since the *Haskalah* could be equally well characterized by continuities, as by radical changes. A summary statement classifying Jewish positions occupied by fields of activity would most likely lead to the conclusion that, even between the two world wars, the majority operated (with variations from country to country, of course) in precisely the same three branches—trade, handicrafts, and the money market—where they were to be found in the eighteenth century, at the start of the modernization process. That allows the inference that a significant portion of Jewry did not, in fact, modernize on the economic plane, or the modernization took its course within traditional sectors in the form of an enhanced or modified reproduction of old economic structures.

The best example of that is trade. Let us take a look, country by country, at relevant basic data for the early part of the twentieth century, the period between 1907 and 1926, for instance. (The apparent precision of the numbers is misleading though, since the statistical surveys quoted showed significant technical divergences from one another.) The proportion in the Jewish working population of those active in commerce, forwarding of goods, and granting of credit (the data often do not permit these activities to be differentiated more accurately) was approximately 67–69 per cent in Bavaria, 50 per cent in pre-war Germany as a whole and the Habsburg Bohemian provinces, 49 per cent in the Austrian Monarchy as a whole, 48 per cent in Latvia, Slovakia and Habsburg-ruled Galicia, 43 per cent in post-Trianon Hungary, 41 per cent in Italy, 33 per cent in Lithuania, and 30 per cent in Soviet Russia during the NEP period (in 1926) as well as in Ruthenia. There are no comparable data at all for Western Europe, though one may postulate that were they to exist, they would be close to the data for the most highly developed of the countries just listed, that is, Germany and the Bohemian provinces. These statistics gain their true significance when we appreciate that during the years in question the proportion of those working in these sectors represented less than one-tenth of the total work force in Eastern Europe (3–4 per cent in Lithuania and Russia, 8 per cent in Hungary), varied from 10 (Italy) to 17 per cent in the rest of industrialized Europe, and only exceptionally exceeded 20 per cent in those few countries (Britain, the Netherlands and Norway) where the economy was more strongly based on international trading relations than elsewhere.

The significantly greater presence of Jews than other economically active adults in commerce is not only striking everywhere but was also the subject of constant controversy, ever since the *Haskalah* and the emergence of enlightened absolutist régimes in the eighteenth century. This is a critical literature in which Jewish reformers also had their say, together with public authorities of nation-states as well as representatives of anti-Semitic movements. One thing on which they all agreed, at any rate, was that the preponderance of commerce was one of the marked signs of the 'unhealthy social structure' of Jewry, the 'remedy' for which would be the induction of Jews into 'productive' sectors, i.e. their redeployment in agriculture, craft industry, mining, and large-scale industry. This reflected a tenet of classical political–economic theory, later also to be adopted by Marxism, that only these sectors could be classed as 'productive' economic activities, whereas commerce, credit and other intermediary branches represented 'unproductive' (if not necessarily 'parasitic') sectors.

The high rates of participation by Jews in commercial and financial services is all the more conspicuous, the less highly developed these sectors were in the national economy. This again applies only to the countries of Eastern Europe, as in this respect the western and eastern parts of the continent were sharply differentiated from one another.

In the West, the non-Jewish, 'indigenous' urban burgher classes, having emerged early on, were to retain a hold throughout on a major portion of investments in trade, banking and transportation, since the realization of major projects of industrialization was dependent on precisely these sectors. Jews too joined in this development, but without achieving leadership positions or dominating particular areas (their demographic paucity and dispersion alone would have precluded this), except may be in a few regions (Alsace) and cities (Amsterdam, Frankfurt or Livorno in Italy), to cite the most prominent examples.

The situation was completely different in Eastern Europe where commerce and credit business, heavily lacking investments, like other 'bourgeois' occupations, lay for the most part outside the sphere of interest of mobile Christians seeking to make their way in the new middle classes. In these sectors, positions taken up by Jews and other entrepreneurs, most of them likewise of alien or immigrant stock (as compared to titular élites), virtually never came under serious competitive pressure. Here, though, it should be recalled that almost everywhere in Central Europe (with the partial exception of Bohemia and Moravia) at some stage—in most cases during the early part of the twentieth century—, boycott campaigns against Jewish traders were far from unknown. They were usually backed up by the establishment of mutual loan societies to underpin the advance of a 'national shop-keeping class,' or by imposing state marketing or monopoly arrangements on the most profitable commodities (as in the case of tobacco and alcohol in Poland during the early 1920s, for example). Undoubtedly, such maneuvers played a part in significantly reducing the market shares held by Jews (notably in Poland). Another factor in the process was a frequent change in professional direction, or restratification proper, on the part of the descendants of the threatened Jewish commercial capitalist stratum. In Ruthenia (previously the most northeasterly part of Hungary), for example, as late as 1921 Jews still comprised 87 per cent of those engaged in trade. Similar data are available for places in several provinces of newly independent Poland (Tarnopol, Volchynia, Stanislav, Nowojenska, Polesie). These are obviously extreme cases because we know that during the same period and elsewhere in the same regions Jews held 'only' around half of all positions in the commercial sector: 63 per cent in Poland overall, 50 per cent in Slovakia, and 45 per cent in Hungary. Those statistics, however, conceal a decrease relative to the recent past, especially in the largest urban centers. The proportion of Jews in commerce in Warsaw, for instance, had dropped from 79 per cent in 1882 to 62 by 1920, and in Hungary from 62 to 51 per cent between 1900 and 1920 (though here the drastic territorial changes must also be taken into account). At the same time, it may be noted that in Poland in 1919, the Jewish work force outside agriculture most commonly—almost 300,000 in all—made a livelihood as small shopkeepers or peddlers, comprising 56 per cent of the national total in these two categories. (The total active Jewish population outside agriculture then amounted to 1,046,000.)

Specialization and capital concentration in commerce and credit

The persistent predominance of Jews in these apparently traditional branches, in reality, also conceals spreading modernization and professional specialization. Jews managed more often than Christian rivals to hang on to their small shops, agencies, and other commercial enterprises. There are also sporadic but concordant data to show that they were also able to accumulate significant commercial capital to invest (as typically in Poland, Hungary and Czechoslovakia) first in banking, later on in the industrial sector. As to proportions of entrepreneurs or proprietors ('independents') and subordinates (commercial employees and workers), it is readily demonstrable that almost everywhere 'independents' were in the majority amongst Jews, whereas the opposite was the case amongst non-Jews. In Hungary, for example, 50 per cent of Jews in commerce were 'self-sufficient' (1920), compared with 35 per cent of non-Jews. In Hamburg the figures were 53 per cent as against 24 per cent (1907); in Prussia, 51 per cent as against 28 per cent (1908); in the Czech provinces, 53 per cent as against 27 per cent (1908); in Slovakia, 42 per cent as against 23 per cent (1921); in Vienna, 30 per cent as against as few as 10 per cent (1910); albeit in Romania, it was 57 per cent as against the virtually identical proportion of 56 per cent of Christians who were active in commerce (1913).

The term 'independent' does not have, though, the same connotations in the highly industrialized West and the more backward economies of Eastern Europe. In the West, the persistence of relatively high proportions of Jews (within the overall Jewish working population) in commerce can be ascribed to the fact that their earlier economic practice changed radically with the foundation of big department stores and chains of retail outlets, often by Jewish entrepreneurs and with Jewish investments. This kind of commercial modernization, however, did not call for large numbers to be involved. As a result, in Western Europe, the proportion of Jews amongst those working in the commercial, credit, and transportation sectors, lumped together, never surpassed a few per cent of the total. In Germany, for example, where, since the nineteenth century, 'western' Jews were present in the greatest numbers, both in absolute terms and (with the exception of the Netherlands) relative to the total population, they made up no more than 6 per cent of the population engaged in commerce in 1907. Subsequently, with general economic expansion, even that fell sharply, to 3 per cent in 1925 (admittedly here, too, following territorial losses). Modernization accompanied by concentration of capital in commerce and credit business was also encountered in some countries in Central and Eastern Europe, such as Hungary and Austria. Nevertheless, a good proportion of Jewish traders in Eastern Europe between the two world wars continued to pursue their old, traditional practices such as itinerant selling, hawking, street selling, dealing in second-hand clothes or waste products (leather, feathers, etc.), pawnbroking, keeping general stores or small taverns, and not uncommonly running these on 'private credit.'

Jews would not have been able to maintain and even consolidate their economic positions without going down the path of specialization, in some places spectacularly but everywhere very obviously so. This primarily related to financial branches in the proper sense (banks, insurance companies, currency exchange agencies), though these only required small staffs. The proportion of Jews, active in the commercial, credit, and transportation sector as a whole, who were engaged in these particular branches was altogether 0.4 per cent in Russia (1897), 2 per cent in Austrian Galicia (1910), 0.9 per cent in independent Poland, 3.7 per cent in Germany (1907), 5.6 per cent in Italy (1900) and 3.6 per cent in Romania (1913).

Nevertheless, the 'ascendancy' of Jews in high finance was most spectacular in the epoch following the industrial revolution. Foundations for this development were laid by the credit–loan activities of court Jews in the European capitals of the early modern age. The

Rothschilds, for example, settled in Frankfurt during the sixteenth century, although up to the eighteenth century and the time of Mayer Amschel Rothschild they operated without any particular distinction as merchants and purveyors to the margraves of Hessen. After withdrawing into voluntary exile to London (1798), they became the biggest financiers for the anti-Napoleonic coalition, then dispersed their operations to Paris (1812), Vienna (1816), and Naples (1820). It was likewise during the Napoleonic wars that most of the big Jewish-owned banks were founded in Germany: in Berlin, the Mendelssohn bank (1795) and the Bleichröder bank (1803), which later became the private banking house to Bismarck; in Hamburg, the Warburg bank (1798); and in Bonn and Cologne, offices of the Oppenheim bank (1789). During the nineteenth century, these were followed by similar banking houses in France, such as the Credit Mobilier, set up by the Pereire brothers in 1852, or the Banque de Paris et des Pays-Bas established in 1872; in Germany, as with the Deutsche Bank in 1870; in Italy, as with the Banca Commerciale Italiana and Credito Italiano; in England, the banks set up by a clutch of famous founders such as Moses Montefiori, David Salomons, David and Hermann Stern, Lazard Speyer-Ellissen, etc. These mighty financial institutions negotiated with governments and invested on international markets, playing a part in the growth of the modern transportation network (above all railway construction) and the establishment of a string of big industrial and commercial enterprises throughout Europe, the Middle East, South Africa, and elsewhere. All the same, as 'Jewish banks' practically nowhere did they manage to gain monopoly market positions. During the twentieth century, the concentration of the international credit business increasingly shifted over to the United States, where the role of Jewish banks (if not that of financial experts) was relatively negligible: their heyday manifestly had been reached in Europe at the middle of the nineteenth century. The composition of their staff remained 'mixed,' however, and in their grandest operations they collaborated with other, 'non-Jewish' capital-management institutions. The positions of Jews were probably at their strongest, relatively speaking, in Central and Eastern Europe, as to high-financial transactions with respect of the capital they owned or invested right up to the eve of the Shoah. In Hungary, for instance, they are estimated to have comprised as many as 85 per cent of bank directors around 1900.

Other aspects of specialization were also decisive in the commercial activities of Jews. Between the two world wars they almost monopolized the international markets in the West for the trade in real pearls and precious stones (with Paris and Amsterdam as major centers) and premier furs (with Paris and Leipzig as centers). Apart from various big department stores, they were also important agents in the trade of grain, *objets d'art*, books, tobacco, textiles, gold, clothing, and leather goods. In Eastern Europe the structure of the commercial sector was far less developed, but here too there were similar forms of specialization by Jews, most notably in the marketing of products of the leather, textiles, furniture, grain, jewelry, gold, lumber, book, metal, and chemical industries.

Archaism and modernization in industry

Outside commerce, participation by Jews in handicraft industries likewise tends more to provide a further example of the reproduction of traditional economic functions. Yet one should not forget the heated ideological debates that accompanied the shift of Jews from commerce to small-scale industry from the eighteenth century onwards. This was the period when the adherents of *Haskalah* and the officials of enlightened absolutist states formulated the first plans for the inclusion of Jews in 'productive activities' within the framework of their program of 'moral regeneration.'

The same duality between West and East was encountered in Jewish small-scale industry as in commerce. In the West, handicrafts had been disappearing from the main areas of occupation for Jews right up to the point when the mass migration, set off from the East, began to arrive, that is towards the end of the nineteenth century. Those masses then proceeded to recreate a veritable subculture of highly specialized craft artisans centered mainly around the manufacture of clothing, in a number of cities like Paris and London during the early years of the twentieth century. As time passed, though, the proportion of Jews engaged as artisans in handicraft industries continued to fall, whilst in Eastern Europe it remained high up to the period between the two world wars. Whereas fewer than one-fifth of the Jewish work force in the Czech provinces and Germany were active in this branch (just 14 per cent in

Hamburg in 1907, and 19 per cent in Bavaria in 1925, for instance), the proportion was still as high as 42 per cent in Romania in 1913, 35 per cent in Hungary and the Soviet Union even during the 1920s, 32 per cent in Poland and Latvia, and 22–24 per cent in Slovakia, Ruthenia and Lithuania. As artisans too, similarly to the experience in commerce, Jews throughout Europe were more likely to be self-employed entrepreneurs than employees, apprentices or laborers. In Vienna, for instance, 38 per cent of Jews active in handicraft industries in 1910 were self-employed, as compared with 31 per cent of Christian artisans. The comparable figures for Hamburg in 1907 were 44 versus 20 per cent; for Poland in 1921, 50 versus 22 per cent (exceptionally, the basis of comparison here is the country's total labor force); for Hungary in 1920, 39 versus 29 per cent; for Prussia in 1907, 41 versus 16 per cent; for Bohemia and Moravia in 1921, 39 versus 13 per cent; and finally, for Slovakia in 1921, 42 versus 23 per cent.

The persistence of such high rates amongst the Jewish population active in this branch in Central and Eastern Europe (and, indeed, for a while still in Western Europe after 1900) can undoubtedly be ascribed to their advanced specialization. This secured for Jewish artisans fairly strong market positions, and occasionally, in Eastern Europe, virtual monopolies in certain categories. Essentially everywhere there was evidence of the peculiar weight being placed on clothing (both making and altering) as a focus of that specialty, with most of them working as tailors, seamstresses, hatters, furriers, and cleaners, less often as bootmakers, cobblers, button-stitchers, and haberdashers. In Western European countries their proportion exceeds, and in eastern ones it approaches, half of all the Jews working in small-scale industries: 60 per cent in Germany (and 69 per cent in Hamburg) in 1907; 54 per cent in Russia in 1898; 47 per cent in independent Poland in 1926; and 40 per cent in Romanian Bessarabia in 1925. Jewish tailors and other artisans in the clothing industry were even more conspicuously overrepresented among Jewish emigrants from Eastern Europe to settle in the West. Contemporary surveys estimated their proportion amongst the local Jewish artisans at around 71 per cent in Paris and 80 per cent in London at the start of the twentieth century. All the evidence points to the clothing trades serving as sanctuaries for the most traditional Jewish artisans in the West, whilst elsewhere on the continent the spectrum of Jewish small-scale industries was much more diverse.

Small-scale food-processing industries (contract distillers for customers' crops, butchers, meat processors, etc.) may have employed far fewer people, but the proportion of Jews here too was very high in all places, as it was also amongst glaziers, watchmakers, jewelers, as well as producers of paper and leather goods or chemicals. The common denominator of all these crafts was that they turned out ready-made, immediately saleable products. Indeed, it would be common to find next door to an artisan's workshop a small shop run by himself, his employees or members of the family.

At the same time, with the gradual accumulation of capital, Jewish small-scale industry would often modernize, many of the small workshops growing into factories, especially when it was possible to attract capital from external sources into the business. A process that showed considerable variation from country to country, its mechanisms have still not been adequately explored, if only because the bulk of the available denomination-specific evidence make no distinction between small-, medium- and large-scale industrialists. What can be established at all events is that Jewish capitalists of the late nineteenth century were taking the initiative to make significant industrial investments in many places. Parallel with this, we also see the emergence of a fairly sizeable Jewish industrial proletariat in Eastern Europe. A relatively large-scale representation of Jews amongst industrial entrepreneurs seems to be clear-cut everywhere, though accurate data are hard to come by in this respect. The industrial investment policies of large Jewish banks would similarly merit separate historical investigations. In independent Poland in the year 1919—when, as a baseline, the proportion of Jews in the entire non-agricultural working population was not more than 20 per cent—42 per cent of industrial entrepreneurs and 44 per cent of other 'independents' were Jewish. For Hungary precise statistics are available on factory directors and proprietors, more than half of whom in the inter-war years being Jewish (and even more if baptized Jews were to added to the score).

The textile industry in Poland (Warsaw, Łódż or Białystok) developed predominantly from Jewish-owned workshops, but co-religionists also made up large numbers of their workers, their proportion, judging from contemporary surveys, being in inverse relation to the size of the plant. Demonstrably, then, Jewish workers, unlike the Christian proletariat, tended to concentrate more in small and medium-sized enterprises and workshops. Some 64 per cent, that is a substantial majority, of Polish Jews classed as industrial workers and miners in 1929 (120,000 out of around 188,000) were engaged by small enterprises, as compared with altogether 28 per cent of non-Jewish workers.

Branches of the textile industry proved attractive for Jewish capital elsewhere too, as in the case of Bohemia and Moravia (Brno and, especially, Prague), Germany and Hungary, as well as Paris and London. Significant injections of capital are attributable to Jews throughout Europe in the production of wines and fine spirits, cigarette and cigar manufacture (where these were not subject to a state monopoly), milling, and especially printing. In Hungary, for example, both before and after 1919, the bulk of the entire printing industry, and particularly the parts connected with book production, was built up by Jewish capitalists, and also very largely run by Jewish skilled labor. In Eastern Europe Jewish entrepreneurs were very active in setting up new branches of industry (e.g. the oil industry) or introducing mechanization (timber processing). There were also exceptional cases where highly specialized and localized branches of industry were almost entirely sustained by Jewish capital and Jewish skilled labor. The diamond industry was one of them in Amsterdam, with beginnings going back to the sixteenth century, the center of which shifted to Antwerp at the end of the nineteenth century.

Traditionalism and restratification in intellectual occupations

A great many entirely or partly intellectual occupations ('intellectual' in the sense of requiring highly specialized expertise rather than manual labor) were also attractive to Jews in not inconsiderable numbers, but not a high proportion either. These are modern activities that are yet linked with some age-old intellectual occupations that flourished in the most traditional Jewish communities.

First and foremost amongst them were vocations serving ritual functions, including the rabbinate, the cantorial office, religious education, and community administration. Especially before emancipation, Jewish congregations usually had rather more social duties than was the case for Christian dioceses and parishes: caring for orphans, widows, the sick and disabled, wide-ranging support for the poor, burials, arranging marriages for unendowed girls and widows, and so on, in addition to collecting taxes and maintaining schools (*chederim* and *yeshivot*). That meant that they needed a relatively large number of employees, especially in the Orthodox communities of the eastern part of the continent. When relevant data pertaining to the era of industrialization are available (as in the case of Hungary, for example), they point, as a rule, to a significantly higher proportion of the Jewish work force finding occupation with Jewish congregations, as compared to their Christian counterparts. Such overrepresentation of intra-community employment is typical even in some countries where Reform congregations predominated. In Germany, Jews accounted for 1.7 per cent of all those employed by the various religious denominations in 1907, when they comprised only 1 per cent of the total population. In Poland the corresponding figure was no less than 17 per cent in 1921, when only 6.8 per cent of the working population was Jewish. In Hungary it was 12 per cent in 1920, with only 5.9 per cent of Jews in the population. Furthermore, it was often members of the intellectual élite who filled some of these positions in congregations. The post of chief secretary to Budapest's 'Neologue' congregation at the end of the nineteenth century was held (more out of necessity than choice, though) by the much acclaimed orientalist Ignác Goldziher who carried out in his spare time the scholarly work which won for him international reputation.

In Orthodox Jewry, amongst the liberal occupations associated with religion, there was a conspicuously high number of *Talmud*ist scholars, either engaged as private tutors for the children of better-off bourgeois families or providing religious instruction supplementary (on weekday afternoons or Sundays) to the state elementary school curriculum. Paradoxically, the significance of those educational services grew temporarily with modernization, most notably in countries such as Austria, Bohemia–Moravia and Hungary where, in the wake of emancipation, the state introduced compulsory public education. During this evolutionary phase, which in the aforementioned region lasted until at least the First World War, the private tutoring that replaced religious study (*Talmud Torah*) provided by the community was often designed to compensate for the perceived deficiencies of compulsory religious instruction provided in public schooling.

A crossover of those in occupations linked to liturgy (or their descendants) and the restratification of specialists taking their inspiration from the traditional arts are likewise demonstrable, albeit to a smaller extent, in music, the fine arts, goldsmithing and architecture. The great respect given to performing arts in the Jewish public (violinists, later pianists and conductors), was a direct continuation of a set of customs and habits deriving from secular Jewish folklore, from holiday celebrations and from folk arts, in which music had played a pronounced role, pointing to a considerable degree of preservation and transmission of that traditional musical culture within culturally assimilated Jewry. The manifestly high demand for musical culture is shown by the throngs of young Jews—and their conspicuous relative numbers (still seen to the present day)—who entered the music conservatoires of Western and Eastern Europe after emancipation and then speedily advanced into the élite of professional music performers. In Hungary, no less than 32 per cent of music and art teachers in 1920 were Jewish (six times their representation in the general population). Jews were even more prevalent amongst Hungarian musicians attaining international fame as emigrants to the West, after being displaced from the domestic musical scene during the post-First World War 'Christian-national' régime or subsequently.

Finally, there was also a secular group of intellectual occupations the modern versions of which could likewise be traced back to distinctive ancient traditions of professional expertise in European Jewry. Mention has already been made of medicine, which in the modern age became one of the most widespread and prestigious liberal professions. Considering that over the course of history there were less obstacles placed in the way of Jews seeking to set up practice in the medical market than in other specialties associated with advanced learning, (so few, indeed, that some universities, mainly in Italy, were willing to accept Jewish students into their medical faculties from the late Middle Ages on), and that in the modern era, well before emancipation (from the 1780s in the Habsburg Empire, for example), the medical faculties were the first to open their doors to Jews, Jewish physicians appeared in the intellectual brackets of European societies both earlier and in greater numbers than in any other professions. Slight though their numbers may have been at first even so, given the rather narrow scope of medical markets at the time, they soon acquired notable reputations for the quality of their services. In several Eastern European capital cities it was not long before they actually achieved even numerical superiority. In Budapest, Warsaw and Vienna at least half of the medical establishment around 1900 was made up of Jews, and the same held for certain Russian provinces, and indeed Hungary as a whole, at that time. No less than 75 per cent of Vienna's physicians in 1936, on the eve of the *Anschluss*, were Jewish (when Jews comprised altogether 8 per cent of the total population). A substantial Jewish overrepresentation was likewise evident from the early days of modernization in other therapeutical disciplines, associated to medicine (amongst dentists and veterinarians, then later on amongst clinical psychologists and, most spectacularly, psychoanalysts) as well as, though to a lesser extent, amongst pharmacists, midwives, and hospital nurses. Their combined presence in these disciplines reached 36 per cent in Romania in 1913 (when only 4.5 per cent of the population was Jewish), 25 per cent in Hungary in 1920 (as against 5.9 per cent in the total population), and 18 per cent in Poland in 1921 (against 6.8 per cent in the active population).

Alongside that, the Jews of the Diaspora can truly be seen historically as the 'people of the Book,' in that the tradition of producing printed texts was likewise a springboard for a broad range of new professional options. Accordingly, throughout Europe, from the nineteenth century on, there was a striking overrepresentation of Jews (albeit with little reliable statistical documentation) in printing, book publishing, the book trade, enterprises producing cultural and scientific magazines, and indeed amongst authors of many genres. Hungarian data show that, even during the era of 'Aryanization' of the interwar years, book publishing concerned with the dissemination of high culture was almost totally sponsored by publishing firms founded by Jews (some 80 per cent in 1935).

That is already to anticipate the subject of the following section, because several more recent cultural pursuits became established rather by breaking with traditional occupations than as natural successors to them. They follow the logic of professional regeneration and creativity, and for that reason deserve separate discussion.

Cultural capital and the 'dual structure' of intellectual markets

Perhaps the most dramatic manifestation of Jewish professional modernization and restratification may be caught in the fact that in most intellectual occupations (new or old) remaining forbidden to Jews prior to emancipation, a sudden leap is seen in the numbers of Jews involved everywhere, out of all proportion to their representation in the general population, immediately after the liberalization of the professional markets concerned. This phenomenon is particularly striking in Central and Eastern Europe, since there it is common to find cases where this resulted in an absolute numerical dominance of Jews in certain local professional markets (e.g. in capital cities). The pertinent data for medicine have already been recalled. In terms of a more comprehensive picture, the only statistics usually available refer, unfortunately, to the far too comprehensive category of 'public officials and freelance professionals,' which is singularly imprecise in this respect (and moreover unproductive, or even counterproductive, in regard to the link that is being sought), since the bulk of the relevant national statistics condense the numbers of all those pursuing any 'intellectual' activity under this heading. By this, they usually dilute the invariably higher levels of recruitment of Jews to the liberal professions with data for the stratum of state and other public officials, from the ranks of which they often remained excluded. Nonetheless, in Germany (1907) the proportion of working Jews belonging to this combined category was 6.5 per cent, roughly the same as the corresponding figure for non-Jews; in Hungary (1920) it was 8.6 per cent, as compared with 4.3 per cent for non-Jews; in Romania (1913) it was 5.3 per cent, as compared with 4.5 per cent in the working population as a whole; in Poland (1921), 12.4 per cent, as compared with 6.8 per cent; in Slovakia (1921), 7.1 per cent, as against 1.3 per cent; and in Italy, where Jews comprised a tiny minority of barely 0.1 per cent of the population, they made up 6–7 per cent of those in the category in question.

These figures serve though more to obscure than throw light on the picture of the sociological reality that forms the background to the previously discussed 'dual structure' of professional opportunities in most aforementioned countries. Before the First World War indeed, in spite of formal entitlements they could hold, Jews had a hard time in most Central and Eastern European countries to accede to posts in public services (including state administration, judiciary, teaching and public utilities as well as the active officer corps in the armed forces), or may have been permitted to fill such positions on exceptional grounds only. Some exceptions aside (like the Soviet Union or the Czechoslovak Republic), that situation persisted and, indeed, worsened in the inter-war years, until the Shoah. Thus, whilst there were relatively few Jews amongst public employees, and still fewer with the passage of time, their representation in the liberal professions exceeded considerably everywhere the levels indicated by the above figures. The proportion of Jews in each of the professions follows, more or less everywhere in Europe, the same rapidly rising trend as soon as they opened up to Jews from the latter half of the nineteenth century onwards. This concerned some classic professions (lawyers, engineers or architects as well as physicians and musicians) together with some newer ones (especially artistic métiers, actors, sculptors, painters, literary authors, etc.), or other equally new intellectual vocations with creative or organizational functions brought about by the very process of modernization (journalists, editors, university lecturers and private scholars, officials and clerks in non-profit organizations, party functionaries, etc.). Still, there were places where earlier prohibitions on entry of Jews into several professions remained in force (like in Russia or Romania, up to the First World War). But in certain countries and areas, especially the capitals and other larger cities, where the markets for intellectual services were mainly concentrated (e.g. Vienna, Warsaw, Prague or Budapest), from the start of the twentieth century, Jewish lawyers, engineers, chemists, and architects were at times in the majority within their profession. In 1926, 30 per cent of liberal professionals within Ukraine as a whole were Jewish, as against 5.4 per cent of Jews in the general population, and in White Russia (Belarus) 36 per cent, as against 8.2 per cent in the general population. The figures were similar or even higher in Hungary, where in 1920 Jews comprised 51 per cent of lawyers, 39 per cent of engineers and chemists, and 34 per cent of journalists, against their 5.9 per cent only in the general population. In Vienna at this time 62 per cent of the lawyers were Jewish, when they made up 8 per cent of the local population.

The example of Jewish lawyers in Hungary gives a good idea of the sweeping success achieved by Jews in an occupation, socially prestigious as it was financially rewarding, that guaranteed a prominent position within the middle classes and, on occasion (in Hungary commonly), served as a springboard to political careers as well. It will suffice to recall that the legal profession was officially off limits for Jews (except in a few individually permitted cases during the early 1860s) prior to their emancipation in 1867. Barely four decades later, however, Jews made up almost half of lawyers in the country as a whole (45 per cent, and even more if the baptized were counted), and as many as 62 per cent of those in the capital. The profession had doubled in size in the meantime, but the growth was almost exclusively due to Jewish jurists. The Hungarian example would seem to be paradigmatic, as parallels are readily demonstrable during the twentieth century in many places for which data are available—at least where the integration of Jews into intellectual occupations did not come up against artificial barriers.

For an appreciation of the main trend in this development, it is necessary to take into account at least four sets of variables directly affecting this disproportionately rapid expansion of the Jewish segments of the professional intelligentsia. Just two of these will be discussed in the present section: the general growth of economic markets, and the role that Jews achieved in those markets and, more particularly, the consequences of capitalist investments made in sectors liable to generate or increase the demand for related intellectual services. (The other two factors are also important, but they served more as preconditions for the development to take place in the first place and, as such, deserve a separate analysis. Specifically, these are the exploitation of opportunities offered by the supply of schooling and university education, on the one hand, and the links that acculturation and assimilation had with intellectual creativity, innovation and inventiveness.)

For Jews, to gain entry to intellectual markets, these had to exist in the first place, and then they had to be opened to them. These simple conditions, in themselves, hint at a fundamentally divergent evolutionary dynamic between the western and eastern countries of Europe, and also at the extent to which opportunities for Jews to gain professional advancement remained or came to be restricted in the very course of modernization, despite emancipation (or through its denial).

This has to do with basic historical conditions of how emerging modern intellectual markets were shared.

The difference in evolutionary dynamic can be well illustrated by the three main regions of the first Czech Republic in the inter-war years, remarkably discrepant as they were in their development. In 1921, the proportion of the Jewish working population engaged in intellectual occupations (apart from public administration and education) corresponded precisely with the different levels of economic modernization of these regions: 7 per cent in Bohemia–Moravia (West), 5 per cent in Slovakia (Center), and 3 per cent in Ruthenia (East). At the same time, however, and leaving demographic factors aside, the more developed the region, the smaller the share of Jews within these occupations: altogether just 6.6 per cent in Bohemia–Moravia but 20 per cent in Slovakia and as much as 39 per cent in utterly backward Ruthenia. Through their western-type level of development, in the three Czech lands (Silesia, Bohemia and Moravia) the competitive edge of non-Jews in the intellectual arena, as in other 'bourgeois' careers, proved to be extremely strong, what obviously limited the Jewish share of the markets concerned, however substantial the drift of Jews to these professions may have been. Their competitive position was most robust in those countries (as in Hungary and Austria after the 1867 'Compromise') and under those developmental conditions, where the new markets for intellectual skills were rapidly modernizing and expanding without much Gentile competition – since the mobility of the latter was directed preferentially towards the more easily accessible 'protected' markets of the public sector. A good example is provided by the markets for legal competence in Hungary. The reason why gross numbers of Christians within the Hungarian legal profession barely rose in the half century after 1867 lay in the fact that Gentile members of the 'nation of jurists' were primarily seeking the sinecures of public office in the emergent nation-state, or careers in county, city, and national politics and administration, which were practically reserved for them. Thus recently qualified Jewish lawyers had virtually no external rivals in competing for most of the newly created legal positions.

The sudden mass entry of Jews into the legal and other professions in Hungary, as in other states that carried out a 'conditional' emancipation (like Germany and Austria), was also strongly affected by this 'dual structure' of professional expectations outlined above. Those excluded from 'protected' markets, however inequitable the arbitrary division of markets under the aegis of the 'dual structure' may have seemed to them, in no small way could thank to this rigid arrangement their success in the liberal professions, since it meant they had only to reckon with relatively weak competition from Christians. Elsewhere, in most countries of belated Jewish emancipation, Jews were hit additionally by the general handicaps of backwardness. Excluded from various intellectual markets, in addition to those that came under the state's immediate dispensation, they continued to be underrepresented in the liberal professions overall. In Romania, Jews made up altogether 2.4 per cent of lawyers and just 3.2 per cent of those in all liberal professions, as compared with 4.5 per cent of the general population in the pre-First World War years. Conversely, in a country like Italy, which conducted a western-type Jewish policy and had stepped onto the path of economic modernization once the unification of the state and a representative system of government had been accomplished, practically all intellectual markets, private or public, were open to Jews: by 1920 no less than 23 per cent of active Jews were classified in the category of 'public officials and liberal professionals.' A comparably high figure could not be encountered anywhere in Central and Eastern Europe, of course.

The cultural industry, assimilation, and intellectual achievements

The move across into intellectual occupations by a growing portion of Jews engaged in the processes of modernization (secularization in particular)—principally the descendants of the mercantile and industrial lower-middle and upper-middle classes—was powerfully stimulated by numerous agencies of the modern cultural industry founded by Jews, or established with Jewish capital. Whether it had to do with Jewish entrepreneurs seeking new markets, or with investors ready to fill market gaps in post-feudal economies, all were endeavoring to exploit a growing consumer demand for intellectual services in the broad sense. Demand in these fields, thanks to the general improvement of levels of schooling and the spread of literacy, was sustained not just by élite groups (albeit primarily by them, naturally enough) but increasingly by ever larger social layers, especially in cities. Jews were regularly amongst creators of the modern press, founders and managers of theatrical and musical enterprises (as commissioners and operators of theatres and concert halls), directors of the first film studios, cinemas, art galleries, photographic studios, antique shops, dealers in antiquarian books and postage stamps, and, indeed, amongst investors in a range of other paracultural facilities catering for leisure-time pursuits and mass entertainment (swimming pools, sports halls, stadiums, music-halls, cabarets, etc.). In emerging metropolises of Central Europe (Budapest, Prague and Vienna) Jewish entrepreneurial participation was regarded as decisive, for instance, in the establishment of coffee-houses, giving a new flavor to everyday life in modern cities but also temples of literary creativity proper and irreplaceable arenas for the socialization, exchanges, development of cultural refinement among intellectual élites and circles of the bourgeoisie (including its lower strata) up till the Second World War.

This vigorous, capitalistic penetration into (and creation of) new cultural markets largely due, from start to finish, to Jewish entrepreneurs, was all the more likely to inspire a sense of vocation for creative intellectual careers among educated young Jews, that many descendants of the first entrepreneurial generations of the Jewish bourgeoisie took a dislike to the purely 'capitalist' pretensions of their forebears, all the more since a significant (and probably ever-growing) segment of the consumers of these markets were themselves urban Jews by origin. The modern mass press in many parts of Europe, therefore, owes its existence to innovations brought by Jewish entrepreneurs, and its products too, in large measure, were under the direction of Jewish editors. It was just as important, however, that, from the very outset, masses of urban Jewry were amongst the most zealous readers of that press. If, as all the evidence suggests, Jews historically showed a keener and more discerning demand for political and cultural information, that may well be because, by virtue of the peripheral position into which they were driven by anti-Jewish pressure, they felt a much stronger need to keep themselves apprised about prevailing social realities that might threaten their marginal existence.

Participation in all these markets either explicitly cultural or having a cultural stamp was always linked to a string of not just economic but also symbolic interests, whether it concerned Jewish capitalists, entre-preneurs, patrons, or consumers, resulting in the appearance of a body of Jewish experts trained specifically for those markets. This kind of nexus applied even more particularly to certain major cultural–intellectual innovations (such as the foundation of the periodicals *Nyugat* /'West'/ and *Szép Szó* /'Fine Words'/ in early twentieth cen-tury Hungary) that were hatched in coffee-houses built and run by Jewish entrepreneurs, and for which Jewish capitalists provided the financial backing, with rich Jewish patrons providing the money to keep them running, and the cultivated Jewish middle class figuring heavily on their subscribers' lists. Initially and for a long period, the chief theoreticians and practitioners of psychoanalysis (and a good number of their patients as well), came from educated Jewish circles throughout Europe, with the Habsburg Monarchy in the vanguard. In Budapest, it was thanks very largely to the Jewish bourgeoisie and intelligentsia, the Jewish audiences in the concert halls, Jewish musi-cologists and music critics, and, on occasion, Jewish patronage, that the musical revolution introduced by Bartók and Kodály (both Gen-tiles, though) won through. It would not be hard to list other similar examples.

This receptivity to culture, whether of the high or 'light entertain-ment' variety, cannot be explained purely by economic stakes Jews may have held. For them, obviously, it was also a voucher of their cultural integration, providing a social space to converse with and understand, to join forces and collaborate with their Christian partners and counterparts of similar station and interests in a spirit of shared aesthetic values or modern norms of spending one's leisure time.

Dance halls, literary circles, coteries of editors and regular writers for magazines, sports clubs, academies of art or music, artistic coffee-houses and their reserved tables for regulars, and so on, informal though they might often be, provided an institutional milieu for Jews to fit in socially and, besides much else, to display 'Jewish creative flair' in a manner that was most readily perceived and appreciated by the outside world, demonstrating their contribution to the current 'national culture,' or fostering modern habits of consumption of that culture. For these reasons, Jews on the way of deserting their tradi-tional lifestyle—more the city dwellers in the West generally, and to a considerable extent in Central Europe as well, to a somewhat lesser extent in Eastern Europe—invested heavily, out of all proportion to their numbers, in intellectual values—in capitalistic, professional and symbolic sense alike. That, in turn, led everywhere to a high level of representation of Jews in occupations aimed at cultural production. (Unfortunately, occupational statistics rarely allow this to be attested in full detail.) Thus, many Jews figured amongst the true pioneers, as well as the rank and file professionals among journalists, actors, playwrights, performing musicians, theatre and film directors, art photographers, or—less often—painters and sculptors, or else in the managerial staff of the cultural industry, like newspaper proprietors, theatre managers, film producers, editors in chief of cultural periodicals, exhibition organizers, and artists' agents.

According to a 1907 statistic from Germany, for instance, the prevalence of Jews in the category 'journalists, private scholars and writers' was more than eightfold (!) higher than in the overall workforce. On the same basis, in 1920 their representation in Hungary was fourfold higher amongst 'poets and musicians' and 'actors,' six times higher amongst 'editors and journalists,' threefold higher amongst 'painters and sculptors,' or five times higher, on average, amongst those with occupations in the field of high culture as a whole. Polish data indicate that in 1921 the proportion of Jews in the arts and sciences was approximately twice as high in the overall working population, and almost four times higher in theatre and music.

What these summary statistics do not show is how often Jews, precisely thanks to their Jewish background or descent, figured in the top flight within the internal professional hierarchy of the various branches of art and science. There is no space here to enter into a detailed analysis of specific cases so as to expatiate on the particular circumstances driving many Jewish intellectuals to usher in innovations of major importance, which often enough brought them to the forefront of their professions. In the following section we shall have to confine ourselves to the evocation of some plausible links between the outstanding intellectual achievements of Jews, their relative overeducation, and the experiences and consequences of their assimilation. The vigor of that creative flair is testified by conspicuously large numbers of leading intellectual luminaries from the cultivated urban Jewish strata who were to be found, around the turn of the nineteenth century, in psychoanalysis, the nascent social sciences, many circles of the artistic and literary avant-garde as well as amongst international pioneers of medical, physical, and other branches of scientific research in a wide diversity of countries—in Weimar Germany, in France of the Third Republic or early twentieth-century Vienna, Prague and Budapest. A mere list of some of the best-known names—Freud and Wittgenstein, Proust and Durkheim, Chagall and Mandelstam, Mahler and Schönberg, Heine and Celan, Einstein and Husserl, Kafka and Broch, Marx and the Frankfurt School, Eisenstein and Korda, John von Neumann and Sándor Ferenczi—is proof in its own right that the series of intellectual achievements ascribable to Jews who had integrated into the markets of cultural production in the most varied areas of creativity was inseparable from intellectual modernity in Europe (and in the world, for that matter).

Social circumstances of Jewish 'overeducation'

These achievements were merely the visible tip of an iceberg, the invisible bulk of which was formed by the broad ranks of an increasingly well educated, mainly urban Jewry that, with time, was becoming ever more closely assimilated into host civilizations. This is basically a matter of two extremely complex processes that may be characterized only with gross simplification under the rubrics 'relative overeducation' and 'assimilatory break with traditional identity,' and can, at best, only be sketched here in rough outline.

A high level of education, of course, is a technical precondition for major intellectual accomplishments in any social group. In the case of Jewry, however, cultural assimilation (or acculturation) served as a distinctive socio–historical condition and major motivation for decisive educational efforts. Had there been no investments in advanced education, accumulation of the cultural capital necessary for selecting the minds capable of exceptional achievements could not have taken place. Had there been no assimilation, cultural activities would have been caught within fields of traditional (principally religious) education, as was largely the case (at least for a long time, up to the early twentieth century) amongst Yiddish-speaking Jewish communities of Eastern Europe. Insofar as the latter would have retained their dominance, the intellectual values created by Jews could not have attained a universal validity and reached large, receptive publics. To be more precise, they would not have accommodated to the universalistic ideological and intellectual trends of European civilization that took their point of departure from the Enlightenment.

Widespread schooling is one of the key phenomena of post-feudal Jewish social history. Though this is already richly documented in the specialist literature, the socio-historical circumstances of its development have not yet been sufficiently explored. Findings agree on the spectacular fashion in which, once Jewish youngsters had gained admission to public secondary schools and universities since the late eighteenth and (in most countries) during the nineteenth century, their ratios of pupil and student enrolment shot up in all accessible élite educational institutions. The statistically generally significant over-representation of Jews in élite education seems to have peaked in most countries in the outgoing nineteenth century, when factors of nine- to tenfold were observed in Prussia, fivefold in Austria, and sixfold in Hungary and the Monarchy's Czech provinces. Throughout Central Europe, in Vienna, Prague, Berlin, Jassy (Iaşi), Czernowitz or Cracow alike, Jews were conspicuous for their inordinately high proportions amongst university students. Depending on the place and faculty, they might make up anything from one-fifth to one half of the total student enrolment. Their presence at French, Belgian, Italian and British universities also went up many times over after 1900, and even more during the years between the two world wars, at least as compared to numbers of foreign students, since western higher education took up the excess educational demand of Jews in Central and Eastern Europe that was ever less readily satisfied in their home countries, due to the overt or masked application of anti-Semitic violence and restrictive quota systems (*Numerus Clausus*). It is not difficult to point to similar outcomes with regard to secondary schooling.

Such data present an inaccurate reflection of the group-specific Jewish demand for education, however, for they fail to take into account the specific social factors, working both for and (sometimes) against a high level of schooling, on which neither the easily available documentation nor the research carried out to date throws sufficient light.

Amongst the positive factors that promoted schooling one has to cite the 'internal' cultural and structural variables, including the previously discussed religious intellectualism, the predominantly urban location of Jewish populations (which put them physically nearer to institutions of learning and cut tuition costs), the smaller and rapidly diminishing numbers of children per family due to the earlier onset of the demographic transition, and, above all, their dominantly middle class, bourgeois or petty bourgeois socio–economic stratification, as compared to other segments of the population. Exploratory assessments, however, have shown for Vienna, Cracow, Budapest, and Hungary as a whole, as for a series of other cities in the Central European region, that when stratification effects are allowed for, or in other words students with similar backgrounds in terms of residence, social class, and family culture are compared, then a higher level of education of Jews does not show up so conspicuously on crude quantitative indicators, but it does not vanish either, at least in the period preceding the introduction of *Numerus Clausus*-type restrictions (in other words up to at least the First World War in the more easterly countries). Moreover, in Hungary (for which my own research results are the most detailed), even after allowing for group specific differences in socio–economic set-up, a significant overrepresentation of Jews is evident prior to 1919 across the whole spectrum of secondary school types (and most notably the 'civic' or 'burgher' /*polgári*/, upper commercial and 'modern' /*reál,* with no Latin and Greek/ schools with the exception of teacher training colleges.

It is perhaps even more to the point that several recently completed studies have made it possible to construct indicators that relate to qualitative measures of schooling. Research findings of this type cover large numbers of university first degrees awarded in Hungary between 1880 and 1939, and also the examination results achieved by pupils in different grammar-school classes (*gimnázium* and *reáliskola*) in a number of Hungarian cities (including Budapest and some 20 other, among them Szeged, Miskolc, Temesvár (now Timişoara, Romania), Arad (Romania) etc. in selected years between 1870 and 1945. Comparable results are, for some pre-First World War years, also available for secondary schools in various towns in Transylvania (Kolozsvár, Máramarossziget), Galicia (Lemberg), Bukovina (Czernowitz, Suceava) and Moldavia (Iaşi). These studies demonstrate that Jewish students attending secondary schools and universities almost everywhere, and in every subject (with the exception of sports), stand out from their fellow students with significantly better average results achieved in their studies. Jewish students both gained university entry and completed their courses at a younger mean age, whilst their failure rates were appreciably lower than those of Christian fellow students. The success of Jewish secondary-school pupils was even more marked, especially in the upper forms where—in Budapest for example—they were on average half a grade ahead of Christian form-mates (with marks of a four-grade scale). That superiority was particularly evident in the intellectually more demanding subjects, such as Latin, German, Hungarian Literature, History, and, to a slightly lesser degree, Mathematics and Physics. All the evidence underpins the hypothesis that one of the distinctive features of assimilated Jews was their drive for more advanced educational attainments (in terms of qualifications), both quantitative and qualitative. Such educational eminence cannot be interpreted without taking into account assimilationist strategies and efforts. Their admission into élite educational establishments, in itself, predicated a significant degree of assimilation and, equally, signified the consummation of their 'assimilationist career.'

That was notwithstanding the fact that in contemporary Europe there was no lack of objective factors militating against Jewish over-schooling. Those who research into this general topic tend to forget about the negative factors, though in reality they placed a great many obstacles in the way of Jews acquiring advanced education. This primarily concerns the major additional costs and social difficulties that Jews were burdened with as the price they had to accept for simply gaining admission into élite schools, at least in Central and Eastern Europe.

Jews were indeed rarely—if at all—granted scholarships, tuition exemptions or reduction of fees as compared to other students. One sector or another of the school system—either the ecclesiastical or state sector, depending on the country—was regularly reluctant to admit Jews, if it was not closed to them altogether. It could also happen that they were obliged to pay specially high tuition fees, in some cases even in institutions (as in many Hungarian Protestant schools), which were in principle more accessible than others to Jews. To give just one example: liberal and highly reputed as it was, and much favored by the Jewish bourgeoisie, the Lutheran Grammar School near Budapest's City Park demanded from Jewish parents six times the standard tuition fee between the two world wars (240 instead of 40 pengős) charged for students belonging to the local Lutheran congregation. In Hungary, where the majority of classical secondary schools (albeit a declining proportion over time) were run by the Churches virtually to the very end of the old régime in 1945, Jewish students were, little by little, excluded from these (almost completely so during the inter-war years), a few Protestant institutions excepted.

The anti-Semitic atmosphere that regularly poisoned the lives of Jewish grammar-school and university students should also be counted among factors that hampered their access to élite training. Violent anti-Jewish movements amongst student bodies in Central and Eastern Europe escalated from the 1890s onwards. During the previous decade, student fraternities (*Burschenschaften*) were already ever less inclined to admit Jewish members in Germany and Austria. A cap on university entry, in the form of an official *Numerus Clausus*, was imposed in Russia as early as 1886, and in Hungary in 1920, well before similar quota systems spread to the greater part of Europe, often under the influence of Nazi Germany. In the inter-war years universities became the sites of veritable pogroms in Vienna, Budapest, Bucharest, Jassy and Warsaw, to say nothing of the discriminatory measures that were inflicted, whether by direct legal means or indirectly by non-observance of legality, upon Jewish youth seeking to study. In Polish universities during the 1930s, after the failure of attempts to get Jews officially excluded, 'Jewish benches' (on the lines of the 'dunce's seat') were established in lecture theatres.

To these unfavorable circumstances must also be added market factors proper, liable to discourage Jews from seeking higher educational entitlements. This has to do with the difficulties, great and small, that were placed in the way of Jewish graduates obtaining gainful employment in most intellectual markets, particularly in those countries of eastern and Central Europe that operated 'dual systems' of professional opportunity. For a Jew, gaining a university degree in Russia or Romania at the turn of the century, or in Hungary during the inter-war period, was tantamount to a passport to probable unemployment. In 1928, the real rate of unemployment amongst Jewish 'intellectual workers' was twice as high as amongst non-Jews in Hungary. In Poland at virtually the same time, in 1929, Jewish town dwellers were four times as likely to be without a job as others. Prospects were no more alluring in the western countries that were traditionally picked as destinations by immigrants, with dismissals of, or refusals to employ, foreign graduates getting under way during the 1920s and 1930s. Many promising careers of young Jews were also broken in mid-course on the reefs of forced emigration. Provinces of professional expertise, such as in law or the humanities, highly esteemed in Eastern European intellectual markets, turned out to be completely valueless in the destination countries for immigration.

These negative factors had the additional effect, when they did not put Jews entirely off the idea of further studies, of pushing them towards transferable intellectual investments of universal application, that is, above all medicine, engineering and some other 'hard' sciences. The general deterrent effect, however, is clear from university statistics. A rapid fall in the numbers of Jewish students after 1930 was typical not just in Hungary (even though there the overtly anti-Semitic provisions of the *Numerus Clausus* law were officially removed in 1928—at least temporarily, till 1938), but in Austria, Romania and Poland as well, even before right radical (*völkisch*) measures took root in universities from the middle of that decade up till complete Nazification.

At the same time, attempts to squeeze Jews out of élite educational institutions set in train, or reinforced, certain compensatory mechanisms. On the one hand, Jewish candidates applying for higher education employed tighter standards of intellectual self-selection. Thus those, who did stay on at school, on the other hand, were spurred to achieve exceptional results. That might be one of the reasons why, for instance, the average grades of Jewish pupils taking the school-leaving examination (*Matura*) at Budapest's grammar schools were significantly better, in relation to other pupils, in 1930 than they had been earlier, like in 1870–1889 or in the first decade of the twentieth century.

'Overeducation,' assimilation and strategies of integration

It is evident that Jewish over-schooling, for all the obstacles, did become a *fait accompli*, at least in Central and Eastern Europe. (To the best of my knowledge, empirical research into this phenomenon has not been undertaken for Western Europe, except for Germany. It is true that the empirical resources for such studies are much more difficult to establish, for lack of denominational information on students.)

Space constraints do not permit a full evaluation of this finding, so I shall restrict myself to outlining the main social prerequisites of the trend.

The first factor worth noting concerns the lure of markets that opened up in intellectual careers and the cultural industry following (and sometimes even before) emancipation, in book publishing, the cultural press, theatres, musical life, art trade, and, later on, in photography, film-making, etc. To that one should add the opportunities that were also unbarred, and not just in Western Europe, to pursue classical intellectual careers in public institutions of learning. The arrival of Jews at the very top of the university hierarchy in France and Italy, from the end of the nineteenth century is indeed striking. In Paris it is betokened by the work of Durkheim, Bergson, Lévy-Bruhl and Mauss. The same is observed in Germany and elsewhere in Central Europe, at least at the level of the *Privatdozenten*, or unsalaried lecturers, since an exclusion of Jewish candidates, along 'dual structure' lines, from appointments to university chairs was fully operating by then. (Even a figure like Ignác Goldziher, the renowned Orientalist, typically quoted as a counter-example, was into his fifties before he was given a chair in the University of Budapest's Faculty of Arts.)

Specific motivations were, possibly, even more important than that to go through an educational path providing palpable opportunities for social integration, indeed, securing a 'gentleman's position,' that is, attainment of middle class rank or status, tied to certified levels of advanced learning, in practice: graduation from secondary school (*Matura*) or from a university. It was typical of Europe as a whole at least up to the First World War, but often much beyond – admittedly more in the eastern part than the western—that principles of social classification and class distinctions, inherited from the feudal system, were perpetuated including a sharp boundary line between the common people and the élite, or the 'gentlemen.' The yardsticks of belonging to the élite included, in addition to, first and foremost, descent from the nobility or patrician, the attributes of a 'genteel' lifestyle and economic standing (like a flat of three rooms or above, a housemaid, etc.), but also, not least, a fixed level of formal education. Now with advancing modernization, university degrees and other educational titles increasingly took over the function of noble titles, to the extent to become, in themselves, a guarantee of most political and social privileges, whether of recent origin or else feudal hangovers formerly reserved for the nobility: entitlement to vote and to stand for political office; eligibility for membership of clubs and entry to salons; qualification to fight duels; abbreviated 'voluntary' army service and admission to the reserve officer corps which was predicated on that. Symbolic entitlements were not the less important, like inclusion in the etiquette of the élite (e.g. the use of the familiar second-person singular when speaking to equals), the right to be addressed by the honorific 'Mr' (and its equivalents), and so on. In this context, obtaining a school-leaving certificate (*Matura, baccalaureat*, etc.), particularly from a grammar school (*Gymnasium*) but also, to some degree, from a modern school or commercial college, was a true watershed, a basis for setting oneself apart from 'ordinary people' or the working class. Such mechanisms of educational class distinction could also be given official recognition. Indeed in some countries, notably Austria–Hungary, even ordinary army enlistees or non-commissioned officers endowed with a grammar school-leaving certificate, were entitled to distinguishing braids or flashes on their uniform.

In this kind of status order, which in Central and Eastern Europe persisted up to the end of the Second World War, it is easy to see how certified educational distinction made possible a rapid and otherwise unattainable advancement up the symbolic social ladder for Jews whom these societies, not so long before, had still treated as pariahs. Even in Russia, as already discussed, the fruit of higher educational qualifications was not merely symbolic since, from 1865 onwards, it conferred the right to leave the 'Pale of Settlement' and, from 1874, entitled one to serve a shorter term of military conscription. No wonder, then, that the number of Jews studying at Russian *lycées* should rise from a mere 159 in 1853 to around 8,000 in 1880, to say nothing of those who left to pursue studies abroad.

For socially marginalized groups like the Jews, attendance at educational establishments patronized by the élite also secured, at one and the same time, a practical chance of integrating into its ranks. Examples of that would be Prague's Akademisches Gymnasium, or the aforementioned Lutheran Grammar School in Budapest, where scions of the 'national' upper classes and the Jewish bourgeoisie and intelligentsia came together. Elsewhere too such 'mixed' secondary schools (i.e. the ones that did not adopt anti-Jewish discrimination) were rather rare islands of 'free competition' between Jewish and Christian youth, largely unhampered by hidden barriers, offering both the opportunity to develop contacts, exchange ideas, get to know one another, make friendships, have a shared social life, eventually, even outside school. It was common for relationships formed between Jews and non-Jews in the classrooms of secondary schools subsequently to cement diverse schemes of economic, cultural, social or existential cooperation, which could find expression in mixed marriages, in the 'mixed' movements of literary or artistic avant-garde, in denominationally neutral political parties (Liberal, Socialist or Communist alike), in liberal freemasonry, and in other organizational forms of modern élites with universalistic value orientations. The long courses of classical secondary schools and some university faculties (especially in law and the humanities), moreover, provided an opportunity for cultural integration at the highest level, by bringing outsiders into the cultural value-system of Gentile host societies. The key role that national languages and literatures played in the symbolic foundation of nation-states is widely recognized. The indication, underpinned by research into Hungary's educational history, that Jewish students excelled more in subjects relating to the 'national culture' than in sciences or mathematics is very telling in this regard. Next to German, they attained their best results in Hungarian, history and Latin—the latter ranking also as a 'national' subject in that it had been (until as recently as 1843) the official language of the state (nobility and administration). Although one has to be cautious about generalizing from this localized indication, it can at least help us to understand how vastly significant it must have been for Jewish students, deprived of equal social status, to succeed, by advanced schooling and scholarly distinction, to appropriate some of the most prestigious cultural assets and values of the old élite.

For ambitious young Jews, then, the long years of study and their often achieved scholarly excellence, whilst all this may also have been amongst motivations for other students attending secondary schools and universities, were invested with a particular function in their strategies of social mobility and integration in the period immediately after (or shortly before) emancipation, when, at varying points in history from country to country, the possibility of achieving success outside the ghetto assumed concrete forms and Jews were allowed to resort to hitherto inaccessible practices of both collective and individual self-assertion.

Assimilatory pressure and the influence of cultural heritage on restratification within the intelligentsia

The foregoing already broaches a whole set of questions that impinge on problems of assimilation.

At a first approximation, assimilation is a process consisting of the forced or voluntary acquisition, taking over by minorities or newcomers of the culture, in the anthropological sense—i.e. way of life, values, social attitudes—, of the host (or majority or dominant) society. This implies a unilateral rapprochement on the part of Jews to their Christian milieu as a first step, with that leading, as a second step, to the emergence of forms of reciprocity and cooperation on the basis of the demonstrated rapprochement, as well as common interests and future plans for society as a whole. I shall essay a more substantial analysis of the process of assimilation later on (in a special chapter), but here it is sufficient to state that there was no Jewish professional intelligentsia in the modern era that was not at an advanced stage of cultural assimilation, at least before the Shoah. In this section my aim is to show that the cultural creativity of educated Jews adopted the logic of assimilation throughout the long historical passage from emancipation (or its beginnings) to the Shoah.

The evolution of a Yiddish-language culture of acknowledged high standard or the appearance of Jewish nationalist intellectual and political movements in the late nineteenth century might seem to contradict that statement, it is true. However, these initiatives, whether anti-assimilationist as a deliberate part of their program or only by incidental effect, drew only apparently on traditional aspects (notably the Jewish languages) of the Jewish cultural heritage. On closer inspection, it is generally found that their instigators had first adopted, to a large extent, the values and dominant intellectual norms of (usually Western) European civilization before returning or moving on, as a result of scholarly or political–ideological, at any rate voluntarist, strategic decisions to the production of cultural goods that could be considered as the exclusive preserve of the Jewish world, or to the elaboration of blueprints for a political future of Jewry including such exclusivism.

Assimilation is, before all else, an effort to alter one's identity, with the aim of conforming to the demands of the host society. Anyone seeking to assimilate wishes to turn into a new person, so as to be 'just like anyone else,' to abolish the distance separating him from his social environment, to become 'normal' and both capable and entitled to abandon discriminatory marks of otherness. Yet this kind of transition to the mode of existence of the majority or the dominant cluster calls for a complex creative act. It requires, first of all, a sustained effort to become acquainted with, and adopt the host culture (its language, eating habits, dress, customs, written culture). That in itself is a hard enough task, especially for Jews rising from a pariah status, since it entails not just working out and successfully managing the modes of behavior for the 'dual affiliation' that characterizes the long transitional phase, but also actively enduring the burden of a constantly reflected experience of difference in the alien world of the '*goy.*' In reality, that latter experience never completely disappears, if only due to the workings of anti-Semitism or, at the very least, the aloofness that is maintained by those within the host society, their tendency to size one up as 'foreigner' ("*le regard des autres,*" as Sartre put it). This sort of duality has important intellectual components. Their specific sources are bilingualism, the need to accumulate extensively what is considered as necessary knowledge about the host society, and all the exertions appearing to be useful for 'staying on one's feet' in an intercultural field of force.

It is clear, then, that the assimilatory enterprise, insofar as it succeeds, predicates the development of certain intellectual abilities in the first place, and in at least two different ways at that. It requires, for a start, the adoption of the actual cultural goods through which assimilation may be accomplished at all (that applies mainly to the national language and symbolic culture of the host society), and second, the acquisition of the behavioral skills needed for the self-definition of those in the position of assimilational 'duality,' the legitimization of their conduct, the accomplishment of day-to-day decisions bound up with this, the interpretation of the experience of assimilation itself. All this separates dramatically those implicated from their traditional community, even to the point of shutting them out. The burden of assimilatory self-reflection in the moral household of those concerned is all the heavier the more the 'assimilated Jewish' identity remains problematic. The very process therefore helps and provokes the development of a body of knowledge and abilities liable to facilitate an understanding of the complexity and frequent ambivalence of power relations, human relationships, and conditions of existence in modern societies. That very body of knowledge and intellectual abilities could be indirectly made instrumental in some of the human sciences springing up during the very period of mass Jewish assimilation (social psychology, demography, social statistics, sociology, political philosophy, etc.), in certain therapeutic techniques (psychoanalysis, psychiatry, social work, the treatment of psychosomatic illnesses), in expressive artistic activities aimed at uncovering and interpreting contemporary social reality and the modern human condition (novels, lyric poetry, theatre, film, photography) or, most commonly of all, in ideological constructs and commitments including programs of universal salvation (Liberalism, humanist freemasonry, Socialism, Communism, pacifism, Esperanto, feminism, etc.). This suggests that a close link can be hypothesized between the multiple cultural constraints endured by assimilating Jews and the creative flair they displayed in most above-listed fields, all the more so, given that it was not uncommon for the existential 'duality' and ambivalence grounded in this manner to form the specific object of their scholarly explorations.

The social position, collective experience, and stance towards their identity of assimilated Jews contributed even more directly to enhanced chances of success in scientific fields connected to activities of intercultural mediation and healing.

Since those concerned were participants in two cultures, anthropologically defined, they also had the opportunity to gain familiarity with two (or, as was not uncommonly the case for emigrants, several) 'high cultures,' thanks particularly to the adoption of bi- or multilingualism. From that acquaintance with multiple cultural construct a particular advantage could be derived in various interculturally oriented intellectual fields. Disciplines of that kind in the realm of high culture include literary translation proper, comparative literature and cultural history, general and comparative linguistics, and so on. But similar activities also exist in the practical world of business, as with

international representation, running foreign branches of banks, trading in a multiethnic setting, etc. All these occupations are indeed not
infrequently outgrowths of old-established and often 'typically Jewish' mediator functions. A multilingual flair remained for a long time
(sometimes down to the present day) a distinguishing mark of members of the assimilated Jewish élite (in intellectual and business occupations alike) in most European countries. Paradoxically, this appeared sometimes most conspicuously in countries where the non-
Jewish élite was either monolingual from the outset or became such
(e.g. in France or Britain). Traces of the 'intellectual mediator' functions exercised by Jews can be discerned in the history of most
branches of modern scientific, economic or cultural activities. '

The same applies to various branches of therapy. Here too the
long-standing historical condition that connects Jewish identity with
very real collective experiences of trauma may well have played a part
in the construction of the professional tradition from the outset. Protracted traumatic experiences inevitably foster a certain sensitivity to
trauma, pain, suffering. Amongst forms of abreaction it is obvious that
the identification with the distress of others, empathy, readiness to
help, and models for the exercising of compassion and mercy have
been elaborated in different subcultures in various ways and with
varying intensities. It must have been markedly so in the case of
Jewry, due precisely to the previously discussed dominance of non-
violent behavioral patterns. These all provide a basis for the dispositional qualities and virtues called for in the effective therapist. That,
too, is why it cannot be regarded as a coincidence that remedial occupations should have been given such great weight in the restratification of segments of Jewry having gained the opportunity to choose
their occupation freely, above all during the era of emancipation and
subsequently, and more particularly amongst those embarking on a
career in the intelligentsia and the professions. Among disciplines
concerned one has to cite medicine itself and its auxiliary branches
(including pharmacy, dentistry or veterinary science), which continued to be major Jewish career choices in modern times. But psychology and especially psychoanalysis must also be mentioned. The latter
recruited its first practitioners overwhelmingly (and in Central Europe,
including Hungary, almost exclusively) among Jews, up till the middle
of the twentieth century, as has already been noted. Later on many

other forms of therapy were affected by preferential Jewish professional options.

Assimilationist compensation and creativity

The results achieved by Jews in these areas often contributed to the establishment of new branches of learning, as well as new markets for social, cultural and economic services. Naturally, the same career opportunities were open to non-Jewish specialists as well, only their professional choices were not motivated by the peculiar social status proper to Jews.

Here it is necessary to return to our starting-point, following which assimilation was a far from spontaneous, 'natural' or self-explanatory process, but a life strategy that often demanded the daily mobilization of energies, with manifestations that can be traced through several successive generations. In point of fact, it was a series of creative acts accomplished within a framework supplied not just by a public transformation of one's self-image and self-presentation, but also by a veritable program (whether it was adopted consciously or unconsciously) for the treatment of a 'multiply constrained' personality always implemented under duress. The assimilationist undertaking extends to everything that shapes one's daily life or the practice of modern occupations, the realm of one's tastes, one's style of self-expression, one's way of life, one's demeanor, one's cultural choices and (e.g. linguistic) competence. That predicates constant self-discipline, if only due to worries that one might 'betray oneself.' That 'state of preparedness,' in turn, necessitates a single-minded attention and self-control, which may be characterized as a subculture of sorts, based on permanent self-reflection and involving an unremitting supervision of one's speech, posture, gestures, and conduct. (Similar behavioral patterns could be of course developed, occasionally, by other minorities as well.) Consistent self-discipline of this kind (the origins of which could be, as suggested above, traced back to traditional Jewish religious practices), may also be manifested in professional accomplishments. Its outcomes were particularly obvious in intellectual fields and in the production of socially recognized cultural goods where inherited Jewish values (and their 'modern' variants) coincided with those of legitimate Gentile civilization. This interpretation can equally apply to the educational excellence observed amongst Jewish secondary-school pupils in Central Europe just as to intellectual peak performances manifested in the disproportionately large number of Jewish Nobel laureates.

Those examples shed light on another important dimension of the connection between assimilation and intellectual success. Through assimilation, an opportunity was opened for Jews to pursue studies and economic or other activities from which they had been debarred in the past, and moreover in such a way as to be placed in direct competition with Gentiles. That competition gained all the more edge the greater the number of successes liable to serve as proof of complete assimilation, the demands of which fed back to those concerned as a self-fulfilling prophecy to further stimulate their performances. It 'behoved' a 'good' Hungarian (or German or French, etc.) Jew to achieve good results in the study of national literature at secondary school, since that would corroborate the commitment to the 'national culture' expected from him, which had to be proved over and over again. Similar commitment was not necessarily expected from a non-marginalized 'native.' In the same way, a 'good' Hungarian (or German or French) Jewish lawyer had to provide evidence of at least equivalent, but preferably higher, abilities in order to be accepted as a peer in the profession. Wherever Jewish descent appeared as abnormal or disadvantageous, in any sphere of social intercourse (economic, scholastic, professional, friendly, and, indeed, emotional or sexual), which was the case up to the Shoah in the bulk of European countries, even in those where political anti-Semitism was officially condemned or actively opposed, the need for recompense for one's 'bad' origin, a veritable 'compensatory mentality' regularly implanted itself in the consciousness of Jews seeking to make their way in public markets that be.

Such 'compensatory' behavior is not explicable in terms of purely psychological mechanisms. It represented a logical response to the challenges with which assimilationist Jews were faced in the most diverse fields of activity within the given—and, from the Jewish viewpoint, nearly always disadvantageous—frame of professional, emotional, and other partnerships and social power relations. In secondary schools (outside the Jewish school network proper, but in the entire, long history of Jewish public education that was only of significance in Poland and Romania) Jews were regularly in a minority amongst pupils and teaching staff alike. However hard an educational establishment might endeavor to demonstrate its even-handed treatment of religious differences (and such even-handedness, a few western democracies excepted, could, by no means, be regarded as typical of all times and places), Jewish students constantly had to 'overachieve,' merely to show that they were 'just like everyone else,' or 'just as good as anyone else,' in other words, that they met the standards expected by the institution. A striving for excellence in studies was all the more indispensable in situations of institutionalized anti-Semitism, which were far from uncommon in the modern age. The previously cited research on Hungarian secondary schools, for instance, indicates that whereas the performances of Jewish pupils in the more difficult subjects (e.g. Latin) were better during the era of growing Fascism than they had been previously, their always perceptibly weaker performance in sports, as compared with others, tended to worsen in the years preceding the Shoah. That in itself reflects a situation in which anti-Jewish discrimination may have been the main element, if only in the form of 'reduced expectations' or tougher marking of Jewish students. To counterbalance that, excelling in intellectual subjects must have become even more important than it had been before the outburst of the anti-Jewish hysteria.

Similar observations may be made in other areas too. In Judaeo–Christian marriages, for example, one finds (specifically in Budapest between the two world wars) that men from the Jewish middle classes were—significantly more often than others—inclined to marry 'beneath their station' to women of 'non-middle class' background. This model of doubly (denominationally and socially) heterogamous marriage may likewise be correlated with a growing need for compensation in the face of a general intensification of anti-Semitic attitudes. There is often documentary evidence that husbands 'offset' their Jewish decent in the power relations of the marriage by being of higher status in the economic–occupational hierarchy. In these cases it is likely that this same compensatory balance left its mark within the marriage, indeed possibly even in better balanced or more harmonious sexual relations. For this there is indirect evidence in the fact that the divorce rate for mixed marriages did not rise significantly, but rather remained constant (at least for Jewish men, according to my own findings), or even fell, during the unhappy ordeal of Fascism. The reason for that is, perhaps, to be sought not just in the emotional 'overinvestment' (already mentioned in the demographic chapter) observable in 'mixed' matrimonial alliances, where there was a more individual element of choice (since these were usually contracted against the wishes of the family). The need for compensation could also exert a positive effect on creative efforts to realize the specific, individualistic values that could be accomplished in the market of marriage and love. At all events, in the new matrimonial model a greater measure of individual freedom is granted in the choice of sexual or marital partner, physical violence is to be deprecated, and it is probable that new forms of cooperation evolve more commonly within the household, and children also take benefit from milder and more 'child centered' pedagogical principles in their education.

All these connections require further research, but it is already reasonable to conclude that 'compensatory' forms of behavior were present in all areas of activity where assimilated Jews could be encountered. It is conceivable that these constituted the main source of creativity demonstrably characteristic of large segments of the cluster.

Chapter 2

The Challenge of Emancipation. Jewish Policies of the New Nation States and Empires (18th–20th Centuries)

Circumstances of political renewal

The position of Jews in European feudalism was not properly problematic in the ordinary sense of the word, though frequent and extreme manifestations of anti-Jewish violence may seem to belie that. The fact is that Jews were constantly squeezed to the margins of feudal societies as a consequence of their non-Christian complexion amongst the recognized feudal estates, and thus regarded as alien elements in the social order, that is when their presence was admitted at all. Given that they were banished from most Western European states and Russia from the fourteenth-sixteenth century up until the seventeenth-eighteenth century, they could hardly be in a position to play a part as a formative factor in European history before the nineteenth century. This is not to say that they necessarily fell completely 'outside the bounds of history,' as some historians assert, for they frequently happened to stand in the crossfire of economic, political and religious struggles that turned the various feudal powers (urban patricians, nobility, sovereigns, church hierarchy, servile peasantry) against one another. Jews were simply left only remarkably limited room to maneuver within these nexuses and conflicting relations, and what room there was came, more often than not, through representatives who engaged in money-lending. That was exemplified by the *stadlanut* (intercessor) system in the Polish-Lithuanian Commonwealth, before its partition in the late eighteenth century. Their ability to act autonomously was therefore trammeled. Even before the advent of the nineteenth century, however, Jews had managed to build up important social positions as economic middlemen between the estates to the extent that in a number a countries (e.g. in Poland or Moldavia) they were essentially performing the functions of an emergent bourgeois 'third estate,' besides everywhere displaying a degree of communal autonomy—unlike the Christian patricians and middle-class guild organizations—in matters religious, judicial and associated moral policing. There were even instances (and in Poland, of all places, where the biggest aggregations of Jews were concentrated prior to the nineteenth century) where they achieved a far-reaching measure of political autonomy and collective representation, together with a large freedom in dispensing justice amongst themselves. At all events, their status was generally not in dispute in the countries from which they had not been expelled, however precarious it might sometimes be locally (specifically in some cities).

This status, which persisted over a long period, was upset by the efforts unleashed with ever more powerful intensity during the eighteenth and first half of the nineteenth centuries to modernize European societies politically and economically, with the goal of eliminating feudal bonds, rigidities and privileges and establishing nation-states, or at least centralized empires run on more efficient organizational (in the West more and more democratic) principles. Highly diverse as the circumstances under which these projects may have been conceived and embarked upon—not surprisingly, since the feudal system itself displayed a remarkable diversity within the European countries with large resident Jewish populations—in each and every case a consistent intention to seek a new definition of the role and the place of Jews in society is nevertheless discernible. In most cases, the projects of modernization urged, first, a far more organic social integration of Jews than previously, via mechanisms of equalization of rights, social reception and accommodation. Second, they designated a new position for them in the fabric of society, involving more limited degrees of segregation from the state and the other constitutive elements of society, the latter being now redefined as the 'national' community. Their separation was intended—and did actually tend—to be restricted to the denominational sphere.

Two general trends are identifiable in these conceptions and programs of social modernization, utterly divergent as they were in many instances from one country to another.

To begin with, Jewry itself, in large part precisely as a result of the modernization programs and the changes that they set in train within Jewish communities, became increasingly active in implementing transformations of its own social position. Descendants of apparently passive or impotent victims of anti-Jewish violence endured in the past, the offspring of weak and subordinated partners of feudal authorities took more and more often and assertively the direction of their fates into their own hands, in spite of many handicaps and con-straining circumstance (which can be epitomized in the absence of civic emancipation) representing still for long a brake on their activities. Whether a move towards emancipation or continued social marginaliza-tion prevailed in a given conflict situation, came to depend increasingly on relations between the local ruling élite and the Jewish leadership. As a result, the formerly uniform marks of Jewish status also lost their va-lidity, whilst the hierarchical stratification and socio–economic division of Jewish communities grew following their newly negotiated relations with the Christian world and, more specifically, in accordance with the strategy that those concerned were able to adopt in response to chal-lenges of a 'modernization' process perceived either as an opportunity or a potential threat. The mutual understanding that the basis of Jewish identity was the religion, the practice and communal organization of denominational ritual, began to break down at an accelerating pace from the late eighteenth century.

Second, it may be observed that the treatment of Jews in Europe became all but 'globalized,' and at any rate—even if this appeared in various forms— 'internationalized,' in the sense that their position in Christian societies was no longer determined by the ecclesiastical and secular authorities of individual countries, at least not by them alone. Three basic factors furnished an 'international' dimension to what, before long, was to be called the 'Jewish Question': an ever more rapid international interchange of views and conceptions related to Jews, the development of inter-state relations, and the stepping up of international migrations.

Improving conditions for the exchange of ideas not only enabled the ideology of western Enlightenment (whether English, Scottish, French, Dutch or German) to reach the eastern and southern perime-ters of Europe, but also contributed to the popularization of modern political and economic models as well as to the spread —within European Jewry, too—of the core ideas of social reform formulated or introduced in the West. Equally, though, new currents of anti-Jewish prejudice (racism, for instance, a major reference for political anti-Semitism at the end of the nineteenth century) came to be propagated along these same channels (admittedly with highly variable efficiency and responses) to every corner of the continent.

From this point onwards, relations between state powers, their alliances and conflicts were to have an ever-growing influence—often a decisive one—on local responses to the 'Jewish Question.' The French Revolution's or Napoleon's expeditionary armies succeeded for a while in implanting everywhere the Jacobinic answer of statutory unconditional emancipation. In general one can state that, for political élites in certain Balkan or Eastern European countries, the move to align with the West (whether voluntarily or under duress), including the problem of granting equal rights to Jews, was both a pawn and the indicator to the success of the modernization process in the latter half of the nineteenth century. At the 1878 Berlin Congress, for example, the Great Powers overtly intervened in the 'Jewish policies' of the new states, that had just gained independence from the Ottoman empire, with their demands for Jewish emancipation (inefficiently in Romania, more successfully in Bulgaria and Serbia).

Finally, modernization of transports and communications, as well as the relatively widespread opening of borders within Europe facilitated and even gave an impetus to mass migrations. Thus crowds of Jews, probably greater than ever before, were able to shift their places of settlement within the empires (Austria–Hungary, Germany or Russia) or, more importantly, towards Western Europe and overseas. The waves of pogroms unleashed in Russia in 1881 induced millions of Jews to flee to the West and to America in the hope of finding better conditions of social integration and improved economic opportunities. The Russian pogroms and growing Romanian anti-Semitism triggered a huge response in the public opinion throughout Europe not just because the western press promptly reported the events, but also because in a matter of years the looted masses of 'eastern Jews' (*Ostjuden*) were swelling the populations of the Jewish quarters of Berlin, Paris and London alike, and the ports of the West witnessed a spectacular increase in the flood of Jewish emigrants boarding ships bound for the New World.

Modernization programs affecting the Jews

What were the socio–historical sources of political modernization with an impact on Jews? In summarizing them we can run through essential points of the programs that were evolved to create nation states, the goal of which was to establish new, politically unified, culturally homogeneous (under the aegis of a 'national' language and culture) societal formations with 'organic' social cohesion, resting on principles of popular sovereignty and equality of rights—all within a geographically unbroken terrain that could be appropriated and sanctioned as the nation's 'natural' living space during the process of nation-building.

First and foremost, these programs rescinded the feudal heritage of privileges and the rigid system of economic regulations imposing barriers to unifying markets, free trade, and entrepreneurial free rein. In the process, the obstacles to industrialization and technological advance were swept away, thereby securing free movement of capital and labor. For ethnic groups, including Jews, hitherto hit by severe feudal prohibitions and exclusions on their trades and professions, this aspect of modernization had a highly favorable impact, insofar as it opened up a number of new possibilities of occupational mobility and economic achievement not existing under feudalism. The leveling of opportunities undoubtedly acted as a boost to the economy as a whole by intensifying the 'creative competition' that characterizes free-market capitalism. At the same time, it may also be presumed to have played a part in increasing tensions between capitalist groups—in this context specifically of Jewish and non-Jewish background—because modernization abolished the protected markets of the guilds, thereby directly exposing the Christian entrepreneurial stratum to competition with Jews.

The abolition of feudal privileges, of course, modified the field of forces in which Jewry operated not merely in economic terms but in a political and symbolic sense as well. The socio–economic power relations, dependence and clientele or other forms of subjection shifted significantly in favor of those hitherto disadvantaged (serfs, Jews, and non-nobles in general) and to the detriment of the nobility and other members of the institutionalized feudal hierarchy (notably the established churches). It is easy to see how this aspect of the program would have given a major boost to the collective social mobility and advancement of clusters hitherto excluded from all forms of executive power—again, primarily the bonded serfs amongst the peasantry, who comprised the largest masses in feudal societies, and the Jews. Philosophers of the Enlightenment elaborated a 'social contract' that not only bound the political leadership strata, who represented the public will, to fellow citizens who were in every respect their equals before the law, but moreover, through the device of elections, made them dependent on the latter and thus removable and replaceable.

These two fundamental provisions of the programs designed to roll up feudalism necessarily strengthened the legitimacy of state powers that no longer rested on an authority reputedly derived from God but on common consent and the will of the majority. They also opened up what was probably a much wider scope for unleashing economic, ideological and cultural productive capacities and creative energies. They thereby initiated a general process of wealth formation, transformed the rules of the game for social reproduction, altered the make-up of the leadership strata, and gradually redrew the balance of power within societies. The annulment of economic prohibitions and the integration of politically excluded or 'marginalized' groups (e.g. the Jews) laid the foundation for, or reinforced, the chances of upward mobility based on the principle of individual merits. This genuinely was a system in which, over time, inherited or collectively acquired (through family or status group) assets for entry into the ruling classes were bound to lose their effectiveness vis-à-vis individually acquired assets (e.g. expert knowledge, education or entrepreneurship). At all events, progressive individualization of the chances of social advancement created a more favorable competitive environment than previously for the 'new strata,' Jews included, to make their presence felt in the élites. The latter profited not only from the elimination of their former handicaps but also from the many centuries of experience in behavioral strategies they had developed to compensate for those very disadvantages.

A third important provision of modernization programs was to prescribe the uncoupling of, or a reduced sphere of influence for, the 'intermediary institutions' (churches, guilds and other corporate bodies) between the state and its subjects. The highest stake in this respect was represented by the churches, since they - albeit to a lesser extent in Eastern Orthodoxy, but most certainly in western Christianity - had built up systems of power and control of their own, in large part independently of other political authorities. Roman Catholics for example, who formed the largest body in Christendom (and also within whose sphere of influence the greater part of Europe's Jews lived), were subordinated to the organizational and intellectual hierarchy with the papacy as its head, that claimed entitlement to universal authority. The process of political modernization therefore everywhere, but (for obvious reasons) above all in countries with a Catholic preponderance, also aimed at the secularization of public institutions and their liberation from church influence. This occurred, sooner or later, either by the separation of churches from the state, a more (as in France) or less (as in Eastern Europe, ere socialism) radical process and/or by encroaching on the churches' competence in its various former spheres of influence and activity, like education, health, charitable work, and moral supervision. This secularization process was again largely favorable for Jews, as it weakened ecclesiastical institutional systems (particularly that of the Roman Catholic Church) which had generally been hostile to them whilst broadening the scope of 'socialized' but denominationally neutral services in which Jews could now have a role or from which they might benefit (hospitals, schools, sports clubs, civil social initiatives, etc.).

However, secularization also undermined the authority of Jewish denominational organizations, most notably the legal (and sometimes political) autonomy of communities, which state authorities were decreasingly willing to recognize. Besides, community members being now subject to common law, had henceforth the means to side-step the jurisdiction of their religious authorities.

The final element of modernization projects was the cultural unification of nation-states, principally through building up various unified markets for intellectual services (the school system, press, academies, scientific institutions, theatres, museums, etc.). Such services on offer were now available, in principle, to all citizens alike (not infrequently irrespective of ability to pay), indeed to some degree (as with schooling or the use of the state language) they were made compulsory. The importance of cultural homogeneity should not be underestimated, especially in countries that were slow or late in joining the modernization process. In these would-be nation-states, endeavors in this direction, more often than not, even preceded the implementation of other elements of the modernization program. The movements of 'awakening nations' sought, first of all, to create a 'national language,' a 'national literature' and other media of 'national' self-expression—

musical, artistic, scientific, etc.—together with institutional agencies to promote them and provide them with more than symbolic existence. The reason was that all this did not cut across, at least not so directly, established political interests and therefore it was generally easier to implement them than to embark upon the political program of nation-building. The construction of a symbolic apparatus for the 'nation' had, besides, a direct impact on the political arena as well, because the cultural homogenization of a populace in itself created a basis for 'national public opinion' (i.e. the organized expression of basic societal interests in the press, in political parties, intellectual movements, and so on). This, in turn, could contribute to mobilize further social forces to translate the other planks of the modernization program into reality. That is why the means of cultural unification, both symbolic and instrumental, came into being very early on in all societies that had difficulty in extricating themselves from feudalism: academies and scientific societies are founded, museums, libraries, music conservatories, opera houses and, above all, 'national' school systems established, often before there can be question of creating any institutions of the 'political nation' proper.

This kind of transformation into a 'cultural nation' invariably presented the Jewish minority with a new type of emergency. Sometimes their 'cultural integration' and adjustment is openly expected and demanded. Sometimes they tend to be excluded from the outset from potential beneficiaries of the nation-building process (and from membership in the would-be nation-state) as fundamentally unfit, unable or simply unworthy to play an active part in 'national culture.' There were states (such as Russia and Romania) that rejected emancipation, or those (such as Hungary after the White Terror of 1919–20) where assimilation was deemed to have been 'far too successful,' hence legal attempts were made to exclude Jews from participating in educated élites via academic *Numerus Clausus* or restrictive quotas on school entry. If voluntary 'acculturation' by Jews was unsuccessful, or not regarded as sufficient by the dominant majority, they could not escape the odium of socio–political discrimination for preserving their otherness and separation, as exemplified historically by the plight of Orthodox Jews throughout Eastern Europe. With others, however, the 'pressure to acculturate' might be prompted by purely internal motives. This could lead to a real sense of achievement, the euphoria of liberation from the cultural ghetto and of admission to 'European civilization,' 'modernity' and the autonomy in mapping out one's individual existence. The accomplishment of 'national acculturation' would also be a tangible proof, at least symbolically, of a successful social integration. This experience gained special importance for Jews in the 'cultural Great Powers' of Europe (like in Germany, with its cultural impact extending all over Eastern European Jewry), since it held out a promise of participating in the boons of a civilization of universal scale, in the vanguard of historical progress.

This succinct presentation of the features of modernization that pertained to Jews is not only selective and abstract but the bounds of its validity, as a matter of course, can only be delineated with various qualifications. Though the ideological wellspring of the programs can everywhere be traced back to the world of Enlightenment ideas, these were interpreted and applied in extremely divergent ways from place to place. The nation-states that emerged in Europe during the nineteenth century adopted in no way the very same organizational model. There are countries in the western and northern zones of Europe where the forms of feudalism encountered in Central or Eastern Europe in practice never existed (even the Balkans under Ottoman suzerainty can also be counted among them). Elsewhere, as in Russia for example, the body politics retained many of its feudal features well until the twentieth century. Right up until its dissolution, the multinational Habsburg Empire did not evolve as a political nation-state and did not permit its Cis-Leithan provinces to transform into nation states, despite the fact that many of its territorial units were ripe for such a development.

Post-feudalistic sources of the 'Jewish Question'

It has been noted that one of the central aims of modernization projects was to integrate all the social elements that had been excluded from feudal types of society. How come, then, that integrating the Jews was regularly seen as one of the most problematic of the set objectives, to the point that it was regularly discussed as a 'Jewish Question'—even if the content of that 'questionableness' did vary from place to place? Three answers can be offered here. All three can be ascribed to the social distance between Jews and non-Jews, often perceived as unbridgeable by both sides, in the predecessor states of contemporary national societies.

The basis for this singular perception of the Jews was, first and foremost, the sectarian sense of Jewish 'otherness,' at radical variance with a civilization marked by the hegemony of Christianity.

Every European current of thought of any significance, or indeed the bulk of social activities, however remotely they may relate to the practice of religion, in some way or another derives from the Christian paradigm (or can be derived, sometimes, from a reaction to this). For most people throughout Europe up until the nineteenth century it was self-evident that one belonged to a Christian Church. Even the ever fiercer contestation of Christianity, ushered in by the Enlightenment and later the *idéologues* of the French Revolution, was unable to step completely outside the intellectual framework supplied by Christianity. In that context, traditional Judaism (prior to the nineteenth-century Reform movements) inevitably appeared alien from European civilization, as an esoteric cultic survivor comprehensible only to initiates— in no small part due to the ritual role of Hebrew. As a result, in the Christian world, post-Biblical Judaic writings (the *Talmud, Kabbalah, Shulchan Arukh*, etc.) were either completely ignored or misunderstood or else harshly disparaged. The inveighing against the *Talmud,* widespread since the Middle Ages, continued both during and after the Enlightenment, with even 'enlightened' writers often suspecting this huge compendium of commentaries on pre-modern Judaism all kinds of concealed messages of low morality or at least defamatory of Christianity. That negative interpretation seemed to be vindicated all the more insofar as the demand for a fixed measure of social separatism does, indeed, figure as one of the religious prescriptions of Judaism. The prohibition on *connubium*, or intermarriage, with those of other faiths is Biblical in origin (proclaimed as far back as the prophet Ezra the Scribe), even if it was not always observed. Other prohibitions that evolved in the Diaspora, whether these derived from the observance of the '*kosher* laws' on eating and drinking, which complicated *convivium*, or eating at the same table, or from the ritual timetable (notably the strict injunction to rest on the Sabbath), contributed further to Christians building up a mental image of Jews as a people irredeemably alien to the core. Thus efforts could be regarded as useless to integrate them culturally. When social philosophers, rid-ing the anti-Semitic tide of the late nineteenth century, put forward the 'Aryan myth' and subsequently the notion of Jews as constituting a separate anthropological race, this could only confirm the thesis concerning the 'essential otherness' of Jews, the original basis of which had merely been religious difference. By dint of this 'scientific' explanation, 'Jewish otherness' became increasingly naturalized.

Notions current in the modern era, of course, time and again are merely haunted by all the anti-Jewish specters inherent to Christian value judgements of the most diverse kinds, often enough sanctioned by the church hierarchy since the Middle Ages onwards. For that very reason, during the nineteenth century a growing proportion of Jewish communities, defying strong opposition from their most traditionalist circles, chose to introduce several liturgical reforms that brought Jewish worship closer to Christian practices. This was clearly an attempt to secure more social 'dignity' to their ritual together with bringing discredit on beliefs about the doctrinal exoticism of Judaism. In point of fact, the reforms were informed by two complementary goals: they softened the divergences between Judaic and Christian public worship (e.g. by introducing the use of organs and choirs, lessening the separation of genders, placing the Holy Ark in synagogues to a position corresponding to that of the altar in Christian churches, etc.), and they 'nationalized' divine service (with sermons and some prayers being said in the national language).

Jewish social integration also seemed problematic on account of specific features of their community organization. Except for Hasidic communities centered around the *rebbe*, this arrangement was based on a sort of division of powers between those learned in Jewish law (the rabbis), and the lay leadership forming the governing body of the *kahal* usually elected from amongst the biggest tax-payers and other dignitaries. The *gevir* or secular chairman served as the community's spokesman *vis-à-vis* outside authorities. Given that every community organization fulfilled a wide range of ritual and social functions—not just as a guardian of moral order and supervisor of dietary rules, but also by making provision for the essential ritual services related to funerals, marriages and circumcisions, for assistance for the poor, widows and orphans, for nursing and visiting the sick, etc.—it represented a force of cohesion reaching far beyond the bounds of maintaining religious order. To this may be added the elective nature of affiliation to communities of the various religious persuasions (like Orthodox as opposed to Reform Jewry), and the independence from one another of communities which, nonetheless, formed close-knit networks. The latter were founded in some cases by a more or less freely chosen cultic affinity, in others simply by territorial proximity, as with the Sephardim of the Mediterranean zone, the Yiddish-speaking Ashkenazim of Central and Eastern Europe, and Jews of Byzantine origin in the Balkans (Romaniots), etc. One has also to take into account that up until rather recently, Jews in practice had no opportunity to participate in any other social agency of mutual services. For all these reasons, Jewish communities appeared to be much more rigid structures than the parishes or congregations of the Christians. Moreover, Jewish communities were opposed, as far as possible, to efforts on the part of states to treat them as simple congregations with an exclusively religious function stripping them of all their earlier competencies, above all the administrative and political responsibilities. In doing so, however, they exposed themselves even more to the charge of forming 'a state within the state,' as leveled against them in overtly anti-Semitic bombast and in the argumentation of ideologists of the liberal nation-state alike. From the viewpoint of the Jews' chances of gaining equality of civil rights, one of the major bones of contention between Judaism and the states was the limitation—aimed at by the states and fought against by the Jews—of the sphere of authority of the communities.

Finally, the third barrier to integration was the ubiquitously anomalous professional-economic stratification of the Jewish populace as compared with the Christian milieu. The structure of feudal societies was pyramidal, with an extraordinarily broad base formed by bonded serfs and other subordinate groups (domestic servants, agricultural laborers). Above them, in ever-decreasing numbers, were placed, first, freeman service providers functioning as artisans and middlemen (guild craftsmen and traders) and, second, commoner professionals (lawyers, physicians, teachers, and public servants) along with the clergy (who, legally speaking, formed a separate estate). The pinnacle of the social hierarchy comprised the landowning nobility, with its own peculiar stratification by rank and wealth, which held a monopoly on political power. Its relative size in the population was no more than 5–6 per cent, even in countries that most abounded in noblemen such as Poland and Hungary.

The Jewish social structure was at variance in every respect with that sort of stratification. It had no real equivalent to nobility, and thus no special nobiliary culture either. Nor did it have an institutionalized, hierarchically dependent or organized clerical order, for priestly functions (and likewise rabbinical authority) were assigned on free-market principles according to profundity of scriptural learning. A rabbi would be invited by a congregation's secular leaders according to what he could offer in terms of Talmudist reputation and established prestige, and, formally speaking, he was an employee of the community. (Members of the dynasties of Hasidic *rebbes*, whose functions are inherited, represent the sole exception to this rule.) Accordingly, there is no specific 'priestly culture,' nor is there a corporate body to further the interests of the 'rabbinate,' since any adult male with the appropriate theological qualifications can perform the role of a rabbi. (Such qualification used to be indeed offered to most young men in traditional Jewry via the dense network of *yeshivot*.) Equally, Jewry did not historically comprise a peasantry bonded to feudal landlords: its active masses consisted of small entrepreneurs in numerous crafts and trades, including shopkeepers, itinerant vendors, artisans, tenant farmers, publicans, innkeepers, alcohol distillers utilizing their own produce (generally also combined with one of the two latter occupations), providers of door-to-door services, and moneylenders, along with their employees and casual assistants. At the top of the economic hierarchy were bankers, wholesalers, and dealers engaged in interregional or international trade, who from the Middle Ages onwards were often acting as privileged partners of rulers ('court Jews') or, as in Poland, agents of the upper aristocracy.

The traditional stratification of Jewish society was therefore, to all intents and purposes, the reverse of Christianity's feudal structures. Though, prior to emancipation, Jewish communities were subject to the whims of the prevailing political power, in many respects they formed a more independent segment of the population, economically speaking, than did the Christians. As part of a free-market middle class in the making, they possessed a rare blend of abilities and professional know-how (a 'feel' for economic speculation, respect for economic rationality, knowledge of the market, geographic and residential mobility), thanks to which they were in an exceptionally good position to perform certain intermediary functions. Through their own artisans and those who were employed to supply intellectual services within the community, they had a broadly based economic self-sufficiency. The substantial capital at their disposal was sufficient for them to be able to control certain money markets (for instance, to supply the extraordinary borrowing requirements of entire state treasuries by mobilizing capital on international markets). From the eighteenth century onwards the 'Jewish Question' was posed on more than a few occasions as a question of what was claimed to be the excessive economic power of the Jews, in other words, in a sense of feeling threatened by their allegedly ever-greater economic ascendancy. This perception was not entirely derived from specters, as it was also fostered by actual economic conditions. In the economic system of Christian society, the Jews—in part due to their exclusion from all other occupations, in part through unfairly savage taxation—were obliged to restrict their economic role to just a few uncommon (and sometimes uncommonly profitable) activities. Whether small-time moneylenders or big bankers, itinerant salesmen or wholesalers, or publicans invested with sole rights to produce and retail alcoholic beverages (in pre-Partition Poland this nobility privilege was usually leased out to Jews), the network of contacts that they brought to dealings with their Christian clients, more often than not, was such that the latter would regard themselves as the weaker party, with poorer insight into the market, and thus the ones who were vulnerable and, indeed, exploited.

The sheer weight of circumstances alienating Jews from non-Jews at the dawn of the modern age, separating them in virtually every respect, was such that nowhere did the process of integrating Jews into societies that stepped onto the path of modernization proceed smoothly. A graph of their integration would be marked by peaks and troughs, along with occasional regressions. All the same, two main phases of development are observable in the 'Jewish policies' of European states. The broad sweep of progress up to the First World War (except in the eastern marches of Russia and Romania) trended towards social integration and legal emancipation, though it should not be forgotten that in every case this emancipation was attended by conflicts (for instance, with intensified political anti-Semitism in certain countries of Central and Western Europe from the 1880s onwards), and that for the Jews of Eastern Europe, who constituted the biggest block in Jewry, that emancipation was only achieved at the end of the First World War, after many vicissitudes and at considerable cost in suffering. This marked the start of a new phase. Though legal emancipation was formally instated everywhere in Europe, the process of integration came to a standstill during the inter-war period. The presence of Jews stirred up conflicts of unprecedented magnitude, and their further assimilation into society almost everywhere took a turn for the worse. (The exceptions here were countries on the geographic periphery of Europe, as in the Balkans, Benelux, Great Britain, and Scandinavia, or even the Iberian peninsula, priding itself on its tiny 're-entrant' Jewish population, where the integration of the Jews in modern times was likewise not accompanied by major tensions.) The rise of revolutionary right-extremist movements (with the exception of the Mediterranean fascist régimes) produced a huge historical set-back in this respect, whilst the Bolshevization of Russia represented a radical change in direction, initially as a liberating force but subsequently in quite the opposite sense.

The evolution of the situation after 1919 will be dealt with in later chapters on anti-Semitism and the Shoah. To gain an understanding of the socio-historical conditions for those phenomena, however, it is necessary to consider the path that led to emancipation and integration. Here, at the risk of a few inevitable simplifications, the various courses of national developments can be grouped around three major models: the western (France, Italy, Great Britain, the Benelux states, and the Scandinavian countries), the Central European (Germany, Austria-Hungary, and the Balkan countries), and the Eastern European (Russia, Romania).

Social circumstances of (near-) unconditional emancipation and integration in the West

The countries lying to the west, north and south of Germany were the earliest to begin constructing the political program of establishing the modern nation-states, the main points of which were summarized by Enlightenment theorists as the separation of the legislative and executive powers, parliamentary government based on popular representation, equality of rights before the law, general and proportionate sharing of taxation, freedoms of enterprise, association, expression and exercise of religion, guarantees of certain fundamental human rights, and a cultural homogenization of the population, backed up by an effective, compulsory and 'national' school system. In France this transition was essentially accomplished by the French Revolution of 1789. Only a tiny fraction of the Revolution's more important innovations were later annulled, whereas some were unambiguously extended further by subsequent forms of government, albeit at the price of severe ideological and political conflicts (i.e. further revolutions). Amongst those innovations was a state-run three-tier educational system (which included an enduring state monopoly on institutions at the uppermost level). Elsewhere in the West, in England, Holland and the Scandinavian countries, with their constitutional monarchies, progress along the same lines was more gradual but had begun much earlier (already in the seventeenth century in several cases) and was accompanied by far fewer conflicts. The only conspicuous exception in this regard was Italy where political unification of the peninsula came later and at the cost of severe outbreaks of violence, likewise under the auspices of a liberal constitutional monarchy. Italy's development thereafter closely followed the French model (without its conflicts).

It is not just because steps to secure emancipation were taken earlier here than in other countries that it seems right to place the 'Jewish policies' of these states in one and the same paradigmatic model, but also because integration of Jews rested on the same principles and ideals as those which served as the basis for the provisions of the nation-state. Measures to implement equality of rights were therefore not generally tied to conditions, that is to say, they were not (or only slightly) preceded by separate negotiations with the local Jewish population, and those were also relatively little debated. Besides that, social acceptance of the Jews in these countries was a more rapid and smoother process than in the rest of Europe. This portended two particular factors above all. First, that the barriers to professional and economic mobility, notably in the markets for careers in public life (the machinery of state, the army, public utilities, etc.), were fully (or almost fully) opened to Jews early on in historical terms. Second, the process of integration, for all the disputes or conflicts that cropped up in all places, was not accompanied by such acute manifestations of anti-Jewish turbulence as elsewhere in Europe. It was much rarer for the crudest types of anti-Semitic incitement (such as imputations of ritual murder, with the attendant trials and attempted pogroms) that arose in many parts of Central and Eastern Europe during the nineteenth century, blatantly proliferating towards the end of the century, to spring up in the course of emancipation in the West: there its likes were sporadic, and in some of the countries concerned unknown, even after modern political anti-Semitism gathered strength at the end of the nineteenth century. In the exceptional cases where they did raise their head (as they did in Alsace, for example, directly after the revolutionary emancipation, and a century later in French cities during the Dreyfus Affair), the constitutional state enforced its norms and protected the Jews who were under threat.

Legal emancipation in all countries was, in fact, preceded by what was generally a lengthy period of rapprochement, cooperation, indeed coexistence and reciprocal support between Jews and non-Jews, expressed in a variety of collective forms, notwithstanding localized tensions primarily of an economic nature, that this sort of reciprocity might produce. The actual experience of social symbiosis between Jews and non-Jews might run the gamut from fraternal harmony to antagonism, but this development prompted Jewish communities ready for more or less active participation in the struggle for emancipation and 'national integration' to undergo internal change, creating common spheres of interest for Jewish and non-Jewish élites. Since the professional and social integration that followed, and sometimes even preceded, emancipation was a good deal more complete in the West, those Jews who entered the public administrative and political apparatus were in a position to participate materially in the modernizing policies of these states. In this way they were able to commit themselves more directly, and certainly at the cost of smaller 'compensatory' efforts than elsewhere, to the values, modernizing program and 'national' objectives of the élites of the nation-states.

It is necessary, before we examine the specifics of each national development in order to elucidate the issue more thoroughly, to say something about the historical conditions for such a development, both in the receiving societies and in the Jewish community.

Before all else, it should be emphasized that all the western states under discussion (with Italy again as a partial exception) were characterized by a historically rapid modernization, most especially in the fundamental sense that feudalism, with its rigid divisions of society into estates, vanished relatively early, or else did not exist in the same form as in the rest of Europe. This was where the industrial revolution started (in England first of all), and also where new technological processes originated and brought the first economic achievements (in France and then Holland). It was also here that the first major centers for world commerce came into being (London, Amsterdam and, later, Paris). Here too that broad entrepreneurial middle classes with considerable social prestige first evolved, and along with them a new urban culture based increasingly on free trade and the reciprocal services of social classes. Development leading to embourgeoisement and urbanization resulted in the break-up of feudal relations and the rise of a new form of civil class system. It was here that the traditional binary division of society into 'masters' and servants, nobles and commoners, landowners and tenured peasants dwindled most comprehensively. The chances for Jews to collaborate with the bourgeoisie of the cities, first economically then socially, and what is more, on a basis of near-complete equality, grew in parallel, for the milieu that everywhere was the earliest in integrating Jews was metropolitan (Amsterdam, Antwerp, Bordeaux, London, and post-revolutionary Paris), and in countries that served as destinations for later phases of migration (Denmark, Sweden) it was likewise the cities that accepted the very first few immigrants.

This partnership with the nascent capitalist middle classes was, of course, founded on a recognition of similar interests and a common ethos of citizens entering competitive markets, but it did not develop without friction. The competitive conflicts did not worsen over time, however, but rather eased for numerous reasons. Jews only ever occupied a rather modest place in the markets of Western European capitalism (at times a completely insignificant part, as in the Scandinavian countries). This was a function partly of their own demographic slightness and partly of the strength of the native entrepreneurial stratum. In no case, then, did they attain a genuine monopoly position within any given country, or even a market domination comparable to their urban investments in a number of large territories of Central and Eastern Europe. They could not therefore present a major competitive threat to the established interests of non-Jewish investors, particularly because they often entered totally new markets (the diamond industry in Antwerp, for instance, which the Jews built up during the nineteenth century). In certain financial markets, such as moneylending in several places, the Jews of the West were able to achieve virtual monopolies (in the Alsace region during the nineteenth century, for example), but these were narrow markets in which they would not have had many rivals anyway. Then too, the splitting-up of markets in the West's economy took place within the context of a dynamic expansion of those markets, unlike in most other European countries where the industrial revolution only got under way in the latter part of the nineteenth century, and up to that point the market conditions were rigidified over a long period of time by the pervasive role of the guild system. In the West there were even instances of Jewish capitalist groups being explicitly requested to enter the country, bringing their capital with them. This was the case in Denmark, for example, where in 1622 King Christian IV invited the Sephardic Jews of Amsterdam to move to the Danish crown territory of Holstein, offering them commercial privileges as an inducement, or in Berlin after 1670, following the expulsion of Jews from Vienna.

Politically speaking, we are dealing here with states that were in general (with the exception of Italy) stable and had centralized the exercise of power, most of which had emerged by the Renaissance era (with Belgium and Italy being the sole exceptions in emerging during the nineteenth century), whilst on the cultural plane they early on achieved a high level of homogenization, mainly as a result of the churches adopting the national language to perform their pastoral and educational activities, and the early spread of elementary education to the general population. This was especially true of certain Protestant countries, notably Scotland, Scandinavia and Prussia. The outcome of the struggles of the Reformation and Counter-Reformation everywhere was for a single denomination to enjoy a monopoly, so that we are dealing with states that were also, for the most part, unified as far as their religious culture is concerned. Furthermore, the states of the West did not have such substantial ethnic minorities, either in isolated pockets or interspersed amongst the rest of the population, as there were in Central and Eastern Europe where they presented a considerable threat to the cultural unity of emerging nation-states. The rare counterexamples to this—the Irish in Great Britain, the Bretons or Basque people in France, or the Sami (Lapps) in Sweden—were, in large part, penned up within territories that were almost exclusively their own, forming historically long-settled populations, and as such merely proved the rule through their very exceptionalness. Nowhere do we encounter a situation like that in Hungary or Bohemia where the ruling class of an ethnic minority populace dominates a large body of peoples of other ethnic origins. Under these circumstances, in some of the western states in question the Jews represented the sole ethnic group of 'different race' in the homogeneous cultural milieu of the majority population. In view of the disparity of demographic and cultural balance of power, there were no major obstacles to accommodating them: the 'national' majority populace had no reason to feel its unity threatened by incorporating the Jews. That is a reason why we observe, first, that linguistic and cultural acculturation of Jewry goes back a long way in the history of the countries in question, in some cases—and Bordeaux, Metz or Amsterdam exemplify this as well as London—even to times before the states actually formulated policies on integration. Second, by virtue of their having relatively little to 'fear,' the states were fairly late to enact steps to force cultural assimilation on the Jewish populace. France took the lead in this during the Revolution, as a direct result of Jacobinic doctrines, attempting to 'Frenchify' all regional or particular cultures (Breton along with Basque or Picardian), but also because Alsace's Jewish populace at this period constituted the largest concentration of allolingual Jews in Western Europe. In the Netherlands a policy of linguistic acculturation was not asserted until the mid-nineteenth century (principally by the introduction of compulsory state primary education for all in 1857). Elsewhere—in Britain or Italy, for instance— Jewry, when it chose to tread the path of cultural unification, had next to no chance of preserving its one-time linguistic and cultural autonomy, insofar as anything was left of it by the end of the early modern era, in the face of a majority population enjoying such overwhelming numerical superiority.

By the nineteenth century, nurturing the ancient Judaic cultural goods did not have the same symbolic returns in the 'developed' West as it did in other parts of Europe that were still bogged down in (semi-) feudal backwardness. In countries regarded as economically and culturally undeveloped, lacking the language and institutions of a 'national' high culture and with illiteracy rife, the preservation of a purely Jewish linguistic, folk-artistic and religious culture in the anthropological sense —in the form of day-to-day use of the language, turns of phrase, jokes, folklore, etc.— must still have represented substantial symbolic advantages to Jewish élites caught in a web of sectarian bonds. The retention and cultivation of a traditional reposi- tory of concepts and cultural goods would have been an expression not only of social segregation but also of positive 'differentiation,' an awareness of a kind of cultural superiority, since Jews in these coun- tries had good reason to feel they were custodians of the patrimony of an ancient high culture of universalistic scope in the face of backward, provincial cultures, so the relation to the majority culture was almost the inverse of that in the West. There, even Jews seeking to preserve their original identity were obliged to concede that integration could offer an undreamed-of advancement in the pecking order of contem- porary European civilization. Adopting the French, English, Italian or German language at the end of the eighteenth or during the nineteenth century connoted, whatever else, the experience of enlisting in a civi- lization that was heir apparent to the cultural riches of the Great Pow- ers that were sharing world hegemony. The same applied, albeit to a smaller extent, to the integration of Jews in countries like Holland or the Scandinavian states which were culturally outlying but maintained intense exchange ties with the 'great civilizations.' In the West, then, there were equally 'sticks' and 'carrots' as factors inducing Jews to move towards linguistic and cultural integration.

Denominational components of integration and emancipation in the West

It is necessary, finally, to touch upon the particular religious circum- stances of western-type integration. The inhabitants of the countries in this zone either belonged to one of the varieties of moderate Protes- tantism (which, outside Holland and Scotland, means Anglicanism or Lutheranism) or were predominantly Roman Catholic (like France, and even there a markedly anticlerical secularizing movement made big inroads even before the Revolution and especially during the ensu- ing century). Italy, where the process of nation-building was only completed in 1870, emulated France in this respect inasmuch as the new state's 'Jewish policy' drew considerably on the secular principles of French liberalism. Social integration of the Jews was none the less playing for different stakes in Catholic and Protestant Europe.

During the centuries that followed proclamation of the Reformation, the Protestant states were more or less continuously at war with the Catholic powers, and thus displayed a measure of covert and not infrequently openly attested sympathy for those Jews who remained exposed to oppression by Catholic institutions (the Inquisition, expulsions, forcible conversion, charges of ritual murder, etc.). That fellow feeling, which has to be judged case by case separately, was further reinforced not just by the principle of 'my enemy's enemy is my friend' but also, in countries that espoused the more radical kinds of Protestantism (such as England's Puritans after their victorious civil war against the royalists), by the common Biblical roots of faith. In Holland, the Calvinist state religion was the ideological vehicle for the war of independence that was fought and won against Catholic Spain in the latter third of the sixteenth century. Part of its heritage were a number of Marrano communities, the forcible converts to Catholicism who had secretly maintained their adherence to Judaism, so for obvious reasons, liberation from Spanish rule was a shared experience for Calvinists and Jews in independent Holland. Yet there were two further factors that promoted ideological rapprochement between Jews and Protestants on occasion, namely, the early adoption of the principle of religious tolerance and the American connection.

One of the reasons why Catholicism harried Protestantism so hard was because it contravened the sole authority of the papacy to interpret the Christian gospel. By placing this church monopoly in question, Protestantism was thus inherently more inclined to religious tolerance, particularly if exercising this did not entail fortifying a rival cultic community (like Catholicism) and posed no threat to the religious unity of the state that came under its influence. That was certainly the case with Judaism which was not a proselytizing faith (i.e. with universalistic pretensions to convert Christians) and, in view of its demographic insignificance in the western parts of Europe, could hardly be seen as rival to established state religions. That was partly why in England, for example, the Catholic presence was at all times seen as a considerably greater danger than that of Jews. It is no accident that the House of Commons there, in 1833, should have made the first in a series of attempts to pass a bill formally removing the remnants of disabilities on equal legal rights for Jews (all thrown out by the House of Lords), not long after passage of the 1829 Relief Bill emancipating Roman Catholics. In Sweden, the right to hold political office (the culmination of the emancipation process) was granted simultaneously to Jews and Catholics in 1870. The readmission of Jews into England as early as 1656 served a dual goal: on the one hand, it offered recompense for the victims of Catholic Spain, England's ancient enemy and initially its main rival in colonial expansion; on the other hand, the symbolic alliance that it signaled with the people of the Old Testament was a notion dear to Puritans as stern and committed as Cromwell was. In 1830, at a very different stage of progressive political modernization of the united kingdom of the Netherlands, Belgium, with its Catholic majority, was separated from Holland, in which the Dutch Reformed Church was still dominant, in order, among other things, to devise two denominationally (if not ethnically) more homogenous nation-states. Naturally, the equality of rights that the Jews had secured earlier remained protected by the basic law of the Belgian constitutional kingdom.

All the western countries in which Protestantism took hold furthermore maintained close links with the New World, primarily through the intermediacy of substantial numbers of kinsfolk who had resettled across the Atlantic. This applies equally to the Dutch, the founders of New York, to England, which supplied the bulk of the pioneers during the first three centuries of emigration, and to the German and Scandinavian states that sent off many emigrants during the nineteenth century. The principle of religious equality, and implicitly the emancipation for Jews, was incorporated into the American Constitution in 1787, thereby setting a precedent, coming as it did even before the equalities proclaimed by the revolutionary French National Assembly in 1790. It was a step that was also bound to affect the reception of Jews in the Protestant countries of Europe, given that the majority of the American population had originated from these, and naturally the example exerted an influence on the moderate ideologues of the French Revolution in their thinking on the 'Jewish Question,' since they had close contacts and considerable intellectual fellowship with the elements who had been pressing for American independence.

The triumph of the Jacobinic modernization program during the French Revolution was equally definitive in the imprint it made on subsequent French liberal régimes right up to the end of the Third

Republic, indeed (after the deviation of the Nazi-collaborationist Vichy state) beyond that. For the Jacobins the denominational issue relating to the Jews was two-edged. On the one hand, they were able to regard the Jews as natural allies in their battle against the Church—to their eyes, that feudally based and, especially in regard to religious, moral and ideological non-conformism, reactionary and oppressive institution *par excellence*. That applied equally to their efforts to secularize the state, the goal of which was to end all denominational inequalities for citizens in respect of rights and obligations. This same Jacobin-inspired policy of emancipation and secularization, however, found itself coming up against Jewish particularism. As a result, during the Revolution emancipation was offered first, early in 1790, to the small Jewish communities of southern France, who were regarded as 'more French' and less insistent on religious distinctiveness, whilst the much more numerous Yiddish-speaking, traditionalist Jews of Alsace-Lorraine (who then made up five-sixths of the country's Jewish population) were only granted equality of status close to two years later, in September 1791. In the decree relating to the latter, however, the revolutionary legislators took pains to rescind recognition of all Jewish corporate bodies, heeding the dictum that Clermont-Tonnerre, one of the deputies, had enunciated in the original debate: 'To the Jews as a nation we must deny everything, to the Jews as individuals we must grant everything.' It is hardly surprising then that Jewish communities should be the butt, alongside other denominations, of antireligious measures during the ensuing Terror. (Synagogues were locked, the practice of religion was prohibited, and in Strasbourg there were even public burnings of copies of the *Talmud*, etc.) French Jewry would continue to be exposed to harassment against religious particularism and the whims of the executive bodies that were charged with supervising religious communities, especially under Napoleon I, but also, on occasion, later on in the nineteenth century.

Local approaches to integration in the West

The conditions for the success of political integration of Jews in the West are fairly easy to summarize. Perhaps the biggest single factor here was the low numerical proportion of Jews in the population.

From a demographic point of view, it was a matter of essentially minority—and in certain western countries negligible—ethnic groups. In England, where Jews were not present at all for 350 years after their expulsion at the end of the thirteenth century, even though there may have been no major obstacles placed in their way once they were allowed to return, they totaled no more than a few tens of thousands during the period of their emancipation (there were some 20,000 of them around 1825). The numbers in Italy were rather similar: there were some 30,000 Jews residing there at the time of Italian unification—much the same order of magnitude as two centuries previously. Somewhat higher populations had to be reckoned with in France (approximately 40,000 on the eve of the Revolution) and Holland (55,000 around 1810). Scandinavia had no Jews until the eighteenth century, and then immigration was slow and selective. The statistics indicate that their number had still not reached one thousand even by around 1838, whilst there were altogether 4,200 Jews resident in Denmark in 1849. In Norway and Finland, the first very small Jewish communities (totaling less than one thousand in each country) only began to appear at the end of the nineteenth century. (Finland, then still under tsarist rule, was a favored place for Jewish soldiers who had served in the imperial army to settle down after demobilization.) One of the prerequisites for conflict-free integration, at any rate, was a restricted number of Jewish settlers. Among the aforementioned countries, only in the Netherlands did Jewry surpass two per thousand inhabitants, and there it made up some 2 per cent of the population.

It is not unrelated to those scanty numbers that the linguistic, cultural and economic acculturation of Jews in the West got under way early on, often well before the process of evolution into a nation-state had been concluded or an emancipation policy was embarked upon. The Alsatian Jews in all likelihood constituted the sole Jewish aggregation in the West whose legal emancipation preceded their complete linguistic acculturation. Admittedly, here, just as elsewhere, elimination of the everyday use of the traditional Jewish vernaculars—Judaeo-Portuguese, the Ladino of Spain, and Yiddish—was a fairly protracted business, with active bilingualism prevailing amongst those concerned over a lengthy period. That development had effectively reached its end in all western countries during the early half of the nineteenth century. For Alsatian Jews, the switch to French greatly facilitated the rapid urbanization that followed emancipation, above all their mass resettlement in the melting pot of Paris. By around 1850 already one-third of all French Jews were concentrated in Paris, and that rose to two-thirds after 1871, when the defeat in the Franco-Prussian war set off a fresh wave of migration to the capital out of Alsace-Lorraine with the annexation of the latter to the German empire. The sizeable Jewish communities living in the Netherlands, or rather in certain Dutch cities, notably Amsterdam, showed no noticeable resistance to government policies aimed at their linguistic assimilation. These were manifested first of all from the 1820s, via the Jewish school network and subsequently around the middle of the century, with the introduction of compulsory state schooling. 'Naturalized' western Jews nevertheless continued to be fairly flexible in using foreign languages outside the constraints to speak their newly acquired national mother tongue. Pockets of speakers of the original Jewish (particularly Yiddish) dialects still persisted for a long time, later providing a receptive milieu—at least transitionally—for the masses of Yiddish-speaking immigrants who arrived in ever-growing numbers after 1880.

Also by virtue of this demographic insubstantiality, and perhaps also because the more far-flung Jewish populations were broken up into a very diverse set of sectarian congregations—in France, Holland and England there were, on the one hand, Yiddish-speaking Ashkenazim and, on the other hand, the 'Portuguese' or 'Spanish' Sephardim, then later on groups belonging either to strictly traditionalist Orthodox or to Reformist congregations—Jews were nowhere in a position to mount an effective defense of their communal organizations against state efforts to control them. The policy of emancipation everywhere was accompanied by state regulation of the functioning of these communities, in practice bringing their earlier rights of self-administration to an end. In France, the previously autonomous communities were first left in abeyance, then radically reorganized by Napoleon I, being provided with centralized administrative bodies, the *consistoires*, along the lines of the imperial state organization. The post–1830 July Monarchy completed the process of imposing state supervision, transforming the rabbinate into a public office that came with a state salary (this lasted up until the complete separation of state and churches in 1905). In the Netherlands a similar process took place in two phases. First, a consistory system on the French model was established, then, during the liberal but interventionist reign of William I (1815–1840), a number of state decrees regulated the training and employment of rabbis and other instructors working in Jewish schools, school curricula, the requirements for public worship, etc. In Sweden, Jews were granted full citizenship as early as 1838, but the same law also abolished the autonomy of their communities. It other countries such as England, a more pragmatic approach to the state supervision of congregations did not entail such a severe rupture with the previous status.

It is opportune at this point to take a look at how the process of emancipation went ahead in the western countries that accommodated the largest Jewish populations.

The return of Jews to England could only commence after the violent removal of the office of divine kingship, since the royal authority, despite the moderate 'Anglican' reform of Catholicism in the sixteenth century, had kept up the thirteenth-century ban on settlement by Jews to the very end. The official authorization of Jewish entry was achieved through its endorsement by the revolutionary régime (in 1656), but the restoration of kingship chose not to rescind the legal protections granted to what were, in any case, only a small number of immigrants. This policy was carried on smoothly and seamlessly even after the installation of a constitutional monarchy (in 1688). Jews were guaranteed unconditional freedom to practice their religion, without being made liable to any special taxation and, indeed, with remarkably few discriminatory measures or economic sanctions being maintained against them. In 1753 Parliament passed into law a Jewish Naturalization Bill that provided procedures to make it easier for foreign-born Jews to acquire rights of citizenship, though it was soon repealed in the face of strong (albeit non-violent) popular opposition. Thanks to the mildness of constraints on entry into the country and professional advancement, Jewish communities expanded, adopting the path of rapid embourgeoisement and occupying an increasingly important role in public life. Following the emancipation of Roman Catholics (1829), a House of Commons faction led by the distinguished liberal historian Macaulay found support in the Lords from a lobby around the Prince of Wales to sponsor the official granting of equal rights to Jews. The Lower House went so far as to pass a bill along these lines in 1833, but the Upper House threw this out on repeated occasions. That proved no bar for Jews to take up important public posts from 1835 onwards, and for all remaining restrictions on their filling such positions to be lifted in 1846, with the sole exception of the right to sit as a member in the House of Commons—a prospect that was again repeatedly rejected by the Conservative majority in the House of Lords. Despite Lionel de Rothschild's election in 1847 as a member for the City of London, he was only allowed to take up his seat in the Lower House in 1858. David Salomon, on the other hand, had been appointed as the first Jewish sheriff of London in 1835 and was elected an alderman of the City Corporation in 1847, going on to become the Lord Mayor in 1855. Other Jews too were subsequently elected to this high office. Meanwhile, Benjamin Disraeli, a converted Jew who had proudly acknowledged his origins, had entered Parliament (in 1837) and eventually, as leader of the Conservative Party, won two spells of office as one of the most eminent British prime ministers of the nineteenth century (briefly in 1868 and 1874–80). In his wake, many other politicians of Jewish faith were also to gain posts in Her Majesty's governments, especially once the remaining impediments to Jews holding public office were definitely removed in 1871. It should be added that British governments regularly gave their support to British Jewry's efforts to protect and aid co-religionists in Eastern Europe and further afield when they came under threat. They did not hesitate, for instance, to intervene diplomatically to secure the release of those falsely accused of the ritual murder of a Capuchin friar in the notorious 'Damascus Affair' of 1840. With the historical Balfour Declaration of 1917, the British government took the first official step to support the establishment of a 'Jewish national home' in Palestine, which was to end with the foundation of the state of Israel after the Second World War (albeit by then against the wishes of Britain as the colonial power mandated by the League of Nations to administer the territory since 1920).

The course of emancipation in Holland in many respects resembled that in Britain, except that here there was a longer history of Judaeo–Christian coexistence and one even richer in elements of reciprocity. The pace of developments in this regard accelerated at the end of the eighteenth century when the country was invaded by the French revolutionary army and the Batavian Republic was declared (1795). A resolution granting Jews equality of rights was passed by the Republic's National Assembly in September 1796. A small but dedicated group of Jewish liberals (notably members of the *Felix Libertate* club) campaigned for the total integration of Jews into Dutch society and the abolition of their traditional communal structures, but—failing to gain the support of a majority of Israelite congregations—felt obliged to establish a dissident religious organization. During the brief reign of Louis Bonaparte their efforts enjoyed wide-ranging official support, and a centralized system of *consistoires* on the lines of the Napoleonic model was established in 1810.

In France, the emancipatory legislation of 1790–91 was followed, as already noted, by the upheavals of the Terror and the imperial régime. Napoleon put the 'Jewish Question' on the agenda again because the indebtedness of Alsatian peasants to local Jewish moneylenders continued to fuel anti-Semitic passions, and because the state regulation of Jewish communities loudly proclaimed since the Revolution had still not taken place. The emperor did not try to conceal his distrust of, and indeed outright aversion to the Jewry for evading supervision and seeking to maintain its autonomies. Community leaders attending an Assembly of Jewish Notables convoked by the authorities were called upon to respond to 12 specific questions that had been formulated by the administration. Their responses would guide the framing of laws that would determine how the communities that were to be placed under the state's protection should operate. The actual fulfillment of that duty was entrusted to a Jewish high council, the Grand Sanhedrin, likewise convened by the authorities, which met in 1807 and set up the consistory system. Every region or *département* with 2,000 or more Jewish inhabitants was to have a central *consistoire*, and these consistories were to be responsible for expenditures and liabilities (including those incurred by communities in the past). A number of decrees, including the imperial resolution dated 17 March 1808 and valid for a ten-year period, which has passed into Jewish remembrance as the 'infamous decree' (*décret infâme*), laid down measures that would impel Jewry to assimilate and restrict their freedom to engage in trade. The decree (in the manner of the *Tötbrief* moratoria of the thirteenth-fourteenth centuries) annulled existing debts to Jews, required families to select a fixed family name, placed restrictions on the place of residence (prohibiting further settlement in Alsace, for example), made military conscription compulsory with no possibility of offering substitutes, and so on. It is hardly surprising that no tears were wasted by these communities when the empire fell. The Restoration and the régimes that succeeded it did not even try to repeal the gains that had been made earlier on the emancipation front, but they did add to the measures that were aimed at further integration. As a result, the mobilization of French Jewry through schooling and official posts commenced fairly early. From the mid-nineteenth century, Jews were even permitted to fill high state offices: in the July Monarchy (1830–48) they could become parliamentary deputies, and from the Second Republic (1848) onwards might be appointed as cabinet ministers. In 1829, the Ministry of Education turned the *yeshiva*, or Hebrew academy, at Metz into a modern rabbinical seminary, then in 1859 transferred this to Paris. By 1831 rabbis were accorded equal status with the priests of the two other recognized faiths and now received a state salary. The electoral system of the consistories was made more democratic in 1844 and again in 1848, when all men older than 24 years were enfranchised. The formula of the humiliating oath *more judaica* that Jews were required to take in courts of law was declared unconstitutional by the French supreme court in 1846. Achille Fould was the first Jew to be elected as a parliamentary deputy to the National Assembly (1834), followed not long afterwards by Isaac Adolphe Crémieux (1842) who was one of the two Jews to win a post in the provisional government at the time of the Second Republic (1848). The opportunities for Jews to enter public life were all but fully unrestricted even before the advent of the Third Republic (1871). Crémieux, who became minister of justice for a second time after the fall of the Second Empire (1850–70), was the signatory of an 1871 decree proclaiming the right of Algerian Jews to French citizenship.

The course of events in Italy has to be seen as exceptional. Official emancipation of the Jews occurred later here than in other western states and, moreover, only at the cost of protracted struggles. Up till 1870, of course, we cannot speak about a uniform Jewish policy, but all the more about the Vatican's stubborn efforts to intervene against emancipation. When Jews were granted full equality of rights, in the immediate wake of unification of the state, this won unconditional support from state and society at large, and brought with it the freedom for Jews to get on with their lives. Under the *ancien régime* the status of Jews had varied considerably from place to place, depending on whether it came under the control of the papacy or some other state. Civic equality was proclaimed on several occasions in Italian territories occupied by the French revolutionary forces (1796–98) and the armies of Napoleon I (1800), but after the 1815 Restoration these decrees were annulled and the *status quo ante* was reimposed. There were even many instances where the walls of the ghetto, having been pulled down, were rebuilt. However, the Jewish élite and the Italian liberal middle classes who were struggling to create a unified nation-state found themselves almost natural allies against the common foe. They achieved their first successes during the revolutionary movements of 1848–49 when all forms of religious discrimination in the constitution of the kingdom of Piedmont were repealed. Although the forces of reaction subsequently regained power in the majority of Italian states, this constitutional change remained in force thereafter. As a result, no small number of Jews were amongst the deputies voted into parliament in the first general elections to be held in the newly unified nation state (fourteen of them in 1871) or gained government posts. Luigi Luzzati held on to his brief as minister of justice for twenty years, and in 1910 became premier (probably the first Jewish head of government anywhere in the world). Others acquired important economic posts—and that applied to much of the Fascist era as well, with even a Jewish minister of finance who served under Mussolini. The Nazi-inspired discriminative measures taken later on were totally at odds with the political traditions of the Italian state and the country's political culture. They were not introduced until as late as 1938, and even then there is no doubt that they were exclusively triggered by a political compromise reached as part of the strategic alliance struck by Hitler and Mussolini. Even then, up until the period that followed the collapse of the Fascist régime in September 1943, the Italian army and government showed the greatest restraint in executing the anti-Jewish decrees, even going sometimes so far as to actually to sabotage them (as happened in German-occupied territories of south-east France and the Balkans). Arguably, Judaeo–Italian symbiosis weathered the historical test of the anti-Semitic hysteria whipped up by Nazism better than anywhere else in Europe.

'Enlightened' absolutism, or historical antecedents of the modern 'Jewish policy' of Central European powers

During the entire period of political modernization that marked the advance from feudalism, most of the territories extending from the Rhine to the Russian frontier divided up between two state formations: the Habsburg Empire and the Prussian-dominated German Confederation (which transmuted into the German Empire in 1871). Reference has already been made to the divergent directions that were taken by these two areas. The Habsburg Empire was a multinational state confronted with a range of national separatist movements that ultimately led to the empire's dissolution into a collection of smaller nation-states. The German Confederation, by contrast, formed what in effect was a huge but culturally uniform nation state. It is therefore worth examining what circumstances would justify us in placing the two state formations within the same model as far as their political handling of Jewish affairs is concerned, this leading to the official proclamation of equality of rights in Austria in 1867, in the same historical situation as it was set down in the constitution of the unified German Empire (1871), *de facto* emancipation having already been accomplished earlier on in most of the empire's constituent states.

To start with, the 'Jewish Question' arose in these countries in two historical eras. Before the partition of Poland there were no major pockets of Jewish inhabitants in the states of Central Europe. Most German cities and states had been free of Jews (*judenrein*) up until the eighteenth century, following their expulsion around 1500. That also applies to the Habsburg Empire outside Hungary and the provinces of Bohemia and Moravia. Even thereafter, reinstatement of Jews into the cities over a protracted period (up until the nineteenth century) was permitted only under stringent selection criteria, usually amounting to a high wealth qualification and heavy tax liability, so that for a long time only tiny groups of rich Jewish merchants and bankers would be found in Vienna, Berlin, Munich, Frankfurt and Hamburg alike. There were naturally also some clandestine immigrants, but even so their total numbers prior to the nineteenth century were in the hundreds rather than thousands. The regeneration of the old communities was, in any event, more often than not made possible through initiatives taken by resident Jews who had contacts with the local reigning prince

(*Hofjuden*), as in such centers as Halle, Dresden, Leipzig, Cassel, and Brunswick. Even by the middle of the eighteenth century, however, there were no more than 2,100 'protected' Jewish families (or a total of some 10,000 persons) in the whole of Prussia, not counting Silesia. The largest Jewish communities in Germany—those in Breslau, Berlin and Frankfurt—did not exceed more than about 3,300 inhabitants each even as late as 1815. In German states such as Württemberg, Baden and Bavaria there may have been a scattering of extant village communities, but their total population was extremely small. The most substantial centers in the region, from this point of view, were Prague (with 7,000–9,000 Jewish inhabitants in the eighteenth century), Bohemia (a total of 29,000 in 1754), Moravia (5,100 families, or around 25,000 persons, in 1725) and Hungary (with an estimated 18,000–20,000 resident Jews on the basis of a partial census of 1735, and 83,000 by the time of the 1787 general census). The Jewish population of Prussia climbed steeply with the conquest of Silesia (1742), with its large number of Jewish inhabitants.

A dramatic change took place in both empires as a result of the second and third partitions of Poland, in 1793 and 1795, when Prussia annexed the region around Poznań, with close to 75,000 Jews, and then for a while (between 1796 and 1806) Warsaw and its environs, with its 12,000 Jewish inhabitants, whilst Austria secured Galicia where more than 212,000 Jews were living according to a rough estimate made in 1785. Since Austria had already also gobbled up Bukovina in 1775, the Habsburg Empire from then until the end of the nineteenth century was home for the largest group of Jews anywhere in the world outside of Russia. The Jewish population of Galicia alone during this period was considerably more than twice the combined number of Jews living in all the states of Western Europe. By the middle of the nineteenth century, Germany's Jewish populace was substantially smaller than was Austria's, but even so it was still more than tenfold the numbers then living in France, Britain or the Netherlands apiece. With the partition of Poland, at one stroke its 'eastern' Jews were pitched *en masse* into the clutches of the two Central European empires. It was this same geopolitical upheaval that set in train, up to the 1880s, the most powerful waves of Jewish migration that had been seen since the Middle Ages, both westwards (into the interior of Germany and later, after 1849, to Vienna) and southwards (into Hungary).

When the Central European empires took over part of the Jewish masses of former Poland and Lithuania, they already had at the ready a carefully worked-out notion of the policy that was to be implemented towards them. These states were governed through centralized administrative bodies in a spirit of enlightened absolutism, in which the personal power of the ruler was the decisive factor. At the same time, however, neither of the Central European empires—unlike the states of the West—was entirely uniform in political terms. The sovereigns of the individual German states (and later the individual *Länder* authorities) always retained a degree of autonomy *vis-à-vis* Prussian predominance. In Austria the hereditary provinces, headed by the kingdom of Hungary, continued to be governed, at least in part, under their own local legislatures. Throughout the entire modernization era, the imperial powers nevertheless managed to hang on to their privileges far better than in the West, even though here too the course of developments over the long term was progressing towards representative democracy, and in Austria this was accompanied by a gradual political decentralization. From 1867 onwards, first Hungary and Croatia, then the Cisleithan provinces won various degrees of internal autonomy, whereas the German states consolidated into a single unit.

This situation had a dual, and in part contradictory, impact on the fate of Jews. On the one hand, the political line taken with them was more or less determined by the central authority, indeed very highly dependent (especially during the eighteenth century) on the sovereign's personal attitude. That holds good for the entire modernization project for that matter, the main steps of which were usually initiated and enforced 'from above.' On the other hand, since Jews everywhere within the empire were faced with local or 'national' élites (in the various German states, Hungary, Bohemia and Galicia) that possessed a (during the nineteenth century growing) measure of discretion to act on their own account, scope opened for them to make special deals with those élites in order to secure their position. As a result they came to have an ever greater say in the molding of their own fate. There are many instances where, in order to assert themselves, they implemented singular collective strategies geared to local conditions, seeking to make common cause with whatever factions of the local élite were more favorable to them. This led, particularly in Hungary but, on occasion, in Bohemia and Galicia as well, to political cooperation between Jews and the local landowning nobility or urban patricians. That compact sometimes even ran to challenging the imperial power at certain junctures in historical development—as in Hungary prior to 1867, for instance—when the local national élite was in conflict with the central authority.

Before the two Central European empires dismembered the historical Polish state, the Jewish policy that they adopted was clearly guided by a threefold goal: first, a crude attempt to restrict their Jewish populations; second, to extract the maximum profit for the state from those who were admitted, or in other words, exploit them economically as much as possible; third, and just incidentally, to bring the functioning of Jewish communities under the regulation of absolutist authority.

Above all, the central powers imposed a strict quota system on settlement by Jews, and placed constraints on procreation amongst those already present that were unparalleled in other places. This was the blatant aim of Austrian legislation introduced in 1727 relating to family size (the *Familiantengesetz*), which in principle, if not practice, remained in force until 1846. This set a precisely stipulated upper limit on the number of Jews who would be tolerated in the Czech provinces (the only areas within the Habsburg Empire where sizeable communities were to be found in that period). To that end, in Jewish families only the eldest son would be granted a marriage license, or in other words, if younger sons wished to start a family, they would have to leave the country. For the same reason, the size of the ghettos allocated as compulsory places of residence for Jews in certain German cities (Frankfurt, for example) was fixed once and for all time, so that increasingly unbearable attendant overcrowding would set limits on population growth from the outset. Placing the granting of settlement permits on an individual basis made effective control of Jewish immigration possible, though it did not stop clandestine settlers, in addition to the officially 'tolerated' ones (*Tolerierte*), dwelling in many places. Under a 1714 Prussian legal restriction, a *Schutzbrief*, or warrant of protection (i.e. privilege), could only pass from a Jewish father to his 'protected' eldest son, whilst younger sons had to pay a tax that rose exponentially with their number (50, 100, 200, etc. thalers), if they wished to acquire the same 'privilege.' Another law of 1730 prescribed that the eldest scions of Jewish families were liable to pay the state a tax of 50 thalers, and the next-oldest twice that, and even that was only with the proviso that the number of 'protected' Jews (*Schutzjuden*) did not increase in any unit of local government at all. In Prague, the authorities in the early years of the eighteenth century ran an office called the *Judenreduktionskomission* which, as the name suggests, had the task of keeping an eye on restricting the Jewish population. Even an 'enlightened' monarch like Maria Theresa had no great compunction about holding the Jews who resided within her domains in constant fear of expulsion. In 1741 she raised the prospect of having them driven out of Moravia (though this did not occur in the end) and in 1745 out of Bohemia (which was actually implemented in part). The greater part of Prague's huge Jewish community was compelled to leave the city in 1744, although that decree was rescinded a few years later, in 1748.

In order to understand the efforts that these absolutist empires made to reduce the numbers of Jews, one has to remind oneself that in the eighteenth century religious wars and the ideological importance of the state religion were still very much live issues in the world picture of monarchs and the ruling class. The need for unity of faith and serving the state religion often overrode the state's other interests— the economy, for example. Maria Theresa had a morbidly ingrained hatred of Jews, and overt manifestations of religious anti-Semitism were apparent in imperial policy up till the nineteenth century. The one exception to this was Joseph II (1770–80) who pursued a Jewish policy that, whilst it could hardly be said to have been inspired by philo-Semitism, was diametrically opposed to his mother's, though he represents a unique case in other respects as well. High imperial officials themselves were equally disinclined to see things from a secular perspective, and that also applies to the local leadership strata. This was much in contrast to most western countries, where amongst the social élite the ideology of the Enlightenment disparaged giving automatic respect for religious doctrine, promoted sectarian scepticism and, in some groups, even deism and theism, especially in those countries (such as France) where the project of political modernization itself entailed a radical trimming of the Church's power.

In a more profound analysis it would be worth taking a closer look at the main counter-examples in this regard. Hungary is one of the few countries in Europe, besides Holland and Switzerland, that preserved its religious diversity after both the Reformation and the Counter-Reformation. Equally, the Catholicism that was imposed by external force as the state religion in the provinces of Bohemia and Moravia after the battle of the White Mountain (1620) was unable to prevent either the survival of a leadership stratum of protonationalist Protestant intellectuals or the early emergence of its secularization. These exceptions had a hand in the fact that during the nineteenth and twentieth centuries some local élite groups, such as the German middle class of Prague or Hungary's liberal gentry, and representatives of the Jewish élite were able to find a meeting of minds on a program of religious tolerance and secularization. The rule in Central Europe nevertheless continued to be one of political dominance, if not outright monopoly, by the state religion—in Germany right up to the end of the nineteenth century and, in certain respects, even beyond, whilst in Austria even after the break-up of the empire. The thoroughgoing exclusion of those who belonged to 'non-established' faiths from the holding of political or public offices (even after the passage of equal rights legislation) was likewise a general phenomenon throughout Central Europe. In many places, even within the Habsburg Empire, it also applied to the matrimonial market, with prohibitions on mixed Judaeo–Christian marriages remaining in force until the first decade of the twentieth century (but only until 1895 in Hungary). This too was one of the factors that were continually inducing, and in some cases indeed compelling, members of the Jewish élite to convert to Christianity.

Yet in shaping their Jewish policies the Central European empires also kept a very sharp eye on material gains that might be accrued. In contrast to some western countries, overtaxation was widespread and remained so essentially up until the granting of equal rights began to bulk large. In the spirit of their mercantilist ideology, states regularly encouraged settlement by wealthy Jews, sometimes even in the teeth of a sovereign's undisguised anti-Semitism. According to their economic interests at any given time, the states might also arbitrarily interfere in the occupational activities of their Jewish subjects. The better off would be granted rights to settle and, later on, even special privileges, including full rights of citizenship in some cases. In Prussia, the first award of a *Naturalizationspatent* to a Jew was made in 1791 to the family of Daniel Itzig, a renowned court agent. By the nineteenth century, they were even bestowing titles of nobility on certain individuals of the Judaic faith, especially in the Habsburg Empire. There were cases where emancipation could simply be purchased by those who wished. In 1811, Frankfurt's city council was prepared to vote in equal rights for its Jewish fellow townsmen and to have the ghetto walls demolished, in return for a lump sum of 440,000 Rhenish gulden. All-powerful officials and rulers would often extort money from Jewish subjects with small-minded and humiliating pettifoggery. In 1769, Prussian Jews were compelled by their king to buy up and retail abroad an annually specified quantity of the shoddy output from the royal porcelain factory that would otherwise have been virtually unsaleable. A Prussian law of 1730 prohibited Jews from engaging in any trade that might bring them into competition with established guilds, though it did permit trading in luxury goods, moneylending, and second-hand clothing. Maria Theresa levied a 'tolerance fee' on the Jewish families of Austria–Hungary since 1743, modifying this to a personal tax liability in 1746, when it was realized that extending it to family descendants would multiply future intakes many times over. Abolition of that particular tax did not take place until 1846. At the same time, the authorities in Austria were pressing Jews with capital to found manufacturing businesses (a decree of 1749)—a goal that was also actively pushed in Prussia, for example, in the wake of the Seven Years War (1756–63).

'Enlightened' absolutism's policy of exploiting the Jews to the maximum was rounded off by the controls on their communal institutions. The *Judenordnung* issued by Maria Theresa still left intact the communities' legal autonomy in religious affairs (that was later to be rescinded by Joseph II in 1784). Against that, however, it regulated both the public and private lives of Austria's Jews, often down to the minutest detail. It prescribes exactly the duties of the *Landesrabbiner* (the official responsible for allocating any taxes levied on the community) and the manner by which he was to be chosen. The *Revidiertes Generalprivilegium* issued by the Prussian King Frederick II in 1750 contained similar provisions, though admittedly these were concentrated primarily on occupational interdicts.

Seeds of absolutist emancipation and Jewry in the Habsburg Empire

The policies of Central Europe's rival powers took a turn for the better towards the end of the eighteenth century, principally as a result of the spread of Enlightenment ideas in élite circles (even reaching as far as the court). The French Revolution indeed had a direct hand in propagating and, through its armed forces, implanting its achievements, including the emancipation of the Jews, in the countries that were conquered. In some German cities such as Berlin, for example, a conspicuous rapprochement in the spirit of Enlightenment ideas got under way between members of the local ruling class and Jewish burghers. The new state policy was directed not just at the arm's length treatment hitherto accorded to Jewish subjects (they should just 'sit tight') but also brought the first real measures to integrate them that had been witnessed in this part of Europe. The development was not entirely novel, of course, nor did those who mapped out the changes necessarily nurture any particular sympathy towards Jews, but it did fit into reform plans that were much broader in scope. Emperor Joseph II, coming forward with his truly revolutionary program for Austria, and proponents of modernization of the Prussian state, such as Wilhelm von Humboldt, Karl von Hardenberg or Karl von Stein, set their sights primarily on mopping up the legacy of feudalism, and specifically on improving the situation of tenured peasants, and even the very institution of serfdom, weakening the offshoots of feudalism, promoting free trade, augmenting entrepreneurial freedom, and creating social unity through linguistic and cultural assimilation of non-indigenous or ethnic minority groups (or at least their élites) by expanding compulsory education. Insofar as the Jews were concerned, this project may have run all the way to emancipation (although in most cases this was seen merely as provisional) in Prussia and in the German states that were directly confronted by the revolutionary challenges and then the political and military threat of Napoleonic France. In Austria the reforms were stopped dead in their tracks when only halfway implemented by the reaction that was mounted in response to the revolutionary threat.

Yet it had all begun in Vienna itself, as a radical reform process instituted from 'the top.' Joseph II's *Toleranzpatent* (1781) and innumerable subsequent decrees, including the *Systemica Gentis Judaica*

Regulatio (1783) for Hungary, are the first great emancipatory acts of modern times in Europe that affected the Jews. These predate the Federal Constitution of the USA and the French Revolution, even if they do not go as far down the path of emancipation as the latter. The measures were, of course, grounded in the modernizing endeavors of the enlightened reformist emperor and were aimed at culturally and politically unifying an empire that was chopped up into provinces highly divergent in regard to their constitutional history and socio–political structures. Joseph II may have picked up some of his ideas from the German philosopher–diplomat Christian Wilhelm von Dohm's famous reformist pamphlet of 1781 *Über die bürgerliche Verbesserung des Juden*—'On the Civil Improvement of the Jews'—which was widely read across Europe, though it may be that the influence was the other way round, with Dohm's pen being inspired by the emperor's projects. In any event, from then onwards Joseph II's decrees were regularly cited whenever calls were made for the emancipation of the Jews, as may be observed with the ideologues who heralded and prepared the way for it, then finally implemented it for the first time in Europe during the French Revolution.

Joseph II did not break completely with the policies of his predecessors, however. He did not abrogate either Charles VI's restrictive law on Jewish families or the personal 'poll tax' (*Leibzoll*) on Jews entering Vienna, levied by Maria Theresa, merely altering the name of the latter to the 'cameral tax' to mitigate its indignity. Joseph's many integrationist measures nonetheless seem little short of revolutionary because they were usually aimed at filling the gulf that separated the Jews from the rest of a feudalistic society. To begin with, he guaranteed freedom of movement and settlement in all territories where Jews were legally resident (except for mining towns which had a special legal status), along with a virtually free choice of occupation, which meant that Jews were permitted to make their livelihood almost any way they wished, even in agriculture (with the sole proviso that they themselves cultivated any land that they leased). He made it possible for Jews to enter Christian schools right up to university level (though in practice this applied solely to medical faculties, since the only professional occupation then open to Jews was medical practice). But Joseph's intention, first and foremost, was social integration of the Jews, to do away with all the degrading external marks of Jewish existence. He made military service compulsory for Jews on exactly the same grounds as everybody else, and insofar as they might attain officer's rank, authorized the wearing of swords, which was otherwise the prerogative of a nobleman. On the other hand, he also ordained that Jews should establish and maintain at their own expense German public schools, whilst making Hebrew the compulsory language for public worship, instead of what he styled the Yiddish 'jargon.' The compulsory adoption of German family names was laid down by a special decree (1787). In his eagerness to 'normalize' the Jews, Joseph went as far as prohibiting the wearing of beards, although this 'reform measure' provoked such a great storm of protest from Orthodox Jewry that he was quickly obliged to rescind it.

With the death of Joseph II the ensuing hiatus in the process of emancipation for the 'Habsburg Jews' was such that cities that had been opened up to them at once tried to close them again, in some instances successfully. Reforms directed at assimilation were still persevered with, however, and of all areas, in none did the 'Josephinian' spirit live on more vigorously, perhaps, than in the empire's Jewish policies during the reign of Franz I. Herz Homberg, his 'enlightened' Jewish inspector of schools, introduced a separate catechism for use in religious education in Jewish schools. In 1820, philosophical studies were prescribed for the training of intending rabbis, and use of the 'state language' was decreed in all public worship. From then onwards, if we discount the reprisals that came in the immediate wake of the bloody suppression of the 1848–49 revolutions, the Habsburg central power pursued a policy towards the Jews that, more energetic as it may have been at times and weaker at others, was nevertheless consistently protectionist and integrationist, often in the face of municipal authorities that saw them as economic rivals and were correspondingly hostile to such a line. During the Reform Era a string of emancipatory measures came into effect, one after the other, either locally or across the entire empire. In Bohemia, the prohibition on Jews owning land was rescinded in 1841, and the law restricting the size of families in 1846. In the same year the personal tax and the *more judaico* oath were abolished throughout the empire. The 'March Constitution' of 1849 guaranteed Jews the same rights as other citizens; however, most of the provisions of this liberal act were suspended in 1851, during the neo-absolutist reaction that followed the

1848–49 revolutions, meanwhile many Jewish young intellectuals were being brought before the courts for participating in the armed uprisings in Vienna and Prague. Nevertheless, the imperial capital, whose gates had been closed to Jews—except in individually permitted cases—since 1670, opened up to new Jewish settlers from 1849, moreover they were also permitted to establish an official community. The principal remaining prohibitions and hindrances still imposed on them were finally lifted between 1858 and 1860. Thereafter the entire Habsburg Empire advanced rapidly towards full legal emancipation, which became general with the Austro–Hungarian Compromise of 1867, even if sanctioned by separate legislation for Cisleithan Austria and Hungary, the latter having attained autonomy in internal affairs under the Compromise.

The central government from then on pursued policies that were increasingly favorable to Jews, especially during the periods of anti-Jewish unrest that occurred towards the end of the century with the emergence of overtly anti-Semitic political parties. From this standpoint, the participation of substantial local segments of Jewry in the revolutionary and independence movements of 1848–49 (notably in Hungary's war of liberation) proved a historical episode with a quite short-lived impact. The authorities looked on the Jews rather as pillars of the dual monarchy's establishment. The paternalist reign of Franz Joseph after the Compromise lived on in Jewry's collective memory as a golden age of peace and prosperity before the spread of the anti-Semitic and inhuman totalitarian régimes of the twentieth century. The Jews' late but tenacious clinging-on to the symbolic double-headed eagle of the Habsburg Monarchy was tantamount to a veritable imperial patriotism. Whilst the empire's nations, from the latter half of the nineteenth century on, were increasingly demanding the various historical regions as exclusively their own, and their search for political direction generally came to comply with the logic of centrifugally oriented, separatist nationalism, the majority of Jews remained true to the empire, the multinational state that guaranteed their safety. As a witticism that made the rounds had it, in the melee of factious minorities, each proclaiming its national and regional identity first and foremost, they were proving the only loyalist 'real Austrians.' Tempted as many may have been by the idea of a nationalism of 'their own' (in the form of Zionism or '*folkism*'), and even more by that of an 'adoptive nationalism' (particularly in Hungary, Croatia and, to a lesser degree, Polish Galicia), the political framework of the empire represented what appeared to be an increasingly indispensable pledge of security in the face of the extremist, exclusionist nationalist demagogy that prefigured the rise of Fascism (in Slovakia and Galicia, for instance, during the early years of the twentieth century) and anti-Semitic mass movements (in Vienna, but also in Budapest, Prague and, repeatedly in Galicia). That is also why, in the period between the two world wars, the Jewish middle classes in the Monarchy's successor states would long for the return of the state formation that had disintegrated in 1918 and swell the by then ever-diminishing camp of imperial and royal legitimists.

Aufklärung, *Haskalah* and 'conditional emancipation' in the German world

In both Germany and Austria, the emancipatory process was part of a series of reforms launched in the spirit of enlightened absolutism. The policy of the German states, however, even more than that of Austria, showed the influence of the Enlightenment's philosophical ideas, developed after the 1760s within German speaking élites, including circles of high state officials. This converged with the idea of 'internal renewal' advocated by Jewish thinkers, themselves under the impact of Enlightenment, who produced a version of their own of Jewish modernization. The outcome was the *Haskalah*, intended to facilitate processes of embourgeoisement, cultural assimilation within Jewry as well as speeding up its integration into sections of the Christian élite.

As noted above, it was Christian Wilhelm Dohm, a royal archivist in Berlin, who first elaborated what became a classic enlightened concept for 'solving the Jewish Question' in a book he wrote at the request of the Jewish philosopher Moses Mendelssohn. Dohm provided a survey of Jewish history, showing how Jews had been subject to oppression at all times, and that persecution brought on 'discord of a moral nature' in its victims, whence the cult of avarice and usury imputed to them. These 'flaws' were only further aggravated by the religious ordinances and Talmudist reasoning that set Jewry apart from their fellow countrymen. Having established the link between oppression and ascribed negative characteristics of Jews, Dohm found nothing to disapprove of either in their religion or in their collective traits. Jews, in his opinion, were clever, highly principled, indefatigable, steadfast, and capable of surmounting their difficulties. He therefore came out in favor of relaxing the restrictions imposed on them, urged an expansion of public education to remedy their apparent shortcomings, and pushed for their assimilation and integration into the majority culture. If the enlightened government were to bestow equality of rights on the Jews, the state would be enriched and the socially useful population augmented. This would also accord with the principle of equity and justice. In any case, it would be more beneficial to support the Jews and promote their integration than to invite other immigrants to replace them, for the Jews had already put down roots in the country and were not longing for another homeland.

Dohm here articulates the *Aufklärung*'s basic principles relating to the Jews, and these were to circulate in Christian and Jewish élite circles alike in all the German cities, Berlin above all. The 'majority' concerned, albeit not entirely without regard to the critical situation in which the German states found themselves after the Napoleonic invasion, was subsequently to pass a number of local laws of emancipation on the basis of these very doctrines. Representatives of the 'minority,' the culturally better integrated circles of Jewish intellectuals and burghers, for their part, founded the key movement for Jewish modernization, the *Haskalah*, around the emblematic figure of Moses Mendelssohn, the Berlin-based German–Jewish philosopher, friend of Lessing and influential beyond Jewish circles. The contact between German legislators and the most progressive minded Jewish reformers thereby assumed extraordinary significance. For both parties, it was a matter primarily of a rapprochement between the worlds of Jews and non-Jews: a diminution of the distance between these groups needed to take place under the aegis of a common secular 'national culture,' through linguistic and cultural integration, in a spirit of whole-hearted acceptance of the political principles of the nation-state, by abolishing the constraints that hamstrung Jewish economic prosperity, by reform of the ceremonial of Judaism to make the service more similar to the Christian ritual and hence respectable to outsiders, and finally through a 'moral renewal' or 'regeneration' of the Jews, which was to be accomplished with the help of modern education and as a direct result of emancipation.

That demand for 'moral renewal' as a condition of emancipation was, perhaps, the most cardinal of all the reforms. Not only did it, so to say, epitomize ideologically all the cultural misunderstandings, the source of which was to be sought in a fundamental imbalance in the nexus between Jews and non-Jews, whether it be a matter of relations between moneylenders and borrowers, sellers and buyers, the incomprehension of Christians on coming up against what, for them, was an esoteric religious cult, or the mutual mistrust and suspicion that cast a shadow on intercourse between the dominant and the subordinate group. Beyond all that, 'moral regeneration' was to become the central issue for the disputes that, over time, grew steadily more acrimonious between the adherents of *Haskalah* (*maskilim*, as they were known in Hebrew) and their opponents (*mitnagdim*), 'integrators' and traditionalists, western and eastern Jews, reformers and the Orthodox.

The *Haskalah* was also an important historical milestone because the processes of acculturation and assimilation that it set in motion provided the main justification for legal emancipation in the eyes of the authorities, just as it substantiated arguments for the demand for emancipation on the part of the Jews. It is no accident that the *Haskalah* should take root and burgeon in Berlin at the end of the eighteenth century. One of the largest of the Jewish communities in the German states at that period was the one in Berlin. The intellectual sway that it exerted across the whole region of Central Europe was considerable, with many of its members— Mendelssohn as a thinker, for example, or the Itzigs as financier—having access to the leading intellectual and political circles of the Prussian state. Highly educated ladies of the Mendelssohn household and the families of court agents—the likes of Henriette Herz, Rachel Varnhagen and Dorothea Schlegel— inaugurated their salons as meeting-places for Berlin's Jewish and Christian cultural élite around the turn of the eighteenth into the nineteenth century. The salons were also frequented by high-ranking officials (including cabinet ministers or even, occasionally, the king), which explains why some of them espoused the cause of emancipation at the first available opportunity.

That moment came in fact when the combined German forces suffered a crushing defeat from Napoleon at Jena (1806), which brought the urgency of fundamental political reforms to the top of the agenda in the German states. In the course of these, Prussia abolished serfdom and the privileges of the nobility, bestowed the rights to citizenship and to hold political office on commoners (1808), and finally, in an imperial decree of 12 March 1812, recognized the equality of Jews before the law and at the same time rescinded all restrictions relating to their occupation in force until then. Some states, especially those that Napoleon clustered into the Rhenish Confederation—for instance, Baden (1808), Frankfurt and a number of Hanseatic cities (1811)— effected emancipation even before Prussia.

These edicts, far from marking the end of the emancipatory process, were more just an initial, albeit crucial act in Germany. Whilst many of the German Jews of Prussia and other states threw themselves enthusiastically into the fight against the French conquerors during the national uprising of 1813, and the 1815 Congress of Vienna which brought the whole Napoleonic era to a close, and endorsed the measures taken on behalf of the Jews, the governments of almost all German states before long reneged on the matter of full emancipation. Over the ensuing half-century, the provisional nature of the hitherto achieved measures of Jewish emancipation came strongly to the fore. The reaction mustered against Napoleon professed a general political conservatism, and supplied a framework for the Romantic conception of German unity, the sources of which were furnished by linguistic and cultural Germanism (mediated by the folklore discovered by the brothers Grimm), Christianity and the Teutonic past (as in the Wagnerian legendry). In a nation-state of this ilk, Jews were acceptable only if they broke all ties to their ethnic and religious identity. By the time of the anti-Semitic disturbances known as the 'Hep! Hep!' movement (1819), mobs in German towns were resorting to violence in order to express their opposition to the economic advancement and the social integration of Jews. Legislators meticulously adjusted their 'Jewish policies' to the level of assimilation prescribed for and attained by the Jews. In Posen (Poznań), in East Prussia, a law of 1833 directly linked the granting of civic rights to 'satisfying obligations' in regard to moral, economic and cultural (i.e. Germanizing) criteria. Coming up to 1846, fully one-third of Prussia's Jews (and more than 80 per cent of the Jews of Posen) had not yet acquired any civic rights.

A decisive fresh boost was given though to the emancipatory process by the revolutions of 1848. The parliamentarians elected to the German National Assembly in Frankfurt included some Jews as well. Its proclamation of the basic rights— *Grundrechte*—of the German people no longer made any distinction between citizens on grounds of their religious affiliation. The ensuing reaction, however, here as in Austria, delayed a definitive act of emancipation. The North German Confederation in 1869 finally repealed all legal restrictions applied to Jews. That example was followed by the southern states after the Franco–Prussian war of 1870. These arrangements were then incorporated into the new imperial constitution in 1871.

A significant role in this 'contingent' or conditional emancipatory process was played by strategies that Jews had employed in constructing their own identity, under the decisive influence of the ideology of the *Haskalah* and, above all, its endorsement of demands for German schooling and cultural Germanization in general. At the same time, however, there were differences in the definition of expected relations to religion.

The growing cult of German cultural values within Central European Jewry, including a veritable veneration and cultivation of German language, literature, sciences, music and other 'cultural goods,' was undoubtedly due largely to the voluntarist and 'compensatory' efforts of Jews, these 'new-fangled Germans.' It was also, however, part and parcel of the liberating experience undergone by many Jews who stepped onto the path of assimilation: release from a circumscribed and what was felt to be oppressive cultural particularism and participation in the German people's *Kultur*, with a capital K, which really did gain ground internationally over the course of the nineteenth century—and tangibly so, especially after Prussia's victories in the wars against Austria and France. The leading place of German universities was increasingly recognized in the European market of higher education. German scholars, men of letters and professors were becoming ever more renowned. German industry was booming spectacularly; and the armies of the German states were growing stronger. Little wonder if the rate of return on 'investments' in German culture for the Jewish communities in German lands appeared as growing apace. On Mendelssohn's urging, a *Jüdische Freischule* operating on then modern educational principles was set up as early as 1778. Several other similar institutions followed suite, such as a modern Jewish school in Frankfurt known as the *Philanthropin* (1804). In 1819, on the initiative of a number of distinguished German–Jewish men of letters, historians and philologists, Leopold Zunz, Isaac Marcus Jost, Eduard Gans and Heinrich Heine amongst them, set up the *Verein für Kultur und Wissenschaft der Juden* as a scholarly society to promote Jewish improvement untrammeled by denominational considerations and to provide an institutional setting for the emerging discipline of modern Jewish studies, the *Wissenschaft des Judentums*. A marked growth in the presence of students who were either Jewish or of Jewish descent was already evident in German secondary schools and universities during the *Vormärz*, the run-up to the revolutions of 1848.

The 'Germanization' of German Jews in the spirit of the *Haskalah* could only be accounted a success, but the transformed relation to the practice of religion led inexorably to schisms and dramatic conflicts within German Jewry, which accompanied the entire historical course of emancipation and modernization. During the nineteenth century no major efforts at secularization were made on a political level in the German states. As a result, members of the Jewish community (notably the Jewish élite) seeking social integration were continually exposed to pressures and temptations to convert to Christianity. Many of the economically most successful and culturally most 'assimilated' amongst them did just that. In Prussia between 1812 and 1846 nearly 3,200 Jews were baptised, including Moses Mendelssohn's sons and daughters. Official moves, such as a decree of 1818 to exclude Jews from Prussian universities, or shortly afterwards, in 1819, to debar Jews from holding civil service posts in Westphalia, set off waves of conversions. This is precisely the period when the poet Heine and Karl Marx's father were baptized.

Most Jews, however, found a compromise solution to the challenge in the religious reforms, which Moses Mendelssohn himself had already championed. Individual communities strove to head off, or curb, the inducement to adopt Christianity or indulge in religious passivity by carrying out more or less radical liturgical reforms. Over the long term, these reform movements were to divide German Jewry amongst competing congregations. In 1845, one reform congregation in Berlin went so far as to move the Sabbath to Sunday. Although the majority of Jews did not support such extremes, 'liberal' or 'conservative' reforms of worship, for all the debates that accompanied them, proved highly successful. The interiors of synagogues were remodeled in reform communities, the use of organs, liturgical hymns and choirs was introduced, sermons started to be delivered in German, women gained admittance to the interior of houses of prayer (even if still separated from men), and so on. The Prussian *Austrittsgesetz* (1876) allowed a person to leave a local congregation without having to re-nounce his religious affiliation, and this facilitated the establishment of new types of communities. There was, obviously, a strong rabbini-cal reaction to these innovations. It came to be organized under the aegis of traditionalist Orthodoxy, gathering round the neo-Orthodox movement of Samson Raphael Hirsch and Azriel Hildesheimer. In a growing number of German towns there emerged parallel Jewish communities of divergent theological orientations, a pattern soon ap-pearing in other Central European countries as well (like Cisleithan Austria or Hungary).

Haskalah and modalities of national assimilation in the Austrian Monarchy

Indeed, the influence of developments in Germany made itself felt strongly within the Austrian Empire as well.

Whole sections of Vienna's Jews—especially those residing in the First (Inner City) and Ninth (Alsergrund) Districts—and large contin-gents of Jews in Prague and elsewhere in Bohemia and Moravia be-came adherents of moderate reforms, meanwhile individual islands of Orthodox reaction consolidated from place to place (e.g. in Vienna's Second District—Leopoldstadt).

In Hungary, József Eötvös, the Minister of Education and Relig-ious Affairs in the first government after the 1867 Compromise, con-voked a Jewish Congress of representatives of local Jewry in order to set up a national organization for their communities. The attempt mis-carried, culminating as it did in sectarian schism. Hungarian Jewry was split into three major networks: the moderately reformist Ne-ologues ('conservative' or 'Congress' Jewry), strictly traditionalist Orthodoxy (among which Hasidic communities distinguished them-selves by their specifics), and somewhat more moderately traditionalists, so-called *Status Quo Ante* congregations. The state was willing to negotiate with all three factions but recognized Judaism only as a single religion.

Many centers of the *Haskalah* were also formed in Galicia, in cities such as Brody, Lemberg, Tarnopol, and elsewhere, but the bulk of the Jewish masses continued to be divided between the various courses of Hasidic and rabbinical traditionalism within Orthodoxy, highly discrepant as they may have been in their own right. Much the same could also be said of Hungary, where the membership of Orthodox communities constituted a formal majority within the country's overall Jewish population, at least on paper, up till 1919. The famous *yeshiva* at Pozsony (Bratislava) became the stronghold of rabbinical Orthodoxy (and the chief seminary for the Orthodox rabbinate), whereas communities in the east and north-east of Hungary were more likely to be drawn to Hasidism. This division was reflected by official policy towards the Jews in two ways. There were numerous occasions when adherents of the *Haskalah* turned to the authorities for support against their rivals, both in Galicia and in Hungary. This happened to the Orthodox as well, who found even a receptive partner in Emperor Franz-Joseph, a conservative Catholic himself. But a privileged link of reform Jewry with local officialdom hinged on their declared programmatic willingness to assimilate. They actually went to considerable lengths to meet the authorities' demands in regard to the expected degree of cultural assimilation and 'modernization,' whilst the Orthodoxy continued largely to preserve its linguistic traditions (Yiddish) and many markers of its cultural identity (distinctive dress, social and educational self-segregation, etc.).

The drift to cultural assimilation within the Habsburg Empire, however, was in itself a problematic proposition in many places, given that the state was made up of provinces inhabited by nationalities often at odds with or even hostile to one another. It is nevertheless possible to make a few generalizations in this regard.

To start with, cultural integration of the Jews was always directed towards the ruling political and cultural élite. Second, insofar as the leadership strata of the various local ethnic groups were at loggerheads with one another, the Jews usually preferred to align themselves to the national élite that was the 'more modern,' that is to say, more open to the West. Whatever the circumstances, the fervor with which cultural integration was pursued was crucially determined by social class positions. The prevailing Jewish élite (Orthodox religious notables excepted) was usually more inclined to assimilation, amongst other reasons because this went hand in hand with the access to vitally important advantages of public élite education. Third and last, the process of cultural integration or acculturation could never be considered as unequivocal and final, indeed (as will be discussed in a later chapter dedicated to assimilation proper) not even invariably unilateral. The 'assimilated' often preserve over several generations what, in many cases, are significant elements of their original culture, such as speech habits, dietary customs, body language, and other aspects of the physical and intellectual cast of their forebears. A kind of tangible objectification of this is provided by the multilinguism widespread amongst Habsburg Jews until the twentieth century. In this domain, however, cultural decisions could be reviewed in the light of circumstances, should local power relations alter or a move be made to another area. The change in sovereignty that occurred in Transylvania and Slovakia after 1919 partly (though in these territories only marginally) modified the nationality options adopted by Jewish assimilees. Equally, the degree of cultural modernization (and, above all, the educational ascendancy discussed in the last chapter) achieved by Jewry in many places was such as to put them in the position of playing the role of mediators of that culture, and thereby assisting the intellectual mobility of rising but 'culturally backward' elements in local majority populations.

For all the above reasons, assimilatory movements in the Habsburg Empire were not linear, except in Vienna and Lower Austria, where there was no alternative to a German-oriented acculturation. Yet even there the main choice concerned Great German (*grossdeutsch*) culture, rather than that of the Austrian provinces proper. Elsewhere there was a dilemma between Germanizing or commitment to the local national culture. The attraction of Germanization was all the greater, that it accorded with the expectations of the central authorities ever since Joseph II had decreed that German was to become the official language throughout the Monarchy. In Galicia, Hungary and Bohemia, from the late eighteenth century onwards, Jewish communities therefore first built up a network of German schools. That Germanization went ahead without particular opposition in Bohemia. The Jews there, from the outset, had spoken a Yiddish–German that closely resembled the dialect of other Germans in the provinces of Bohemia and Moravia, on top of which they found in the German bourgeoisie of some cities, Prague included, a political ally against the radical nationalism of the 'Young Czechs' who were gaining in strength during the nineteenth century. (In its early phase, extending even beyond the nineteenth century, Czech nationalism was indeed just as anti-German as it was anti-Jewish.)

'Modern' schooling of the Jews in Galicia, too, started in German. That sprang from the fact that in the centers of the Galician *Haskalah* a network of Jewish public schools arose following Joseph II's measures. In 1797, they numbered no less than 104. The drive to Germanization pushed by the elementary schoolmasters and by the Jewish school inspector, an outright *maskil* (reformer) Nafthali Homberg, soon abated, however. Twenty years later, not even the slightest trace remained of the grandiose initiative, with some community leaders going back to the traditional form of Jewish education, as dispensed within the walls of a *cheder* (elementary) and then *yeshiva* (high school). Later on, however, there came another round of setting up German schools. A segment of the Jewish élite was not to be shaken off the path of German cultural assimilation, and even during the 1860s and '70s showed a preference for sending its sons to German-language universities (to Vienna first and foremost, but also to Prague and cities in the German Empire). In parallel with this, particularly at the end of the nineteenth century, the Jewish élite in the provincial centers of Cracow and Lemberg (Lvov/Lviv) often had recourse to Polish schools, particularly when—after 1870—these two cities were the only ones to have a Polish language university. In Galicia, as elsewhere, endorsement of the local political, or indeed cultural nationalism did not rule out reverence for the cult of German and, in some cases, French high culture. That too could serve as a basis of symbolic fellowship with the Polish national élite, themselves often German-oriented in their culture as well as traditionally Francophile. As a result, a sort of genuine Judeo–Polish understanding and cooperation developed within the cultivated bourgeoisie and the new middle classes (which did not hold for the masses), with the Polish side regarding this rapprochement as equally in their own interest—almost up to the end of the nineteenth century. At that juncture, however, the political mainstream of the Polish nationalist movement reformulated its objectives and re-assessed its alliances before finally plumping for an exclusive and exclusionist (i.e. anti-Semitic) conception of their nation.

Hungary and the Balkans: more or less successful examples of national integration

In the dual Monarchy, like elsewhere in Eastern Europe, from the Black Sea to the Baltic, Jewish modernization unfolded within a balance of forces characterized, on the one hand, by what, for many, was the irresistible pull of German high culture and, on the other, both the need and the opportunity to cling to the local culture of host countries, increasingly defining themselves as 'national.'

In this connection, Hungary appeared to be in a unique position amongst the hereditary provinces of the Monarchy. So singular was the character that development assumed here that Hungary could be categorized as standing midway between the western and the eastern models of integration.

It has already been mentioned that contemporary Jewish presence in Hungary was determined initially, from the early eighteenth century, by a substantial wave of immigration from Bohemia and Moravia, then increasingly from Galicia later on, from the partition of Poland right up to the 1850s. This immigrant population seems to have been selected from the most dynamic elements of Habsburg Jewry, which made it easier for them to adjust to local conditions and prosper economically. Cultural assimilation here too began within a frame of German orientation. In the late eighteenth century, Jews began establishing a network of German-language schools, which was all the easier to do since a substantial segment amongst them had settled in the less backward and relatively more urbanized western and north-western areas of the country. Those with 'western Yiddish,' closely akin to German, as their mother tongue, could easily fit into German-speaking milieu. (This was a large cluster of the population in the kingdom which had received, during the eighteenth century, masses of settlers from German lands, additionally to 'Saxons' and other German speaking groups established since the thirteenth century.) These 'western Jews' were later to constitute the core of the Hungarian-Jewish Neologue (conservative reformist) community. From the outset, the settlers cultivated and maintained good relations, based on mutual interests, with the landowning nobility, just as they had in Galicia or back in the times of the Polish–Lithuanian Commonwealth. This concordance of interests later evolved during the Reform era into a veritable (not only symbolic, but also economic and political) alliance of sorts, which can be qualified as an 'assimilationist social contract' between the most liberal segments of the nobility and the swiftly assimilating Jewish middle-class stratum.

The socio–historical foundations of that concord, equally beneficial as it was for the emancipation of Jewry and the modernization of the country, are readily definable. It should be noted here that the balance of denominational powers in Hungary was much more finely poised than in other European nation-states, with even Roman Catholicism, in spite of its status as a quasi state religion, embracing only a minority of the population (some 48 per cent during the nineteenth century), thereby facilitating the implantation of religious tolerance. One must also bear in mind the historic weakness of traditions of institutionalized hostility to Jews (e.g. the Inquisition) as well as the multiethnic complexion of the population, which obliged the ethnic–Hungarian noble ruling class, representing a minority population (some 40–45 per cent only of the total at the beginning of the nineteenth century), to seek ethnic allies for the realization of its program of nation-building and modernization. Jews proved to be reliable allies. In return, the liberal nobility (the future ruling class), extended protection against manifestations of violent anti-Semitism and offered a plan for a tolerant, secularized, modern political constitutionality which, besides free exercise of religion, guaranteed Jews almost full freedom of occupational and economic mobility.

On the strength of this unwritten 'social contract,' Hungary's Jewry committed itself *en masse* to Hungarian assimilation. This included the provision of money and blood by many for the success of the 1848–49 revolution and war of independence: they also shared thus, along with other supporters of the national struggle, the heavy price to be paid during the absolutist reprisals that Austria inflicted on the defeated country. Following the 1867 Compromise, Jews also supported the initially liberal, later ever less liberal objectives of Hungarian nationalism, among them the chauvinistic program of forcible Magyarization of ethnic minorities (who, in their totality, represented up to 1900 the bulk of the population). By 1910, a mere 24 per cent of Hungary's Jews (mostly the Yiddish-speaking communities living in the easternmost counties) professed themselves to be non-native Hungarian speakers. The Jewish primary school system, a network of some 500 institutions of public status at the beginning of the twentieth century, was completely Magyarized. By then Hungarian was the language of sermons in 87 per cent of Neologue synagogues, but even in 13 per cent of Orthodox temples. The 'nationalization' of Hungarian Jewry in the core country, especially in cities, was as complete as anywhere in Western Europe.

The Hungarian nobility, hegemonic as it remained in the political arena, for their part, continued to respect their commitments to Jews throughout the long nineteenth century. As early as 1840 a law of semi-emancipation was promulgated, which finally granted Jews freedom of movement, settlement in towns, free enterprise and large (if at that time not complete) liberties as to the choice of occupation. One of the very last acts of the revolutionary parliament in 1849 (the 28th of July) was an official proclamation of full emancipation in recognition of the services that Jewry had rendered during the fight for national independence. Admittedly, the law—the first of its kind in Central and Eastern Europe (discounting the short-lived Habsburg imperial constitution promulgated in the spring of that same year)—was annulled by the absolutist reaction. But the first parliament to assemble after the Compromise passed full emancipation into law, without a single dissenting vote, before the end of 1867.

Hungary (along with Croatia, which was constitutionally connected to it up till 1919) went further still in its consolidation of the legal framework for Jewish integration, outstripping other states in the region, including Austria's Cisleithan territories. Secularization of the state was largely accomplished by a string of laws on ecclesiastical policy passed in 1894–95: obligatory civil marriage, state run public records (for births, marriages and deaths), reciprocity between the protected (so-called 'received') denominations (on matters like mixed marriages, conversions, determination of the religion of offspring in mixed marriages). Judaism was endowed with the protected status ('law on Jewish reception' in 1895) meaning the same rights as other 'received' religions (and thus entitled to the same support from the state). On every occasion that Jews came under threat of mass violence, as they did during April 1848 in some towns where ethnic Germans formed a majority of the inhabitants, or during the infamous 'show trial' of Tiszaeszlár on trumped-up charges of ritual murder (1883), governments intervened vigorously against the trouble-makers. Even after organized anti-Semitism had made its entry into the European political arena, Hungary, although certainly not escaping the influence of that movement, remained a haven of liberal tolerance, as Theodore Herzl himself, the Pest-born and educated founder of Zionism, openly conceded. Political anti-Semitism could not rely on any official complicity in Hungary prior to the break-up of the Monarchy in 1918.

The Balkan countries that were liberated and gained independence from the Ottoman Empire during the nineteenth century (Greece, Bulgaria and Serbia), together with the European part of Turkey itself, may also be classified as belonging to the Central European model, at least in the sense that the construction of their nation-states was accompanied by Jewish emancipation without major hitches or serious opposition. True, the new national leadership strata in the Balkans had little to fear from them, since their presence was small and highly scattered. In Turkey the Jews had traditionally been treated equally as—if not somewhat better (since they were not regarded as potential enemies) than—all other non-Muslim minorities. On that strength they enjoyed the Porte's protection and thus never encountered significant discrimination. Amongst the various reforms introduced to modernize the state apparatus during the nineteenth century was an officially accepted charter of religious tolerance which proclaimed equality of all citizens, irrespective of religious affiliation. The equality of rights proclaimed in 1856 in regard to taxation, schooling and public office brought the effective emancipation of Jews in the European part of that empire. Nevertheless, it did not secure for them the same opportunities as Jews of Central Europe enjoyed. The Turkish political régime remained indeed profoundly autocratic, with very few representative institutions, and it continued to be marked by corruption and arbitrary use of power, usually at the expense of non-Muslim minorities.

Amongst the Balkan states, as far as Bulgaria and Serbia were concerned, they more or less promptly took their lead from Central

Europe, and all the more so, that the legal emancipation of Jews was one of the conditions imposed by western powers that were guaranteeing their integrity. That said, the Serbian parliament ratified the equality of rights in 1889 only, a good decade after the country's representatives had accepted its principle at the 1878 Berlin Congress. But thereafter no impairment of Jewish legal securities was experienced until the drift towards Fascism. In Bulgaria, emancipation was included in the founding charter of the nation-state. This constitution was formally accepted in the immediate aftermath of the Berlin Congress. It was symbolically countersigned by the country's chief rabbi, also appointed an official member of the constituent national assembly. The situation was far more conflict-ridden in Greece, where in the eyes of the Greek nationalists, Jews had usually been regarded as allies of the Ottoman Empire, ever since the start of the 1821 uprising and war of independence. Whilst legal equality for Jews did slowly achieve recognition, a succession of anti-Jewish excesses, fabricated charges of ritual murder, and other manifestations of anti-Semitic violence, often linked to real local rivalries between Greek and Jewish traders, remained not uncommon political features of modern nation-building throughout the entire nineteenth century. Still, such developments notwithstanding, anti-Semitism in Greece never reached such hysterical proportions as, occasionally, in most of Central Europe. In that respect though, the Greek developments deviated somewhat from the far more successful other cases of Jewish integration in the Balkans (outside Romania).

Political sources of the rejection of emancipation in Russia and Romania

The final model of the treatment of Jews is applicable indeed to Russia and Romania, the two easternmost countries on the continent. Only here were subjects of the Judaic faith denied full legal emancipation during the process of political modernization of the long nineteenth century. The two countries had virtually nothing else in common, except their adherence to Eastern (Orthodox) Christianity and the increasingly inflexible 'apartheid-style' policy that they adopted towards Jews. But the Jewish policy of tsarist Russia developed within the framework of an archaic system of government, a continuation of the multinational feudal empire. Romania's policy arose in a manner that was unique in Europe. By virtue of its singular concept of a 'Christian' nation-state (unparalleled in Europe), Romania's new ruling class would not countenance accepting Jews into the ranks of the 'nation,' even though the political modernization that followed the unification of the country could be accounted a success. Russia was a military great power with a say in the settlement of international relations in Europe and further afield, and in a position to conduct its internal affairs with a completely free hand. Romania, on the other hand, was a new state formation, put together under the protectorate of western powers, from component parts broken off from both the Russian and Ottoman empires in the course of their disputes. The western powers, consequently, retained considerable influence on Romania's internal politics, including the treatment of Jews.

Russia formed an independent autocratic régime, its ruler's supreme power being permanently sustained, with hardly any institutional checks. Essentially both legislative and executive power were concentrated in the tsar's hands, the continuance of which was a condition for allowing a relatively autonomous judicature to be set up only in the latter half of the nineteenth century. The feudal hierarchy of the aristocratic and economic ruling class, with its strictly defined spheres of authority and obligations, survived and, indeed, in some respects was bolstered even further during the nineteenth century. An elected legislative body was not established before the revolutionary uprisings of 1905. But even then, the state's executive power was still unequivocally wielded by the tsar. The régime bestowed very little in the way of collective rights on the huge mass of ethnic minorities. Its refusal to entertain the idea of full emancipation of the Jews can thus be accounted for partially by the fact that the régime actually denied equality of rights to the rest of the Russian people as well, especially to most of its non Russian minorities. In other words, the Jewish policies here can be best interpreted considering the fact that no western-style political modernization took place in Russia before the renewed stirrings of revolutionary unrest in February 1917.

Romania's development followed a completely different path. This nation-state was only formed during the second half of the nineteenth century, from Moldavia and Wallachia, two principalities inhabited by ethnic Romanians that had been Ottoman imperial protectorates. Following the 1821 revolt, they had exchanged Turkish for Russian suzerainty and later, after the suppressed revolution of 1848 and the 1856 Paris peace conference ending the Crimean War, extricated themselves from colonial status as well. In 1861 the two territories, by then again part of the Ottoman Empire, united as a single autonomous principality, which eventually, following the 1878 Congress of Berlin, became a kingdom fully recognized by the Powers as a sovereign state. The new nation-state was governed on the principle of representative parliamentarism, with the privileges vouchsafed the king being weak to begin with, but growing over time (ultimate veto on the passage of legislation, the right to take independent political initiatives). This régime, officially liberal but in practice based on an ascendancy of traditional noble élites (the boyars retained up to 1877 the large majority, later a sizable minority of government positions), refused to grant citizenship to Romanian Jews. Thanks to the lobbying of Moldavian deputies, the 1866 constitution introduced a unique 'Christian Clause' (Article 7) stipulating that Christians could only become citizens of the state. After 1878 there were no fewer than seven attempts to redress that situation with meager results. Jews could demand henceforth individually their naturalization. Some 2000 only were eventually accepted before 1919. Finally, under heavy outside pressure and extraordinarily late in the day, after the peace treaties that ended the First World War had been concluded, a decree of emancipation, issued on the 22nd of March, 1919, was put into statutory force under the new constitution of 1923, following much prodding from the signatories to the Versailles Treaty.

It is also instructive to compare Russia and Romania in regard to the sources of their 'Jewish Question.'

The Jewish communities of Romania came into being in several stages, from the fourteenth century onwards, as a result of migratory flows that headed for Moldavia. During the sixteenth century, the princes of Moldavia expressly invited in the Jews of Poland, with offers of various privileges and fiscal immunities, in order to restart the economy of war-ravaged towns, to build up new commercial centers or boost the existing ones. Many small towns, such as Suceava and Focșani, developed as veritable Jewish settlements. The Jews were received so cordially by the authorities, and the local markets so favorable, that when Austria occupied Bukovina in 1775 and Russia took Bessarabia in 1812, substantial segments of Jewry in those territories moved across Moldavia. The much more scattered Jewish populace that settled in Wallachia had originated from Spain at the time of the expulsions in the late fifteenth century, gradually topped up over subsequent centuries by further, mainly Sephardic groups. Jewish small shopkeepers here, however, soon found themselves under fire from other strata also functioning as middlemen, with Greek, Bulgarian and Armenian rivals often being supported by an Orthodox Church that promulgated an implacable hostility to Jews on theological grounds. But only in the nineteenth century was that anti-Judaism raised to the level of state policy by the political forces that acquired decisive influence in the fight for independence and state unity. In a Romanian nation-state that was essentially religiously and ethnically uniform at the time of its establishment, the need for unity of national culture, and the alleged threat to this posed by 'the enemy within,' served as a pretext for a policy of isolating the Jews and excluding them from public life.

In Russia, like most of those classed as foreigners in regard to their ethnicity or religion (the only exceptions were invited settlers and other groups that enjoyed special privileges), Jews were not allowed to settle at all until the eighteenth century. From then onwards, however, there was a gradual change, which took a decisive turn in the wake of Russia's successive military conquests. The tsarist power seized the Crimea and Black Sea littoral from Turkey in 1768, and more particularly took its share from the dismemberment of the Kingdom of Poland after 1772. As a result, what was then the largest Jewish population in the world, together with other large blocks of indigenous peoples (Poles, Ukrainians, Balts, Germans, etc.), came under the supremacy of the Russian Empire. Hence, the 'Jewish Question' and the 'Nationality Question' were both raised simultaneously inasmuch as, due to the expansion of the Empire at the end of the eighteenth century, the hitherto more or less homogeneous country in its religious and ethnic composition was transformed, all of a sudden, into a multinational state formation. Policy towards the Jews thus developed as part of the control of ethnic minorities, though in many respects in quite the opposite sense. The Polish, Lithuanian and Ukrainian peoples had their own landowning (noble) class, a past with states of their own, specific, territorially demarcated areas of settlement as well as strong military traditions. The Russian authority regarded these ethnic élites as natural negotiating partners, even as it mercilessly crushed their revolts against the central power. (From the time of the first partition of Poland onwards, during which the largest chunk of Polish territory passed under the tsarist crown, there were major uprisings within Polish-inhabited areas alone in 1793, 1830 and 1863.)

The Jews were in a very different position. Their areas of settlement were much more scattered, their lack of a tradition of belligerence meant that they did not pose any military threat, and they had no collective plans for the future or demands other than liberty of worship. To boot they were religious aliens in a country marked by the Orthodox Christian state religion. Thus they could be and indeed were treated in a far more cavalier fashion. Being judged to have little ability to resist, they were laid open to the frequently arbitrary actions of the tsarist administration, in line with the momentary interests of the authorities, and thereby ever more at the mercy of the personal whims of tsars, often imbued by many centuries of Judeophobic fanaticism.

Integration and exclusion under Russian absolutism

The Jewish policies pursued by the tsarist autocracy were not coherent, however, as they fluctuated between conflicting objectives. These included the territorial segregation of Jews, with their being confined to their earlier areas of settlement and geographically restricted zones of the recently conquered Black Sea region which remained to be colonized. Other aims of this policy were directed towards their maximal economic exploitation, linguistic and cultural Russification, a degree of social integration through occasional bouts of forcible conversions, their restriction to towns, and their political suppression and incapacitation through police intimidation and, in cases, pogroms left uncontrolled by the authorities. It is perhaps needless to remark that the pogrom, that officially tolerated, encouraged or even overtly organized manifestation of collective violence against Jews, had strongly rooted traditions in both eastern and western Christianity. During the political modernization in Western and Central Europe, however, that tradition, along with other public acts of anti-Semitic violence, was either done away with completely or made illegal. Tsarist autocracy, by contrast, not only re-vived this weapon during the nineteenth century but showed a predilec-tion for it, more than once as part of a deliberate policy of maintaining divisions amongst the downtrodden minorities. The Jews proved all the more suitable to be placed in the role of the treacherous public enemy or made scapegoats for the state's own failures, since they were also set apart economically, through their particular intermediary functions, from the masses of a peasantry still in serflike bondage (with elementary civic rights granted only in 1861), a feudal (petite) bourgeoisie, and a proletariat that had begun to emerge at the end of the century. On top of that, in an autocratic régime, intransigent in its resistance to seculariza-tion, the special stigma of being branded 'enemies of Christ' continued to fall to their lot. That, then, was the general framework in which the Jewish policy of tsarism was articulated. But the actual treatment ac-corded to Jewry might change significantly during the reign of any given tsar.

During the decades immediately following the partition of Poland, Russia for a while sustained the Jews in their earlier, relatively favor-able status. Catherine II at first inclined even to expanding their privi-leges, insofar as she wished to allow them to pursue their commercial activities in the empire's old territories. She abandoned that intention under pressure from the merchants of Moscow and Smolensk, who feared Jewish competition. She nevertheless confirmed their commer-cial freedoms, including their right to be represented in the local mu-nicipal councils of 'New Russia.' That imperial policy only took an anti-Jewish turn at the end of Catherine's reign in 1794, when the Jews were subjected to double the rate of taxation levied on Chris-tians, and severe restrictions on their settlement were introduced. Thenceforth they were allowed to live only in the former territories of Poland and the regions beside the Black Sea that had been taken from the Turks. In 1812 the Russian Empire gobbled up Bessarabia, with its large Jewish population, which fixed almost definitively the limits of the compulsory Pale of Jewish Settlement stretching from the Black Sea to the Baltic, into which those who had already settled elsewhere were subsequently driven. After 1859, residence outside this zone was permitted in exceptional cases, on an individual basis and under strict (albeit locally variable) conditions, for those who were entering higher education or Jews regarded as belonging to the élite on account of their wealth or economic activity. For the Jewish masses however, the Pale of Settlement was retained, and indeed consolidated, right up to Russia's involvement in the First World War (1915). Its final abolition was only proclaimed in March 1917, along with the lifting of all other impediments to which the Jews had been subjected, due to the Provisional Government formed after the February Revolution.

The clauses in the 'Statute for the Jews' proclaimed in 1804 were a miscellany of measures for forcible integration and prohibitions of draconian severity. Jews could be admitted to a school at any level, provided the education was given in one of the three official languages (Russian, Polish or German). Many of them were compelled to settle in the sparsely inhabited southern regions, but remained excluded from villages, even when they had previously made a living there as innkeepers, estate administrators, distillers or purveyors of spirits. This policy drew to some extent on the program of 'productivization' promoted by supporters of the *Haskalah* too, according to which there would be a chance for Jews to 'normalize' their economic position in Russia, as elsewhere in Europe, if they would give up in favor of agriculture the intermediary occupations that they had traditionally pursued. The war against Napoleon may have delayed the translation of this draft program into practice, but when it did get off the ground it brought large segments of the economically active Jewish population to the very brink of ruin. Expulsions from the villages and redirection to the south, to a constant chorus of exhortations to convert, became ever more energetic from 1822.

The reign of Nicholas I opened a new phase of Jewish oppression. The infamous cantonist system of conscription into military service was introduced in the provinces of Lithuania and the Ukraine in 1826 and remained in force right up till 1856. Under this, young Jewish boys were pressed to serve periods of 25 years in the army—a practice bound to lead to their losing their Jewish identity. The expulsions from villages and from certain geographical zones continued. From 1827 Jews were forbidden to live in Kiev, and from 1843 anywhere within a 50-kilometre perimeter from the borders with Austria and Prussia. Since families, fearful that their children would lose their Jewish attachments, were chary about sending them to state schools, the government made an attempt during the 1840s to set up a Jewish school network under supervision of the communities and at their expense (through a tax levied on candles). An 1844 resolution to that effect was only partially implemented, yet even so teachers' training colleges, founded in Vilna and Zhitomir, were to grow into important educational centers for training a staff to run the Russified Jewish school system. The government also interfered in the organization of Jewish communities themselves, permitting them only a limited autonomy and obliging them to comply with a whole series of decrees affecting every little detail of Jewish communal activities. Communities themselves were allowed to collect taxes, and in every administrative district they could nominate a chief rabbi, made responsible to the government for keeping the register of births, marriages and deaths as well as delivering loyalist sermons on state holidays.

In 1851 a long-gestated official system of discrimination between 'useful' and 'non-useful' Jews was instituted, despite the general outcry that it aroused both within Russia and in the West. The category of 'useful Jews' included the wealthiest groups, whether merchants, artisans or farmers. They were even granted exemption from military service for encouraging their settlement in the southern regions. Everyone else counted as a 'non-useful' Jew. In principle, they were liable to conscription for military service and could be compelled to learn and pursue a 'useful' trade. The unfortunate outcome of the Crimean War (1854–56) may have prevented the full implementation of this discriminatory system, but at the same time it exacerbated the brutality of 'cantonist' recruitment drives still further. Even more boys were carried off (30 'cantonists' for every 1,000 adult male Jews) to shore up the ranks of an army that was on the point of total collapse.

The reign of Alexander II was a period of great reforms, which for once involved a moderation of anti-Jewish policies, in part forced on him by the military catastrophe suffered in the Crimean war. The system of pressganging into 'cantonist' battalions was ended, whereas the discrimination into 'useful' and 'non-useful' categories was revised to the advantage of the best-off strata of Jews. The wealthiest merchants (1859), those with university degrees (1861), skilled artisans and medical practitioners (1865) were granted the right to settle wherever they wished within the country. Following the abolition of serfdom (1861) Jewish civic inequalities were also formally abandoned, without the lifting though of most other restrictions inflicted upon Jews (notably the enclosure in the Pale). To the latter, new ones will be added in subsequent decades. This bundle of measures, as well as the reduction in the period of military service to four years for those who had passed the school-leaving examination (1874), produced temporarily a substantial rise in educational demand of Jewish youngsters. In addition, a significant growth in the Jewish population got under way in the bigger cities (principally Moscow and St Petersburg). Even if they represented only a slight layer of Jews in the Pale, under the impact of all these trends, a Russified and secularized Jewish intelligentsia emerged in the Tsarist Empire.

As a consequence of reforms, Jews began to appear—in some cases with spectacular success—in intellectual markets that until then had been the sole preserve of educated Russian or Russified Christian strata, including journalism, theatre, music, visual arts, legal and medical professions. That was inevitably met with hostility by conservative circles, without the liberal or revolutionary groups in the Russian intelligentsia daring to mount any effective defense of their 'objective' Jewish allies for fear of losing the support of their core public. This Slavophile anti-Semitism, to which even such a major writer as Dostoevsky lent his prestige, raked up the old accusations that the Jews 'exploit the Russian masses,' 'constitute a state within the state' and, despite being 'foreign elements,' still managed to hold control of the nation's economic and cultural life. A 'modern' line of reasoning, its main targets were assimilated urban Jews—precisely the people who had been relatively successful at integrating into the ranks of the new Russian intellectual and economic élite. Meanwhile, however, the traditionalist masses, stranded in the *shtetl*s continued to be plagued by old-fashioned, religiously-motivated anti-Semitic bigotry—a harassment that intensified particularly after the Russian–Ottoman war in the Balkans (1877–78), and rose to its highest pitch after the assassination of the tsar in March 1881.

Pogrom policy and state anti-Semitism at the end of the tsarist régime

The year 1881 was a real turning-point in the history of Russian Jews and, indirectly, the whole of European Jewry. The new tsar, Alexander III (1881–1894), made short work of deflecting towards the Jews the general discontentment with the government. From 1881, more or less with connivance of the authorities (though government participation remains a debated issue), virtually coordinated orgies of looting, murder and rape broke out in many of the towns of South Russia (Kiev included). Other manifestations of anti-Jewish violence were to follow these pogroms in subsequent years, without the victims finding anyone to stand up for them, even within political opposition circles. Indeed, the latter endeavored to exploit the disorders to stoke up a revolutionary atmosphere. Government commissions investigating the events did their best to pin the blame for the disturbances on the victims themselves. The 'Temporary Regulations' of May 1882 relayed, as it were, the autocracy's presumptions by restoring old anti-Jewish oppressive measures: a ban on settling outside the walls of towns, the annulment of Jewish purchases of property.

With the pogroms being brought to an end in 1884, these were supplanted by administrative badgering of Jews. All along, this was being accompanied by an unprecedented campaign of anti-Semitic vilification by the officially censored press. Konstantin Pobedonostsev, chief secretary to the Holy Synod of the Russian Orthodox Church, publicly expressed his hopes of a final solution being found for the Jewish Question in that 'one-third of the Jews convert, one-third die, and one-third clear out of the country.' The banishment of Jews from villages was indeed again reinforced, and from 1887 a stringent *Numerus Clausus* was introduced on school entry, under which the ratio of Jewish pupils in state schools within the permitted zones of settlement was not supposed to exceed 10 per cent, and elsewhere 3–5 per cent. In 1891 most of the Jewish inhabitants of Moscow were expelled.

It should be noted that these drastic measures to relegate Jews to the background of society as well as impede their socio–economic prosperity and integration, were being brought in at precisely the time when Russia was setting off down the path of large-scale reforms aimed at removing the feudal impediments that were piling up in the way of mobility between social strata and equality before the law. Since the country's industrialization was gathering pace at the end of the century, it does seem as if economic leaders of Old and New Russia were in league with one another in seeking to deprive Jews of the fruits of modernization, maintaining that otherwise the Jews would take over control. It is true that Jewish entrepreneurs, particularly from the 1860s onwards, had taken a significant share in the construction of the road and rail network, working mines, developing the textile and food industries, exporting grain and timber, to say nothing of setting up modern credit banks. In the Ukraine, the main center for industrialization, Jewish capitalists in 1872, to take one example, controlled 90 per cent of distilling (an ancient Jewish activity, it is true), 57 per cent of the timber industry, 49 per cent of tobacco manufacturing, and 33 per cent of the sugar production. It was precisely the Ukraine where anti-Semitic violence on the part of locally whipped-up and mustered mobs reached their pitch. There the hostile passions fostered against the Jewish bourgeoisie were further fuelled by nationalistic resentment at the Russification of the Jews. The memory of assorted infamous Jew slaughterers of bygone centuries, epitomized by figures like Khmelnitsky (celebrated as a national hero) and other *hetman* butchers of Jews in the seventeenth and eighteenth centuries, were thereby invested with a new political function.

Mob violence, direct or indirect incitement by officialdom, local boycotts of Jewish commercial wares and other oppressive measures all contributed to the impoverishment of the Jewish masses and social isolation of their leadership strata. The Jewish bourgeoisie was forced into liquidating its investments on more than one occasion; the willingness of Russian-schooled, cultivated Jews to assimilate dwindled, although there were some whom exigency drove down the path of 'self-denial' to conversion. As a consequence of this, an emigratory movement far outstripping all earlier ones in intensity got under way within the entire population affected. Previous migrations had, for the most part, taken place within the borders of the country, with the capital cities as the much desired goal (for the privileged few), or were directed from north to south, towards Odessa and other Ukrainian towns that became major Jewish colonies over the course of the century. Beginning with the great Lithuanian famine of the 1870s, however, the number of migrants setting off for the West also proliferated. The ensuing pogroms of 1881–84 sparked off a veritable 'exodus.' Up to the First World War, unparalleled masses of Jews—over two million souls—set out, the majority of them towards the United States of America. The bulk of the young men upon whom the *Numerus Clausus* bore most directly were soon turning up at universities in Germany and France, with many of them having no intention of returning to their native land. At the same time, political radicalism grew amongst the young Jews who stayed behind, in part with the appearance of Jewish nationalism in various organizational forms (like Zionism, *Folk*ism, *Bund), but also by fair numbers of young Jews coming from the assimilated élite joining Russian revolutionary movements.

The reception and assistance of Jews having left Russia or destined to do so was efficiently supported by some members of western Jewish élites. An open-handed French philanthrope, Baron Maurice de Hirsch, entered a contract with the tsarist government in 1891 to facilitate the resettlement of three million Russian Jews in Argentina... The lavishly funded Jewish Resettlement League set up for this purpose may not have come even close to that goal, still it played a useful role in training up (principally as farmers) many young people who were preparing to emigrate. Demographically, the mass departures did not fully offset the high birth rate and the declining mortality, with the population of around 2,350,000 Russian Jews in 1850 more than doubling over the next half-century. But the exodus did help ease the abject poverty of the Jewish masses, since cash remittances from emigrants helped out many of those left back home.

The need for western intervention on behalf of the people of the *shtetl*s grew from year to year. There was no let-up in the pressure on the Jews from the Russian authorities during the reign of Nicholas II (1894–1917) either, and the 1904–05 revolutionary unrest was an occasion for further pogroms, much bloodier than before. Anti-Semitic mob violence at Kishinov over Easter 1903 claimed some fifty dead, with many more over the ensuing years. Pogroms organized, sometimes with powerful assistance from the army and police, were part of the authorities' strategic moves to divert and release the pent-up reserves of revolutionary forces. The wave of pogroms reached its peak in the days following the promise to give the country a constitution, made by the tsar in his 'October Manifesto' of 1905. Forced into making concessions, the government set up a legislative parliament, the State Duma, in which even the Jews gained representation. This did nothing, though, to alter the situation. Against a handful of Jewish delegates and their Social Democratic allies stood the Union of the Russian People (which was to achieve notoriety under the name of 'Black Hundreds'). This strong, far-right political grouping proclaimed an increasingly radical anti-Semitism until it ended up demanding the complete removal of Jews from the country. It was in order to incite the Union's supporters that the *Okhrana*, the Russian secret police, in 1905, brought out the now infamous forgery entitled *The Protocols of the Elders of Zion*, which was dressed up as an exposé of Jewish ambitions to gain world domination. The inflammatory document had been cobbled together with meticulous care at the end of the preceding century, and although even the tsar himself was unwilling to give it credence, it was to become a primary reference source for militant anti-Semitism (especially in the aftermath of the First World War) right up to the present day.

The State Duma rejected any reform that might have been favorable to Jews. The hatred for Jewry of a parliamentary majority dominated by extremists went as far as stipulating that descendants of Jews, down to the third generation were disqualified from serving as officers in the imperial army (1912). On the eve of the First World War, the government again resorted to the device of spectacular anti-Semitic propaganda by attempting to resuscitate the calumny of ritual murder in a trial that created a stir around the world (the Beilis Case of 1913). The authorities' efforts misfired, however, because the jury of twelve peasants acquitted the accused in the end.

Under these circumstances, the First World War could only bring further tribulations for the Jews of Russia. The young men were sent off to the front, which, as a result of the advances made by the Central Powers, soon split the Pale of Jewish Settlement into two almost equal parts. On the home front, the tsarist authorities intensified the burdens falling on Jews in an attempt to counteract the society-wide reaction to war-time privations and military defeats. The slightest pretext might expose Jews to charges of treason or spying, and suspicion was enough for the Jewish populace in whole districts to be brutally expelled from sectors close to the fighting, as from Kurland in Latvia and from North Lithuania in June 1915. With the compulsory Pale of Settlement no longer tenable, the residential constraint on Jews was thus brought to an end in 1915, paradoxically not by an act of emancipation but by military emergency. Typically, as the Pale of Settlement was wound up, a ban was announced on publications with the Hebrew alphabet, which choked off the entire thriving Yiddish and Hebrew-language press. But these decrees, as well as the conscription of Jewish young men into the army, in their various ways, suddenly accelerated the process of Russification of the Jewish population. At the same time, as a result of the Russian war machine, large masses of Jews were now cut off from their major religious and cultural centers in Poland and Lithuania. Right in the midst of the war, this brought about a fateful (and, as history was to show, permanent) division in the network of communities in Eastern Europe. Adherents of Hasidism that encompassed the western parts of the former Russian territory became separated from their co-religionists in the east.

Emancipation and forced assimilation after 1917: the ordeals of the Russian Civil War and Bolshevik dictatorship

The defeat of the tsarist armies culminated in the complete collapse of autocracy. The February Revolution of 1917 brought a turning-point, not only in Russian but also Jewish history. One of the very first legislative acts of the Provisional Government, on the 16th of March, 1917, was the abolition of all restrictions related to Jews. For them, this represented an immediately perceptible rise in standing with respect to their legal status and role in society alike. They were now able to move around and settle anywhere within the country, hold public offices, gain promotion as officers, etc. The government classed anti-Semitic propaganda as incompatible with the spirit of the revolution and banned it. It is no wonder thus, that Jews gave initially such enthusiastic support to the new régime. Their representatives were to be found in the general staff of the reorganized army and in the ranks of all parties urging change. This concerned not just the Bolsheviks (Trotsky, Kamenev, Zinoviev, Sverdlov) and Mensheviks (Martov, Dan), but also the Constitutional Democrats (Vinaver) and the Revolutionary Socialists (Steinberg, Minor).

For Russian Jews, the months between the February Revolution and the Bolshevik seizure of power in October 1917 amounted to a Promethean time that, brief as it may have been, was rich in cultural initiatives. A Congress of Russian Zionists held in Petrograd during May was a great success. The Jewish press and book publishing were able to operate again; new newspaper titles and publishers were founded, thanks to the abolition of censorship; the foundation stone was laid for a Hebrew theatre to be called *Habima*. In parallel, the newly proclaimed freedom of organization made it possible for the Jewish masses to build their own self-governing, organizational and military self-defense bodies. In the Ukraine, with some 60 per cent of Jews of the former tsarist empire, it went as far as putting forward the idea of declaring autonomy. A Jewish National Council was formed at the end of 1917. Later on, after the declaration of Ukraine's independence, one of its members became, temporarily, a minister in the first provisional government.

The power of the Provisional Government of revolutionary Russia weakened though from month to month, and a collapse in public order was a looming threat. The military coup staged by Trotsky in early November 1917 (the 'Great October Revolution' of the Bolsheviks) brought the peaceful transition to a close. Civil war broke out between 'Reds,' 'Whites' and other combatants, whilst the embers of external war were rekindled against the renascent Polish state. Hostilities dragged on until early 1921, with a good part of the densely Jewish-inhabited territories once again being turned into a theatre of operations.

The new war left a horrendous legacy of destruction, with a large number of Jewish communities (over 530 on the evidence presented by the Jewish–Russian historian Simon Dubnov) amongst those to be devastated. In this climate of chronic anarchy, Jews were afflicted by an unending succession of pogroms, armed attacks, arbitrary murders and plundering raids. Since the perpetrators usually came from the ranks of the White Guards, it is hardly surprising that the Bolsheviks should have enjoyed a broad base of support amongst those Jews who resisted the call of emigration: 4.4 per cent of the Red Army's officer corps in 1926 was Jewish (more than twice their representation in the general population). The Bolsheviks did indeed punish anti-Semitic excesses, prohibited anti-Jewish agitation, and made efforts to rein in mass outbursts of anti-Jewish violence (though in 1920, during the withdrawals from the advancing Poles, some of the Red Army units themselves took part in pogroms). Uncontrollable peasant gangs, prone to attack and rob any Jew who came near, aided and abetted the White forces. The atrocities committed by the men under Petlyura, commander of the Ukrainian national army, and by some Polish troops became indelibly inscribed in the memories of survivors. The officers of counter-revolutionary units who were pushing towards Moscow in the summer of 1919 resuscitated the old tsarist rallying cry: 'Thrash the Yids and Save Russia'! Neither the protests of the Ukrainian government's Jewish minister, nor armed self-defense by prospective victims was able to ward off the anti-Jewish violence which in some settlements—in Zhitomir, Berdichev, Proskurov (Khmelnitzsky), Fatov, and other places—claimed tens of thousands of victims. Jews in that region had not suffered such immense losses since the great Cossack rebellion in the Time of Troubles during the seventeenth century. The total number of victims of this bloodshed has been put at between 60,000 and 100,000 (indeed some authors speak of as many as 200,000 dead). That amounted to some 3–4 per cent (or even more) of the reduced Jewish population of around 2,500,000 living within the borders of the Soviet state, as they stood around 1920.

The ultimate victory of the Bolsheviks opened a fresh chapter in history. In their policies towards the Jews, the Soviet authorities, with many leaders of Jewish descent in their ranks, championed full assimilation. Since the new power had advocated the cause of equality of rights for Jews, and during the Civil War had given them protection, it could rely on a ground swell of sympathy from that quarter. That, however, in many respects did not stand to the test of the Bolshevik intervention against Zionism and other forms of Jewish nationalism. Opposition to the atheistic Soviet régime within circles of traditionalist Jewry was only further stepped up by the nationalization of industry and commerce during the period of 'war Communism' and by the abolition of the services supplied by the *shtetl*s to villages. These steps cut the economic ground from under independent Jewish shopkeepers, service providers and artisans. Collectivization of the economy also condemned the masses of bourgeois and petty-bourgeois clusters to accept distressing forms of forced occupational mobility. Only the New Economic Policy, introduced in 1921–22, temporarily breathed new life into small Jewish businesses, but that did not stop large numbers of them from trying their luck in the non-Bolshevized successor states of Poland and the Baltic states, Romania, or, whenever possible, in the West. Figures of around 300,000 Jewish emigrants are quoted for the 1920s. To this should be added the large number of those who fled abroad for purely political reasons, due to the Bolshevik Party's ruthless crushing of democratic organizations seen as rivals.

Whilst they were settling into power, though, the Communists were offering Jews previously unheard-of opportunities within the state machinery, the party apparatus, and management of the reorganized economy. They also recognized officially, after some hesitation, the national status of the Jewish people, similarly to that of other ethnic minorities. For all that, Soviet 'Jewish policy' always remained equivocal. Stalin, in a 1913 article (later expanded) under the title *Marxism and the National Question* defined the characteristics of a nation as 'a language, territory and economic life that have evolved historically in common.' Jewry could hardly be said to fit that definition, as the Austro-Marxist philosopher Otto Brauer remarked already at the time. Furthermore those belonging to the Jewish intellectual élite were not, as a rule, themselves demanding an autonomous national existence for Jewry but, in the spirit of assimilation, made do with the self-definition of 'adopted' nationhood. Communist ideology was urging the development of a 'new type of socialist man' for which the point of reference was precisely a universalistic set of ideas, independent of cultural, national, let alone religious or other 'particularistic' connections. Soviet 'Jewish policy' strove for forcible cultural assimilation (in practice, continued Russification) of those in question, far more than it did in the case of other, equally diasporic but 'territorially based' national minorities (like the Volga Germans, Armenians, etc.). War was declared, first and foremost, on the Judaic faith, whilst scraps of 'cultural autonomy' were temporarily left untouched. Indeed, a sort of artificial territorial basis was even proposed for purposes of giving Jewry 'national' representation in the officially multinational Soviet state.

The tasks of organized assimilation, including the forceful elimination of all institutional agencies of Jewish political autonomy, such as the *Bund* and Zionism, was entrusted to a Jewish Section of the party, the *Evsektsiya* founded in 1918 and made up of tried-and-true Communist Jews. Its main activity was directed against Jewish communities, religious institutions and those elements of cultural heritage that clung to them, notably religious faith and the Hebrew language. The anti-religious drive revived the worst practices of the tsarist autocracy (although the tsars rarely attacked Judaism as such), following the logic of a policy of radical secularization : extraordinary taxes were levied on rabbis; Hebrew theological colleges, the *yeshivot*, were closed; notables of the communities were imprisoned or expelled from the country (that was the fate of, amongst others, Yosip Isaak Schneershon, head of the Lubavich dynasty of Habad Hasidism). The publication of writings related to religious practice was banned (1928); teaching of Hebrew and the Hebrew-language press were suppressed; institutions that transmitted Hebrew culture (such as the *Habima* Theatre, the Jewish Historical and Ethnographic Society) were shut down. Around 1930 most Hebrew-speaking authors and artists were placed under tight control which, within a few years, was to pass into savage persecution. Having accomplished its main tasks, the *Evsektsiya* itself was disbanded in 1930.

The other main aspect of that same strategy, however, was the official support given to 'Jewish proletarian culture' in the vernacular (i.e. Yiddish). A Yiddish press had life breathed into it (though only with a phonetically transcribed print, not the traditional Hebrew lettering, in order to facilitate control), Yiddish-language theatres were set up (including the showcase Jewish State Theatre of Moscow, under the direction of the famous actor Solomon Mikhoels), departments of Jewish cultural history were set up at the universities of Minsk and Kiev, and a network of elementary schools with Yiddish as the language of tuition was organized. It was permissible to use Yiddish as a national language in law courts. Yiddish literature flourished transiently during the early 1930s, thanks to some noteworthy writers, several of whom had even returned from exile abroad. Those developments were arbitrarily halted in 1935, and the institutional basis of Yiddish culture was totally expunged well before the Stalinist era had ended. Many of its distinguished creative exponents were physically wiped out.

As, so to speak, a bureaucratic illustration of the aforementioned Stalinist concept of nation, which ordained that every recognized national group had to possess its own territory—a national territory goes with national existence—a 'Jewish Autonomous Republic,' known as Birobidzhan, was brought into being in the Far East, on the border with Manchuria, without any historical precedence whatsoever. At the time, this experiment was presented as one of the practical alternatives to Zionism. (It did, incidentally, rouse the interest abroad of so-called 'territorialist' Zionists, who were not committed to Palestine.) The creation of the Jewish Autonomous Republic at one and the same time harked back to certain ideas deriving from the *Haskalah*, with its attempt to mobilize or 'productivize' Jews in agriculture. The project of an 'autonomous territory' was officially adopted in 1928. Birobidzhan came into legal existence in 1934, but since it was located a huge distance away from the actual centers of Jewish population, its colonization proved extremely difficult and ended in complete failure. The number of Jews living there never exceeded 30,000, even at the peak of the migratory influx that coincided with the Second World War. The 'Jewish' character of the territory faded away all the more in the wake of the two great purges— those of 1936–37 and 1948–49—that were conducted in a climate of semi-officially fomented anti-Semitism. The project of a 'national homeland' in Birobidzhan, in other words, underwent the same fate as the encouragement of Yiddish culture following the Bolshevik seizure of power.

The treatment of Jews in Russia always had two fundamental trends. To the very end, the tsarist régime set its face against civic emancipation, and it strove to subject and humiliate Jewry to the utmost. To that end, it deprived them of a whole string of cardinal conditions of social existence that were permitted to other, economically similarly placed citizens. The ephemeral 1917 revolutionary episode brought western-style liberation, but the subsequent Soviet régime resumed a policy of forcible integration and assimilation, even though it formally recognized Jewry as a nationality (which was also displayed in the 'internal passports' of all concerned). Above all, in the early days it provided a certain scope, albeit carefully controlled, for Yiddish culture. Jewish representatives, however, never had any effective say in any of these processes. The political treatment of Jewry in Russia was thus always dictated by an omnipotent state, organized in a spirit of 'Oriental despotism' which was no more ready to grant Jews civic emancipation than it was to respect the autonomy and other collective rights of any ethnic minority.

United Romania, or a case study in Judaeophobic nation-building

The Jews of Romania, for a while, shared the same fate as their co-religionists in Russia. Earlier Ottoman protectorates, between 1819 and 1834 the Danubian Principalities were under occupation by tsarist forces, and until 1856 remained submitted to the Muscovite empire. The almost invariably restrictive or overtly oppressive elements of the hegemonic empire's 'Jewish policy' thus inevitably had an impact on the local élites, who were laying the ground for the country's independence. The framework of what was to be the official ideological and legislative approach to handling the Jews had already been mapped out before independence was gained. Under this, the Jews were to be seen as foreigners who should be denied citizenship and whose immigration should be restricted. Since the Jews were allegedly notorious for exploiting indigenous populations, they could not be allowed to live in villages, to lease land or to set up industrial businesses. The 'Organic Statutes' (*Règlements organiques*) approved by the 'protecting power' in 1839 and 1843 contain a meticulously elaborated set of anti-Jewish measures which, on the Russian pattern, empowered local authorities to decide which Jews were 'useful' to the country; the rest could be declared 'vagrants' and expelled on that score.

This system vouched the authorities far-reaching arbitrary powers of decision at every level, with corruption as the sole means of easing the gravity of abuses. The prince of Moldavia, for example, resuscitated medieval traditions in pursuing his anti-Jewish actions in 1835 and 1839, until he had compelled his Jewish bankers to cancel his debts. Blackmailing Jews with threats of expulsion was thereafter a weapon regularly used against Jews who failed to comply with corrupt authorities. During this era, Romania and Russia were the only two countries in which a central institution was maintained to supervise the Jews and mediate between the state and Jewish communities. The system of the *hakham bashi*, or chief rabbi, was a late relic of the Ottoman protectorate that survived until 1834 and was charged with a wide range of functions (tax collection, administrative head of the communities, representation of state power, etc.). Ensconced at Iaşi, he had an emissary in Bucharest. His authority within Jewry was virtually minimal, and his powers came under ever-growing fire from Jewish emigrants from Galicia, for the most part influenced by Hasidism, until they finally succeeded in getting his jurisdiction abolished.

Russia continued to intervene, even after the unification of the Principalities, in the discriminative Romanian 'Jewish policies' in order to apply pressure against plans for emancipation. This happened during the crucial negotiations (the 1856 Peace Conference of Paris ending the Crimean War) that paved the way for independence in 1859, and also after international recognition of the country's independence was granted at the 1878 Berlin Congress. Between these two dates, Romania's leadership perceptibly vacillated in the line it took. The revolutionaries who had risen against Ottoman suzerainty in 1821, and in 1848 against the Russian invaders who succeeded the Ottomans, had counted on backing from the Jews, and had not been disappointed. The Paris Peace Treaty had even proclaimed the principle of equal rights for all citizens born within the country, irrespective of religion. Due to opposition of the ruling classes, enforcement of that clause was indeed thwarted when it came to the Jews. During the rule of Alexandru Ion Cuza, the 1848 revolutionary and, from 1859, the liberal head of both principalities, native Jews were granted rights to vote in local elections ('lesser citizenship'), but the multitude of immigrant Jews were denied even that. After the departure of Cuza, overthrown by an 'unholy alliance' of liberals and conservatives, relations with the authorities took a distinctly unfavorable turn for Jews. Under the new constitution, which was confirmed on the installation of King Carol of Hohenzollern–Sigmaringen, a supporter of conservative restoration, civil rights were only due to Christians. This stipulation was unique in European legislation during the modern age, although it was reminiscent of the various provisos that remained in force, even after emancipation of Jews, in the less secularized countries of Central Europe and, whether overtly or covertly, preserved political and high state offices for adherents of the state religion or other 'protected' Christian denominations. The Romanian authorities, in order to justify their attitude, did not balk at resorting to the well-tested repertory of anti-Semitic agitation. One example in Bucharest was the razing of a big synagogue by a mob, with police complicity in 1866. In 1867, despite protests from western governments and Jewish organizations, Minister of the Interior Ion Bratianu—likewise a liberal back in 1848—resumed the removal of Jews from villages and expulsions of those not born in the country.

In 1878 the Romanian and Russian delegates at the Berlin Congress failed to prevent the western powers from making the emancipation of Romanian Jews a condition for granting recognition to an independent Romania. Back in Romania this was followed up by country-wide street demonstrations in favor of the authorities' discriminative anti-Jewish policies. Under pressure from the Great Powers, though, the parliament in Bucharest was nevertheless obliged to accept the change to the 'Christian clause' in the constitution. The possibility was thereby opened, in principle, for Jews to acquire citizenship rights, except that each case had to be dealt with individually by act of parliament, requiring assent by both chambers of the national assembly. Thus, even though 883 Jewish veterans of the 1877 'war of independence' against Turkey were instantly granted citizenship, the complicated procedure had only allowed a total of around 2,000 Jews to acquire citizenship before 1919. During the Berlin Congress, the western powers would not budge an inch on the principle of emancipation, and the crisis that was developing between them and the new state was resolved, not for the first time, by the interplay of financial interests. Romania bought back, at a huge mark-up—six times the rate quoted on the stock exchange—the blocks of shares in the Romanian railways owned by the Junkers of Silesia (including members of the imperial court at Berlin), in return for which Germany agreed to grant the country diplomatic recognition, leaving France and Britain no choice but to follow suit.

Sure in the knowledge that it could act with impunity, the Romanian state allowed the constitutional status of the Jews to deteriorate during the decades that followed the Berlin Congress. They were unable to acquire any sort of political rights, treated as aliens and remaining subject to numerous occupational prohibitions. They were indeed highly restricted in their opportunities to make a livelihood at all, since they were no more permitted to hold public office, be employed by public utilities (in transport or hospitals, for instance), become teachers or lawyers or to trade in any commodities covered by state monopolies (salt, alcohol, tobacco). In 1885, several influential and completely Romanized Jewish intellectuals (the ethnographer Moses Gaster and the historian Elias Schwarzfeld) were expelled from the country, accused of not giving up the struggle for emancipation of their co-religionists. In 1893 a strict quota system was introduced into state schools: This prompted, with the support of the Alliance Israélite Universelle and other European Jewish organizations, the establishment of an independent network of Jewish schools. The peasant uprising of 1907 was directed primarily against Jewish landowners and leaseholders (on this occasion, of course, not at the instigation of the authorities). As far as the two most influential political parties were concerned, there was nothing to choose between liberals and conservatives in their anti-Semitism. In 1910, the National Democratic Party, founded by two respected academics, Alexandru C. Cuza and Nicolae Iorga, used an overtly (albeit not extremist) anti-Semitic platform in its propaganda.

In view of the failure of foreign pressures, brought to bear to obtain emancipation, a Jewish opposition began to be formed. In October 1872 a Fraternal Society of Zion was set up, which convened a conference of the world's Jewish organizations in Brussels to aid the cause of the Romanian Jews. Under the influence of those factions that espoused assimilation, the congress rejected the idea of mass emigration from Romania as being an unpatriotic solution. In 1890, a Romanian General League of Native Israelites came into being. First of all it pushed for civil rights for Jews having performed military service. Pressurized by the socialist wing, it expanded that demand to include all Jews born in the country, but the League was then disbanded, due to threats and acts of violence aimed against its members. The baton was taken up by a Union of Native Jews, which set both assimilation and emancipation as its goal. Despite its efforts, the flow of emigrants heading for the West and overseas continued to multiply. The total number of emigrants between 1900 and 1914 has been put at 70,000, or more than one quarter of the country's Jewish population, which meanwhile—despite the high natural increase—declined from 267,000 to 240,000. According to other estimates, during the thirty years between 1899 and 1928 some 135,000 Jews left Romania, more than one-third of them to settle in the United States.

The battle for emancipation grew in intensity during and after the First World War. That was due, on the one hand, to more resolute intervention by the western powers, and on the other hand, to stiffened resistance by the Romanian authorities, since, from a demographic standpoint, the territorial expansion of the country was entailing the admission of larger masses of Jews. The stake for allowing emancipation was therefore far more serious than it had been earlier. The annexation to Romania of Transylvania, Bessarabia and part of Bukovina under the terms of the Versailles Treaty, in fact, more than tripled the Jewish population concerned. Legal emancipation was only won, at last, after fierce struggles, in 1923. That, however, did nothing to alter the increasingly more extremist anti-Semitism that was current in Romanian society. Political life and the evolving balance of forces in the enlarged Romanian nation-state during the inter-war years were accompanied throughout by ever-cruder forms of anti-Semitic incitement and outbreaks of anti-Jewish violence.

According to the romantic and xenophobic self-definition of Romanian nationhood, it was necessary to demarcate itself both from external or 'historic' enemies (Turks, Russians, Hungarians, Poles) and from the internal ones (Greeks, Gypsies and, above all, Jews). Consequently, anti-Semitism too finds itself amongst the popularly recognized organizing principles of the Romanian nation-state, and in that concept Jews are presented as posing a permanent 'ethnic threat.' Major literary figures (including Mihai Eminescu, who fulfilled the role of a 'national poet') as well as most influential politicians shared and propagated these anti-Jewish views. (It is a sign of how rare the exceptions were, that they are usually referred to separately, by name, as in the case of the politician Titu Maiorescu or the famous playwright Luca Caragiale.) Anti-Semitism appears to be a subject of far-reaching general consent within Romania's political leadership throughout the entire period of the old régime.

Chapter 3

Identity Construction and Strategies since the *Haskalah*. Assimilation, Its Crises and the Birth of Jewish Nationalisms

Inherited group identity and the challenge of assimilation

Practically up to the very end of the eighteenth century, almost all of European Jewry lived in closed communities, governed internally by traditional laws and externally by the jurisdiction regulating the legal status of those who fell 'outside the estates' of feudal societies. Collective identity could not have been problematic for Jews in that situation. In an expression that Marcel Mauss, the father of French anthropology, used to characterize a group identity of that type, Jewry's collective individuality, and its demarcation from other sections of society, was a 'total social phenomenon,' since it comprised simultaneously aspects of religious, social, political, economic and (at least by virtue of matrilineal descent) biological distinctiveness alike. If Jews did become separated from their original community, for one reason or another (they fell into the hands of pirates, or were driven off by Ottoman conquerors, or entered the personal service of a feudal lord or prince, etc.), that did not pose a threat to the cohesion and collective survival of the group as a whole. A sufficient guarantee of solidarity was provided by the moral armor donned to counter the external pressure weighing on every Jew, as a Jew, together with the prestige of the Judaic religious authorities. To such factors of cohesion may be counted the high 'costs' of the step of secession, always possible in principle, by converting to Christianity (even in cases of forced mass conversions linked to collective persecution). Secession entailed indeed a number of dire consequences, such as the sheer difficulties of joining the Christian world, the peculiar burden of an 'intermediate' state in feudal society, the sense of shame over deserting the community, etc. In feudalism individual switching from one estate to another was anyway an extremely rare phenomenon, and it in no way affected the invulnerable unity of the estates.

Both the 'internal' and the 'external' conditions of Jewish group identity were radically altered by the collapse of feudalism. The external change comprised legal emancipation—achieved first of all in western countries, in the wake of the French Revolution, but becoming part, or a planned goal, of social reform programs throughout the rest of Europe. With that, a rapprochement of Jews and non-Jews to one another was set off, or accelerated, in a series of areas, with Jews finding it increasingly possible to enter into non-Jewish domains of economic, cultural, artistic and ideological activity. Secularization and the spread of secular attitudes multiplied the chances for Jews and non-Jews to work together and form communities of interest, as factors influencing denominational separatism increasingly retreated to the realms of private life. With the abolition of feudal privileges and with the industrial revolution (a fair number of whose initiators were self-made men), achievement came increasingly to be seen as the cornerstone of the rules governing social mobility. The diminishing influence of inherited status in the reproduction of social relations opened up for Jews all sorts of opportunities to make a way in economic and public life, even in domains until then reserved exclusively for non-Jews.

The previously rigid barriers separating Jews and Christians from one another also tumbled down, some of them even before emancipation was granted. Residential and school segregation, some prohibitions on settlement and profession, brakes on economic investment, restrictions on entering public places of entertainment, such as nightclubs, theatres, and concert halls, indeed even class-specific institutions of social life, like clubs, casinos and salons, increasingly lost their rigor. That development was rapid, especially in urban environments, even in countries that opposed the political project of emancipation, including in many respects Russia and Romania. In European cities that grew into true metropolises during the nineteenth century new, more secular and more 'democratic' models of the use of urban spaces and communications were established in coffee-houses, social circles, dance schools, theatres, opera houses, clubs, and sometimes in brothels, later on in swimming pools, stadiums and sports grounds. Members of aristocratic or middle-class strata, and of ethnic or religious groups, bit by bit eased back, at least in part, on the habitual segregationist reflexes that had been handed down from feudalism, and their ways of life at the equivalent levels of wealth, income and education moved closer to one another (though the differences did not vanish altogether in many places before the Shoah).

A similarly gradual yet thorough overhaul of professional markets in line with free trade conventions made further inroads on the system of inequalities associated with feudal status that they had sustained for so long. Whether as citizens who had the right to vote or not (depending on the country), as 'burghers,' or simply as solvent clients and customers, Jews were increasingly admitted to participate in public social life. In this new situation, the 'cost factors' of withdrawing from one's community decreased all the time, despite the fact that in the course of building up their 'external' social connections Jews would at times continue to come up against crude debarment. That, however, was something they had to reckon with in many places even after legal emancipation. One can even argue that social mixing—allowed by the very process of emancipation—conducted precisely to the multiplication of possible situations of friction between Jews and hostile Gentiles in Gentile dominated environments.

Nevertheless, from the end of the eighteenth century—albeit at differing points in time from country to country, and under highly divergent conditions—Jewry virtually everywhere throughout Europe, and especially in the towns, encountered a growing 'integrationist challenge,' being subjected to growing demands to comply with the requirements of a process of more or less 'conditional' emancipation, as initiated by the majority community, by eliminating the marks of self-distinction, cultural particularism and self-imposed seclusion. The 'integrationist challenge' turned into political pressure to assimilate in many places, to some extent even in western countries that granted, in principle, unconditional emancipation, but all the more so in the Central European empires, which planned to give this more or less 'conditionally' only, or in Russia and Romania, which refused to entertain such project. Jews everywhere were upbraided for clinging on to specific attributes of their affiliation and encouraged to abandon them. Those incitements might have either positive or negative under-tones, however. A positive sense predominated with some of the leading personalities of Hungarian liberalism during the Reform Age, as in the case of Lajos Kossuth or József Eötvös. By way of contrast, during that same era, Havlíçek-Borovsky, the nationalistic publicist for the 'Young Czech' movement, cast doubt upon the 'assimilability' of Jews into the Czech nation. A negative perception prevailed else-where too, even if not over the long term, as in the case of Napoleon I. That is what gave pretext to the *décret infâme* of 1808, which sus-pended certain provisions of the revolutionary emancipation in the hope that the Jews of Alsace–Lorraine (the sole group to whom the decree applied) would meet the assimilationist expectations of the state within that period.

Within Jewish circles the 'integrationist challenge' was perceived by some as a risk, a source of danger, by others as a chance. In the traditionalist communities of Eastern Europe, encompassing the most enclosed and most populous camp, the advocates of resistance long held the upper hand. This was served by a consolidation of group boundaries (attended, amongst other things, by the expulsion of dis-senters and 'reformists'), a strengthening of rabbinical controls, and the accentuation of the traditional, peculiarly complex definition (at once religious, '*folkish*' or ethnic, cultural and, indeed, racial) of Jewry. Judaic Orthodoxy locked itself in behind the rigid bastions of tradition, refusing for a long time to countenance any compromise with modernity, even when that would have brought foreseeable ad-vantages on the political or economic plane. In a number of countries preparing for emancipation—Hungary and several German states in the mid-nineteenth century may serve as examples—many Orthodox community leaders preferred to reject the extension of rights, or showed a professed indifference towards it, out of a fear that legal equality might incite their faithful to take stock of and reappraise the traditional rules governing their lives.

Even as Jewish communities hung on unbendingly to their tradi-tions, new strategies for the conduct of one's life and interpretation of the self were emerging, particularly within élite groups of Jews, who had a greater degree of latitude in this area. Their prototype, and also the most influential movement, was the Berlin *Haskalah*. The centers for such strategies, as a rule, were smaller congregations within Western and Central Europe, many of whose members maintained economic partnerships, and occasionally even social relations with the Christian élite (court Jews). Christians too could be found, for instance, amongst those who frequented the tactfully run salons of cultivated upper-class Jewish women in Berlin, Vienna and Paris in the early nineteenth century. These local Jewish élite groups, having already achieved a certain level of integration into the receiving society, seized every means to reconcile the demands of Jewish life and modernism, strove to revise earlier definitions of Jewry in Gentile society as well as they were prepared to reformulate the norms governing Jewish identity.

These novel strategies of symbolic self-assertion exploded any uniform notion of group identity. The concept of Jewish identity as a 'total social experience' ended. Henceforth progress led through a miscellany of collective self-interpretations to major new models of identity. The paradigmatic constitutional framework for these was supplied initially by 'denominationalism,' that is, the idea that 'Jewry' was merely one of several religious aggregates in society. Later on though (with influence persisting still to the present day), the converse notion of a fully secular interpretation of 'Jewry' came to prevail, Jewry as a community of fate or descent, a people or nation, that is, a group endowed with a particular historical experience and corresponding values and sensibility, regardless of the devotion and formal religious commitment or even, in the extreme case, denominational affiliation of its members. Moses Mendelssohn, father of the Berlin *Haskalah* remained faithful to the religion of his ancestors, and was quite prepared to defend it in his writings against external attacks. His children however, along with many of their Jewish contemporaries, accepted Christianity, though in most cases retaining a link with their original identity, albeit often at the cost of conflicts, tussles with their conscience, and sometimes conversions back and forth. At all events, for all European Jews up to the end of the eighteenth century, the dismantling of ghettoes and other mechanisms of segregation, that signified their social separateness, upset the hitherto prevailing consensus regarding their collective self-definition.

Concomitants of the new identity strategies

The causes of this development may be summed up with a number of observations.

To begin with, over the course of the seventeenth and, even more so, eighteenth centuries there developed what was, in some ways, a historically unparalleled social gulf between those Jews who could get established in the cities of Western and Central Europe (Berlin, Vienna, Frankfurt, London, Amsterdam, Bordeaux), with their legal securities and sometimes even actual privileges, on the one hand, and the main body of Jewry in Eastern Europe, on the other hand. The gulf was manifest in respect to their ways of life, living standards, and levels of social integration and cultural assimilation. Certain sections of urbanized Jewry in the West became partners (and often financial equals or even superiors) of the Christian élite, well before emancipation. For them, further acculturation and, in more favorable cases, admission into the Christian élite were attended by a much smaller measure of self-denial or symbolic sacrifices. Socio–economic advancement, and the prospects of integration into highly prestigious national leading strata that this in itself enhanced, amply compensated for the incidental risks of a loosening of religious and community links. For the first time in European history (at least since the Iberian peninsula's Arabo–Judaic heyday), in the wake of emancipation certain host societies, under the rubric of the broader application of the law and legal equality associated with modernization, formally offered Jews virtually complete socio–economic mobility without demanding in return, as they had earlier, an official breach with their original community. That proposal, what is more, stemmed from prestigious leading circles of states whose cultural heritage was in the process of transition into a 'national' culture. For many Jews in these clusters, all set to integrate, the allures of actively participating in these 'grand' and open national cultures proved stronger than the symbolic advantages anticipated from preservation of the backward-looking Jewish tradition.

It will not be possible here to outline a full historical typology of modern Jewish identity options. It should be emphasized, however, that these new possibilities also entailed a break with the previous practice of identity transmission and confirmation. From then onwards, Jewish identity was passed on less and less as a simple heritage from one generation to the next, but—increasingly – it became a matter of strategic personal or group choice (e.g. proper to families or social strata). The generalization of the optional principle applied to Jewish Orthodoxy as well. Indeed members of communities, officially committed to preserve tradition, were themselves ever more frequently exposed to the temptation of 'deviations,' as well as to the constraint of choosing among various patterns within the Orthodox way of life. In Hungary, for example, there were the dilemmas, nationally speaking, of joining either a rabbinical (western) Orthodox, a Galician type Orthodox, a Hasidic or a *Status Quo Ante* community. In bigger towns (Budapest above all), there was indeed a vast choice between synagogues distinguished by very diverse forms of worship. From the early nineteenth century on, in most European cities, traditionalist and a variety of 'Reformed' communities operated more and more often alongside, competing with one another—whether tacitly or at the cost of open conflicts—to hold sway over souls. Those must also be taken into account here who, quite apart, had converted to Christianity, entered into mixed marriages, or gone otherwise against tradition (for example by 'nationalizing' their surnames), or else, simply by their growing religious indifference—all of whom their Jewish and non-Jewish milieu alike nevertheless continued to consider as still Jewish, if only as being 'of Jewish descent,' 'of Jewish blood,' or 'Jewish at heart' or having a 'Jewish cast of mind.' The range of those affiliated to Jewry in one way or another became vast and diversified to the extreme.

In the European map of Jewish identity options alternative models appeared thus in ever-widening bands, but their adoption continued to be, even at the very personal level, as it were 'overdetermined' by factors tied to the social and communal position of each one concerned. These factors included, obviously, the sectarian options offered by the local Jewish milieu, the cultural and religious heritage of the family, the intellectual capital and academic qualifications obtained by the person concerned, his or her occupational and ideological commitments and constraints as well as his or her specific network of contacts. It is no wonder, then, that the frequently fierce antagonism and competition between adherents of the various models of identity should become and remain (in many respects to the present day) a structural feature of the new situation.

Thus, affiliation strategies in the wake of that development became ever more highly individualized, with at least three types of major consequences worth noting.

First, it was not only communities of divergent persuasions that might find themselves opposed to one another, but school class-mates, neighbors, business partners, members of large families, possibly brothers or—fairly typically—parents and their children, with the different generations reflecting the historical evolution of their identity choices and, at one and the same time, their relationship to inherited identity.

Second, those decisions and strategies related to identity options were liable to change even within a person's life. In most 'assimilationist paths' it is possible to find examples of such modifications as a result of historical experiences. In situations of dire necessity, as in Budapest during the German occupation in 1944, there were converts even from traditionalist Jewish circles, who would have hardly ever thought of baptism before. In this context we can speak about an intra-generational mobility in relation to identity, though inter-generational mobility appeared to occur more frequently. This has its own distinctive conventions and types (for instance, by gender and age, following the parents' life-span, etc.).

Third and last, an individual identity strategy also embodied the possibility of individualizing one's relationship to the accepted pattern of group identity. With everyone concerned thereafter, the choice of an identity could also signify an ever more varied specific experience of that identity. The bigger the social stake of the adopted degree of modernism in identity matters, the more varied were the models of that experience. For both inherited and chosen patterns it holds that these could be sustained actively or passively; one might be ashamed or proud of one's Jewishness, hide it or openly demonstrate it; it might arouse distress and anxiety in the person concerned but equally generate, on occasion, a liberated feeling of joy and satisfaction.

In order to understand the complexity of the situation, it is necessary, first of all, to sketch briefly the chief ideal types of the historical process stemming from assimilation. We can then turn to a few specific manifestations of that process and a discussion of certain forms of assimilationist conduct, liable to be qualified as pathological. That will bring us to problems of the historical crisis of assimilation and the reactions this evoked, the outward forms of which were mapped by modern Jewish nationalism (primarily Zionism) and other ideological models of political dissimilation, or separatism (such as cultural autonomism or the Socialist *Bund*). These all unfolded under the auspices of the modernization of Jewish identity.

Assimilation as an impossible undertaking

The very first, and perhaps the key element of every kind of assimilation process, as already mentioned, was the unilateral rapprochement of Jews to their Gentile environment on terms laid down by the latter. The word 'rapprochement' in this context is used in a restricted sense merely to denote the direction of the change in behavior. The process in reality never comes to an end. Ultimately, an assimilated Jew, appearances notwithstanding, often does not 'change his existence' in order to be 'exactly like every one else' (or in other words, he does not turn into a simple Hungarian burgher, a French senior civil servant, an Italian intellectual or a German patrician), even though the ideological picture of the process, as created by the states promoting assimilation and, equally, by Jews committing themselves to the movement, apparently refute that fact.

There are at least three reasons why the outcome of assimilationist rapprochement, all things considered, is regularly imperfect, defective, or remains incomplete.

The first reason is that, however successful 'unilateral rapprochement' may be, insofar as it produces social actors who really do identify with (chosen) corresponding strata in the majority society, those actors nonetheless continue to preserve a profound consciousness of their otherness, if not otherwise, at least in the form of memory, the recollection of the collectively traversed historical path. They are able to play the part of the Hungarian burgher, French civil servant, etc., because that is what they became at some point in history. But the peculiarity of their social affiliation does not merely lie in their collective memory. The host milieu also regularly makes it clear to them, often in a coarsely brutal fashion. Such outside reminders mostly suffice—especially in historical moments of anti-Semitic threat, even much before the Shoah—for a strong sense of otherness to evolve or persist, even within the framework of what seems, above all 'outwardly,' to be a perfectly well functioning assimilated identity. In reality, the transformation of ideological and objective criteria of af-filiation, however radical and 'successful' it may be, does not, or only exceptionally, alter the life experience of 'assimilees' to such an ex-tent as to make the change in identity complete, through a person's 'forgetting' his Jewish origin. The evidence of the Shoah is a reminder that even what seems to be the most thoroughly accomplished assimi-lation is reversible, especially under the impact of a trauma relating to identity. That can occur even in generations that manage to evade the direct impact of a historical trauma, or amongst whom every objective criterion of the original identity is lacking. Recent decades have pro-vided numerous examples across Europe of how members of genera-tions that have completely lost touch with Jewry, with an assimilation-ist past going back several generations, may return, sometimes to even the most archaic models of their ancestral identity.

The second reason is that the vigor with which the rapprochement came about was far from uniform in every area, nor did it produce uniform results. Even amongst the 'most perfectly' assimilated Jews it is common to discover relics of traditional ways of thinking or behav-ing, at times smothered and suppressed, at others more or less actively admitted or even cultivated. They can be related to models of con-sumption, child-rearing, celebration and mourning or customary eve-ryday conduct (gesticulations, intonations, preferred poses, body lan-guage, eating habits and other aspects of private life). Amongst Jews, as with other secularized communities, these form part of what sur-vives, anthropologically speaking, from an ancient cultural patrimony in modern living conditions. Often the 'give-away' is precisely the fact that new or first-generation assimilated Jews (not differently from all other 'newly assimilated,' of course) scrupulously strive to follow the supposedly prescribed or 'normal' patterns of behavior (e.g. in language usage), and that conformism sometimes backfires in dis-torted 'over-performances,' easily shown up by the host environment. These distinctive models of behavior can sometimes be discerned even amongst remote descendants of assimilees, even though the ones con-cerned may be unaware of the models, or ascribe consciously no significance to them. As has already been noted, one of the historically distinctive features of members of the assimilated Jewish élite in Central Europe is that they were either teetotal or conspicuously more moderate in their drinking habits than their average social equals. Indeed, they were often inclined to justify that abstention on moral grounds, even when copious consumption of alcohol and a generous drinking culture was an integral part of the conventions of the stratum they aimed to assimilate to. It is only in recent times, with the Russification of sorts of Central and Eastern Europe, that this inbred and radical temperance relented in the most assimilated sections of Jews concerned. The fact is observable among immigrants in Israel arriving from the former Soviet Union or its satellites.

The third reason for the impossibility of the rapprochement in question being completed is that assimilation, as we shall see later on, generally consists of Jews—despised, socially excluded, and subordinated on account of their 'alien' nature—doing everything to creatively alter the face of the personality they present to the 'external' and 'internal' public, most often also for enhancing their social class position. Those involved in making the 'rapprochement' will go to whatever lengths seem necessary to achieve that revaluation of their social status. The criteria for success of their strategy, however, are set by the demands of the host society. Failure to meet the expectations of their milieu exposes them to the accusation of not having tried hard enough. If they 'overstep the mark' and start to act too much 'at home,' as if they had been 'born' to their position, that too may be taken amiss. One would consider them as 'parvenus,' 'interlopers,' social 'misfits,' or in other words, people who 'don't know their place.' In the field of assimilationist actions and associations, furthermore, Jews, precisely because of their social position, cannot follow or adopt but certain models of conduct—generally the 'most modern' ones—amongst those current in the target group: in the political arena, for instance, those that are not anti-Semitic—hence the attraction of liberalism or socialism; in the religious domain, those that are tolerant of the practice of Judaism or favorable to converts – hence, among other reasons, a degree of 'overconvertibility' to Protestantism (even in some Catholic dominated societies), etc. Yet these choices do not necessarily correspond to the outlook or values prevalent in the majority of host societies. Consequently, however successfully assimilated Jews may conform to the basic cultural features and expectations of their target groups, the latter may still judge disapprovingly their assimilationist performances.

As a broad generality, assimilationist mobility may assert itself in three forms: the first is acculturation (the learning and adoption of the essential elements of the language, high culture and everyday culture—in the anthropological sense—of the majority society); the second, identification with the political nation of the majority society ('nationalization'); the third, a 'denominationalism,' invariably associated with a certain measure of secularization (the concept of Jewish identity being restricted to the religious domain). Under favorable circumstances these might be supplemented by social integration (more or less secure, harmonious and irreversible) of those committing themselves to assimilation into the target groups. Integration might be associated with apostasy (baptism), mixed marriage, change of surname, adoption of Gentile first names, residential mixing in non-Jewish quarters, attendance of Christian schools, etc. Finally, after the main determinants of social distance between Jews and non-Jews had been eliminated, albeit without that ending the perception of the assimilees as 'different' in the social arena, and it became clear at the same time that the assimilated Jews had reached a more advanced 'stage of modernization' than a large part of the majority society (in bourgeois lifestyles or economic efficiency emulating western patterns, for example), it was possible for 'counter-assimilationist' processes to get under way. Thus the 'assimilated' themselves became, under certain conditions, targets for assimilation, a model group in their own turn, as happened primarily in certain central and east European societies with both big Jewish clusters and heavy deficits of modernization.

Paradigms of rapprochement: acculturation and 'adoptive nationalism'

The initial element of assimilationist mobility, then, comprises acquiring the language and lifestyle of the majority, and adopting the values of the host culture. The chief means for this was formal education, the learning process being associated with living together with Gentiles, cultivating relations with Gentile partners, accepting Gentile cultural norms. Economic and other kinds of cooperation could possibly also have a role alongside that in the acculturation process. Acculturation invariably occurs, if not immediately under explicit pressure from the milieu, then at least under power relations that are unfavorable for the socio–economic and, incidentally, cultural autonomy of Jews. That does not mean, though, that those concerned necessarily experienced that unilateral rapprochement—forced, expected or manifestly obligatory as it may have been, and in any case ranking as a product of symbolic violence—in a negative dimension as suffering, forcible 'deculturation' or 'de-Judaization.' Quite the reverse. Insofar as the acculturation did not bring a person up against elementary group loyalty (e.g. through the odium of constrained 'conversion'), it could be a doubly liberating experience. On the one hand, it could be a liberation from very real obligations in relation to a Jewish way of life and religious practice, perceived as increasingly onerous under modern conditions, as well as a relief from the burden of symbolic otherness. On the other hand, the liberating experience may have been further enhanced by the social advancement that it most commonly served for or promoted. By virtue of his altered mode of life, the 'acculturated' Jew, now in possession of the new linguistic and cultural assets and competence, was able to participate in the most important symbolic achievements of the majority society. From being a despised 'other kind,' he became a real or virtual member of the majority cultural community.

A transformation of that nature presented itself as an especially impassioned experience when, as has been discussed, this took place in a prestigious cultural great power within the symbolic hierarchy of European nations. In Western Europe or Germany, the intellectual capital that had been accumulated in university institutions, scholarly societies, in 'national' literature, artistic and scientific creativity, to say nothing of the prestige of modern statehood in advanced democracies or powerful empires, became potent assimilatory attractions. To switch from Yiddish to French, English, German, or even Russian, would have signified, along with exchanging a 'patois' for an international language, not just participation in the creative worlds of the cultural heroes belonging to recognized high civilizations—that of Molière, Shakespeare, Goethe or Tolstoy. It also signified the desertion of the intimate but closed circle of ghetto culture for the dynamic prospects offered by one of the world's 'leading' civilizations.

The process of creating 'national cultures' only began to unfold in Eastern Europe during the nineteenth century. That is when the political and symbolic apparatus of national statehood was developed and, before all else, local vernaculars started to function via linguistic modernization as 'national languages.' Societies in the East naturally could not exercise as big an 'acculturational attraction' as those of the West. There Jewish cultural integration was justifiable by the prestige of the historical élites—princes, aristocracy and bourgeois stratum—with whose assistance it was possible to enter into socio–economic partnership, and sometimes (as in Hungary or in Prague during the nineteenth century) political alliance, with clusters of the élite implementing programs of modernization. Contributory to the advantages of acculturation in that part of the world were the orientation of the national cultures towards universal values, and their endeavors to catch up with the West. In the late nineteenth century, all these countries saw translated literature start to expand by leaps and bounds, a nationalization of the canons of western civilization, and many cities of Central and Eastern Europe—not Vienna alone but Prague, Budapest, Cracow, St. Petersburg, Warsaw, Lemberg and Odessa as well—themselves became centers of highly original cultural production. The main thrust of cultural integration for the Jews of Eastern Europe turned towards a leading stratum that avowed the same intellectual direction, especially in places (as in the liberal nobility of Hungary or amongst the German bourgeoisie of Prague, etc.) where this did not encounter anti-Semitically motivated rejection. All the while, assimilating Jews were able to keep more than one iron in the fire at once. They could hang on to their multilingualism and western high-cultural values, more particularly as this coincided to a large degree with the scale of values of their new partner groups in Central and Eastern European 'national' élites, many of whom had been trained at western universities and were themselves under the spell of western culture. Whilst a growing part of French, British and German Jewry settled into the 'adoptive national' monolingualism over the course of the nineteenth century, an overwhelming majority of eastern Jews committed to cultural integration remained actively multilingual for successive generations (right up to the Shoah in the case of the élite). In addition to the local language they also spoke German (this was typical of all countries) or French (in Russia, Romania or Poland), and many also retained Yiddish–German for private use (in family circles as a means of communication across generations) or as a lingua franca with co-religionists living in other countries.

In many instances, a considerable degree of linguistic and cultural integration, in the usual anthropological sense of the term, might occur even in Jewish circles that in other respects—particularly religious, but sometimes also as to main elements of their way of life—, remained faithful to their traditions. This happened, for example, in Hungarian Orthodox communities living within Magyar ethnic boundaries, or in some town or other in Bohemia, Galicia, and even Romania. The reason was, that over and above the symbolic gain deriving from such a demonstrative 'nationalized' self-assertion, this was associated with important practical advantages in various fields, like everyday business activities, advanced professional studies and relations with the authorities. The degree of integration liable to be achieved depended on the size of the community, the personal attitudes of the Jewish leadership and the rabbis, residential dispersion, and the acceptance of Jewish acculturation by society at large. In big and tightly knit communities the chances of mass acculturation worsened if the local grandees did not support it or where political anti-Semitism raised its head. In liberal Hungary of the nineteenth century, those factors happened to act, on the contrary, in favor of rapid acculturation. That explains how a 'Hungarian national' reformulation of Jewish identity could occur even in some of the most Orthodox Jewish circles, finding advocates even amongst some Hasidic *rebbes*.

There could have been little question about the direction of cultural integration in western countries regarded (sometimes wrongly, it is true) as ethnically uniform, or on the way of rapid cultural homogenization during the nineteenth century, especially with the introduction of state directed or supervised school systems, teaching in the 'national' language. In Eastern Europe however the same process of 'national' cultural modernization often inevitably created severe conflicts in the not uncommonly multinational populations of nascent nation states. In Hungary, for political reasons that we shall return to later, Jews most often opted for the path of Magyarization, following demands from the hegemonic Magyar élite. In Galicia, which in principle simultaneously offered opportunities for Polish, Ukrainian and German acculturation (the latter being represented, amongst others, by its Austrian public administration and the educated German bourgeoisie of some towns), the Polish orientation turned out to be ever more problematic as the nineteenth century went on under the pressure of intensifying local anti-Semitic agitation. The Jews of Bohemia initially (in the eighteenth and nineteenth centuries) chose German assimilation, which offered the combined advantages of partnership with the locally dominant German urban middle class and of loyalty to the empire. Subsequently however (during the twentieth century, and especially between the two world wars), when the liberal Czechoslovak state guaranteed better circumstances for integration, the link to the Czech nation was reinforced and Czech loyalties prevailed among Jewish identity options. Similar dilemmas of cultural orientation and commitment cropped up during the nineteenth century in the Prussian province of Posen (Poznań, with German and Polish poles of assimilation), in Lithuania (with Lithuanian and Russian poles), in the towns of Ukraine (with Ukrainian and Russian poles), in Trieste (with German and Italian poles), and after the First World War in Slovakia and Transylvania (with the influence of the older Hungarian and German and the new Slovak and Romanian assimilatory pulls, respectively). In every case, Jews, just like all other assimilees, generally solved the problem following the prevailing balance of powers, at least as they perceived it. They opted in favor of the language and culture of the dominant élite groups that appeared to have the greater attraction (for instance, were less anti-Semitic). Often enough, however, an élite consciousness that involved sheer snobbism proved more influential in this domain than real or imagined practical advantages. That explains why, for example, the assimilated Jewish bourgeoisie of Central Europe engaged in, and in some places actually spearheaded the Wagner cult, which in other milieus was a trail-blazer for racist anti-Semitism. Irrespective of that, conflictual situations generally operated as obstacles to the social integration of Jewry.

The most decisive elements of the power relations referred to were of a political hue. The unilateral rapprochement of Jews to their milieu was more likely to be crowned by success in places where, thanks to support from the political authorities, that was accompanied not just by symbolic gain; in other words, where the state assured them protection against anti-Jewish violence, abolished disadvantageous economic discriminations, did not obstruct their social advancement into élite circles, and made it possible to assert themselves in public social, administrative and educational markets, hence in schools, universities, civic societies, political parties, etc. Cultural integration was more complete when a mutual political interest and agreement of Jews and the determining majority served as its basis. That was the case in western countries and, at least partially, though with a highly divergent tenor, in nineteenth-century Germany and Hungary. In those countries, Jewish acculturation was by no means restricted to the cultural and linguistic levels alone but was complemented by an important political aspect too. Its basis was a notion that, whilst leaving Jews in their Jewishness, now regarded their identity as 'national,' and thereby compatible with the projects and interests of the nation state. This new definition of Judaism was grounded on two factors that carried equal weight: its religious uniqueness was retained, but it was stripped of its earlier political concomitants; Jews constituted a religious grouping but not a people or nation. Jews could be affiliated to a national minority, indeed a national entity, and become 'French Israelites' or 'Germans (Hungarians, etc.) of Mosaic faith.' Patriotic identification with the host nation states—or 'adoptive nationalism'—was the chief element in the new model of collective self-interpretation, both in Reform Judaism and in the Jewish neo-Orthodoxy established by Samson Raphael Hirsch in Germany.

The other variant of national–political acculturation, which was not necessarily at odds with this model, can be seen in the Germanization of the Jews of Bohemia and Moravia, which at the same time corresponded to a political and a social class alliance between the German and Jewish middle strata against Czech nationalism in Prague and other cities during the latter half of the nineteenth century. The political projection of that same acculturation was incorporated in the monarchist idealism of the Jewish masses throughout the Habsburg Empire, which persisted in the form of legitimist nostalgia even after the collapse of the empire.

Religious indifferentism and religious reform

Acculturation and political 'nationalization' might, at the same time, assume a distinctively religious guise, inasmuch as these processes were regularly (albeit not universally) accompanied by religious reform movements. It should be recalled that the intellectual progenitors of the *Haskalah* already raised this problem. This is why they proclaimed the importance to minimize the esoteric ritual and intellectual components of Judaism, like the *Talmud* (i.e. those that were the most 'alien' to Christians), and to put its moral teachings to the fore instead in order to reduce the sectarian gulf between Jews and non-Jews. The religious reforms initiated in Germany at the beginning of the nineteenth century, later to be diffused throughout Europe, set themselves two main goals. One was explicitly in the sense of secularization, or 'denominationalization,' in that it cut back the time budget allocated to religious observance and attempted to adapt ritual ordinances to the secular circumstances of a modern way of life. The second was a more or less radical rapprochement to Christian practices of worship. Jewish religious reform can therefore be considered an institutionalized element of acculturation.

Accommodation to the secular surroundings primarily meant that the amount of time devoted to religious observances was reduced. The religious regulation of public and private activities was hence relaxed. This concerned activities as diverse as education, leisure time occupations, sexual and family life or business exercises. Each and every instigator of Jewish religious reform held to this course. Amongst the major reformist ideologues, however, Samuel Holdheim was the only one who advocated wholesale abandonment of ritual conventions that went back to pre-*Talmud* times, on the grounds that these were unworkable and invalid under contemporary conditions. Orthodox leaders who were unwilling to make any concessions over the strict demands of tradition were not entirely unjustified in their mocking of co-religionists who accepted such reforms as '*Kippur* Jews'—people who only observed their faith on high holidays. The other reformist enterprise was obviously directed, though this was not always admitted, at making Jewish religion more 'presentable' in some manner to Christian eyes. During the decades running up to 1848, reform synagogues started to employ organs, to introduce the use of choirs in services, to reorganize the interior layout of the temple on the Christian pattern, and to permit, indeed in many places (as in the case of Hungarian Neology) systematically encourage the use of the national language in sermons.

The reforms provoked interminable conflicts between Orthodoxy and the supporters of reforms, whether moderate or radical. The dissensions eventually spread throughout Europe, with considerable time-lags, perhaps, but always closely on the heels of acculturation and construction as a political 'nation.' Reform communities, that had seceded and become institutionally separated from the Orthodox, were officially recognized by the Hungarian government on the occasion of the 1868 Jewish Congress in Budapest. The German *Reich* adopted a similar liberal legislation in 1878. In the cities of Germany and Hungary (indeed also in Bohemia, Galicia, Bukovina, and some of Russia's Polish and Ukrainian territories) Orthodox and Reform communities thereafter often operated alongside one another (generally self-sufficiently while studiously ignoring one another). The strongholds of Reform Judaism were to be found in the cities of Western and Central Europe, or in the belt of Russian cities outside the 'Pale of Settlement' where, prior to the February Revolution of 1917, only the most acculturated and wealthiest Jews obtained residence permits. At the same time, with the move of parts of the *shtetl* populace into towns, larger and smaller pockets of Orthodoxy began to arise in big cities as well, alongside Reform congregations.

Factors influencing social integration and 'counter-assimilation'

As is evident from the foregoing, the progress of integration, political 'nationalization' and religious reform in opening up the way towards a secular mode of life considerably reduced the social gulf between Jews and non-Jews in post-feudal societies. Opportunities arose for ambitious Jews to enter into social circles, institutions, and occupational spheres appropriate to their proficiencies. Those who had completed their 'assimilationist alignment'—ever-expanding circles of European Jewry in the nineteenth century—now sought to reap the fruits of the efforts they had made to integrate into national societies.

In that matter, however, it takes two to drive a bargain. In other words, the chances of Jews being integrated also depended on the 'integrating party.' The latter term in practice covers manifold social components that did not always have a uniform effect on Jewish integration, although there are demonstrable systematic coincidences between them. Before exploring the discrepancies, it is necessary first to stipulate the general conditions for successful integration.

It has already been established that a unilateral rapprochement by Jews to the majority society was not, of itself, a sufficient condition for success. Cooperation on the part of the hosts was also required for mutual understanding, the assertion of common interests and forms of social intercourse satisfactory to both sides to be able to develop. That process of harmonization was supported by various ideologies of modernization. In the nineteenth century these could be grouped around essentially two types of program (even if, subsequently, this ideological field would become more complex): one had to do with secularism, the other concerned projects for a utopian harmony of future societies, whether that be liberal-democratic, anarchist–egalitarian, socialist or Communist of various sorts in inspiration. A foundation for all these programs was given by universalistic (and usually also secular) values derived from philosophies of the Enlightenment. Conservative utopias, antithetical to the ideals of the *Aufklärung* and also, more often than not, Judaeophobic, would emerge later, particularly in the last quarter of the nineteenth century.

From the Enlightenment onwards, secularization became ever more distinctively one of the acknowledged main trends of modernization in the West. The French Revolution made a first radical break with clericalism, the institution of the Church being invested hitherto with substantial public service and social supervisory functions. In the nineteenth century Western Europe as a whole was moving in the direction of secularization, admittedly with variable determination and success, even in France, the pioneer in this domain. Be that as it may, the prohibitions and restrictive provisions that penalized minority cults lapsed, one by one, and there slowly emerged legal frameworks for freedom of denominational choice, voluntary religious adherence, and freedom of dissent from all creeds. Ever larger groups of the élite and the lower classes extricated themselves from the influence of Churches, at times rejecting it fiercely. A liberal freemasonry, antagonistic to Catholicism and independent of Protestantism, found growing numbers of adherents in Europe's ruling social classes, even in Central and Eastern Europe. Education, family and matrimonial law, and care of the sick and poor had earlier been exclusively ecclesiastical preserves. Even in countries like the Habsburg Monarchy or Germany, where other church privileges, passed down from feudalism were hardly curtailed at all, these functions were now sometimes taken over by secular institutions (thanks to the institutionalization of national school systems, civil marriage and social security provisions, for example). It is typical of this process that from the mid-nineteenth century onwards, national statistics in Britain, France and other secularized countries no longer recorded religious categories. (The complete legal separation of Church and State was actually enacted in France in 1905). One of the most significant achievements of secularization was precisely the elimination of religious differences from public life. It is easy to see, then, how the ideology of secularization and the bodies of civil society that sustained it—freemasonry, liberal parties, socialist movements—would also have served as agencies of the social integration of Jews.

Three qualifications must be noted in connection with that statement, however.

First, not all forces that were fighting for secularization gave unequivocal support to the integration of Jews. It is possible to identify *foci* of outright anti-Semitism in the Proudhonist French socialist movement, and even amongst Marxists, in some masonic lodges as well as certain circles of the French bourgeoisie (not surprisingly, since anti-Jewish views also turn up amongst their intellectual predecessors, the *philosophes* of the Enlightenment). At the end of the nineteenth century, some movements of political anti-Semitism, out of which Nazism was later to grow, exploited the anti-Jewish tendencies of the secularization program touted by right-wing anticlericalism.

Second, even when secularization did not turn into Judaeophobia, in some countries it still envisaged the social integration of secular Jews only. Social acceptance of Jews was thus very much tied to the condition of their advanced level of Jewish secularization. This was tantamount to the exclusion of those who remained faithful to their religious commitments. The secularization of societies, especially in cases where this was associated with extremist political consequences (as with French policies of Jacobinic inspiration), contributed in substantial measure to the de-Judaizaition of Jewish masses. (Elsewhere in Europe, as in Holland or Great Britain, for instance, such pressures were milder, since the secularization of the whole society made only limited progress.) In any event, disparities in the timing of secularization gave rise to growing tensions everywhere in Europe between Jews having converted to a secular way of life and traditionalists. Such conflicts erupted especially at the turn of the century, during and after the First World War, following the immigration of massive waves of Eastern European Jews into France, Britain, Austria (Vienna) and Germany through which the ranks of traditional Orthodoxy were replenished.

Third, secularization benefited only within a certain time span unequivocally to Jewish integration. That varied from country to country, but it generally applied only during the nineteenth century (up to the First World War at the latest). That implies that the integrating role of secularization could change over time, and sometimes even reverse. Strongly permeated though it was with the ideals of liberal freemasonry, the Polish élite, for example, up until around 1863 and the failure of the anti-tsarist uprising, had no objection to entering into an alliance of interests with their Jewish counterparts. So, early Polish nationalism did not obstruct the integration of Jews into Polish society. Later on, however, that same nationalist and, in part, secularized outlook debouched into a furious Jew-hatred, which found expression in organized anti-Semitic boycotts and political agitation at the beginning of the twentieth century. During the inter-war period, the heirs of that trend in the new, independent Poland returned to a church-bound, exclusivist, ethnocentric and xenophobic chauvinism. The Catholic Church thereby assumed the function of the 'national religion,' and Catholicism became a complementary but essential determinant of 'Polishness.'

Modernization of society at large and chances of assimilation

The large-scale programs of social modernization—liberalism, socialism, Communism, and so on—that unfolded in the wake of universalistic teleologies underwent a similar transformation. Most of them were sympathetic at first to the social integration of Jews, but later on (above all in the twentieth century) the plans for the future that they entertained for Jewry began to diverge, with one or another occasionally being perverted into an anti-Semitic movement. The earlier reservations notwithstanding, the fact remains that projects of modernization aimed at secularism (and in this respect it makes no difference whether one is speaking of eighteenth-century absolutist, nineteenth-century liberal or twentieth-century Soviet-style socialist endeavors) all prepared the ground for the social integration of Jews.

This holds especially for those states where the secularization in education, public administration or politics was launched early on. In the Austrian empire, a start was already made on drawing the school system under state supervision in 1777 (following dissolution of the Jesuit teaching congregation), during the reign of the bigotedly Catholic Maria Theresa. During that same period, the principle of religious neutralism was realized in Prussian schooling. As indicated above, a major sustaining force of modernization and social integration amongst Jewry was represented by their admission to public higher education. This was accomplished from the late eighteenth century at an ever more rapid pace in Western and Central Europe, following Emperor Joseph II of Austria's Patent of Toleration and the French Revolution. Indeed the earlier exclusion of Jews from secondary schools and universities was done away with during the nineteenth century everywhere in Europe: Their educational segregation ended even in Russia and Romania during the 1860s (until various *Numerus Clausus* quotas were reimposed a quarter of a century later). During the nineteenth century denominationally neutral western states opened up for Jews the possibility of holding public office and advancing into high political or administrative positions. The presence of Jews amongst middle- and high-ranking state officials in unified Italy, France of the Third Republic, and England was sometimes remarkable (even though it was spread extremely unevenly within the various branches of activity). Jews took full advantage too of the proffered opportunities for getting ahead socially, with some of them, as already noted, rising to the very highest offices in the land. By the early twentieth century, Italy, France, Britain and other countries had appointed Jewish ministers and, in some cases, heads of government. This could demonstrate for Jews the reality of their social integration and justify the costs they had to pay for 'national assimilation.'

Germany and the Habsburg Empire did not pursue with similar determination a program of secularization, but even there, the slower pace of evolution triggered similar effects. In liberal Hungary of the years running up to 1910, despite the 'dual structure' that continued to prevail in the professional markets of the middle classes, Jews were represented in similar, or even somewhat higher, proportions to that in the overall population in most branches of public service. (The proportions were lower in the armed forces, slightly higher in the judicature, in education and in municipal governments). Yet there was just a single minister of the Jewish faith in the entire Monarchy—at its very end at that, due to the extreme liberalism of the new emperor. (This could obviously not happen in imperial Germany, where Jews remained practically excluded from prestigious branches of civil service, like the officer corps.) After legal emancipation, shared political commitment would furnish Jewish and non-Jewish élite groups fresh occasions for cooperation, pooling of ideas and (demographic) intermixing. The organizational means for that were assured by liberal and socialist parties themselves, or the social circles, clubs and civic agencies that often drew their membership from the supporters of those parties (like, typically, freemasons' lodges).

Similarly, outside the sphere of state-related public service, intellectual modernization also created opportunities for cooperation and relations of interest between Jews and non-Jews that favored social integration. Secularization had a liberating effect on social intercourse that in the past had so often been impeded by a heavy burden of religious exclusivity, discrimination and segregation. From the end of the eighteenth century it had already been possible for Jews, according to their wealth, cultural capital or professional position, to gain admittance to some salons of the upper-middle class and high state officials in Berlin, London or Paris. Indeed, the more 'enlightened' of the non-Jewish members of such circles began to visit the higher-ranking Jewish salons, such as those of Moses Mendelssohn or the renowned 'socialites' Henrietta Herz, Rachel Varnhagen, and Dorothea Schlegel. Important amongst the wide range of purchase points for integration were shared economic interests in stock exchanges, professional associations of lawyers, physicians and engineers, and chambers of commerce and industry. Many of these, especially in the liberal West but sometimes even in Central Europe, retained their 'mixed' and 'integrating' character right up to the rise of Fascism (in Hungary only up to 1918).

Gradually, though, there was no longer any need for formal means of integration. Religious, ethnic, and sometimes even class differences tended to count for less and less in places of everyday relations and communication. The walls of ghettos were often physically dismantled as well, and if a certain degree of residential separation of Jews might continue to be observed, that was a voluntary rather than imposed self-segregation, and it increasingly diminished. In the cities of Western and Central Europe, Jews started, bit by bit, to abandon the quarters earlier reserved for them and to disperse to other residential suburbs. This process followed their upward social mobility in the middle classes. Sometimes it also gave rise to new, densely Jewish-populated quarters and neighborhoods due to the intensity of the social life of those residing there. Such development of residential self-segregation obviously depended on the access opportunities offered by the non-Jewish milieu in the locality as well. From this point on, proximity in fact became an important social factor in integration. Apart from denominationally mixed schools—these were perhaps less prevalent in elementary education but certainly predominated at the secondary level throughout the West, but usually elsewhere too—playgrounds, amusement places, dance schools as well as sports halls and grounds often had just as important a role in this process. Denominational intermixing, as has already been discussed, thus became increasingly generalized throughout nineteenth-century Europe, especially in the public space of cities: promenades, parks, coffee-houses, restaurants, theatres, swimming pools, and other venues.

To give a sense of the dimensions of the historical path that had been traveled, it is sufficient to recall that settlement by Jews in many towns outside the West was prohibited from the fifteenth century right up till the period of emancipation, and even where it was permitted, that was mostly in exchange for special levies and under extraordinarily finicky and strict conditions, usually with the 'tolerated' having compulsory dwelling places designated for them (ghettos). In the feudal era, almost everywhere, officially 'tolerated' Jews were forbidden to set foot in the Christian districts of towns on Sundays and holidays, for example; even in such an 'enlightened' city as Frankfurt am Main that prohibition was only annulled in 1798. In the Papal States the walls of the ghettos, the gates of which were closed overnight, were only pulled down in 1848, but the obligation to live in the ghetto (albeit not the nightly locking-up) was reimposed later on in Rome for a period, so that this drastic restriction remained in force right up until the unification of Italy was accomplished. The fading of, or growth of indifference to, religious boundaries in everyday life was therefore a novel and important milestone for Judeo–Christian relations in the nineteenth century.

Rather than picking up pace after emancipation, however, this trend tended to slow across the entire central zone of the continent, from France to Russia, starting in the 1880s and 1890s, under the pressure of increasingly strong anti-Semitic movements, and came to a complete halt, at least for a while, with the growth of Fascism between the two world wars.

'Counter-assimilation'

Having looked at the main processes of assimilation, like accultura- tion, political 'nationalization' and social integration, it is now neces- sary to refer to a phenomenon observable in all countries that vigor- ously pushed for and achieved that assimilation, namely, a reaction to assimilation, which may also be described as a 'counter-assimilation.'

Up to this point, we have had to emphasize how strongly assimila- tion was tied to conditions, dependent on power relations over which the Jews themselves had little control, as well as the very one-sided character of the change in Jewish identity. It is now time to draw attention to some of the paradoxical repercussions in host societies of differential modernization of Jews and Gentiles. If the emphasis hitherto has been placed on the mostly uneven power relations to the detriment of Jews in the process of assimilation, it is necessary now to clarify how host societies reacted to the fact that the moderni- zation of Jews generally turned out to be more rapid and successful than their own.

Since assimilation generally occurred within a framework of mod- ernization of society as a whole (or at least during the course of some degree of modernization of majority élites in terms of secularization and 'bourgeois' professional mobility /*Verbürgerlichung/*), the con- spicuous success of Jews along these lines—whether that is attributed to 'compensation,' 'in-built cultural capital' or skills drawn from other resources—, regularly drew a line of demarcation between Jewish and non-Jewish clusters belonging to the same occupational and social circles as to the level of modernity they had actually achieved. That difference was objictified in many ways. In Central Europe one can refer to differences in terms of foreign language capital, familiarity with western civilization and high culture, receptivity to universalistic salvation ideologies, entrepreneurial and innovative flair, quality of housing, etc. On the strength of such differences Jews could become from assimilees model agents of assimilation, as potential moderniz-ers. They could offer for an example to follow their accumulated as-sets of 'modernity.' That is why assimilated Jews everywhere, but of course much more conspicuously so (just by virtue of their demo-graphic weight, for a start) in the more backward countries of Central and Eastern Europe, rather than in the West, could be perceived to be often actively instrumental in the modernization of their host societies themselves.

One can distinguish at least three major areas for these sorts of 'counter-effects' of assimilation: 'adoptive nationalism,' intellectual and mental as well as techno–economic modernity.

The adoption of nationalism ('guest nationalism') was typical of Jews in both Western and Central Europe. During the nineteenth cen-tury, assimilated Jews reached accommodations of interest with some of the national élite groups that had instigated political modernization (e.g. the bourgeoisie of the French Third Republic or the liberal nobil-ity of Reform Era Hungary), in the sense that they took the project of nation state building as their own. In order to bring the project of a Hungarian political nation-state into being, members of the Ma-gyarized Jewish middle class, for example, actively pushed for forcible Magyarization of the local Slovak majority in Upper Hungary after the 1867 Compromise. In response, the 'awakening' Slovak na-tionalists acted even more antagonistically towards Jews, heaping politically motivated Hungarophobia on their traditional anti-Jewish attitudes. The same logic explains why many Frenchified Alsatian Jews continued to back the French cause in Alsace–Lorraine itself or in their 'emigrant' circles in Paris after the German occupation of the territory in 1871. Jewish young men fought with equal enthusiasm and nationalist convictions in defense of their chosen homelands on the First World War battlefronts right across Europe. Many examples could be listed of how the 'assimilated' offered the right hand of a fellow combatant to their 'assimilators' in some of their most chauvinistic political ventures.

The reaction to assimilation is perceptible in even more general terms in the model of bourgeois ways and manners that Jewish circles of the professional, commercial or industrial middle classes—educated and completely 'nationalized' culturally (e.g. in their language), yet more 'westernized' and partially secularized in their mentality—offered to semi-feudal societies of Central and Eastern Europe. Undoubtedly, a concurrence of two historical phenomena played a part in this: on the one hand, the lack or frailty of a bourgeoisie (modern middle class) in the majority or host society and, on the other hand, the predominantly— and many places markedly—'modern middle-class' stratification of Jewry in the late nineteenth century. The upshot of deficiencies in modern professional social mobility ('bourgeoisification') on the Christian side and 'over-bourgeoisification' on the Jewish side was that what could be considered 'modern' elements of mentality and behavior— which were usually developed or acquired by the educated middle classes first and foremost—were either promoted or mediated by assimilated Jews on the basis of foreign (usually western) patterns. There are numerous telltale signs, and not just in the economic and political arena, but also in such domains as child-rearing (the introduction of new pedagogical methods, the culture of academic excellence), demographic behavior (birth control, the model of the 'nuclear family' consisting of just parents and a small number of offspring), housing conditions (better standards of comfort, modern furniture), hygiene, urban sports, suffrage for women, and the introduction of new female roles (performed by the educated, independent, sexually liberated and professionally active women), amongst others. As discussed above, some of the revolutionary changes in twentieth-century mentalities – due to psychoanalysis, for one—were directly, and for a long time almost exclusively, associated with assimilated Jewry.

Last of all, since many Jews perfected their knowledge and acquired much expertise in new middle-class activities in the course of assimilation, they could be the pioneers or initiators of various new technologies, management techniques, political ideologies, or even entire scientific disciplines and branches of enquiry, again principally in Central and Eastern Europe. There, Jews are acknowledged to have had a decisive role in transmitting and importing essential intellectual goods from the West. This was due, as discussed earlier, to their knowledge of languages, their 'international contacts' cultivated via family diasporas, and the fact that their economic élite groups in Europe, since the very beginnings of modernization, had remained active in maintaining avenues of commercial relations between states. Classical Jewish competences as economic intermediaries could be converted, unexpectedly, into modernizing functions proper, in the framework of the 'counter-assimilationist' importation and introduction of intellectual, mental and other assets of modernity.

Self-denial and conversion: a forced path of assimilation

Deep as the imprint that assimilation may have left at times on the modernization of 'assimilating' societies, within Jewry, at any rate, it most frequently manifested itself in forms of behavior that, whilst individual, conformed to collective patterns and signified a more or less radical break with traditional identity. Of these, it is worth studying somewhat closely three in particular, that can be tracked in certain European countries on the strength of fairly accurate quantified evidence: conversion to Christianity, mixed marriage, and nationalization of surnames. These are strategic acts of assimilation that, though showing a strong statistical correlation with one another, each in its own right carried a specific weight in the assimilatory rapprochement between Jews and non-Jews. At the same time, all three should be classed as 'negative' patterns of conduct—modes of 'self-denial' of sorts—since they all are public demonstrations of a breach with and a refusal of traditional Judaism. The actual achievement of the status mobility—as expected from assimilation—did not absolutely necessitate any of these steps in most circumstances (especially in the West). So it would be more accurate to say that they represent an 'over-fulfillment' of assimilationist demands. Far from uncommon though they may be in certain situations, they have to do with extremist strategies. It is therefore worth examining the circumstances under which they might be resorted to.

Of all these strategic actions under discussion, conversion to the Christian faith or formal desertion of Judaism is the most unequivocally 'negative' in character. In the symbolic field of assimilation it amounts to 'betrayal,' to 'going over to the enemy's camp,' even if, at a later historical phase (for the most part, commencing after the Shoah), following a partial decoupling of the definition of Jewish identity from religious Judaism (in Communist or post-Communist states, for example), this negative significance could be attenuated. In this late phase and in borderline cases, a Christian religious status may be reconcilable with even a strong sense of Jewish identity. Historically speaking, though, that latter situation not only emerged late, but involved only small brackets of those affected. Prior to that, Jewish communities could place no other interpretation on it than as an odium-laden, shameful desertion of the endangered faith, given that it occurred most often in periods of mounting pressure on Jews, (as discussed in the chapter on demography), especially when such pressure reached critically high levels. True, converting Jews could always cite a change of religious beliefs as the public justification for their act, that being a potent legitimating argument in an era of individualism, but their motivations have a whiff of interests that are very much of the moment, as is not uncommonly discernible from the actual accounts given by those concerned. More light is likely to be thrown on conversions to Christianity by a brief historical typology, however sketchy, of the real social reasons than by the declared motivations of the converts themselves.

In investigating this topic, the historian has recourse to data that are of extremely variable reliability from country to country and period to period (remarkably little information is available from early secularized western countries). Nevertheless it is possible to dissect out at least three types of motivation. The main reasons for conversion to Christianity, according to these data, are flight from threat, followed by a 'strategic' change of faith destined to secure certain socio–economic advantages (expected from status mobility, consistently with the very logic of assimilation), and lastly, in fairly rare cases, a step due to purely religious, spiritual conviction. These reasons may supplement one another in a range of variants, of course, but the first can be shown statistically to be the most pressing of them (with the second coming next). If that were not the case, waves of conversions would not track so closely the intensification of anti-Jewish pressure and crises of anti-Semitism. In all countries for which reliable data are available for annual trends in the numbers of converts over the long term (as in the states of Central Europe), it can be shown that the overwhelming bulk of twentieth-century Jewish converts left the faith of their ancestors during years of anti-Jewish hysteria. In Hungary, more such switches occurred in the two years 1919 and 1920 (an average of over 4,500 in both years) than had taken place over the previous twenty years (when the annual average was just 440). Likewise, over the period 1938–1942, the first five years that the so-called 'Jewish Laws' were in force, the rate of conversions (at an annual average of 4,920) was six and a half times what it had been during the 'Christian–national' period from 1921 to 1937 (773 per year)—which itself had not been lacking in anti-Semitic pressures. What may be gathered from this is that the explanations for turning to Christianity are by no means as simple as one might be led to suppose on the basis of the interpretations given by those concerned or their opponents.

To start with, since conversions most often occurred in response to external pressure, the role of genuine religious 'conviction' could, perforce, only be slight, if present at all. Although there are known 'converts' who became enthusiastic proselytes of Christianity, such cases were rare. Forced and 'strategic' conversion alike had the substitution of social status as a Jewish for that as a Christian as its goal, first and foremost. In analyzing that swap, it is necessary to take into account, as those implicated normally did, how the balance of anticipated gains and costs was likely to turn out. Amongst the possible advantages and losses—a full listing of all the factors cannot be attempted here—one should consider the symbolic returns of 'putting down roots' in, or joining, a new religious and social milieu, the specific opportunities it opened up for getting ahead (economic, social, matrimonial, etc.) via integration into the new denominational community. Equally, one should not overlook the possible losses that conversion may bring at the time or in the foreseeable future. Acceptance and instigation of the switch to Christianity are only likely to take place when the anticipated benefits outweigh the drawbacks—rational considerations that are at total odds with the idealism of piety. Forced or strategic conversions conform much more with the logic of social interests. For that reason, most of them implicitly also signified a break from religious observance, either preparing the way for a process of secularization or directly marking its close. In that case we are dealing simply with an act that aimed at 'normalizing' one's social position, the precipitating cause consisting in the fact that Judaism was at variance with the majority's norm, or frankly roused its disapproval.

It is clear from the logic of secularization why those contemplating conversion, particularly in countries with a Catholic majority (such as Austria or Bohemia–Moravia), should tend to favor Protestantism (as compared to the negligible numerical strength of Protestants), even though the social returns for choosing Catholicism would be a good deal more 'rewarding.' The chief denominations of the Reformation were themselves in a minority position in Catholic countries, albeit still within the 'Christian norm.' Conversion to one of the Protestant Churches therefore assured the key benefits associated with Christian status without attracting the same degree of odium of 'going over to the majority' as Catholicizing would. Besides that, the practice of most of the Protestant Churches, from the nineteenth century onwards, permitted a greater measure of internal secularization than Catholic parishes. Conversion to Protestantism, moreover, entailed surmounting a much smaller 'ritual distance' for those who still felt a need to practice a religion. The absence of a holy iconography and a cult of intermediary saints, the emphasis placed on the Bible, especially the weight of Old Testament references, including a stress on monotheism, etc. are common to radical Protestantism and Judaism.

Second, the outcome of conversion in regard to a person's social position and affiliation (just as with self-assessment) always remained ambiguous. New believers received into the bosom of a Christian Church are often ringed about by an air of suspicion or mistrust, and they may be expected to 'merit' their acceptance by furnishing evidence of the sincerity of their faith. That expectation may be disconcerting for Jews who were usually more open to a secular outlook, especially when they converted for 'strategic' reasons, and could hit even harder those who have converted under duress. It may have driven them into maneuvering, seeking opportunities to eschew their new religious obligations, or at least reaching an acceptable compromise with their milieu in this matter. In western countries with secular arrangements, France of the Third Republic being the exemplar, it was a relatively easy matter to achieve such a compromise. They merely had to fit into anticlerical circles, which would welcome them with open arms, thereby putting the cap on their choice of secularization and abandoning any sort of public worship. That is why masonic lodges and anticlerically inclined republican, socialist, radical agencies of civil society as well as liberal movements and parties exercised such a great attraction, not only for secular but also converted Jews. A more moderate variant of maintaining one's distance from the adopted religion was to restrict the observance of conventions solely to religious consecration of the main rites of passage—birth, marriage and burial.

Equally, and independently of that, the social acceptance of converted Jews was itself equivocal. For reasons that are readily understandable from the foregoing, those converted to Christianity, perceived this as an act of conformism driven by self-interest. Other Jews understandably would often maintain a reserve towards them or put them in a separate category. That could also apply to Jews having merely taken the path of secularization. As a result, if the converts came into conflict with their new milieu, the latter could at any time dig up the matter of their 'origin' and, indeed, disparage them for it. The fear that a Jewish background was being kept on record might haunt a family for several successive generations, always bubbling to the surface at times when anti-Semitism was gaining ground. An example of this paradox is supplied by the fact that the only way the conservative, but also anti-Nazi, political camp in Hungary was able to get rid of prime minister Béla Imrédy in 1939, a right-wing extremist and one of the chief authors of the 'Jewish' laws, was by obtaining proof that one of his remote ancestors had been of Jewish descent. Imrédy, allegedly, collapsed under the accusation and immediately resigned from his post (only to rejoin later the pro-Nazi government in 1944). Under such circumstances, then, the official adoption of Christianity was, in most cases, unable to alter the experience of being Jewish, and all the less so that the behavior of those from the abandoned religious environment—immediate family, friends, clients, neighbors and acquaintances—would also provide a standing reminder of what, when all things considered, was still the shameful essence of the conversion (whether forced or 'strategic'). A breach with the denominational bonds of Judaism was, therefore, usually far from marking a complete end of the social experiences that went with Jewish identity. For one thing, a baptized Jew was hardly ever able to 'wash off' the fact that he had only 'converted' as an adult; for another, he was obliged to come to terms with the usual consequences of his action, the threat of 'falling between two stools.'

Conversion, mixed marriage, 'nationalization' of surnames

Those difficulties might, no doubt, be counterbalanced or compensated for by a sense of liberation or (for those who converted out of 'conviction') spiritual elation, or else by the symbolic and, in some cases possibly, material gains (e.g. new career opportunities) that would derive from meeting the majority norm. Most of those concerned (unlike those converting on 'spiritual' grounds) would however be unable to make a success of their 'rootedness' in the new religion. In the case of adults, that would often not be the intention anyway, even though they would usually (at least in weakly secularized countries) make an effort to raise their children in the faith of the majority. For those who had distanced themselves from faithful Jewry, and yet found they were not fully accepted by their Christian milieu either, usually all that was left in regard to their symbolic (and most commonly also social) integration into majority society were constrained courses of action. For the most part, these may be classified into two categories.

They might make a break 'forwards,' towards identity options offered by universalistic and secular ideologies, by accepting the world view, underlying ways of thinking as well as conditions for integration of circles and agencies (e.g. political movements or parties) professing such philosophies. That is why so many joined liberal freemasonry and likewise the socialist, Communist, Esperantist and pacifist movements, or other currents with universalistic or/and humanist claims. Such movements were indeed generally open to all groups and social strata. In fact they appealed mostly to those struggling with difficulties of social integration. Some of them—notably tightly knit underground organizations that aimed at overthrowing current political régimes, or the cliques vying for power in the Soviet Union—called for ideological, political and emotional commitment of an intensity equal to that of the highest degree of integration into a traditional community. To be sure, blind, fanatical acceptance of those trends, and the unqualified loyalty they could inspire, was very comparable to the sort of 'primordial bonds' for which only religious communities provide a basis.

The other constrained solution was to identify oneself with others 'tarred with the same brush,' that is to say, converts to Christianity, mixed married couples, or those with ambivalent identities for other reasons. This often leads to the emergence of close-knit circles of friends, partners and neighbors who keep company and are always able to come up with some 'common denominator' in order to overcome the standing risk of 'losing touch' with their proper place, and hence of social isolation. It could happen, then, that Jews who had voluntary left the ghetto would create another kind of self-made, 'in-between' ghetto, unwilling, even as a formality, to surrender their honestly held identity commitments, particularly in countries and historical situations where, through a lack of secularization, religious affiliation retained its social effectiveness. The identity that their descendants received as a heritage would be weak in every respect, and for that reason they would sometimes be driven to far more compromising opportunism or more strenuous 'searching for roots.'

The position of those living in mixed marriages would be similar in many respects as to their self-perception or self-assigned identity, all the more so as such heterogamy often led to the Jewish partner becoming sooner or later Christianized, though examples of the opposite—of the Christian partner, more usually the wife, becoming Jewish—did also occur. This type of 'Christianized,' to avoid the official label of a mixed marriage, might take place either before or after the marriage ceremony. This was a widespread practice in non-secularized countries, where 'mixed' marriages offended the norm of religious uniformity, or at least represented an exception that was to be avoided.

Mixed marriages nevertheless had a different rationale from baptism, even though, statistically, they affected virtually the same circles of assimilated Jews. Admittedly, from the viewpoint of Judaic commitment, mixed marriage was seen as almost comparably damageable for Jewry as conversion to Christianity, because it resulted in just the same weakening of the religious community, by breaking the continuity of the chain of descent and the group's physical reproduction. That statement actually holds, historically, for the majority of cases up to the Shoah, though it might happen that the children would later enter the Jewish community. Sometimes even a reversionary clause in the marriage contract (e.g. the one introduced in Hungary in the 1894 law that made a civil ceremony compulsory for all marriages) might properly stipulate that any offspring were to be brought up in the Judaic faith. (In practice, in most cases the stipulation in question, an option in the marriage contract, was made in favor of the Christian upbringing of would-be offspring.) Mixed marriages, at any rate, provided concrete examples that integration was possible. Both partners to the marriage accepted the other in his or her otherness, even if they could protect themselves, later on, from the social ordeal of official heterogamy by one of the spouses converting to the other's religion. In the first instance they jointly accepted the 'dual' social affiliation of their offspring. Besides that, they would also make an attempt to pool, and together exploit, the network of contacts and alliances (their 'social capital') that each brought as 'dowry' from their respective extended families and circles.

In the latter undertaking, more often than not, they would expose themselves to the risk of failure, depending on how decisive group interests appeared embedded in the religious and 'interreligious' (i.e. manifesting in relations between Jews and non-Jews) spheres. That naturally applied more in social circles and countries backward in secularization (as in pre-Communist Eastern Europe). In Orthodox Jewish families it was not uncommon, as already noted, to conduct public mourning ceremonies for one of their number having entered a mixed marriage, just as for converts to Christianity. They expressed thereby, for their part, the irreversible nature of the break with them. Negative reactions might be just as acute in families that had already practically abandoned the practice of Jewish faith, but still cherished strong links of identity with Jewry. Both partners in mixed marriages had often to accept the risk of a similar 'social death sentence' on the side of the Christian relatives as well (the weight of which, in terms of their proneness to exclude a couple, would again be a function of the rigidity of that community's sense of self-identity). Families that rejected mixed marriages would cite as justifiable counter-arguments the difficulties of social integration that were to be expected for the couple, the conceivably higher risk of divorce and the difficulties of bringing up children with dual identities. (The latter argument could be actually instrumental in the inclination of mixed couples to restrict drastically the size of their family, so that more protection could be

extended to offspring who had to go through the sometimes not uncommonly cruel experience of 'dual' descent). Thus, the same danger
of becoming isolated, and thus having to live with split identities, rent
by inner conflicts, in a sort of social no man's land, would be lurking
for mixed couples, just as for persons converting to Christianity under
duress or for 'strategic' reasons. (Similar strains could be weaker for
converts out of religious conviction.)

For many assimilated Jews, the 'nationalization' of family names
was likewise regarded as a milder form of 'self-denial' of sorts. Both
Jews and non-Jews alike tended to be much more lenient over that
than they were over mixed marriage or conversion, and for several
reasons. In the Jewish world, names rarely carry a strongly distinctive
connotation (except in the case of the sacral functions associated with
the Kohanim and Levites). Indeed, for broad groups of Jews of Central and Eastern Europe many of the 'typically Jewish' family names
were actually products of the whims of state authorities, as in many
places the adoption of fixed surnames, often selected quite arbitrarily,
was made compulsory at some stage or another during the modernization of administrative systems (in 1787 in the Habsburg Monarchy, for
instance). For that reason, from the very outset, they did not carry the
same significance for those concerned as the symbolic patrimony of
ancestry in noble or even other families of patrician or otherwise
middle class background. That obviously had a part in explaining why
many Jews perceived 'nationalizing' their name as one of the least
illegitimate ways of constructing a 'modern' identity, a token adoption
of a purely symbolic or demonstrative 'guest nationalism,' indeed an
act of conformism that did not contravene essential Jewish traditions.

Indeed, waves of name changes of greater or lesser import occurred
at those points in time when broad swathes of Jews who had settled in
a country accepted liberally disposed assimilationist programs. That
was the case in most western countries and in Hungary throughout the
nineteenth century. But in the West, like France for instance, such
demonstration of symbolic nationalism was never seriously expected,
let alone enforced. In Hungary, Jewry was part of a wider movement
of name nationalization ('Magyarization') that the authorities not only
supported but on more than one occasion, actively initiated and organized, with mandatory effect for civil servants and other state employees. This was the case during the government of Dezső Bánffy, fol-

lowing the country's millennium in 1896, or the post–1933 Gömbös era, marked by decisively proto-Fascist nationalist policies. An indication of the extent to which Jews shared an interest for the movement is offered in the statistic that they made up close to 60 per cent surname Magyarizers between 1894 and 1918. Since they were rarely among civil servants and other state employees, who could be forced to do so, it is reasonable to suppose that Jews were among the most 'voluntary' participants in the movement with an over-representation of around ten times their proportion in the population.

Possibly no reminder is needed that even the purely linguistic stake in changing to a 'national' name was far less important in Germanic, Scandinavian and Anglo-Saxon countries, where the Ashkenazi nomenclature of the bulk of Jewish immigrants did not jar so markedly with the national stock of names. Hence such moves to nationalize appeared mostly in non-Germanic countries of strong assimilation (like inter-war Estonia, for instance). To some degree, the weak interest for surname nationalization also applied to Sephardic Jewry—historically the majority within Jewry in Latin countries. In any event, it can be concluded that, in places for which thorough surveys on the subject are available (Hungary, for example), 'naturalization' of the family name did play a part in the success of assimilation and other strategies planned or implemented for social advancement. Although it was mostly Jews who had set off down the path of assimilation who provided its social base, a smaller fraction of Orthodox Jewry also effected changes of name. That was certainly much less likely to spark off discord over religious affiliations than other, more radical modifications of formal identity or relinquishing tradition.

Crises of assimilation as psychic disturbance and traumatic experience

As has already been mentioned, the process of voluntary assimilation was associated not just with disengagement from communal bonds and a release from oppressive social degradation, but also with subordination to new norms, which, after the initially uplifting but often illusory satisfactions of success, might well discharge into an experience of failure and frustration. Many Jews, longing to achieve assimilation, experienced occasionally both aspects, either successively or even simultaneously. So marked is this phenomenon that two periods may be in this respect distinguished in European history, with the positive experience of assimilation coming to the fore in the first, the negative experience in the second.

The first developmental phase, then, was an essentially positive or optimistic contact with assimilation. Precedents for this were to be found in launching the *Haskalah* movement and elaborating programs of emancipation. Palpable manifestations of the latter can be perceived in the Josephinist integrationist measures that came into force in Austria–Hungary during the 1780s, or the first ever laws to grant civil rights to Jews enacted in France and Holland in the 1790s. Where this type of assimilation took place, it neither came into conflict with the dominant ideology of the key host circles—the western and Scandinavian élites, the German bourgeoisie of Bohemia, the liberal nobility of Hungary, the 'new strata' fighting for the country's unification in Italy—nor were the Jews in question skeptical about the idea of participation in the process of nation-building and socio–economic modernization. The situation was the most complex in Germany, in that there political unification was, finally, executed not by the liberal camp, the secularization process stalled during the period of imperial rule, and implementation of other aspects of the modernization program occurred by big fits and starts, whilst an ethnocentric, if not outright racist, exclusivist nationalism took hold early on. That greatly narrowed down the circle of partner groups willing to accept the assimilation of Jews unreservedly. Eastern Europe does not even enter the frame, since neither Russia nor Romania instituted western-style programs of assimilation. Even discounting these exceptions, growing masses of Jews took over the idea of assimilation during the nineteenth century, placing their trust in its in-built historico–teleological promise of an imminent solution to the entire 'Jewish Question.'

The initial impetus carried on only up to the turning-point of the 1870s and 80s, however. That decade saw the rise of political anti-Semitism across the whole of Europe. An increasingly violent Judaeophobia emerged and generated major political crises, all but foreshadowing the later historical phases of anti-Semitism. To make matters worse, it happened precisely in countries where assimilation had seemed to be proceeding with the greatest success. One has in mind here republican France, where the final decade of the century was overshadowed by the crisis provoked by the Dreyfus Affair, or how the political climate of triumphant national liberalism in Hungary was poisoned, albeit only temporarily, by the anti-Semitic disturbances that accompanied the Tiszaeszlár 'show trial' of ritual murder calumny (1882–83). Assimilation kept on going ahead, of course. Indeed it even speeded up in some countries, such as Hungary, Italy or the (lightly Jewish-populated) Scandinavian states. But from then onwards, the outcome of the assimilationist process was marked by uncertainty and doubts multiplied about its success. Skepticism and disillusionment at the prospect of the obstacles, piling up in the way of assimilation, henceforth limiting the effects of the movement. This was a period in which paths became both muddled and diversified. The upcoming crisis of national assimilationism deflected ever greater numbers of Jews, earlier committed to the assimilationist ideal, from their original choice. More and more of them were swept 'beyond assimilation,' that is, either towards leftist and revolutionary universalistic utopias (socialism and Communism) or towards Jewish nationalism.

Even those Jews who plumped for philosophies of universal or ethnic prosperity, however, were at one with their more skeptical compeers in sensing that, whatever real successes may have crowned their integration into what were often Europe's most cultivated and prestigious élite circles, their assimilation was no more than a route-march that had lost its direction, a fundamentally tragic experiment, doomed to fail. Indeed the popularity of such universalistic utopias, in itself, was a product of the frustration of national assimilation, which only enhanced the fervor of their adoption.

Previously, there had been basically two courses of action available for Jews, with regard to their affiliation. The first one pointed 'ahead' (towards 'progress' and a correspondingly reformulated Jewish identity), the other 'backwards' (towards tradition). From the latter half of the nineteenth century on, similar choices started to proliferate. That alone complicated all subsequent identity strategies, not just because hope in a comprehensive, unqualified, and irreversible integration into European societies had faded away, but also because competition between the proffered 'solutions,' each more extreme than the last—a return to Zion, ethnically based class war, revolutionary struggle for universal happiness—increased the pessimistic conviction that no helpful solution to the matter of Jewish identity should be counted on in the foreseeable future. From that juncture, the assimilationist experience began to lose its previously unequivocally positive character, becoming instead an option of uncertain outcome. Those concerned were forced to concede, however painful that might be, that their degree of assimilation already attained might be thrown into question and rescinded at any moment.

With the deepening crisis of assimilation in the late nineteenth century, all forms of modern Jewish identity became saddled with some kind of psychic disturbance. These transformed the assimilationist drive into a potentially traumatic experience. The pathologies proper, which arose from it, occupy a place on a scale running between the two extreme types of identity concept: one had to do with an obsessional, paranoid cult of the collective self, the other boiled down in self-hatred.

The culture of self had its own historical merits, but the ideological realm and collective imagination of the newly established nation states of Central and Eastern Europe, small and large, were no strangers to pathological fears of external aggression or, indeed, destruction and 'national death.' A common method of abreacting to these was to paint a diabolical picture of neighbors, and show their intentions and policies in a bad light. Throughout this part of the world, in order to create or reinforce internal solidarity, the ideologies of nation-building play on dread of external enemies and internal aliens. Poles have their fear of the Russians, Ukrainians and Germans; Romanians, theirs of Hungarians, Bulgarians and Poles; Hungarians, theirs of being 'engulfed' amidst 'Slavic hordes,' Ottoman power, and Germanic expansion, and so on. Some of those countries—Poland, Lithuania, Czechoslovakia, Bulgaria, Serbia and, in part, Hungary too—did actually undergo the historic experience of seeing their medieval state torn apart and drawn into a hegemonic foreign empire. Thus, genuine precedents for 'national death' were very much alive in collective memory in those countries. Modern nationalism could hence appear there as promoting a national 'renaissance' and, indeed, 'regeneration' (in much the same way as Jews embarking on the path of modernization regularly used that expression from the time of the *Haskalah* onwards). Equally, it is common to find the discourses of nation-building bringing up the great 'historical errors' that have been committed, as

well as 'weaknesses' and other negative aspects of the national character lying heavy on collective conscience. Pathological self-veneration
as well as (to a lesser extent) self-loathing, then, are mental dispositions and disorders that, during the nineteenth century, were present
not just in Jewish communities. Assimilated Jews over much of
Europe, however, having no means of defense at their disposal, were
obliged to deal with very real violent crowds or face the vicious hostility of Judaeophobic newspapers. All this undoubtedly reinforced the
sense of danger and helped pathological reactions to develop. Without
dwelling on the images of collective narcissism, a cult of collective
self, as constructed in nationalist imagery, became general in movements of political and cultural autonomy amongst Jewry just like
amongst other peoples.

Self-hatred appeared to be however far more characteristic in the
Jewish setting during the nineteenth century, to such a degree that it
may be regarded as the typical pathological product of assimilation. It
might be encountered in at least two forms—one projected onto fellow
Jews, the other asserting itself inwardly, in the self-image of assimilated Jews.

Assimilated Jews had an aversion to their past, which did no favors
for their present contacts and future plans. They would have liked,
after all, to emerge from the 'darkness,' from the past. This was why
they could experience the progress of assimilation as a sort of redemption. They recalled with horror the oppressive burden of ghetto
life, and the torments they had suffered there, although the denial of
collective past might sometimes be compounded by dashes of nostalgia. That led to resentment towards those who had stayed there. Traditionalist Jews, on the one hand, could never be seen with the eyes of
a complete 'outsider' by the assimilated ones, since the latter might
still be attached to the former even by family ties. Yet, on the other
hand, they also might, precisely through their traditionalism, imperil
the chances of social integration for the assimilated. When 'eastern
Jews' began arriving *en masse* in 'western' cities (first in Berlin and
Vienna, then elsewhere too) during the late nineteenth century, assimilated Jews set upon them with what, at times, was a revulsion that
bordered on truly anti-Semitic frenzy. That 'self-hatred,' in the extended sense, was an almost natural product of discrepancies produced
by rapid modernization. They were encountered everywhere in

Europe, and not at all only amongst Jews. Whenever the modernization of any given group occurred at a precipitate pace, rifts arose in the
identity of its various geographically and socially dispersed fractions,
each of them being in a different stage of development at a specific
historical moment. Jewish 'self-hatred' was invariably directed against
'archaic' Jews who rejected 'progress' (at least before the revaluation
by Jewish intellectuals since the early twentieth century of the cultural
assets secured by eastern coreligionists). Much illumination, from this
point of view, can be gathered from the texts of Bernard Lazare, an
intellectual hero of the battle to rehabilitate Captain Dreyfus, or the
reactions of Jewish socialists and freemasons of that era, which were
often replicated piecemeal several decades later in activities and messages due to people's commissars of the Jewish Section of the Russian
Bolshevik Party, once it had been installed in power. The same attitudes of contempt, disdain, and disrespect for traditionalist Jewry
marked the Jewish cadres in the state apparatuses of post–1945 Communist states.

Antipathy and aversion of a different kind was directed against
Jewish 'cultural atavisms,' that is to say, the primitive character traits
seen as being typically Jewish that persisted in assimilated Jews. Any
elements of the inherited cultural *Lebenswelt*, perceived by outside
groups as being typical of Jews, whether external (elements of worship, ritual objects, Yiddish words, rests of the observance of dietary
customs) or incorporated, 'internal' manifestations (locutions, gestures, body language or everyday behavioral patterns, as perceptible in
attitudes to money, sexuality, violence, etc.), might be the object of
such hatred. Otto Weininger, a brilliant young philosopher of Vienna
in the early twentieth century, put together a whole theory from a rag-
bag of virulently anti-Jewish and misogynistic ideas before, drawing
the tragic lesson from his own conclusions, he committed suicide at
the age of twenty-two. In many respects, the self-hatred current in
assimilated Jewry assumed elements of the stereotyped images of
Jews as being 'weak,' 'cowardly,' 'avaricious,' 'effeminate,' etc. that
were developed in the anti-Semitic literature of the day. A plethora of
examples of personality disorders in relation to identity is to be found
equally in historical anthropological works dealing with assimilated
Jewish circles as in memoirs. Various forms of self-hatred, an extreme
attitude it might appear though, was a recurrent topic of such writings.

Other pathologies of assimilation: dissimulation, compensation and dissimilation

These deformations of personality lead to the emergence of three types of (not equally) pathological self-reflective forms of behavior, namely self-imposed concealment of one's origins, a compensatory 'over-fulfillment' of assimilationist expectations, and, through the adoption of less simple patterns, an obsessional preoccupation with one's Jewish identity and conspicuous flaunting of one's Jewishness.

The hiding of telltale signs that might 'give away' one's origins (that is, Jewish descent) was one of the perpetual elements of self-adjustment amongst assimilated Jews. Given that the lines of force charted in the course of assimilation are almost invariably unfavorable for Jews, concealment of the 'Jewish part' of one's personality from the public (and often its elimination from private life as well) becomes, after a while, a kind of predisposition, a basic norm governing everyday conduct. It may be justified as a desire for 'normality,' an avoidance of 'standing out,' a precaution against a possibly anti-Semitic milieu, and a way to apparently suppress personal identity issues—that those around one would not understand in any case, if they are outsiders and thus not concerned. This type of dissimulation followed behavioral patterns that could be partly strategic but also partly unconscious. The degree of the compulsion to cover up generally depended on the balance of power between Jews and non-Jews, as it stood at the given time, the extent to which dissimulationist attitudes were expected in the Gentile environment, and also the extent to which that might assist further integration of the assimilee. At all events, in most 'host' institutions and organizations—Christian schools, 'mixed' masonic lodges, left-wing movements, and especially ruling Communist parties—the matter of a person's Jewish origin or the 'Jewish issue' as such would be taboo subjects *de rigeur*. In other domains of everyday life the obligatory nature of such external censorship would depend on circumstances.

The mildest form of concealment applied generally also (especially in the pre-Shoah era) in 'mixed' circles, where any mention of the subject of Jewishness was habitually headed off in the presence of non-Jews, even though it might feature heavily in verbal exchanges of the in-group. The indirect reason for such reserve was a fear (sometimes vindicated) that the person raising the matter might hold anti-Semitic views. Possible prejudice of that kind was used as a pretext by many of those concerned for regarding any reference to Jewishness in a non-Jewish milieu, however well intentioned, as anti-Semitic in principle. In the interests of perfecting the concealment, a whole metalanguage could, occasionally, be developed among assimilated Jews to circumvent any explicit reference to the group by mentioning only terms like 'us' or 'ours' in public discussion, even inside Jewish circles proper. (The term *Unsereiner* and its equivalents amongst the Jewish petty bourgeoisie of Central Europe served similar functions).

Compensatory behaviors would be indispensable concomitants and indeed a most common outcome of the need to hush up a person's Jewish descent. The essence of such behaviors was the maximization of conformism and perfection in various public activities and performances. Assimilees would seek to fulfill as completely as possible the presumed expectations of their Christian milieu in regard to 'normal' cultural practice, lifestyle, manners, opinions. An assimilated Jew would thus not just desire to be the equal of non-Jewish fellow members of the milieu in question by simply aping their ways, but would do his or her best to 'outdo' them and thereby discharge what is believed to be his or her 'obligation to assimilate.' It was noted earlier that such attitudes may have, occasionally, contributed to the burgeoning of intellectual creativity. Here I would like to stress possibly grotesque forms of behavior (often caricatured in literature), a hypercorrect use of the 'national' language, maximal conformism in dress and public self-presentation (e.g. avoidance of 'laxity' according to station and occupation). There may have even be cases of imitating Christian traits that turned out to be utterly improbable, pointless or misplaced in a Jewish environment (e.g. a military bearing and gait, excessively genteel social manners, heel-clicking Prussian style, etc.). Proclamations of chauvinistic bombast or other excessively 'guest nationalist' conducts belonged to that lot. This was why assimilated Jews felt in Dualist Hungary a calling to act as representatives of Magyar rule in ethnic minority areas before 1918.

Behind these varieties of assimilationist self-denial lied an obsessional conviction that a Jew was best advised to do everything possible not to be Jewish, or at least not appear to be that. That logic, in the end, would lead many Jews to cease being Jews in any sense that the word may have had in the course of history. The endeavor did, indeed, produce the desired results in many cases: many descendants of 'strategic' converts to Christianity, or from mixed marriages, did actually succeed, albeit usually only after several generations, in expunging or completely covering up any traces of their descent. The need to pay constant heed to fitting in, however, paradoxically drove those engaged in such strategies of concealment to an obsessional preoccupation with identity. That can only be understood if one bears in mind the fear that real or supposed anti-Semitism could arouse, especially when reinforced by the beady and, at times, malicious gaze of surrounding society. 'Over-fulfillment' of the norms of the group to which one wished to belong sprang not just from the difficulty that assimilating Jews had in steering a middle course between the demands made on them by the majority society and an elemental sense of self-esteem opposing total self-denial, but also from the very real risks run by Jews in a hostile environment.

Yet even if dissimulation was successful, that could not necessarily mean an automatic alleviation of the anxiety involved. Thus, Jewish cadres of the Communist era may well have squirmed in the grip of the same 'fear of disclosure' as 'new Christian' Marranos of former times in Catholic Europe. It was just that whereas Communist leaders did their best to ignore or at least to make their children forget, or else—if possible—not even learn about their Jewish origins, seeking thus to make political capital out of it, insofar as their background might 'discredit' them (due to possible anti-Semitism of 'populist' cadres), the Marranos continued to nurse their roots, regarding the purely symbolic advantages of clandestine fidelity to their ancestry to be more important: they did indeed believe in the God of Israel, and piety was the all-powerful spiritual component of their being.

Only the emergence of new models of Jewish nationalism in the final decades of the nineteenth century brought European Jewry the possibility of an intellectual way out of such dilemmas. Different variants of nationalism also offered new choices of Jewish affiliation that broke with assimilationism, along with its consequences, that for many, up till then, had been the preferred route at any cost. Amongst these models some (Herzl and Nordau's Zionism) could be regarded, by virtue of their decisively modernist components, as a continuation of assimilation but in the brand new, nationalist key. Others (the *Bund*, for instance) combined a universalistic model of class struggle and the principles of Jewish particularism at one and the same time. Still others (the *folk*ism, or doctrine of Jewish cultural autonomism, propounded by Dubnov) foresaw a modernization of Jewish identity through a cult of particularism and the assertion of its rights. The common point in all of these programs, as we shall see, was the fight for the liberation of Jewish identity. This included the possibility of freely living out one's Jewishness and—from a group-psychological stance—the accentuation of a positive Jewish self-image via the development of a collective narcissism of sorts. This was also meant to eliminate hitherto frequent inclinations to compromise with the temptations, now discerned as pathological, of self-hatred, self-denial, identity concealment or compensation for one's part of the collective self.

The crisis of assimilation and the nationalist responses

Since the *Haskalah*, assimilation had been Jewry's biggest hope for a normalization of their position in European societies. Throughout the nineteenth century, their image of the future was determined by expectations related to the final success of their cultural integration and 'naturalization' in Western and Central Europe. The results that came in the immediate wake of the extension of civil rights, or sometimes even prior to that, and the actual outcomes of the social integration of Jews could be spectacular, even in countries with political arrangements as disparate as France and Hungary. In the West integration became the rule and few of those concerned expressed doubts about its eventual success.

The unequivocally unfavorable circumstances of Eastern Europe notwithstanding, it was evident by the latter half of the century that the most acculturated strata (or the wealthiest) of local Jewry were gaining access to higher education in ever-growing numbers, and also obtaining rights of settlement even in Russian capital cities, which remained still prohibited for their less 'assimilated' co-religionists. The *Haskalah* began to exert indeed an influence in the largest Jewish community within a single country, the circles of Russian Jewry, although certain opponents, such as the Hebrew novelist Peretz Smolenskin, were early proponents of the necessity of keeping separate the modernization and the 'national' development of Jewry. During the 1870s the ranks of Jewish students swelled in Russian public educational institutions, and signs of cultural integration of Jews and the political 'normalization' of their position were multiplying, not uncommonly thanks to the complete secularization of their economic and intellectual élite. Most of those concerned were likely to have felt, at all events, that assimilation was starting to bear fruit even for eastern Jewry.

That belief in the effectiveness of assimilation, however, was shaken during the 1880s throughout Europe. In this respect, an air of crisis hung over the decades around the turn of the century. Hopes of assimilation that had previously been fulfilled, one after the other, were now shattered in a crossfire of crude assaults, the repercussions of which spread across the entire continent. In Russia, though pogroms were unleashed against some big Jewish communities at intervals during the whole of the nineteenth century—occurring in Odessa alone in 1821, 1859, 1871 and 1881—, this very year of 1881 and succeeding years brought an even more tragic turn of events. As was discussed above, this marked the start of a concerted wave of attacks against Jews in the Russian empire that far surpassed the earlier ones both in its extent (160 communities were devastated) and its fury (there were hundreds of victims). Many of these anti-Jewish atrocities were properly organized by the Union of the Russian People (the 'Black Hundreds') with the overt support of the tsar. A new type of anti-Semitic propaganda showed its colors in 1905 with the forgery known as *The Protocols of the Elders of Zion*, which proclaimed war on the whole of world Jewry from the very outset. The 'Temporary Regulations' of May 1882, the *Numerus Clausus* of 1886 and other anti-Jewish measures of the tsarist authorities put the ideas of assimilation beyond the bounds of possibility.

Yet the general climate of Jewish opinion was even more gravely discomfited by the spread of public anti-Jewish agitation in countries where assimilation had seemed to be most advanced. In 1896, even Prague was the scene of violent anti-Jewish riots and demonstrations (albeit without any fatalities). When concocted murder charges against members of a local Jewish community were cleared by the jury in Hungary's notorious Tiszaeszlár case (1882–83), that not only sparked off country-wide attempts to whip up pogroms, obliging the government to mobilize military detachments to quell them, but even led to a National Anti-Semitic Party rearing its head, if only for a short while. The age-old libel that Jews were engaging in ritual murder cropped up ever more frequently across Central and Eastern Europe. Still retaining a chilling resonance in legal annals are the Hilsner Case in Bohemia (1901), if only because the defense attorney was T.G. Masaryk, later president of the first Czechoslovakian Republic. In this case too he was going against the general anti-Semitic drift of his own party, even though he failed to gain an acquittal. The Beilis Case in Russia (1913) likewise stirred up a world-wide furore.

During the very same decades of the outgoing nineteenth century a number of political parties appeared in the East and the West, pushing openly anti-Semitic platforms. They gained mass support from voters in Austria (Karl Lueger was elected mayor of Vienna in 1895) and Germany (the *Reichstag* had 13 anti-Semitic representatives in 1893). Around the turn of the century, from 1894 onwards, France, the first country to proclaim equal rights for Jews, was convulsed by the storm provoked by the Dreyfus Affair and the attendant anti-Jewish smear campaign, culminating in the year 1898, the likes of which had hardly been seen before in the West in the modern era.

A sense of being under threat kept on rising; new obstacles were piling up in the way of its efforts to assimilate, and official policy in regard to social integration of Jews was now equivocal, even in the few countries, like France or Austria, where settled Jews had long enjoyed full citizenship rights. Jews reacted to this crisis situation in essentially four different ways, two of which were continuations of older strategies, while the other two were new developments, embodying new, nationalist definitions of Jewish identity.

The first reaction was to redouble efforts to assimilate (possibly even by refocusing the direction of assimilation on local élites or ethnic majorities hitherto neglected, as in the Czech provinces in the late nineteenth century). In order to avoid or fend off threats, those adopting this course would always lend their support to potential allies, that is to political parties and social forces (active in ideological, literary, aesthetic or other arenas) that appeared to be the least tainted by anti-Semitism, if they did not roundly reject it. This pattern of behavior became generalized in Hungary, France, and elsewhere in the West, in Germany's Weimar Republic, and in Czechoslovakia under Masaryk—in other words, wherever guarantees of safety offered by 'allied' forces looked to be relatively the most effective.

That intensification of assimilation gained distinctive expression in the political radicalization of broad sections of Jewish youth. Many joined socialistic or Communistic movements, founded on universalistic ideologies that broke with classical parliamentarism. That happened particularly in countries—Russia, Hungary, and Germany, amongst others—where the 'first generation' of Jews to undergo the process of national acculturation were still more or less excluded from the professional roles to which their qualifications and skills should have entitled them. Let it not be forgotten that this 'internationalist,' or 'left-wing,' option was no more than an alternative to 'nationalist' assimilation, generally only gaining prominence when the latter appeared to be fully achieved but also to run into a *cul-de-sac*. In reality, however, there was no contradiction between 'internationalist' and 'nationalist' assimilation, except for the ideological and political options adopted, since both predicated compliance with fundamentally identical assimilationist strategies in private life, schooling, secularization, occupational mobility, matrimonial customs, and so on. The 'labor movement' may well have brought more couples together in Judaeo–Christian 'mixed' marriages than did civic assimilation itself, helped along by the speedy deracination and early secularization of those involved in it, whether they belonged to the industrial working class or to the frustrated Jewish intelligentsia.

The second type of reaction was traditionalist by nature and consisted in a form of return to religious orthodoxy. This may be characterized as a conscious redoubling of efforts to expunge all assimilationist inclinations. This intellectual trend began to assume shape in organized movements that emerged at the beginning of the twentieth century, attaining their most unequivocal expression in *Agudat Israel* ('Alliance' or 'Union' of Israel), which grew into a huge world organization of Orthodox Jewry in Central and Eastern Europe. *Agudat Israel* was founded between 1909 and 1912 by a united front stitched together with quite some difficulty by representatives of German neo-Orthodoxy and Lithuanian, Polish, and Hungarian rabbinical Orthodoxy. Though it managed to win over several currents of religious Zionism (the adherents of *Mizrachi* affiliated in 1912), indeed even some Hasidic authorities, and proved to be systematically able to put across its main goals—preservation of the religious *status quo*, and opposition to any kind of religious reforms and to policies advocated by adherents of assimilationism—the key constituents of *Agudat* were unable to reach agreement on the practicalities as to the norms destined to govern Jewish identity. Divisions arose over language (the use of Yiddish advocated by Polish and Lithuanian Jews being opposed by Central European moderates, who argued for the adoption of the languages of host societies), the acceptable degree of modernization of religious instruction, the ideal of returning to Zion (which aroused mistrust at first, being accepted by many only after the Shoah), and whether there should be any participation in local social struggles. Since the movement as a whole was unwilling to adopt this, *Po'alei Agudat Israel* split away as a distinct workers' organization. The divisions notwithstanding, *Agudat Israel* served as a supreme organizational frame for movements which took issue with the modernist experiments seeking and urging a reformulation of Jewish identity. Because it was far from simply an upholder of the entirely archaic stances of old-style Orthodoxy, it was able to find grounds for compromise, through its political recommendations, its social base, and its religious commitments, between the officially irreconcilable standpoints of moderate and unbending traditionalists. It thus retained a huge influence between the two world wars in Poland, which then (Soviet Russia being cut off) served as the major creative ideological workshop within traditionalist European Jewry.

A third response to the crisis of assimilation was given by Zionism, which from its very beginnings held out the prospect of a mass emigration of European Jewry to overseas, whether that was to Palestine (as a historical 'return from exile') or elsewhere (as a so-called 'territorialist' solution). In retrospect, Zionism, having seen its basic goal of the creation of a Jewish nation state crowned by success, now looks to have been the most important of the movements that broke with assimilationist aspirations at the turn of the nineteenth into the twentieth century. From a historical perspective, however, the situation was not so clear-cut as that. To begin with, the eventual success of the Zionist project should not hide the fact that, initially, it was regarded by many as just a fantasy. Furthermore, during its early decades it managed to win over only a rather negligible fraction of educated or middle class Jewish élites in Central and Western Europe. It undoubtedly had a larger camp since the beginning in the East, though this too was for long insignificant compared to the size of the total Jewish population. Right up to the Shoah many regarded it as a utopia from first to last. In the ideological contest between assimilationism and *Agudat* as well as other Jewish nationalist movements, Zionism was for a long time relegated to the fringes, so far as to its capacity to mobilize masses was concerned. Finally, according to its authors and representatives, Zionism was unequivocally a brainchild of the most highly assimilated intellectual circles of Central and Western Europe, whilst its main goal—the creation of a modern, secular, democratic nation state on the western pattern—points quite clearly to the ideology of modern nationalism sprang from the Enlightenment.

The point at issue, after all, was the provision of a framework for national autonomy for a dispersed group (the Jews)—being looked down upon everywhere as an alien ethnic and religious minority—, in the same way as other diasporic or 'dismembered' peoples had managed to realize it in Europe during the nineteenth century (with the unification of Germany, Romania, Italy and the foundation of nation states in the Balkans) or in the twentieth century (with the establishment of Czechoslovakia, Yugoslavia, Poland or the Baltic states). The Zionist project, however, differed from the listed European examples in that Jews could not command an equivalent 'national potential.' Indeed Jewry did not have a recognized territorial basis with a demonstrable element of historical continuity, since Palestine was an Ottoman possession, in which Jews anyway had formed a minority for far too long. They were neither linguistically nor culturally united or uniform, and they even displayed decisive religious divisions. To boot, most Western or even Central European Jews felt sufficiently attached to their host country, in spite of difficulties they met, not to plan a radical change of residence and of national loyalties, as proposed by the Zionist ideology. For all these reasons Zionism was considered stubbornly by many as a generous but utopian enterprise.

It was in order to dispel that notion that Zionists first of all set about elaborating a politically and organizationally credible international agency as a deliberate means of bolstering the movement's 'national potential.' As elements of that scheme, after some vacillation, they settled on a location for the future state (Palestine), proclaimed Hebrew to be the would-be 'national language' (the acceptance of which did not go at all smoothly), chose a set of symbols for the movement (hymn, flag) and drew up a long-term action program destined to bring the new state into being.

Each of the main components of the Zionist project underwent significant changes over time; nevertheless it retained throughout its doubly universalistic character.

First of all, Zionism sought to establish itself as an ideology ranking alongside the nationalisms of nineteenth-century Europe in terms of territorial, cultural and ethnic unity, which was in the era of the Romantic concept of nationhood the organizational principle regarded as universally valid for modern societies. Second, Zionism saw its ultimate and practical goal as the gathering together of all Jews scattered across the world, and thereby to mould the ethnic–religious Diaspora into a 'nation.' Zionism therefore proposed a radical, universally valid reformulation of Jewish identity in the name of a nation-building people. In this respect it broke perhaps the most decisively with all other previous identity options or projects of affiliation that had been accepted up till then in the Diaspora.

The fourth response to the crisis of assimilation was given by other forms of Jewish nationalism, more local and less 'universalistic' in nature. Foremost amongst them one has to mention autonomism (or *folk*ism) and the socialist *Bund*. These movements placed their enterprises on both ethnic and cultural (though not religious) and also (particularly in pre–1917 Russia and independent Poland) territorial foundations. They also accepted, indeed advocated, the principle of secularization; indeed, in some cases (as with the *Bund*ists) they conducted explicitly antireligious propaganda and followed political models regarded as among the most secular ones, whose legitimacy was increasingly recognized in the European ideological market, especially after the Versailles peace treaties which endorsed or at least paid lip service to some of them: the rights of ethnic and linguistic minorities to cultural self-determination and freedom within the borders of nation-states—the fundamental tenet of *folk*ism—, or of working Jewish masses to fight for their economic, trade-unionist, cultural, and political rights (as in the case of the *Bund*). The goals of these nationalist movements were thus more modest, but also more precisely and, in temporal terms, realistically formulated. To put it another way, they were not carried away by the 'double universalism' of Zionism. That also applies to the matter of identity. Unlike the Zionists, they did not commit themselves to a seemingly utopistic concept of the 'new Jew,' but made do with Jews as they were already. They restricted their goals to defending clearly defined collective interests. It might be that one or the other would serve up their demands with a garnishing of philosophies of history presented as being of universal validity—examples of that would be Dubnov's autonomism, to be discussed later on, or Marxism—but all this was meant to mobilize the Jewish masses for large-scale political action.

These non-Zionist nationalist movements represent an original model of Jewish identity. For one thing, they preserved, and indeed programmatically elaborate upon a distinctively secular (or 'popular') cultural heritage of traditional Judaism (including the cult of Yiddish, often disparaged by assimilationists or Zionists as a mere jargon), even if they minimized the religious dimensions of this tradition. For another, they attuned themselves culturally to whichever local social élite was seen as the most progressively educated. Their projects espoused the defense of local Jewish interests, close to the day-to-day aspirations of people they tried to represent and to whom they belonged in concrete terms. Similar forms of this 'ambiguous' social status can also be identified in certain other 'belated' nationalist movements (amongst the 'national awakeners' of Slovakia, for example), or amongst European trade union leaders who had 'risen from the masses' and, despite their limited schooling, often became men of considerable reading and serious if only 'down-to-earth' political experience. Here too a difference is discernible between the inventors of 'particularist' nationalism—the *Bund*ist or *folk*ist leadership—, and the Zionist establishment, with its 'universalistic' pretensions, especially in the early years, whose members originated primarily from the ranks of the highly educated bourgeoisie and heavily 'westernized' Jewish intelligentsia.

Main socio–historical dimensions of Jewish nationalism

However much the various currents of Jewish nationalism appearing at the end of the nineteenth century may differ from one another, all share the common feature of containing within themselves elements of rupture, both with religious traditionalism (which had held most of the

Eastern European Jewish masses in its thrall up to that juncture), and with assimilationist aspirations, which built on 'host nationalism,' the adoption of the local nationalism of host societies. At least four kindred aspects may be recognized in the visions of the future and social programs propagated by Jewish nationalist movements.

First of all Jewish nationalisms were all based on the identification of Jewry with a modern national community. All of them built on hidden dimensions of cohesion, or nation-forming potential, of the populations they sought historically to reach and mobilize. The most important of these latent factors, ironically, was precisely their sectarian solidarity, and thus, indirectly, the piety that Jewish nationalisms publicly ignored or (as in the *Bund*'s atheistic ideology) flatly rejected. The religious dimension was nevertheless an indispensable ingredient of Jewish nationalism, not by virtue of its articles of faith or ritual customs, but because the sectarian community was the only concrete definition of the target populations for the movements. Moreover, this was also the principal 'reason' offered for the adverse discriminations they had to endure. Equally, the messianism imbedded in religious Judaism was readily 'translatable' by a secular gloss into an optimistic philosophy of history appropriate for constructing a new vision of the future and self-perception. The center of this vision was here no longer the 'chosen people' of religious dogma but a self-confident, modern national community that was taking its fate in its own hands and able to control it. The idea of a 'return' to *Eretz Israel*, accordingly, became in the Zionist political program grounded in the 'natural' right of the Jewish people to reconquer the country that constituted its legitimate historical property. This is a good example of how religious mythology and past references could be exploited for secular, nationalist goals as a means of mass mobilization. It goes without saying that reference to the anti-Semitism present all around, the collective enemy that all too palpably attacked members of the Judaic community, played a major part in bringing to the surface the nationalistic inclinations of Jews living in the Diaspora.

In the second place, by alluding to 'national' features ascribed, to a greater or lesser extent, to the Jews, or at least to the collective interests that bonded Jews together into a single camp, all of the nationalist movements professed separatism, a kind of dissimilation, a disentangling from the intertwinements binding them to non-Jews. Thus, even as they formed part of the movements of political modernization in contemporary Europe, Jewish nationalist movements were conceptually mapping out for the 'Jewish people,' for which they were seeking to give an ideological grounding, a future that was distinctive, if not necessarily at odds with that of other nationally based societies. As far as Zionists were concerned, the organization of all Jews into a nation in some ways transcended assimilation, since it actually aimed at gaining admission for Jews into the 'community of peoples' as an independent nation. Others rejected assimilation rather on grounds that it was not working appropriately. One of the early forms of Russian Jewish assimilation, for instance, manifested in joining the outlawed opposition to the tsar, until it became clear that most of the anti-tsarist movements were often equally unprepared or unwilling to offer protection against pogroms and arbitrary anti-Jewish measures of the authorities. Even within the framework of socialist movements could Jewish interests be asserted and defended. Thus, both *folk*ists and *Bund*ists promoted separatism because they could see no other possibility of achieving their specific objectives of Jewish self-defense, but also—and here they concurred with Zionism—because separatism alone carried the promise of putting an end to the 'assimilationist alienation' and assure the collective dignity of Jews. This appeared to be the only way to stand up successfully against humiliations and, more particularly, to proudly assume the Jewish cultural heritage.

That primary cultural concern of separatism was manifested in endeavors to update Jewish idioms (Yiddish in the case of *folk*ists and *Bund*ists, Hebrew in the case of the Zionists) into national languages that would sustain a high-level literary culture, so important in every modern movement of 'national awakening.' In the situation as it had evolved at the turn of the century, such a change in attitude was nothing short of a cultural revolution. In the past most supporters of the *Haskalah*, and the Jewish élites within its sphere of attraction, had looked down on Yiddish as an argot of the lower, 'uncivilized' strata, whereas Hebrew was preserved purely for widespread ritual use and intellectual exchanges between *Talmud* scholars. It is sufficient to recall that even Herzl himself, when he began to elaborate his project, had foreseen German (being the 'natural' vehicle of culture for 'westernized' Jews like himself) as the official language of the would-be Jewish state.

Thirdly, every Jewish nationalism covertly sought to 'historicize' the Jewish people, in other words, to turn Jewry into a history-making people, rather than puppet-like participants in a history 'made by others.' That aspiration had both a philosophical and a practical aspect. In the philosophical conception of the situation, Jewish history arrived at a turning point. The millennia of wandering of the Diaspora in exile (the *Galut*)—while the group had been stripped of its chief means of autonomy, starting with those that served for self-defense – must be ended in a way that Jews themselves should be put in a position to control their own fate, either as a political nation (for the Zionists) or as an ethnic group possessing a distinctive culture, history, and the means of collective action (for non-Zionist nationalists). Practically speaking, in order to realize that goal, the Jewish masses must be mobilized to fight for and defend their distinctive regional, national, or (given that everywhere they formed a marginalized cultural community) supranational interests.

That aspiration can be put down to the fact that from early in the twentieth century, Zionists, *folk*ists, *Bund*ists, etc. did their best not just to intervene in political disputes between Great Powers but also embarked on a path of direct political action. They especially took part in the battles of progressive trade-unions against the tsarist régime and later in the parliamentary struggles of independent Poland. The birth of armed self-defense movements to counter the pogroms in Russia, during the difficult period between 1903 and 1905, was a tangible evidence of this change. The same message was given out by the build-up of new institutional networks for Jews, often global in scale, which were no longer set up for protection of local interests only, as earlier, but as interregional or international agencies of mutual assistance: locally they supported the Jewish school system, mutual aid and insurance reserves, strike funds (amongst *Bund*ists), endowments for emigration (amongst Zionists), health care providers and hospitals, theatres, press centers for the association, indeed (between the two world wars) even academic initiatives, the most significant of which was the *Yidisher Visenshaftlikher Institut* (YIVO—Institute for Jewish Research), founded at Vilna in 1925. It would be fair to say that, in this way, the nationalist revival led to the creation of a veritable national infrastructure proper that, over and beyond its symbolic significance, was able to offer important collective services to Jewish populations, much in need of them, especially in Eastern Europe and Palestine. All this was achieved, what is more, well before the national movements could have any hope of realizing their political goals.

Fourthly, it was a final general feature of Jewish nationalist movements that they tried to do away with the factors of Jewish historical 'exclusiveness,' and thereby to 'normalize' the status of Europe's Jews, in both the socio–political and the anthropological domain, under the aegis of modernization.

Most public figures in the national movements, except the *Mizrachi* brand of Orthodox Zionism, refrained from any kind of religious commitment. They were indeed mostly indifferent (and sometimes antagonistic) towards religion, precisely because it was considered to have had a decisive hand in making discriminations historically possible in the first place. The liberation of Jewish identity from narrow religious determinism, and a new kind of self-definition that referred to joint interests, collective dangers, and common 'fate,' descent and history, all meant creating the widest possible accord amongst Jews, forging into a unity a 'people' that had become ever more divided since the *Haskalah*, mostly on account of irreconcilable differences of opinion surrounding religiosity. That is why the concept of a 'community of destiny' (*Schicksalsgemeinschaft*) became one of the guiding principles in the reformulation of Judaism. Unlike with other nation-states-in-the-making, there was no other way for the Jews to assert a linguistic or cultural identity, due to the growing socio–economic (and indeed demographic) weight of 'westernized' (that is secularized, culturally 'de-Judaized') elements amongst them. At the same time, paradoxically as it may appear, this overtly secular concept of a 'Jewish people' went against the intellectual heritage of the *Haskalah*, which supported assimilation in every domain except that of religion, thereby reducing Judaism to a religious affiliation within nation-states formed by 'host peoples.' The gaining of recognition from European powers for the special interests of Jews and, in that context, for their internationally representative bodies established around the turn of the century (Zionist institutions throughout Europe, various nationalist associations and parties mainly in Eastern Europe) formed part of the process of 'historical normalization.' It also proved that an overhaul of Yiddish and reform of the Hebrew language were indispensable for this purpose, essentially on the basis of the principle that 'a nation lives through its language.'

A similar motive guided Jewish nationalists in their thinking about the 'new Jew,' and in their working out of practical guidelines relating to this. The ideal of the 'new Jew' was laid down by a complex definition. Politically, the 'new Jew' would organize self-defense, fight for his rights, etc. Economically, he would give up 'unproductive' commercial, financial, and intellectual activities and—much in the spirit of the *Haskalah*—, move into 'useful' industrial or agricultural occupations, or manual work more generally, just like the majority of other, 'normal' European peoples. Anthropologically speaking, 'regeneration' would require the 'new Jew' to give up his culture of acquiescence, complaint, and non-violence. Instead he would react to the wrongs done to him. As to identity assertion, he would stand up actively for his Jewishness, be proud of it, and see other Jews as comrades in (mis)fortune. At all events, according to all the nationalist philosophies (and also the contemporary universalistic utopias, including Marxism), a historical 'normalization' of Jewry, could only occur through a fundamental transformation or revision of relationships towards traditional Jewish identity. A break with religious traditionalism was just as inevitable as that with secular assimilationism.

Voluntarist notions of 'normalization' are thus, in part, corollaries of ideas of the *Haskalah* but also, in part, with regard to nationalist separatism, at variance with these.

Intellectual forerunners of Zionism

The birth of the political Zionism leading up to the creation of the state of Israel in May 1948 is customarily tied to the work of Theodor Herzl, as exemplified by the publication of his book *Der Judenstaat* (1896) and his convening of the first Zionist Congress in Basle (1897). We know that the word itself was coined by the Viennese editor Nathan Birnbaum, whose newspaper *Selbstemanzipation*, which he had published since April 1881, began appearing with the subhead *Organ der Zionisten* from May 1893. As soon as the Zionist ideal made its appearance on Europe's ideological stage, its declared political goal was organizing the emigration of Jews from Europe, specifically to

Palestine (Zion, by ancient Judaic tradition, denotes Jerusalem), in order to found their own state there.

By the time political Zionism emerged, however, there already existed a movement with a global network of contacts, particularly in Eastern Europe, which, except for the notion of founding a state, was effectively striving for the same objective. More than that, this movement had already been of assistance on numerous occasions to émigrés seeking to settle in Palestine. *Hibbat Zion* ('Love of Zion') and its activists, *Hovevei Zion* ('Lovers of Zion'), to start with, would be the Zionist movement's first rivals at one and the same time as they were supplying Zionism with its first members. They concentrated their activities on giving financial aid to those setting off on the journey to Palestine, whence their earliest characterization as 'practical Zionists.' They were to differ from their 'political Zionist' fellows both in their approach and their ideas right up to the Tenth Zionist Congress (1911), where the two trends were successfully fused by the adoption of the concept of 'synthetic Zionism' suggested by Chaim Weizmann. These movements can therefore be regarded as the direct pioneers of Zionism, though this also had many other forerunners besides them. It is worth examining the legacy they left to Zionism.

The chief sources of the Zionist ideals can be captured in three historical forms: in religious messianism, amongst proto-Zionist thinkers, and in the *Hibbat Zion* movement.

The first thing that should be noted is that the idea of a 'return to Zion' formed an integral part of the religious thinking of Jews living in the Diaspora. The customary parting phrase, "Next year in Jerusalem," of those who gather together for the festivals celebrating the Passover is an expression of the constant timeliness of the messianistic promise, according to which with the coming of the Messiah 'at the end of time,' all Jews will be reunited in Zion. The practical nursing of that hope generally manifested itself in the fact that intellectual, demographic and, indeed, financial links between the communities of the Diaspora and *Eretz Israel* were never broken. There were also periods, especially from the sixteenth century onwards, when, as a result of great outbursts of messianistic fervor, large numbers set off for Palestine (although there were also times of migrations in the opposite direction). Diaspora communities always ranked as one of their chief moral duties giving financial assistance to those who were preparing to set off, or had already departed, on that journey. Active and prolific advocates of the idea of 'returning' were to be found, even in the nineteenth century, amongst the great figures of the *Haskalah*— Zevi Sneersohn was one such—who themselves moved to Palestine.

When the blood libel of the 'Damascus Affair' in 1840, having raised a huge outcry throughout Europe, was eventually settled after prolonged wrangling, a widespread rumor of the coming of the Messiah threw masses of Jews of Eastern Europe and the Balkans into a frenzy. It is no coincidence that several proto-Zionist thinkers started their work in this period, including Judah Alkalai, rabbi of a small Sephardic community near Belgrade. Alkalai stuck to his guns with sincere conviction and was indefatigable in propagating a scheme that lay very close to the future Zionist project. He indeed expressed the need to organize a 'return home' of world Jewry to *Eretz Israel* to bring a modern nation into being there, with Hebrew as the common language. Alkalai demonstrated his allegiance to his scheme by personal example, spending the final phase of his life in Palestine. It needs to be remarked, however, that the 'return' that he proclaimed, at root, amounted to a demand for religious revival, having barely any political complexion. Alkalai was an optimist, his venture taking place at a time that was still before the first pernicious waves of political anti-Semitism swept across Europe between 1870 and 1880. His program was thus not yet a response to the challenges of the violent anti-Jewish agitation typical of later years.

The same applies to the work of Zevi Hirsch Kalisher and Moses Hess, two major ideologues, who can be regarded as direct forerunners of Zionism. Still, the cultural and ideological milieus that shaped them were very different from one another: Kalisher was a rabbinically trained German scholar of Polish birth, whereas Hess was a 'Young Hegelian' philosopher disillusioned with socialism, though remaining personally close to Marx. They nevertheless both came to the view that a Jewish nation should be revived in Palestine. In Kalisher's view, the legal emancipation that Jews had already achieved in several countries, and which could be hoped for in others, along with the growing economic power of big Jewish banking families, would create the opportunity to keep the prophetic promise of 'redemption,' that is to say, liberation from exile and a return to *Eretz Israel*. Hess's philosophy drew on the fashionable Romantic nationalism of his age and its corroboration with the unification of Italy and Germany, respectively. In his eyes, Jewry was the last European people to be still tormented by the insolubility of its 'national question.' To both authors it seemed outrageous that the ancient Jewish people was behind even the 'young' peoples of the Balkans in fighting for its national rights.

From the 1860s on, the ideas that Kalisher and Hess had elaborated (the two were acquainted and maintained contact with one another) found increasing resonance in Jewish intellectual circles, but no organized bodies emerged to implement them. The situation changed radically in the late 1870s, with the renewed outbreaks of anti-Jewish violence in Romania, the advances made by anti-Semitic politics in Germany, and particularly during the first big Russian pogroms of the 1880s. It was then that the ideologues' thoughts of a 'return,' previously classified as utopian, started to chime with the practical steps that the supporters of *Hibbat Zion* had instituted under the influence of the anti-Jewish oppression in Russia.

'Lovers of Zion,' or 'practical Zionists'

Hibbat Zion came into being under a dual set of circumstances. It was, on the one hand, a response to the acceleration of assimilatory efforts in Central Europe (above all, in Germany and Austria-Hungary) that had come with Reform Judaism and relegated messianic prophecies about Zion to the background in favor of religious teachings carrying a universalistic moral message. On the other hand it was an obvious reaction to the failure of assimilation in Eastern Europe. The latter both triggered off and offered the chance for an ideological counterblast of sorts to be unleashed.

As early as 1868 the journalist and novelist Peretz Smolenskin had used the columns of his monthly *Ha-Shahar* to condemn the disinterest shown towards Zion. This journal would become the main propaganda vehicle for the renewal of spoken Hebrew. The lexicographer Eliezir Ben-Yehuda used it to publish articles in which he linked the modernization of the Hebrew language with the rebirth of Jewish national unity in *Eretz Israel*. The succession of Russian pogroms in 1881–84 provoked intense debate amongst the Russian Jewish intelligentsia about how Jews might be extricated from the tragic mess they were in and set on the path of emigration. That discussion was carried on not just in Hebrew. Russian-language periodicals also participated in the movement, such as *Rassvet* ('Dawn'). In their wake philanthropic discussion circles and associations quickly sprang up and started to provide tangible assistance in organizing emigration. All were agreed on the notion of a Jewish national rebirth, the importance of a shift towards 'productive'—primarily agricultural—occupations, and the rejection of assimilationism, but there were differences of view regarding the destination that was to be set for emigration.

The *Am Olam* society, founded at Odessa in 1881, managed to arrange for hundreds of emigrants to get to the United States, where they set up four short-lived settlements based on Communistic socialist principles. The *Bilu* movement, established at Kharkov in 1882, soon transferred its headquarters to Odessa as well, since from there it could more effectively organize the embarkation of those wishing to leave. With its assistance, the first settlers disembarked at Jaffa in July 1882. They would help in setting up many Jewish colonies in Palestine, such as that at Gederah. Founded in 1886 by young Jewish intellectuals in Berlin, the *Ezra* Society was to extend its activities in support of emigration to the whole of Germany. *Ezra* published newspapers and propaganda booklets, as well as ran a fund for settling Jewish farmers in Palestine and Syria.

The international activities of a number of rich philanthropists who lived in the West fit into this context. The largest-scale colonization programs were those bankrolled by the French Baron Maurice de Hirsch. Western European instigators of such aid lent their support to the efforts of Jewish agricultural colonists, indeed, even to their settlement in Palestine, despite the fact that they generally thought the creation of a national pocket in the Near East—or anywhere else for that matter—was a day-dream. Thus, the Jewish Colonization Association, maintained by the Hirsch Foundation, from 1891 put up huge sums of money to finance the voyages of volunteering Jewish emigrants and their placement in well-equipped agricultural colonies in Argentina, Brazil and, to a somewhat lesser extent, the USA and Canada. Most of those colonies, it should be recorded, were not long-lived.

In that respect, there is no question that the most influential activities were due to Leon Pinsker. Pinsker had been one of the very first

Jews to be admitted as a medical student to Odessa University. He was a co-founder of the Russian-language periodical *Rassvet*, also writing widely for other Russian newspapers to propagate the ideas of the *Haskalah* and urge the more rapid integration of Jews into Russian society. That approach was transformed by the widespread pogroms, starting with that of 1871 in Odessa, which he lived through himself. Returning from a tour of western countries in 1882, he put out a famous pamphlet, *Autoemancipation*, which called for the establishment of a Jewish national center outside Europe, even though it gave no indication of where that was to be located geographically. Pinsker remained, to the end, a supporter of the emancipation that had been prescribed by the pioneers of the *Haskalah*, but he was forced to admit that the intensification of anti-Semitism made it impossible to expect any fulfillment of the hopes attached to assimilation. Jews would be condemned to live in a state of subordination and estrangement, in the literal sense of the word, until they, like other nations, brought about the conditions for recognition of their equality by creating their own national state.

Pinsker's call served as a reference point for *Hibbat Zion* circles that began to form, one after the other, in Russia's 'Pale of Settlement' (with Odessa as a center) and in Romania (where no fewer than 30 local cells were in existence by the end of 1881), with Pinsker as overall head of the alliance of societies. The movement mounted several international conferences in order to widen its base to the West without meeting much success. Their plans became more focused, and their readiness for action was greatly boosted, once agreement had been hammered out between the various sections of the movement at Focsani in Romania (1882) and Katowice in Galicia (1884). For spiritual, theological, and practical reasons—its relative proximity and the low land prices—and not out of any political considerations, the members of the movement (the 'lovers of Zion') soon began to channel their activities into organizing emigrations towards *Eretz Israel*. Thus it was *Hibbat Zion* members who founded (or refounded) the towns of Rishon le-Zion, Rosh Pinnah, Petah Tikvah and others in Palestine, from 1882 onwards, even though the Ottoman authorities had, in principle, prohibited all immigration.

The new colonies managed to gain financial backing from Baron Edmond de Rothschild. Those sums were incomparable to the modest funds collected by *Hibbat Zion,* opening up the possibility—although it led to clashes with Baron Rothschild's trustees—of keeping the initially tiny colonies going and founding new ones. In 1890 the movement succeeded in gaining recognition from the tsarist government of its interests in Jewish emigration as a 'society for the support of Jewish farmers and artisans in Palestine and Syria' in the Odessa district. With the help of the donations that flowed in, they set up the Rehovot and Haderah foundations (1890–91) and in 1891 directed to Palestine many Jews who had just been expelled from Moscow. When Herzl's 'western' Zionism made its appearance amongst the trends of thought in Europe, the 'lovers of Zion' were overshadowed, as dissimilationist aspirations made headway in Jewish élite circles. Herzl in person declared that their activities—that is to say, their 'infiltration' into *Eretz Israel*—were downright 'illegal,' given that they were formally prohibited by the Turkish government. However, *Hovevei Zion,* guided by the essentially humanitarian motives of saving fellow Jews in misfortune, living under threat, carried on their work as 'practical Zionists.' Their official fusion with the 'political Zionists' occurred only in 1911.

The most direct critique of *Hovevei Zion* activities came from one of their own number, the essayist Ahad Ha-Am (pseudonym, 'One of the people,' of Hirsch Ginsberg). This originator of the 'culturalist' trend within the then-emergent Zionism (*Kulturzionismus*) exercised a profound influence on the early activists in the movement. To Ahad Ha-Am's way of thinking, *Eretz Israel* could not be the end-goal for mass emigration, but it would have an all the more decisive role as a gathering place for a self-aware Jewish élite, or in other words, an intellectual center for new Jewry. In this view, Palestine would be the womb for the renaissance of a Hebrew culture appropriate to modern times, which would embody the national ideal to be disseminated within the ranks of the Jewish masses. As far as Herzl was concerned, he represented a view diametrically opposed to the efforts of *Hibbat Zion.* He laid the main emphasis on political projects over fundamentally humanitarian endeavors. At the same time, he did acknowledge the cogency of Pinsker's ideas, which in their final formulation, shortly before the latter's death, he felt to be very close to his own. He even admitted that he would never have written his own book, *The Jewish State,* if he had already come across Pinsker's *Autoemancipation.*

Establishment of political Zionism and its initial dilemmas

The existence of a copious specialist literature of high quality on the development of Zionism dispenses us from the need to delve into the details of the complex history of the movement. Zionism truly did open a new chapter in the cultural and political history of world Jewry, but it did not have exactly the same effect, at least not immediately, on the social history of Jews. That is why reference will be made here only to the most salient phases in that evolution, which, as will be seen, when all is said and done, still attained only a secondary role amongst the political options for European Jewry prior to the Shoah. In this outline of trends that were, in themselves, highly complex, the emphasis will be primarily laid on the new norms of collective self-definition and cohesion to which they gave rise.

The first great inspirers of Zionism, Theodor Herzl, Max Nordau, and others, had initially been wholehearted advocates of assimilation, and it was essentially the crisis provoked by anti-Semitism at the end of the nineteenth century that turned them against the ideals of their younger years, and even then not in every respect. It is relatively simple to trace the 'external' ideological influences affecting the formation of the main ideas developed by the fathers of Zionism (secularism, Romantic territorial and cultural nationalism, major importance attributed to the national language and the symbolic infrastructure of nation-building, the project of a modern state organization with democratic institutions). It was perhaps even more symptomatic, though, that during the lifetime of Herzl himself Zionism appeared only as just one of the possible answers to the 'Jewish Question' that was conceived as a solution under the pressure of anti-Semitic violence.

At the very beginning, Herzl, still following the assimilationist logic, supposed the 'solution' in the complete desertion of Jewish identity, that is, a movement of mass conversion. In the course of their lives, both Herzl and Nordau had moved from the East (Hungary) to the West (Vienna, Paris). The latter had even changed his family name, from Südfeld to Nordau, an act of highly assimilationist symbolism. Both would have liked to retain the benefits of European civilization and extend them over the whole of Jewry, in line with the socio–symbolic and geopositioning strategies of a fair number of

Europe's Jews. Both came from Hungary's capital, where they had completed their secondary education (and Nordau also qualified as a physician) before Herzl settled in Vienna, Nordau in Paris. Both were bilingual (and Nordau multilingual), publishing regularly in the press in Austria, Germany, and elsewhere, and were thoroughly at home in the best editorial offices, salons, and liberal political circles of Europe's capital cities. By upbringing and by the society they moved in alike, both were cosmopolitan publicists, German-language writers, preserving hardly anything from the cultural or religious legacy of traditional Judaism. They worked within the orbit of Pan-German culture, sharing enthusiastically its universalistic values and aspirations. At the beginning of his studies at Vienna University, Herzl was actually a member of a students' fraternity oriented to the Greater German ideal, until the anti-Semitism manifested by some of his fellow members obliged him to resign.

The dissimilationist program that the fathers of Zionism envisaged for Jewry, then, essentially began to take shape when anti-Semitism flared up towards the end of century, as both men had opportunity to witness at first hand at the time of the Dreyfus Affair in Paris, Lueger's election as mayor in Vienna, and the anti-Semitic demonstrations of the Young Czechs in Prague, all in the last years of the outgoing nineteenth century. They were thus far more Zionists by necessity (*Notzionisten*) than their predecessors, who had floated the idea of a 'return to Zion.' As a result, they were unable to enter into a cultural community with traditional Judaism, viewing it as a whole only with considerable reservations and some of its elements, such as the Yiddish jargon, with a certain condescension. That may explain why the 'solution' that they proposed to the 'Jewish Question' was, essentially from the outset, so decidedly political in nature, tailored to bring the interests of the various factions of contemporary Jewry, with their diverse cultural and religious alignments, down to a common denominator. That is why Herzl put the emphasis on the creation of a nation state, not just in his celebrated programmatic tract, *The Jewish State*, but also in the action program for which he gained acceptance at the first Zionist Congress (Basle, 1897), a task to whose implementation he was to devote the rest of his life. Summing up the lessons of that gathering, he was already noting in his diary, 'Here in Basle I founded the Jewish State.'

He was justified in so referring to the program, actually stitched together by Nordau, that had been passed at this first major meeting of representatives of the chief 'families' of European Jewry. It indeed contained all the preliminary political goals necessary for the creation of a state. These objectives could be very quickly realized. The congress itself was made a central institution, as the Zionist movement's supreme deliberative and decision-making body (a kind of periodic parliament elected by all financial contributors). There was an executive apparatus, under an elected president and working like an incipient government, with a global sphere of authority. In accordance with the program, it was not long (at the Fifth Congress in 1901) before the Zionists were setting up their own bank to take care of the movement's financial affairs, the resources for which were to be guaranteed by a Jewish National Fund. Financing was to be obtained by the sale of so-called 'shekels,' the fee for membership of the Zionist Organization, with the proceeds being allocated above all to implementing the policy of mass emigration to Palestine. Finally, for purposes of keeping the Jewish and non-Jewish public informed, a multilingual press was established.

In short, up until his premature death, Herzl strove, first, to find a territory for the resettlement of European Jews that would be suitable for setting up a quasi-state apparatus. In pursuit of this end he entered into negotiations, ultimately unsuccessful, with the Porte to secure autonomy for the Palestinian Jews (to start with). Second, he achieved to equip the future state with all the seemingly indispensable symbolic appurtenances (a national language, flag, anthem, etc.), which appeared to be indispensable for mass mobilizations, following the experiences of other movements of national awakening in the nineteenth century. Just in the official air of its external trappings alone (parliamentary-style deliberations, dark suits as obligatory dress, etc.), the Basle Congress bore the stamp of a symbolic system of projected state dignity from the outset.

One may discern overtly modernist political choices in many of the details of Zionist notions and at the same time, in the spirit of Zionism's 'dual universalism,' an intention to reconcile the traditionalist outlook and the sensitivities of 'western' Jews. A good instance was the incorporation of seven stars into the design of the 'national flag,' which were envisaged not just as an obvious symbol for the seven days of the week but also to express the then utterly utopian ideal of a seven-hour working day. Similarly, the choice of Hebrew as the national language was a highly strategic act, not just an expression of the purely political desire to preclude any attempt to make some foreign (i.e. 'non-Jewish') tongue the official language of the would-be Jewish state (German, for example, towards which even Herzl himself was inclined, finding it improbable that Hebrew could be made suitable for everyday use). It was principally meant to block the adoption of Yiddish, or for that manner any Jewish dialect that had its derivation in another European language, imbedded as such in a particular locality, which might have sown division amongst immigrants, as some of them would have had to acquire it as a foreign tongue while others would have been advantaged as 'native speakers.' The stake here was the need not merely to break with Jewry's historic disunity, diversity and splintering, but also to avoid any one Jewish group acquiring a status of symbolic, intellectual or political domination or preeminence over others, making the future state unequally attractive for all clusters of the world Jewry. To that end, it was important to create a totally new, as it were 'pan-national' Jewish culture that, to boot, did not in any way resemble the traditions of societies that had hosted the Diaspora, except in respect of political and economic modernization.

All these 'nationalist' principles did not suffice to change the fact that the language of debate at Zionist Congresses was to be almost exclusively German even well after Herzl's death. The proceedings of the meetings were likewise recorded in German right up until the 1930s, when, for both practical and political reasons this was given up for English. The obvious reason for that was not just that German had become compromised by the ground being gained by Nazism, but also the growing importance of Anglo-Saxon Jewry amongst the movement's financial supporters.

The founders of Zionism thus treated the creation of a political framework as overriding all other considerations. It was only for want of better immediate solutions that they lent support to the 'practical Zionists' in the settlement of immigrants. That is probably also the reason why neither Herzl nor Nordau ruled out the idea that their dream of a 'Jewish national homeland' did not necessarily (at least in the short term) have to be realized in Palestine. Following the collapse of their negotiations with the Porte, they did not turn a hair in giving serious consideration to accepting a territory in Uganda offered by the British government, though meanwhile not abandoning of course formally the idea of a 'return' to *Eretz Israel* as the ultimate goal of the movement. This so-called 'territorialist' concept, which disregards the symbolically overinvested notion of a 'return to Zion' (though not showing indifference to these) well illustrates that priority, in principle, was always given to practically accomplishable and seemingly acceptable political solutions. As Herzl put it, the Zionist movement's main goal was 'to direct a people without land to a land without people,' wherever that might be located. Much ink was spilled in arguing over the 'territorialist' option, and it gave rise to no little dissension within the nascent movement, but in the end it was rejected, as it came up against the furious opposition of a majority of members, especially from Russian Zionists. The 'territorialists,' led by the English writer Israel Zangwill, having been outvoted at the Seventh Zionist Congress (1905), in fact resigned from the movement and set up the Jewish Territorial Organization. Thanks to later distinguished representatives, Isaac N. Sternberg amongst them, 'territorialism' rose again from its ashes on the threshold of the impending Nazi menace and made desperate but unsuccessful attempts to find a place for Europe's threatened Jews in Australia or the Dutch colony of Surinam. In any event, the temporary interest shown in 'territorialism' is testimony to the political pragmatism that governed the actions of the founding fathers of Zionism.

The ideological complexion of Zionism and the 'Zionist synthesis'

Nordau spent his whole life searching for possibilities of effective defense against the threats and blows of anti-Jewish violence that he could observe in Eastern Europe during the First World War and directly afterwards. He devised the concept of 'muscular Judaism' (*Muskeljudentum*) to express the ideal of the physically strong 'new Jewish man,' willing to use force, whom Zionism would want to emerge in *Eretz Israel*. In 1919, he pushed for an operation to be mounted to pressurize the competent authorities to grant the permits to undertake the emergency evacuation of 600,000 Jews fatally threatened in Ukraine and Russia as a result of the civil war. The movement's other leaders rejected this 'scare-mongering Zionism' and Nordau duly withdrew from the leadership. Jabotinsky, the leading figure of right radical Zionism, was later to recall Nordau's undeviatingly 'practical' posture and, not long before the Shoah, was to give the name the 'Nordau Plan' to his own program for mass rescue of Polish Jews to Palestine, part of the purpose of which was to achieve a demographic predominance for Jews in the country.

The political pragmatism of the movement came under fire from 'cultural Zionists,' under the sway of the highly influential publicist who used the by-line Ahad Ha-Am. The followers of Ahad Ha-Am were convinced, above all, that the resettlement of the millions of Jews living in the Diaspora had to be ruled out, as an unrealizable daydream. Let the Jews of Eastern Europe set off, as and when that became realistically possible, for America or other, more tranquil lands, but the solution for their main problems was 'spiritual.' What was needed was mainly to restore the sense of historical continuity of the 'Jewish people,' for the Jews always had constituted a single 'nation.' This was, in essence, the battle cultural Zionists had to wage. The solution was to be sought, first and foremost, in education. If religion could no longer be relied upon to bring about and sustain this 'spiritual unity,' then a new framework was urgently required within which Jewish identity might receive the same dignity ('glory') that religion had provided in the past. Ahad Ha-Am questioned the effectiveness of Herzl's diplomacy and criticized the estrangement of the founding fathers of Zionism from the fundamentally moral and cultural nature of Jewry's inherited values.

Chaim Weizmann, leader of the adherents of a 'Zionist synthesis,' was one of Herzl's adversaries whilst the latter was alive. But subsequently, after David Wolffsohn and Otto Warburg, he took his succession in the presidency of the World Zionist movement in 1920. It was also Weizmann who achieved the completion of a 'synthesis' between what, until then, operated as antagonistic trends within Zionism. One of those main wings comprised the 'practical' Zionists, whose primary aim was to realize the *aliyah* (the 'ascent' or 'going up' to *Eretz Israel*) – as efficiently and for as many emigrants as possible, whilst seeking to improve everyday living conditions for the *yishuv* (Jews settled in Palestine). The other influential wing was that of the 'spiritual' or 'cultural' Zionists who, by contrast, gave priority to the educational work to be pursued amongst the Diaspora masses, though not neglecting the organization of the political framework of the future state as planned by the founders. Weizmann was a central figure in the negotiations with the British government that resulted in the so-called Balfour Declaration of the 2nd of November, 1917, the first official statement on the part of the Great Power (that was soon to accept the League of Nations' supervisory mandate over Palestine) concerning "the establishment in Palestine of national home for the Jewish people" favorably considered by the British government. One token of the 'synthetic' Zionists' success was the establishment in Jerusalem of the Jewish Agency to represent the Jews of Palestine, the *yishuv*. In 1922 this won recognition from the League of Nations as an official negotiating partner for the authorities governing Palestine.

By effecting a partial reconciliation between the two antagonistic camps, the 'synthetic' Zionists succeeded in coming to the fore themselves and simultaneously widened the institutional framework of the future state. The Jews in Palestine gradually gained autonomy during the inter-war years in the educational system (as exemplified by the foundation of the Hebrew University of Jerusalem in 1925), in organizing armed self-defense, and indeed in various forms of actual self-government. The renaissance of Hebrew as the modern official language was from that point on a *fait accompli*. Even more significantly, the Zionist movement became an internationally respected, global mass organization that most governments were willing to recognize as a negotiating partner. Foremost amongst them was Great Britain, which after the First World War took over from the Ottoman Empire the administrative mandate over Palestine. The movement managed to win over a substantial portion of Eastern European Jewry, at least in terms of regular financial donations, and, to a lesser degree, Western European as well as American Jewry.

The authors of the 'Zionist synthesis' indeed took a leaf from the 'cultural Zionist' book in devoting considerable attention to propaganda work, education and training, and also to developing mutual assistance within the Diaspora (especially in Eastern Europe where this was most needed). That 'on-going work' in diaspora circumstances (*Gegenwartsarbeit*) was attended to by a huge network of Zionist circles, clustered into regional or national alliances, its cells

increasingly present throughout the world, wherever Jews were living, since the inter-war years. Due to their activities it was possible
to turn traditional elementary schools (*cheders*) into modern educational institutions (in the Polish territories and Romania), to found a
whole series of sports and youth clubs (Bar Kochba Association, the
Maccabi movement, etc.) in order to cultivate skills in a Zionist
spirit outside school, and to launch numerous explicitly political
initiatives to secure the election, in target parliamentary or local
government seats, of representatives whom they could count on to
stand up for 'Jewish interests.' That is what happened in Russia
during the post–1906 constitutional period, in the Cisleithan region
of the Habsburg Empire, when universal male suffrage was introduced in 1907, and later on in inter-war Poland, Czechoslovakia and
Romania. Pressure from Weizmann was likewise responsible for the
broadening of the Jewish Agency's social base in 1929 to admit to
its ranks non-Zionist European and American Jews, who had shown
considerable personal commitment to rescuing endangered Jews in
Central and Eastern Europe.

The First World War threw the geostrategic situation of European
Jewry into confusion. With massacres in Ukraine, the dismantling of
empires, the 1919–20 revolutions in Central Europe and the consolidation of Bolshevik power in Russia, fresh contradictions, conflicts
and debates arose within the Zionist movement. The main issue under
discussion was the economic strategy to be followed in the course of
Palestinian settlement. Weizmann and his European allies continued to
advocate a broadening of the political base of the Jewish institutions
set up in *Eretz Israel* and also of financial sources to support colonization. This problem area lost increasing ground, however, to a new
program, sponsored by the Zionist Organization of America (ZOA),
that put much more emphasis on problems of economic efficiency.
During the war the ZOA was headed by Louis Brandeis, the first Jewish judge to be appointed to the US Supreme Court. In Brandeis' view
the political phase of the Zionist movement had ended with the Balfour Declaration. The next phase would be that of intensive settlement, the success of which depending on the economic success of the
Jewish colonies. For this, the return on investment had to be the para-
mount principle to be respected, just as in any other business enterprise. It was Weizmann who emerged the victor from the clash with

Brandeis. Behind their difference of opinions, though, stood two distinct socio–political concepts of the future state: one of a strong, social and liberal constitutional state, the other aligned to American-style free trade capitalism.

At the dawn of Zionism, under the sway of Nietzsche, other intellectuals who carried weight had rejected any idealization of the Jewish past and the 'values' associated with it, seeing, on the contrary, the foundation of a Jewish state as a condition for the inevitable break with the past. Derided by others as 'Canaanites,' these Zionists also wished to see a 'new Jewish' man come into being, whom they envisaged as being strong and hard, but also indifferent to rabbinical doctrine and the traditional values it espoused. They may have made little headway, but other thinkers who hove onto the intellectual horizon in the initial era of Zionism, including the Tolstoyans—represented by labor leader Aharon D. Gordon—, adopted closely similar positions. Gordon, who had been one of the first immigrants to arrive in *Eretz Israel* in the modern age, likewise recommended for settlers in Palestine a practical rupture with Jews' historically determined 'basic character.' In his opinion, the Jewish state had to be founded on the free and creative decision of the masses in order that the 'new Jewish man,' true to his land and hardened by manual labor, should come into existence.

In reality, the most influential of all currents of thought within nascent Zionism were the socialist trends inspired by Marxism and organized labor. Their first leaders, Nachman Syrkin and Ber Borochov, put a new critical twist on the already much-discussed 'inverted pyramid' stratification of Jewry living in the Diaspora, which even the first adherents of the *Haskalah* had considered the main source of all evil visited on Jews in the modern age. In the very first hours of the creation of a new Jewish society in Palestine, socialist Zionists believed, it would be possible at last to get rid of that 'accursed historical legacy' and set up a normal economic pyramid, resting on a broad base, provided that Jews themselves, like any other people, attended to all the tasks that classical (and hence also Marxist) political economists saw as 'genuinely productive,' above all in the agricultural and industrial branches that had been 'neglected' in the Diaspora.

The organization of Zionism in Europe

Through Herzl's efforts Zionism became institutionalized into a world-wide agency, whilst simultaneously, by virtue of its status as an ideological umbrella organization, it succeeded in unifying most circles and currents of thinking within European Jewry hostile to assimilation, whether in the West or the East—irrespective (at least partially) of their specific religious or political alignments. That was just the product of a conjunction of circumstances, however, with Zionist unity just about being held together only under the pressure of external threats and the tiny ideological core shared by all. The entire remaining history of the movement was to be marked by a twofold endeavor: firstly, a struggle to win over and gain support from those segments of Jewish public opinion in various countries and social strata that were mistrustful of, hostile or indifferent to Zionism, and secondly, to construct and gain acceptance for a minimal common program, that would make it possible for the movement to maintain its constantly threatened unity.

Zionism, to the present day, has been extremely selective in its enrolment of members. Even following the foundation of the state of Israel, the movement has had only a limited attraction for a large part of its potential target audience, for at least three overlapping socio–historical reasons: the structure of the 'host' society of the Jews in question (more particularly, the weight given to local anti-Semitism in the ideological mix that went into the process of building the nation state); the conditions of life, anthropologically speaking, of the Jewish communities in question, that is to say, the extent of their cultural assimilation, their attitude to religion and their relationship to those in power—or the nature of political integration they enjoyed—; and finally, the social class stratification of those concerned (their financial and economic status, level of academic qualification, etc.). To this must be added that the cyclical nature of historical development could sometimes alter the character of the anti-Semitic threat from one day to the next (as was the case during the revolutionary unrest and civil wars in Central and Eastern Europe after the First World War, or throughout Europe during the incursions of Nazism). These circumstances could have a direct impact on the appeal of the Zionist movement at any given moment.

To attempt a detailed analysis of the factors involved—research is anyway still a long way from having clarified them in every respect—, would be to bite off more than can be chewed here. What is both possible and necessary, though, is to identify some general connections through an outline of the socio–geographical topography of Zionist influence up to the Shoah.

It has already been shown that the Zionist concept was originally elaborated and promulgated by highly assimilated Jewish intellectuals from both the West and the East. Its largest camp of supporters, however, was mustered primarily in Central and Eastern Europe. This was the case especially in Romania and the tsarist empire, above all amongst Lithuanian Jews (*Litvaks*) settled in former territories of the Polish kingdom and Ukraine (where movements preceding political Zionism had already prepared the ground from the 1870s onwards). But, to a lesser extent, many opted for Zionism in Germany and the Habsburg Monarchy (specifically in Galicia, where a proto-Zionist movement had likewise been organized well before the time of the first Basle Congress). Even after the First World War, these strongholds of Zionism in Jewish public opinion were retained within the successor states of the great empires, in Poland and Lithuania in the first place, but also Czechoslovakia and Austria in the second place. As has already been noted, the worst of the ever-cruder anti-Semitic agitation, becoming part of local state policies from the end of the nineteenth century, was borne by Jews living in Russia and Romania. Mass emigration to North and South America did little to alleviate the appalling living conditions of the remaining Jewish populations, stricken as they were by the general backwardness (and at times total dysfunctionality) of the local economies and undergoing explosive growth of their population in the initial phase of demographic modernization. Slow economic growth, or long-term relative stagnation, and the early expanding phase of the demographic transition, the pressures of which were not much eased by emigration, played a similar role in Austrian Galicia. They made local Jewry peculiarly receptive to Zionism as a veritable salvation ideology, since it promised deliverance from their present predicament. Here too there was a further contributory factor, of course, in the shape of Polish nationalism holding the local political hegemony, which in the final decades of the nineteenth century spilled over into a sort of aggressive 'ethnic war' directed partly against the 'national awakening' of the Ukrainians (who constituted a majority of the population in East Galicia) but partly against local Jewry.

The living conditions and possibilities of social advancement for Jews were incomparably better in the Czech provinces and Austria proper than in underdeveloped and economically backward eastern regions of the Habsburg Monarchy. For a long time the anti-Semitic threat was also not so directly palpable here under the shield of the liberal empire (though both Vienna and Prague were scenes of acute anti-Jewish agitation from the end of the century). That sense of threat was to recede even more in democratic Czechoslovakia of the inter-war period, whereas it intensified with the rapid growth of indigenous Fascism in Austria during the 1930s. This impacted particularly on opportunities for Jewish intellectuals caught within the 'dual structure' of the professional job market, and all the more because, during the inter-war years, obvious discrimination against educated Jews, usually encouraged by the public authorities and dominant political parties, became general throughout Central Europe, particularly in Austria ('Red Vienna' excepted), Poland, Slovakia and Hungary. Its emer-gence had already started to become perceptible amongst those enter-ing higher education from the 1880s onwards.

It was in response to such aggression, whether symbolic or physi-cal, that Jewish university students began to band together in proto-Zionist or explicitly Zionist circles. In Vienna the Kadimah students' association was led, from 1882, by Nathan Birnbaum, credited with having coined the term 'Zionism.' In Prague the Bar Kochba associa-tion was founded in 1893 and served as a forerunner of 'cultural Zion-ism.' Even in Budapest a Maccabi circle was established in 1903. None of that, however, meant that an appreciable Zionist camp devel-oped around such initiatives in those countries. The course of events in Germany too was much the same. A few high level assimilated intellectuals, who had grown up within German culture—including such major figures as Martin Buber or Gershom Scholem—, became convinced through personal reflection that a commitment to Zionism and, consequently, emigration to Palestine, represented the sole ac-ceptable strategy, in that it enabled them to transcend the contradic-tions in identity of an assimilated status fraught with sickly de-formities. For Jews caught in the force-field of conflicting nationalistic ideologies in the multinational regions of former Austria–Hungary—like between Czechs and Germans in Bohemia–Moravia, Hungarians and Romanians in Transylvania, Hungarians and Slovaks in Slovakia, Poles, Germans and Ukrainians in East Galicia, Romanians, Ukrainians and Germans in Bukovina—Zionism offered itself as a natural platform in their struggle to find a 'separate path' in their assertion of identity and to achieve a measure of political unification and autonomy.

Jews in the Balkan countries remained already at a lower level of acculturation during the era of modernization for nation states. Equally, the pressures to which they were exposed were not, on average, comparable to those in Central and Eastern Europe. They responded to the Zionist call more for cultural reasons. They had long-standing relations with the Ottoman Empire, belonging to the same Mediterranean life world and civilization (*Lebenswelt*) stretching from Palestine to the Iberian peninsula. For them, the project of a 'return to Zion' was not attended by the huge change in living conditions that it was for most of their fellows in fate elsewhere in Europe. In Bulgaria, Zionists already constituted a majority within the leadership of Jewish communities by 1920, one consequence of which was that regular instruction in Hebrew was introduced into local Jewish schools.

Everywhere else, Zionism could not have a strong impact up until the time of the Shoah, even though certain groups amongst the assimilated Jewish bourgeoisie of Western and Central Europe, guided primarily by motives of philanthropic solidarity, often showed readiness to provide financial aid to the movement. They therefore tacitly accepted Zionism, and occasionally were even willing to support it, but only as an attempted solution to the 'Jewish Question' applicable 'to others.' A good case in point was Hungary, where Zionism not only found no mass response in the decades prior to the country's 'Jewish laws' (1938 and after), but actually ran into opposition from the strong 'adoptive nationalism' (indeed Magyar chauvinism proper) of community authorities. That, however, did not hinder the considerable success of campaigns run by the Pro Palestina movement to raise money to help those leaving for *Eretz Israel*, or already living there, during the years between the two world wars.

The anti-Zionist camp and its points of reference

We are now in a position to turn to the question of why the Zionist program met (and continues to meet) with, at times, such vehement rejection on the part of broad sections of European Jewry, often even in Eastern Europe, and not just from circles that stuck by strategies of 'national assimilation.' Anti-Zionist stances were grounded in at least four basic principles.

First and foremost, broad groups of Orthodox Jewry, both those under rabbinical and those under Hasidic influence, perceived Zionism from the very outset as an antireligious enterprise, not just on account of its neutrality, indeed indifference to 'religious values' and interests, but also following purely religious considerations. For the majority of Jews who strictly observed the regulations of Orthodoxy, the project of a Jewish state, preceding the coming of the Messiah was an outright sacrilege. In their view, the writings of the Biblical prophets were unequivocal in stating that the Messiah alone would be able to unite the Jewish people in *Eretz Israel* 'at the end of time.' From that per-spective, modernization of the Hebrew language, with its sacral func-tion, and its application to the profane purposes of a medium of 'national' communication were tantamount to a denial of religious norms. The main mouthpiece for this traditionalist anti-Zionist objec-tion was to be *Agudat Israel*. It became organized as a political party in independent Poland and fought for the authority of the Orthodox rabbinate to be strengthened, gaining committed support for this amongst certain large Hasidic communities, especially the followers of the Gur dynasty. *Agudat*'s ideological influence, curiously enough, even stretched as far as Orthodox circles amongst settlers in Palestine itself. Though a fringe group, the ultra-religious faction known as *Neturei Karta* ('guardians of the city'), actually split from *Agudat* in 1935 and set up its headquarters in one of the suburbs of Jerusalem. It did so principally in order to act as an extremist censor of the Zionist program. With descendants of the Szatmár Hasidic dynasty (from the former east-central territory of Hungary) numbering amongst its members, it continues to this day to stick intransigently to outright rejection of a secular Israeli state.

Secondly, Zionism was generally spurned by the various wings of Reform Judaism rooted in the ideology of the Berlin *Haskalah*.

'Conservative,' 'liberal,' and (in Hungary) 'Neologue' (or 'congress') communities alike – whatever their names—were dominated right up until the Shoah by those advocating national assimilation within the framework of the state in which they lived. The greatest numbers of Jews lived in such 'reform' communities prior to 1945 in Austria (at least up till 1932, when Zionists attained a majority within the leadership of the Viennese *Kultusgemeinde*), Germany as well as Hungary, to say nothing of Western European countries. It was indeed the strong protests of the German rabbinate that dissuaded Herzl from his original intention to choose Munich as the site for the First Zionist Congress. Though Vienna was to remain the center of World Zionism whilst Herzl was still alive, relations between the movement's founder and the Viennese rabbinate remained throughout on a tense footing. In Hungary, the membership of Neologue congregations became numerically stronger after 1919 than that of Orthodox communities, and their official representatives instituted a veritable witch-hunt against Zionists, squeezing them entirely out of control of representative bodies. Zionists were looked on there as undesirable elements even in the two secondary schools under Neologue control, to the extent that the profession of Zionist beliefs could be grounds for expulsion.

Thirdly, the socialist and Marxist movement, as another contender in the ideological ring of the times, likewise intervened with ever-growing vigor against Zionism even before, but especially after, the Bolsheviks' accession to power in Russia. As was discussed in the previous chapter, the institutionalized far-left was, in reality, a direct successor of policy-makers of forced assimilation and, moreover, ready to resort to the harshest of devices to that end. The victorious Bolsheviks proceeded to extirpate the buds of every ideology competing with or opposing their own within Russia. They thus declared war on Zionism along with the rest. They heaped accusations on it, with the *Evsektsia* set up within the propaganda department of the Communist Party passing severe sentences on Zionist adherents even in the 1920s. A much more bloody campaign to liquidate Jewish intellectuals merely on suspicion of Zionist sympathies got under way, on Stalin's order, in 1948. In 1952, the Slánsky trial in Czechoslovakia, the first in a series of anti-Semitic show trials, was accompanied by virulently anti-Zionist rhetoric, whilst in Romania and Poland anti-Jewish purges were undertaken, ostensibly to root out 'bourgeois' elements that had infiltrated into the ranks of the Communist Party—often a euphemism for Jewish cadres suspected of holding Zionist sympathies. In the eyes of Communists in power, the movement was a contrivance of 'bourgeois imperialism' and no more than a western-inspired 'colonialist venture.' In Hungary, too, official anti-Zionist hysteria competed with the campaign against Titoist Yugoslavia in the vehemence of its sloganeering.

It is true though, that there was a short period between the end of the Second World War and the start of the Cold War when the Soviet Union, simply to oppose the policy line that Great Britain was taking in the Near East, gave its support (side by side with the United States, ironically enough) to Zionist aspirations regarding the partition of Palestine and obtaining the international recognition of Israel. That brief interlude apart, the Soviet power and its allies pursued a systematically anti-Zionist line. Both during and, indeed, after the Cold War, that line was also slavishly adhered to by most Communist parties and left-wing movements in Western Europe and elsewhere in the world (not uncommonly on the urging of leaders who were themselves of Jewish descent). It was not just identification with Communism that adversely affected Zionism, but also assimilation within the ranks of 'left-thinking people,' since the notion of a 'return to Zion,' from its moment of birth onwards, was antithetical in its very principle to the internationalist and universalistic commitments of the secular left wing of its time.

It should not be forgotten, however, that in the first two decades after their assumption of power, the Bolsheviks too did make an attempt to establish a local Jewish national home, acceptable to them, as was noted earlier. The basis was the requirement, firstly, that loyalty to the 'Soviet homeland' be maintained and, secondly, that the Jewish 'national culture' should use Yiddish, to which end a special educational network was set up in the early days. Indeed, although it was of purely symbolic significance for the tiny population involved, they even granted the formalities of territorial autonomy, under strict supervision, to the Far Eastern province of Birobidzhan regarded for some time as an experience in 'Soviet–Jewish' statehood.

Finally, mention should be made of the various forms of Jewish cultural and political nationalism that presented themselves as rivals to Zionism. Most important amongst these both political and cultural initiatives were the doctrine of autonomism, as propounded by Dubnov, and the Yiddish-based, socialist *Bund*. The ideological competition from both these quarters helped considerably to limit the influence exerted by Zionism within tsarist Russia and Habsburg Galicia, as well as, later on, in independent Poland.

To these should be added a number of other schools of thought which, likewise, represented some form of 'practical cultural nationalism,' specifically by pushing for the emergence of a high-level Yiddish literary culture, in contrast to the efforts the Zionists were putting into developing Hebrew as the exclusive Jewish language. One of these trends, headed by the philosopher Chaim Zhitlovsky, showed some affinities to the autonomists (*folk*ists) in regarding the modernization of Yiddish as a major intellectual stimulus, capable of uniting various Jewish minorities of Eastern Europe. For understandable reasons, that ideology exerted an influence on the organizers of the first 'Yiddish Congress' (Czernowitz, 1908) and on the founders of the first center of research into Yiddish culture, the *Yidisher Visenshaftlikher Institut* (YIVO) established at Vilna (1925). These different circles all emphatically rejected the role Zionists assigned to Hebrew, viewing it purely as a sort of 'Jewish Latin'—a language for scholarly disputation and the liturgical idiom reserved for the religious élite. For them, Hebrew was not only remote from the spoken language of ordinary people but excessively archaic: a vehicle for an ancient, traditional civilization, it was quite unfit to meet the linguistic needs of a modern society. They also objected that Hebrew, over and above the genuine difficulties presented by its practical use and its need for extensive 'reform,' was also too closely bound to Judaic religious culture—an influence from which most advocates of the development of Yiddish (except for the committed traditionalists in *Agudat Israel*) wished to be freed.

Emigrants and those taking the path of *aliyah*

By the start of the twentieth century, the social integration of Jews who sought assimilation (new immigrants apart) had largely come to a close in western-type democracies. Nevertheless even those who would still not accept a strategy of national assimilation and its lure of social advancement, or who had become disillusioned and broke with that (as many in France did in the wake of the Dreyfus Affair), were more likely to turn to the political left, with its appeal to prevailing universalistic values, than to Zionism. Thus, in the West Zionists had for a long time to look for recruits to their cause primarily amongst new immigrants from Eastern Europe either struggling with the difficulties of adjustment or having clearly lost any sense of bearings. Even amongst them, most ranged themselves with Zionism merely out of agreement in principle, for purposes of giving moral or financial support to candidates for *aliyah*, usually without themselves giving any consideration to leaving for Palestine. It was no light matter to pass up the quality of life that the economically developed West offered, the spell of universality emanating from a 'great national' culture, and the possibility of integration into a democratically ordered nation state for the dubious project of constructing a 'new homeland' in the deserts of the Near East, the achievement of which, until the close of what, for Jews in particular, was the catastrophe of the Second World War, could only appear as a pipe-dream rather than a realistic program.

That explains why, before the United States introduced a strict quota system in 1924 to control immigration, the majority of Jews leaving Eastern Europe headed for North America or, to a lesser extent, other overseas or Western European countries, whilst only relatively small numbers set off for Palestine. In the years 1919–24, directly following the First World War, for example, no less than 290,000 Jews entered the United States, whereas altogether just 49,000 went to Palestine—large as that body was in itself, as compared with the earlier numbers of settlers in *Eretz Israel*. Admittedly, as a result of the American restrictions, the direction of emigration switched sharply thereafter towards the Holy Land. In 1925–26 there were 48,000 arrivals in *Eretz Israel* and just 20,500 in the United States—a general shift towards the *aliyah* which was to be maintained right up until the outbreak of the Second World War. Contrary to Zionist hopes, however rapid this growth was, the number of Jewish inhabitants of Palestine, rose from 78,000 (out of a total population of 650,000) in 1900 to 475,000 only (out of 1,450,000) by 1939. Thus, Jews continued to remain in a minority against an overwhelming Arab majority. All things considered, the size of the Jewish population in

Eretz Israel, which was partly a result of natural increase as well, proved to be virtually negligible relative to the roughly 2.8 million Jews who had found a home in the United States alone during the decades on either side of the turn of the century.

Then, during the Great Depression of the 1930s, one western country after the other closed the door on immigrants. The year 1933 marks the start of the advance of Fascism in Central Europe (using the word to denote the take-over of power in Germany by the Nazis and the subsequent expansion of the Third *Reich*, rather than in the original—Italian—sense). From 1935, anti-Jewish agitation turned increasingly violent in Poland, Hungary and Romania, to say nothing of the authoritarian (and anti-Semitic) régime of pre-*Anschluss* Austria. The ideological attraction of Zionism was undoubtedly enhanced as a result, despite the fact that the masses who sought to emigrate were, in many cases, still far from adopting the movement's goals for themselves. For the majority of refugees from Hitler's Germany, settlement in Palestine tended to come into the reckoning only as a 'last resort,' or in other words, only when the possibilities for immigration elsewhere became blocked. The climate of the Near East was hard for those used to that of continental Europe, its economy underdeveloped, its cultural infrastructure weak. On top of that, the British authorities mandated to govern Palestine were arbitrarily limiting the number of immigrants, for fear of Arab reactions. In the same time anti-Jewish pogroms carried out by the Arabs (in 1929, for example) served further to scare off or discourage those who might be contemplating flight to *Eretz Israel* both before the Shoah and for some time afterwards, even following the establishment of the state of Israel in 1948.

The ideological spectrum of the Zionist movement

The Zionist movement, by its very design, came into existence as a coalition of many ideological trends, which led during Herzl's lifetime alone to several major shifts in internal alliances and the emergence of schools of thought often at odds with one another. There were some factions at the very center of the Zionist World Organization. They got established from the beginning as independent international bodies, whereas others—the 'territorialists,' for example—promptly left the

movement for good. Others again emerged during the decades following its start to gain highly variable measures of influence in different
countries. The strands by which they were tied to the parent body
were often so feeble and tangled that the link was often severed after
internal quarrels within a given faction. The entire history of Zionism
is thus characterized by kaleidoscopic complexity and by the fact that
there were often irreconcilable conflicts between multiple factions,
despite the supposedly common 'ultimate objective.' The differences
might be ideological or political in complexion, or they might relate to
the manner of the 'return to Zion.' On top of that, the links of the local
organizations of the Diaspora to factions that had set up within *Eretz
Israel* itself, and to branches of those factions operating in other parts
of the world, were not uncommonly fraught with conflicts of their
own. It complicated the situation still more that every political trend
sponsored its own string of youth organizations, women's associations, sports clubs, etc., and some of those acquired a historical significance in their own right. It will not be possible here to trace in any
detail all the ramifications of this complex institutional history. To
oversimplify somewhat, we shall have to make do with outlining the
make-up of the most important parties, groupings, and trends in
chronological order of their appearance.

The oldest amongst them was *He-Halutz*. The date of its foundation goes back to the era preceding Zionism proper. The circles around
Bilu and *Am Olam*, proclaimed themselves to be Russian members of
the movement when they started operating in the 1880s, though the
transformation of *He-Halutz* into real international organization can be
dated to 1905, as a result of being invited to do so by Menachem Us-
sishkin. That was invariably the pragmatic way *He-Halutz* proceeded.
Its aim was to provide young, unmarried men who were prepared to
settle in Palestine (at least for a while) with the specialist, moral and
military training that the *yishuv*, the Jewish community in *Eretz Israel*,
called for. Though *He-Halutz* never spelled out a precise political
stance, it is best regarded as one of the early left-wing or properly
socialist initiatives that primarily urged and prepared their adherents to
set up agricultural cooperative communities (*kibbutz*es and *moshav*s)
and gave their political commitment exclusively to Zionism.

The establishment of model farms was of fundamental importance
to ensure that they would train up the future farmers who would, at

one and the same time, exemplify the 'new Jew.' The movement's main bases were initially in Russia, Romania, and the United States, amongst immigrant Jews of rural origins, and later on, between the two world wars, in independent Poland and Lithuania. The setting up of a world alliance of *halutz*es occurred at the 1911 Zionist Congress. Their program, in essence, was to launch regional associations, give practical instruction to potential 'returnees,' and organize the *aliyah*. The latter became ever more difficult to carry into effect between the two world wars, due to the restrictions imposed by the British authorities to check immigration. As a response, from 1919 onwards, experienced *Halutzim* activists became masters at spiriting people clandestinely into Palestine. Their pedagogical work alongside that placed stress on the qualities expected of the 'New Jew': courage, acceptance of sacrifices and self-sacrifice for the good of the collective, peak physical condition, respect for manual work, and total commitment to the ideal of *Eretz Israel*. The 'curriculum' was partly ideological (Zionism, social sciences, Hebrew language, geography) and partly practical (training in some trade). The branches of the movement were remarkably diverse, depending on the country in which they operated.

During the 1920s, big *Halutz* groups fleeing the Soviet régime set off from Poland bound for Israel, where their reception was often organized in collaboration with other left-wing Zionist bodies. In Russia itself the movement at first tried to work together with the Bolshevik authorities, until a split in its own ranks occurred in 1923, with one faction subjecting itself to the régime whilst the other went underground, transforming itself into an independent Jewish workers' movement. Both wings were remorselessly annihilated in 1928, with only a few cadres managing to escape to Palestine, either via Poland or somehow making their way through the infernal regions of the *Gulag*.

The first party to be formed officially within the bosom of political Zionism was religious in its aims, openly proclaiming that the 'return' had to be squared with the commandments of the *Torah*. *Mizrachi* ('spiritual center') was founded at Vilna in 1902 as a religious branch of the World Zionist Organization for purposes of mobilizing Orthodox Jewry. Its leaders, such as Isaac Reines or Ze'ev Jawitz, were all distinguished rabbis. *Mizrachi* had an important function in the movement's success, as substantial segments of Orthodoxy, especially in the strongly Hasidic-influenced communities of the more southerly territories of Galicia, Ukraine, Romania and eastern Hungary, were adamantly opposed to Zionist aspirations for theological reasons discussed earlier. Geographically, its influence quickly spread throughout Russia (where no fewer than 210 local branches of *Mizrachi* were operating in 1903), Galicia and Romania, as well as other European countries and the United States. In 1923, the alliance set up its global headquarters in Palestine, the first of all Zionist organizations to do so. Having almost immediately come to an understanding with the World Zionist Organization, it was granted wide-ranging autonomy in the field of education. Making the most of this opportunity, it established many religious schools in Palestine, which were only integrated into the Israeli state educational system in 1953. That system extends to all levels, from elementary and secondary schools to institutions providing higher specialist training and *yeshiva*s, offering advanced theological instruction and rabbinical education. In Israel, with the help of religious groups that entered subsequently, *Mizrachi* has to this day managed systematically to resist attempts by other groupings (always in the majority) that have sought a complete secularization of the state and public administrative institutions.

Yet even before political Zionism came on the scene, a number of the schools of thought that were urging a 'return,' all decisively under the influence of the socialist and anticlerical movements of their time, concurred with the proposition that linked the 'gathering to the ancestral land' with constructing a new society, to be created in line with socialist principles.

Attempts to couple Jewish socialism and Zionist messianism can be traced all the way back to the 1890s, with strong elements being found in the writings of Zhitlovsky and Syrkin, as well as in the political proclamations of various local organizations set up for this purpose within the Russian 'Pale of Settlement' towards the end of the nineteenth century. Even before that century was out, these movements had felt obliged to break away from larger movements that were seeking to mobilize Jewish workers. The first such occasion occurred when the Russian Social Democratic Party (the precursor of the Bolsheviks), citing the principle of 'internationalism,' refused to recognize the specific interests of Jews. Then later on the *Bund* itself, the General Jewish Workers' Union, declared that membership of its trades unions was incompatible with support for the Zionist alliance (1901). That marked the start of the fateful clash between Russian Jewish socialists and the Bolsheviks on the one hand and between the Russian–Jewish socialist movements and Zionism, on the other hand.

Thus, as a reaction and around that same time, a number of other associations were raising the idea of uniting socialism with Zionism. The first Zionist socialist movement, *Ahva*, was founded by Saul Raphael Landau in Vienna in 1898. The World Union of *Po'alei Zion*, was born in 1907, with a large sphere of activities extended into Russia, Austria–Hungary (mainly Galicia and Vienna), Romania and other countries, including Palestine. It wavered continually between alliance with the Communist movement and aspirations of independence, as it strove to represent both Jewish socialists and nationalist workers. Splits ensued in the movement in Russia, its original cradle, as a result of the revolutionary events of the stormy years of 1903–05 and the growing anti-Semitic menace, with some groups advocating 'territorialist' solutions and others putting the emphasis on organizing local self-defense against pogroms. Between 1903 and 1905 a new group emerged within the Russian *Po'alei Zion* under the name *Vozrozhdeniye* ('renaissance'). The choice of a Russian name was no accident, as its program was centered on defending the interests of Russia's Jewish workers and eschewed the idea of a 'return.' The movement may have been rapidly wound up, but many of *Vozrozhdeniye*'s plans—Yiddish language education, Jewish national autonomy, 'productivization' of the masses (i.e. retraining for agricultural production in particular)—had a powerful influence on the *Gegenwartsarbeit* ('on-going work' of Zionists in the Diaspora) that was officially adopted as a program by the Third Conference of Russian Zionists at Helsingfors (Helsinki, 1906).

In 1906 another faction of Russian *Po'alei Zion*, under the leadership of Ber Borochov, exerted considerable influence within the Zionist labor movement, but the party effectively disappeared from the political arena when counter-revolutionary political and police reactions were stepped up. Its active membership was decimated by the harassment, those who were left being forced into emigration *en masse*. After the First World War, *Po'alei Zion* was reorganized in independent Poland and Soviet Russia, but the original party continued in other parts of Central European and also (as a result of fresh immigration) in Palestine, Britain, the United States, and even Argentina. The Bolshevik take-over, however, was the source of a further split in the international movement. Certain branches, following instructions from the Comintern, joined organizations controlled by local Bolsheviks, whilst others insisted on sticking to their independence. Before long, though, all were to be swept from the political stage by Soviet state violence.

The broad conglomerate of 'General Zionists' came into being following the emergence of the two opposed wings of political Zionism, the religiously inspired *Mizrachi* and the *Po'alei Zion* labor movement. Their delegates to the Zionist Congresses founded an association that had very little in the way of a specific political platform, and their numbers dwindled more and more over time. Despite that, in 1920 they set up the *Ha-No'ar ha-Zion* youth organization and a labor movement faction whose members later established several *kibbutzes* in Palestine. Up until 1930 they did not possess an officially recognized independent organization, but then, at their first conference in Basle, they founded a World Union of General Zionists. The platform that they proposed placed the emphasis on principles of political liberalism (in defiance both of radical socialist tendencies and of the religious line of Zionism), that is to say, it highlighted the general interests of the inhabitants of *Eretz Israel* over specific class or cluster-bound interests, pushing for cooperation between labor and capital, encouraging private enterprise, and seeking in the name of freedom of thought to end the sway of parties in the Palestine educational system. As a result, the movement experienced numerous schisms and changes of alliance, but the various factions of 'General Zionists' continued to represent a major centrist-party constituent within the Zionist movement as a whole.

Other movements cannot boast of such lengthy histories, though they may at times have succeeded in gathering notable support. Amongst those worth mentioning are the *Blau-Weiss* ('Blue-White') youth groups in Germany, first established in 1912. They had close links with the non-Jewish *Wandervögel* youth movement (initiated in 1901), until anti-Semitism gained a hold on the latter, like many other organizations in the German middle classes. Recruiting its members from amongst Germanized Jewish youth, *Blau-Weiss* urged them to rebel against the assimilationist aspirations of their families. It took over the cult of nature and manly virtues from the Boy Scouts movement, but added observance of Jewish holidays, instruction in the Hebrew language as well as encouraging closer familiarity with Yiddish *folk* culture. During the 1920s the movement organized its own emigratory sorties to Palestine but failed to set up an independent community there on the pattern of those established by other Zionist youth groups. It was disbanded in 1929, continuing to operate further, though in greatly reduced numbers, elsewhere in Central Europe (Austria and Czechoslovakia) in countries of strong assimilationist traditions.

The Zionist extreme left and extreme right

In 1916 a new arrival appeared on the Zionist scene in the shape of *Ha-Shomer ha-Za'ir*, a revolutionary-minded socialist youth movement formed from two branches, operating in Galicia and Vienna. The sources from which *Ha-Shomer ha-Za'ir* drew its inspiration were other prominent youth movements from earlier in the century and of its time: the Boy Scouts, the German *Wandervögel* associations, and some of the secret societies of anti-tsarist, young revolutionary intellectuals. In their endeavors to reform education they adopted their forerunners' principles and methods of personal development, though they were not averse to citing Nietzschean voluntarism either. To this they added the importance of a pioneering spirit, a socialist-style universal humanism as well as the Zionist project. They contended against assimilation, whether that was of the 'nationalist' or Communist variety, and guided their members towards *aliyah* and, more specifically, the establishment of collectivist *kibbutz*es in *Eretz Israel*. Much of their doctrine was, in fact, taken from the stock of ideas that had been developed by *He-Halutz* and more or less orthodox Marxism. The beginnings of a more global reach came at Danzig in 1924, when, in order to complement branches that were operating by then in Poland and Austria, they set up groups in Romania, Latvia, Lithuania, and the Soviet Union. The organization was further widened on the eve of the Second World War to bring in Jews living in other countries under Nazi threat, Hungary included. *Ha-Shomer*'s followers offered leftist-inclined Jewish youth a Zionist alternative which, with the advances of Nazism, increasingly came under the seductive influence of Communist extreme leftists. The *Betar* youth movement, which was allied to the Union of Zionists–Revisionists led by Vladimir Jabotinsky, may be regarded as a right-wing counterpart to *Ha-Shomer ha-Za'ir*.

This period between the two world wars was, indeed, a time when the 'Synthetists,' led by Chaim Weizmann, who comprised a majority with the World Zionist Organization, had to contend with the growing influence of Zionist 'Revisionists,' sharply turning against them. Their leader, the writer and orator Vladimir Jabotinsky, was an unusual and charismatic personality. His faction had emerged from a Russian Zionist group which adopted Jabotinsky's plan to establish a 'Jewish region' on the side of the Allies for purposes of overthrowing Ottoman rule over Palestine. The chief base for this party and the Zionist circles affiliated to it, was always Eastern Europe, and they propagated their ideas through the Russian-language weekly *Rassvet* ('Dawn'), published initially in Berlin (1921–33) and then Paris (1933–34). The basic ideological principles advocated by the 'Revisionist' party were linked to a maximalist and militant notion of accomplishing the 'return,' which regarded recourse to any means to that end as legitimate, including violent intervention against the authority mandated to govern Palestine. Their plan was to settle as many immigrant Jews as possible on both banks of the Jordan so as to gain a Jewish demographic ascendancy in the region. From the very start, this program contained a list of very precisely formulated demands, amongst which were: the formation of Jewish military units in Palestine, land reform, state protection of enterprises, tax concessions for immigrants, a policy of mass immigration, and centralized measures to stimulate economic growth, including a ban on strikes, throughout the entire period of constructing a Jewish state. The 'Revisionists' repudiated charges that they were anti-British, as well as the reproofs of Zionist left-wingers that they were adopting 'Fascist methods' and that their ideal was an authoritarian state on the pattern of Mussolini's régime.

Their actions, in any event, did indeed take an increasingly violent form, with the avowed aim of exerting pressure on the British authorities in Palestine, and additionally—which was not so freely admitted—on other factions of the Zionist movement. It was not uncommon in *Eretz Israel*, as in Europe, for open clashes degenerating into fisticuffs to take place between 'Revisionists,' especially members of its *Betar* youth movement, and left-wing Zionists, who were not shy of drawing attention to one highly eloquent item of their opponents' uniform: the brown shirts that were also part of the Nazi storm troopers' apparel... In 1933 two 'Revisionists' were put on trial for the murder of a Labor Party leader. Certainly, Jabotinsky's resolute militancy found considerable resonance in the Jewish masses of Poland and elsewhere in Eastern Europe, though at the same time he had already put numerous associates off even before 1925, when the movement was officially founded in Paris. It then expanded rapidly, with many viable organizational cells sprouting up, which were organized separately in order to draw in veteran front-line soldiers, Orthodox Jews, women, secondary-school students and Jewish youth in general (in the *Betar*).

Jabotinsky fighting as a lieutenant in a Jewish detachment alongside British units in the Near East during the First World War had been one of the first to cross the River Jordan, for which bravery he was decorated, stayed on in Palestine, working hard from the spring of 1920 to set up an underground Jewish army, the *Haganah*, to fight the rebellious Arabs. He was arrested for that activity and sentenced to 15 years' imprisonment. He was reprieved and went back to a veritable hero's reception in London, joined the Zionist movement's Executive Committee, and picked up his earlier work on behalf of Russia's Jews. Pragmatic in his politics, Jabotinsky had no hesitation about allying for a while with Petlyura's White Russian army, later held responsible for a string of anti-Semitic massacres, in order to win protection for his endangered co-religionists. Equally, as an implacable anti-Communist, he did not shrink from adopting methods that were modeled on the 'leader principle' (*Führerprinzip*) when it came to strengthening *Betar* or bolstering his own authority within his party. From 1933 he took over single-handed control of the movement, autocratically relieving its elected executive body of any power and even going as far as to have his decision ratified directly by the membership.

When Hitler rose to power the 'Revisionists' announced a total boycott of Nazi Germany, then in 1934 organized a huge 'Jewish petition,' addressed to the governments of the democratic European powers (primarily the king of England and other British authorities), collecting six hundred thousand signatures in 24 countries. In 1934 the 'Revisionists' left the Zionist trade-union movement organization, and in 1935 seceded—in principle definitively—from the World Zionist Organization as well. In 1940, however, at the moment when the Nazi peril became extreme, they showed a willingness to rejoin the main body of the movement on certain conditions. It was again Jabotinsky alone who, having recognized the gathering danger, had already started working in 1938–39—on this occasion striking a deal with the increasingly anti-Semitic Polish government—on a plan for the emergency evacuation of a million and a half Polish Jews to other countries. Although the plan foundered on the incredulity and hesitation of the bulk of public opinion, Jewish and non-Jewish, Jabotinsky's party still managed to get substantial groups of Jews out to *Eretz Israel*, many of them illegally, by getting round the ban on immigration imposed by the British authorities.

Cultural autonomism, or the liberal branch of Jewish nationalism

Right up to the Shoah, Zionism had to compete with two assimilationist ideologies, that of national assimilation ('adoptive nationalism') and that of left-wing or liberal universalism (socialism, social democracy, Communism), whilst its influence was further cramped by other Jewish nationalist schools of thought. A common feature of the latter was that they drew essentially their entire support from amongst 'eastern Jews,' particularly those in the two Eastern European multinational empires or their successor states, whereas Zionism and the trends of thought that it embraced, as we have seen, were pan-European from the very start, indeed often growing into world-wide networks. That almost exclusive rootedness in Eastern Europe, along with the ostracism that was accorded both by the victorious Zionist movement and by the Communists that attained power in Eastern Europe, may be the reason why these intellectual and political movements have barely left a trace in the collective memory of present-day Jewry.

There can be no disputing that the oldest liberal manifestation of Jewish nationalism, the least hidebound in adhering to abstract principles and also the most heterogeneous in the membership base that it attracted, was the creation of a group of authors around Adolf Landau, editor of the weekly paper *Voskhod* (Sunrise) between 1881 and 1906. This was the only significant Russian-language Jewish periodical of that era, with 4000–5000 permanent subscribers (most of them living in the southern regions of the Russian 'Pale of Settlement'). *Voskhod* was a cultural journal, put together by intellectuals for other intellectuals, publishing literary reviews, historical essays and political reports dealing with problems affecting their contemporaries. Its imprecisely defined and broad ideological posture was trained at a few simple goals: fostering Jewish national and cultural values, defending the human rights of Russia's Jews, disseminating Russian culture within Jewry, and in that context encouraging the development of a Jewish literature in the Russian language. For all that the journal favored Russian 'acculturation,' it castigated every form of assimilationist self-denial and, after some wavering, supported the notion of reevaluating the Yiddish language, with the understanding that this was the grounding for the everyday life of ordinary Jewish people, and thus intellectuals had a duty to remain close to it. It likewise came out in favor of rabbinical training in seminaries with higher, western-style standards, and even made its own contribution to that by publishing translations of scholarly works produced by the *Wissenschaft des Judentums* group in Germany.

Like most reformist trends beholden to the *Haskalah*, *Voskhod* also urged an economic 'productivization' (industrial and agricultural) of the Jewish masses. At the time of the first great pogroms, in 1881, it also advocated dauntless self-defense, and was to continue doing so subsequently. As a result, the tsarist authorities imposed temporary bans on its publication on several occasions. The paper's partly contradictory goals were permeated by an abiding hope that the problems of Russia's Jews would find a definitive solution within the country when their long-awaited emancipation was achieved. That was why the *Voskhod* circle repudiated equally the notions of Zionism (already back in the time when its precursor, *Hibbat Zion*, first emerged) and 'cultural autonomism,' even though the chief spokesman for the latter was the journal's own full-time literary critic, Simon Dubnov. It is a mark of the journal's liberalism that Dubnov could find an outlet for his early writings on the history of Hasidism (1883–93) in its columns, indeed it even published his manifesto-like *Letters on the Old and the New Jewishness* (1907), the article in which he set out the platform for the movement of 'cultural autonomism.'

It was indeed autonomism, or *folk*ism, propounded by the very same Simon Dubnov, that prolific and at one time highly influential man of letters, historian, and essayist, which constituted the other great liberal current of thought linked to Jewish nationalism. Self-educated, Dubnov led a checkered career as a journalist and scholar. He was born in Belorussia and lived illegally in St. Petersburg for a while before moving to Odessa, where he joined the circle around the 'cultural Zionist' thinker Ahad Ha-Am. From there, his path took him to Vilna, before he finally settled down, this time legally, in St. Petersburg. He taught Jewish history at the Jewish Academy of Oriental Studies founded there by Baron David Ginsburg and subsequently, after the fall of the tsarist régime, at the Jewish People's College, which was party-subsidized by the Bolshevik government. He was a founding member of the Jewish Historical and Ethnographic Society (1908), likewise established by Ginsburg, and edited that society's journal between 1908 and 1918. Seeking to escape the hardening grip of the Bolshevik régime, he left Russia in 1922 to settle in Berlin, where he lived until the Nazis' coming to power, when he was obliged to move to Riga. He lost his life during the deportations of Jews from the Latvian capital, the rumor being that he was murdered in the open street by a former student from Berlin days, who had meanwhile become a Gestapo officer.

The basic concept of autonomism in Dubnov's wide-ranging oeuvre is constructed on two approaches to the philosophy of history. The first of these is his theory of historical evolution, in which he distinguishes three phases: an epoch of ethnic tribes, an age of territorial nations, and finally an era of communities organized on both cultural and ethnic kinship lines. The latter stage would only be attained by groups that had reached an exceptional maturity, such as the Jews, and they would be able to reach that stage because their historical experience was marked by 'an uninterrupted chain of autonomy.' The foundation of this tradition of autonomy had been provided first by the ancient Hebrew state and, subsequently, by the network of Jewish communities. The Jews had therefore never ceased to exist virtually as a nation, not even following their dispersion, for they had preserved their religious and cultural autonomy all along, and they should now gain recognition of that from the states in which they had settled. Here Dubnov was following the positivist doctrines developed by such masters as Renan and Taine, who propounded an organic concept of the nation, which in the terminology current at that time was seen as a 'race' endowed with an autonomous 'spirit.'

Secondly, Dubnov built his political ideas on a theory he had elaborated about the historically variable centers of Jewish creativity. These had been, in turn, Babylon (after the exile from Judah, when the Diaspora was first formed), then Spain and the Rhine region (during the early Middle Ages), and finally (in the early modern era) Poland and Lithuania under the Council of the Four Lands, the supreme body of self-government for the network of Jewish communities living there. The relative political autonomy that the Jews had realized in Poland and Lithuania showed the path that should be taken in future within Europe's multicultural empires, where the majority of Jews were still living in Dubnov's time. In this Dubnov was openly drawing on ideas that had been evolved in Central and Eastern Europe during the nineteenth century by various movements pushing for 'national awakening' and political emancipation of oppressed minorities. Traces of these ideas could also be found, from the 1890s onwards, in the Austrian Social Democratic Party's platform of multiculturalism for national minorities. Otto Bauer, the Austrian Marxist, was later to undertake a survey of this concept in his treatise *Die Nationalitäten-frage und die Sozialdemokratie* (1907), the cardinal ideas of which were endorsed by other influential writers of the democratic left at that time, including the leading Hungarian sociologist Oszkár Jászi.

Similar considerations led Dubnov to his demand for a political settlement in which Jews would retain self-government in the domains of religion, culture, and education, whilst being granted basic rights as to their means of self-defense and assertion of their collective interests. This plan was explicitly anti-assimilationist, yet at the same time set itself in opposition to both the Zionist program of a 'return to *Eretz Israel*' and the class-war objectives of the *Bund*ists.

In the past, Dubnov said, Judaism had been an indispensable means of self-defence in preserving the unity of a Jewish people deprived of every other possibility of collective security. Under modern conditions of life, however, Jewish creativity was finding expression less and less in religion and increasingly in secular culture—despite the impressive counter-example offered by contemporary Hasidism. That was why the modernization of Yiddish was so important, given its place as the lingua franca of the majority of Jews in the two multinational empires of Eastern Europe. Dubnov certainly concentrated his attention on the problems of the communities amongst which he himself moved. After the horrendous outcome of the 1903 Kishinev pogrom in Bessarabia, he joined the Zionists in order to help organize armed self-defense, but also supporting their efforts to set up an independent Jewish school system. For all that, he never rated Zionism as anything more than a pseudo-messianic political fantasy, even though the autonomists' policies concurred at more than a few points with the program of *Gegenwartsarbeit* that Russian Zionists had been vigorously promoting since their 1906 conference at Helsingfors.

The autonomists' dealings with the *Bund*ists were just as complicated as those with the Zionists, even though the *Bund* too, in the end, adopted the principle of their demand for cultural autonomy and took an active part in developing the Yiddish language. The strains in their relation, already apparent earlier, deteriorated further during the 1905 revolution in Russia. Indeed Dubnov stood up for Jewish parties to run in the elections for the First Duma (where he himself was later to be found amongst the 'Sejmists' of the Jewish Socialist Workers' Party), whereas the *Bund*, which was still largely operating underground, was against this. In order to give his own ideas organized political form, Dubnov supported the establishment of a Jewish wing of Russia's Constitutional Democratic Party (the *Kadets*) and himself joined the Society for the Attainment of Full Civil Rights for the Jewish People in Russia. Having left that body soon afterwards, in 1906 he founded a Jewish populist party, the *Folkspartei* or *Folk*ists, which remained in existence right up until 1918, though without exerting any appreciable influence on policy towards the Jews in Russia. Subsequently, denied the possibility of playing any political role in Bolshevised Russia, the *Folk*ists set up camp in independent Poland to present a distinctive ideological shade in the spectrum of Jewish parties there during the inter-war years.

The Jewish socialist movement in Eastern Europe

Of all the strains of Jewish nationalism outside Zionism, it was in-
dubitably the *Bund* (founded in 1897) which exerted the greatest
influence, both ideological and political, on Jews of Eastern Europe
right up until its brutal liquidation: this happened in Russia during
the initial phase of the Bolshevik régime and in Poland during the
Shoah. The activities and goals of the *Bund*, a Yiddish abbreviation
for 'General Jewish Workers' Union in Lithuania, Poland, and Russia,' were directed to representing the interests of the Jewish working classes from a socialist viewpoint, but allying to it the autonomists' cultivation of the Yiddish language, an autonomous secular
(in practice antireligious) nationalism, and a committed political
stand against tsarist autocracy. The *Bund* thus set itself apart both
from assimilationist aspirations (including its Communist versions,
which was its reason to turn against internationalist Bolshevism) and
from the inveterately 'bourgeois ideology,' as it put it, of Zionism
and any form of its emigratory project. The *Bund* saw its main task
in the fight for the improvement of the ordinary living conditions of
the Jewish masses—a policy of what it called '*doikeyt*' (literally
'hereness,' including the determination to stay put). Starting off
from Vilna and other places within Lithuanian and Belorussian
provinces of the Jewish 'Pale of Settlement,' the *Bund* had already
spread to Jewish communities across the whole of Russia by the turn
of the century.

The *Bund*'s historical roots went back to the very first, as yet
strongly corporatist labor movements of Jewish workers, which
emerged in the textile and tobacco industries during the 1870s. Those
actions were given support from Jewish intellectuals, Marxist and
others, close to traditional Judaism, but at the same time maintaining
links with anti-tsarist revolutionary circles and non-Jewish labor organizations. During the 1890s these movements reached a decisive
point in their development. With anti-Semitic violence becoming ever
more acute in the cities, there was a recognition that Jews had special
collective interests, and they needed to mobilize their own resources
for their defense. Accordingly, rather than advocating Russian-
language assimilation as up till then, they should revert to using Yiddish for purposes of political mass mobilizations. As a result, the first

'jargon committees' were brought into being in Vilna, and the idea was born that the 'class war' of Jewish workers should tie up with the struggle for cultural and, ultimately, 'national' emancipation of all Jews in the tsarist empire. Mutual assistance funds were set up by trade unions, independent Jewish labor-movement newspapers were brought out, such as the *Yidisher Arbeiter* (1896–1905) and *Arbeiter Shtime* (1897–1905), and finally the *Bund* itself was formed, taking part in the first conference of the Social Democratic Labor Party in 1898.

Its expansion reached a peak during the stormy revolutionary years of 1903–05. Sister organizations were founded in Galicia (1905) and the United States (by emigrant sympathizers), despite the fact that the *Bund*, which spurned Judaism's global pretensions, was unwilling to collaborate with such foreign bodies, taking great care to confine its activities to Russia alone. During the revolutionary period the party was the main agency of Jewish self-defense against the pogroms, as well as an indefatigable campaigner in the struggle for equal rights for Jews. Its membership around 1904 lay between 25,000 and 35,000, with no less than 4,500 of those being political prisoners.

Under the influence of autonomist ideas, the *Bund*'s leadership was already by the turn of the century coming round to the conclusion that it was one of their obligations to raise the issue of gaining recognition for Jews as a national minority. Since the Bolshevik-dominated Labor Party was not inclined to lend its support, the *Bund* withdrew from it in 1905. Although it officially rejoined the 'internationalist' camp in 1906, it preserved a wide-ranging freedom of action. From that point on, nevertheless, its influence within Russia diminished continuously, in part on account of official police repression, in part because of its voluntary abstention from parliamentary party politics. It remained within the Menshevik orbit of influence, especially after the latter's final break with the Bolsheviks in 1912.

Thereafter the *Bund* devoted all its energies to cultural advancement and education of the Jewish masses, setting up literary and musical societies, free universities and amateur dramatic circles—with Yiddish invariably as the language of communication. All along, though, the party still considered it a duty to make a stand on 'Jewish affairs.' In the Polish territories it spoke out against the anti-Jewish boycott campaign that Polish nationalists instigated in 1912, organized a strike to protest against the libel of ritual murder that had been brought in the Beilis trial (1913), and pleaded the cases for Jewish workers who were threatened with dismissal from their jobs.

On the eve of the February Revolution in 1917, the *Bund* numbered about 40,000 members. It played an active role in the renewal of political life that followed the overthrow of autocratic rule, though shifting its allegiances between the Mensheviks (who were in a majority in the *Bund*'s leadership) and the Bolsheviks. In March 1919, an organization known as *Kombund* was set up from one of its factions in Ukraine, and later on in the year, from an alliance with the left wing of the United Jewish Socialist Workers' Party, another known as *Komfarbund*. In August, the United Jewish Socialist Workers' Party affiliated to the Ukrainian Communist Party. At the *Bund*'s USSR congress in April 1920 most of the leadership voted for the merger with the Bolsheviks, with only a minority sticking by independence. The consolidating Bolshevik régime soon ruthlessly wiped out both factions, regardless of their inclinations.

Poland's achievement of independence enabled the establishment of a separate Polish *Bund*, to which the Galician Jewish Social Democratic Party affiliated. This party operated legally, with its own press (e.g. *Naie Folkszaitung*, 1921–39), a range of specialized organs and institutions (for youth, children, women, sports, etc.), like any of the other Jewish political clusters. On some issues, however, they could not come to agreement within the movement, including the problem of cooperation with the Communists (which most accepted), the establishment of a united front with other socialists (the left wing rejecting this on grounds of the alleged nationalism and revisionism of the fraternal socialist parties), or search for parliamentary representation (as urged by the moderates). Within the political arena of Jewish life, the *Bund* was constantly at odds with both Orthodox Judaism and Zionism, though that did not stop it from forming an alliance with the Zionist left wing, *Po'alei Zion*, during election campaigns for seats in the Sejm. It managed to secure a convincing majority within the Jewish trade union alliance, and in 1921 it participated in the Central Yiddish Schools Organization. Whilst continuing to oppose teaching in Hebrew, it raised no objection to the inclusion in the curriculum of elements of Jewish history and the study of the ritual significance of Jewish holidays.

The *Bund*'s political influence in Poland was at its height during the years immediately preceding the German occupation. It paid a heavy price for the resistance it displayed to the Nazi invaders, as it had done earlier for its participation in the Soviet civil war (a number of its leaders becoming victims of the Stalinist purges). The *Bund*ist representative on the national council of the Polish government-in-exile in London, Samuel Zygelbojm, committed suicide in 1943 as a protest against the indifference that western Allied Powers were showing towards the atrocities that they knew were being carried out against the Jewish people in Nazi occupied Poland.

Chapter 4

The Road to the Shoah.
From Christian Anti-Judaism
to Radical Anti-Semitism

Making sense of nonsense

In earlier chapters it has been noted at several points that anti-Jewish violence, which actually raises a veritable 'non-Jewish Question,' cannot be considered a secondary factor in the social history of European Jewry. Since the final decades of the nineteenth century it was indeed—more than anything else—instrumental in determining the course of events relating to Jewry, even though it is also important to distinguish it from the traditional Christian variant inherited from the Middle Ages. However long the 'historical traditions' that it looks back on may go, a new era of anti-Jewish violence opened in recent times. This change may even be pinned to a particular year, that of 1879, when Wilhelm Marr, the German publicist introduced the term 'anti-Semitism' into public discourse. This was the precise historical moment when the first, new-style anti-Jewish mass movements, organized on bases at once both national and international, had begun to crop up in the political and ideological arena of the European Great Powers—more particularly in Germany, Austria-Hungary, France and Russia. Divergent as their points of departure may have been, as will be discussed, it is fairly easy to discern a continuity between earlier and novel manifestations of Judaeophobia, insofar as they most commonly resorted to similar forms of aggression. With political anti-Semitism, however, that violence acquired new dimensions, becoming secular, justifying itself with arguments often remote from Christianity (indeed, often antithetical to its fundamentally universalistic tenets). As its finishing stroke, Nazi Germany and its allies made a concerted murderous attempt—largely successful at that, through the employment of industrial methods—to wipe out European Jewry as a collectivity.

The tools of social history are undoubtedly far less effective than in other areas when it comes to an interpretation of the historical events associated with anti-Semitism. For a start, it is an extraordinarily hard job to wade through the heaps of patent gibberish that is the hallmark of anti-Semitic rhetoric, often close to mental outpourings reminiscent of a produce of delirium tremens. Sociological approaches that have proven themselves elsewhere likewise come to grief because no causal relationship at all, or only just the faintest trace of such, may be established between the justifications recited by modern anti-Semites and their devastating consequences. Moreover, there is a great diversity of forms of violence together with a large variety of supportive discourses, which may be cumulative, complementing one another, though it occurs also that they exclude one another or are grounded in mutually contradictory logic of justification: this was the case of traditional Christian anti-Judaism as opposed to its—from a Christian standpoint 'pagan'—Nazi-motivated equivalent. Diversity is the rule as to the nature and degree of anti-Jewish violence regarded as 'permissible' in a given global society or in various social clusters. Thus, it may well appear problematic even to discuss all the phenomena customarily treated under this heading within the framework of one and the same category.

Certain manifestations of Judaeophobia are limited to the objective of separation of Jews from non-Jews (to exclude their mixing) in various walks of life: the matrimonial market, circles of friendship, residential areas, political or civic activities, sports clubs, etc. In other words, this is to distinguish Jews from non-Jews with a symbolic and social distance that sets them apart. Others take a demonic image painted of Jews as their starting-point to apply crude discrimination against them in everyday life, in the workplace as in the playground and elsewhere. This may be substantiated as a rejection of otherness in the public or private sphere on the strength of various theories endowed with supposedly historio–philosophical or scientific credentials (e.g. 'race theory'), or with reference to real or imagined competition or conflicts of interest between Jews and non-Jews in personal or communal relations and occupational or economic markets. Under some régimes or in some historical situations (in tsarist Russia, during the changes of government in Eastern Europe following the First World War, in countries coming under Nazi influence), discrimination against Jews was channeled from an earlier, usually verbal and symbolic level into physical violence against isolated individuals, the ransacking of Jewish institutions, legalized persecution, and finally mass murder. Obviously, it would be wrong to regard such actions, with their widely divergent consequences, as having equal weight. One cannot equate a refusal to enter into marriage with Jews, or to share the same playground or residential area, with organizing their deportation to death camps. Nevertheless, in attempting to interpret the modern history of anti-Semitism, it would also be wrong to disconnect them entirely. The milder forms of discrimination made the murderous ones finally possible. The first led often directly to the second. Those ready to separate Jews and brand them symbolically could accept, in a different historical juncture, criminal acts to be perpetrated against them or even to become willing accomplices of the murderers.

Lastly, one has to evoke the fact that the ultimate outcome of European anti-Semitism in the modern age—unparalleled in human history—was the disappearance of the great majority of Jews under horrifying circumstances from the face of the continent, leaving an indelibly traumatic legacy in the minds of their descendants, Jewry in its entirety and other contemporary witnesses. One of the difficulties of the chronicler's tasks, and by no means the least one, lies in the obligation to dissociate himself from the ineluctably tragic gravity of his subject in the interest of narrative objectivity. 'For whatever has passed on, death alters its perspectives,' the Hungarian Miklós Radnóti wrote in his poem *À la Recherche* at Lager Heidenau, on 17th August 1944, not long before receiving a bullet in the back of the head during his forced march towards Germany and thereby joining the ranks of the millions fallen victim to the Shoah.

Since there is no scientifically satisfactory theory for a general explanation of anti-Semitism, we shall content ourselves with a simple interpretative presentation of the main phenomena put under this heading, though with the hope to demonstrate the genesis of major forms of modern anti-Jewish violence. The approach applied here deliberately avoids to take the anti-Semitic discourse as its point of departure: in contrast to most authors working in this field, I doubt that the 'reasons' cited by anti-Semitic propagandists could seriously serve for comprehending these phenomena. The chasm between the credibility and weight that can be placed on the justificatory pretexts and the actual consequences of the violence that they unleashed still gapes so yawningly that, disregarding some exceptional cases already mentioned, it is impossible to hypothesize any reasonable cause-and-effect relationship between them. It is precisely the hollowness of the 'reasons' that feed on the most deeply ingrained beliefs, in some cases spouted obsessively for centuries on end, which is the easiest to expose. Two examples may suffice to prove this point.

An example among many of that kind is the blood libel or the calumny of ritual murder. This is based on phantasmagoria that have been able to fuel murderous anti-Jewish passions from the pogroms of the late Middle Ages through to the massacre at Kielce in Poland in June 1946 without any verifiable basis whatsoever in reality.

Turning to the accusations of an economic character, customarily leveled against Jews—that they are 'rich' and 'money sticks to their fingers,' or 'parasites,' 'capitalist exploiters' and 'shy away from productive work'—,we may diagnose that—although they refer to genuine socio–historical components of the modern era (though more particularly just from the eighteenth century)—, they can in no way be considered as exclusive features of Judaeo–Christian relations, for at least three reasons.

To start with, they cannot explain the extreme, remorseless and mindless pitch of hatred directed towards Jews. Even if there was any shred of substance to the accusations, the severity of the prospective sanctions is totally disproportionate to that of the alleged offences. What we are dealing with here would thus represent a case of complete dissociation of an 'ideological superstructure' from its economic foundations, in the Marxist sense.

Second, let us, for argument's sake, stay within the conceptual framework of the anti-Semite and accept the totally absurd supposition that all Jews live in clover as greedy speculators on the stock exchange, lisping bankers, exploitative factory-owners or profiteering wholesale merchants, who are judged and condemned for that reason by the ruined victims of capitalism. (A temptation of this kind was present amongst the early French 'utopian socialists,' as with Fourier and in the Proudhonist syndicalist tradition.) In that case, however, how does one account for the fact that no comparable rancor was ever directed against non-Jewish beneficiaries of capitalism. After all, even within the most fervidly anticapitalist movements (with the possible exception of the Bolsheviks), there was never talk about the total social exclusion or physical 'eradication' of non-Jewish capitalists, industrialists and bankers.

Third, it is important to bear in mind that the sort of anti-Semitic hysteria which has periodically carried away broad strata of the public, whether 'underpinned' by economic or any other 'reasons,' has only gathered momentum in certain European societies, while others of similar set-up or level of development remained unaffected. It has either barely existed at all, or never attracted any considerable camp in Scandinavian, Anglo-Saxon or Mediterranean countries (including the Balkans, with the single exception of Romania), even though, historically speaking, the economic strength achieved by Jews often bulked just as large there as elsewhere. It might be said, of course, that far fewer Jews lived in those countries than in, for instance, Central or Eastern Europe, but then the spectacle of their economic success was counterbalanced by their high degree of civic integration. In reality, however, it is hard to demonstrate any correlation between the intensity of political anti-Semitism and the relative size of the Jewish population. The demographic significance of Jews in nineteenth-century France, the setting of the unprecedented crisis of the Dreyfus Affair, was much smaller (indeed negligible) than in the haven of peace and tolerance that their co-religionists experienced in the Netherlands.

The logic of stigmatization and the Christian precedent

Rather than accepting the 'explanations' touted by the proponents of anti-Semitism, even as a point of departure, it seems far more expedient to turn the reasoning round and hypothesize that anti-Semitism can be best understood as nothing but a basic ideological disposition in certain sections of modern societies, an attitudinal factor, an in-built need, the 'reasons' for which are merely the products of contingent rationalizations. This is the only way of interpreting the irrational phantom world of anti-Semitic discourse, replete as it is with utterly unfounded, indeed often fantastic generalizations. The primacy of passion over reasons, as a rule, is also demonstrable in the anti-Semite's behavioral patterns. Yet it is nevertheless always possible to discern two tenets behind the reasons offered, even when they are not always explicitly adduced. Of the two tenets, the second is predicated on the first, and so does not arise without that being present; the existence of the first one, however, does not necessarily lead to the second.

The first tenet is the maintenance in everyday social contacts of a radical anthropological discrimination between Jews and non-Jews—'them' and 'us'—in a historical situation where in social reality inter-group differences of all kinds are tending to weaken, to vanish or to change. What we are dealing with, then, is a fundamentally imagined notion, a figment or a fiction related to allegedly ineradicable differences which, for those concerned, requires no explanation. Equally, though, that figment does never come 'out of the blue.' Rather it is always an outgrowth of earlier, historically 'functional' precedents, a henceforth non-functional extension and amplification of the latter, as it were, possibly even a cult that (in anti-Semitic practice) is supplied with a new function.

The precedent is the institutionalized sectarian separation that has existed in Christianity since its very inception, aggravated by the legacy of discrimination against Jews, their forced ghettoization, their exclusion from normal social intercourse, and, on many occasions, their brutal persecution. That all belonged to the past, however, albeit the recent past of feudal societies, in opposition to which the 'civil revolutions' of late-eighteenth and nineteenth-century Europe had brought into being nation states that were culturally integrated, egalitarian in regard to political rights, secularised, based on legal codes that did not recognize ethnic and religious differences, and stratified by economic class. Within these nation states, in accordance with the integrationist logic of their systems, the main goal of which was precisely to 'civilize'—that is to say, grant civil rights to—those elements of society which were stranded outside the 'protections of the constitution' (most notably the bonded peasants who made up the bulk of the population) and, by throwing open the doors to advancement, allow them to narrow the gap between themselves and the former ruling strata, at least in the long term, cultural assimilation and social integration of Jews into the strata that corresponded to their skills, got under way during the nineteenth century, and in many places in Western and Central Europe was also largely achieved before the century was over. In other words, the social distance between Jews and non-Jews diminished to an unprecedented degree in regard to lifestyle and in the domains of the economy, politics, schooling, mixed marriage, social initiatives, and (with ever more general religious indifference, the growth of Reform Judaism, and conversions to Christianity) even religious practice. In this historical context, the postulate of a rigid division between 'us' and 'them,' or a continued insistence on this, in the face of contemporary norms of social co-existence and, indeed, the experiences of actual mixing and integration, gained a new role in relations between Jews and non-Jews.

Distinction of Jews on account of their allegedly fundamental otherness did not necessarily mean, however, that they had to be looked on as an implacable enemy. There were certain Christian groups—for example anti-Trinitarian, liberal Protestant or Catholic and, later on, ecumenical circles, to mention only some sectarian formations—that consistently demarcated themselves from Jews, though without developing any aversion to them. Above all they tended to refuse that acknowledged differences could serve as grounds for the resort to violence against them or accept any justification of anti-Jewish violence. This was an attitude uncommon in other quarters.

That notwithstanding, the other side of the coin must also be emphasized. Any classing of affiliation of this sort contained a potential principle of radical rejection, especially when an 'essentialist' significance was ascribed to it. That is how the logic of discrimination actually functions. For any time that we set up categorically opposed camps of 'us' and 'them,' there is generally, albeit tacitly, a notion of a hierarchical ordering behind this. When the 'us' gains a distinguishing character, there is at once a high probability that the 'them' group will be invested with a negative sign. It is but a short step from that to their being treated with contempt, looked down upon, their exclusion or aggression against them being urged. There is every reason to conclude that it was once again Christianity which, through its prolonged ideological endeavors to make the difference between Jews and Christians a fundamental or an absolute one, prepared the historical terrain that opened the door to the abuses of modern anti-Semitism as well. The aforementioned exceptional groups were able to remain aloof from that, precisely because they had voluntarily opposed to the dominant Christian ideology (not lastly because they themselves were often—as a minority—subject to exclusion or persecution by authorities of the Christian majority). A contraposition of Jewish and Christian 'natures,' mentalities or cultures carried to extremes became the basis for a 'doctrine of contempt' directed against Jews (to use the expression of the French historian Jules Isaac). From the Middle Ages onwards, into the post-Enlightenment era, that licensed the subjection of the Jews to the whims of Christian powers, marked by arbitrary exiles, forced conversions, often murderous 'spontaneous' mass outbreaks of violence, humiliating coercive measures on the part of ecclesiastical authorities, exclusion from the nexus of feudal society, disadvantageous economic discriminations, occupational prohibitions and public anti-Jewish invectives of hired pen-pushers and fanatical preachers. In most European countries both during the century of the Enlightenment and thereafter (in many parts of Eastern Europe right down to the present day), one way or another, this 'tradition' made the Jews the chosen victims of subsequent waves of violence regarded as implicitly justified, even before their perpetrators were obliged to seek any sort of 'motive' for their actions, since they were directed against elements defined as 'aliens,' marginals or social outcasts. The pariah status assigned to Jews comprised the legitimization of discrimination as well.

Christianity placed the Jews in a position where, for a very long time, they were obliged to bear a radically negative badge of otherness. In that position any prejudice, suspicion, slander or accusation was acceptable as justification for cases of anti-Jewish violence. For the most part, it is fairly easy to identify the mechanism of these as self-fulfilling prophecy, or self-induced and self-justifying passions. That is why the more absurd the calumny (classically, the blood libel) that is cited as a 'reason,' the greater the 'yield,' the more authentic, indeed credible, it appeared. The most baseless fabrications could indeed fulfill the best their real function, that is, to justify even the most extreme violence as 'counter-violence.'

What is most important in this connection, though, is the final legacy of the Christian tradition in this respect. Christianity, by making veritably in-bred—as something that goes without saying—the hatred of Jews, allowed the maintenance of the intensity of anti-Judaism after secularization. Indeed, the rejection of Jews could be conserved fully, once it was removed from the system of concepts and motives drawn from Christian doctrine, that served as its foundation, without changing in the slightest either its nature or the measure of its scale. As a result, even the most convinced, enlightened and, for that matter, anticlerical advocates of human and civil rights, such as a Voltaire or a Holbach, found it difficult to avoid (nor did they avoid) presenting the Jews as irremediably harmful 'others.'

At the same time, the historical modes of treating the Jews in the Christian world provided ready-to-hand models and, simultaneously, concrete legitimation for objectivations of anti-Semitic violence in more recent times. As far as the 'spontaneity' of the violence is concerned, there is virtually no discernible difference, even in the degree of ruthlessness, between the pogroms of the Middle Ages, the anti-Jewish 'Hep! Hep!' disturbances that broke out in southern and central-western Germany during 1819, the mass attacks launched against Jewish town-dwellers in Russia throughout the nineteenth century (especially after 1881), the massacres of the Russian civil war, the Nazi atrocities that were orchestrated in connection with *Reichskristallnacht*—'the Night of Broken Glass' (9th–10th November 1938), or the collective murders committed in the Polish town of Kielce or the Hungarian village of Kunmadaras in June 1946. Up to the eighteenth century, several thousand Jews and converted Jews (*conversos*) lost their lives on the pyres of the Inquisition, thus foreshadowing the crematoria of Auschwitz. To make an even more figurative and at once more concrete analogy, it was as if the embers of those pyres had burst once again into flame during the Second World War at those places on the Eastern Front and elsewhere, where units of the German army and their local accomplices took such delight in locking their Jewish victims into a local barrack, military hospital or synagogue and then proceeding to burn them alive. The massacre of Jed Nabve, the Polish village where the inhabitants themselves exterminated all their Jewish neighbors shortly after the German occupation of Poland, was not lacking precedents in Christian Europe, neither in the East, nor in the West. As for the less barbarous manifestations of anti-Semitism in recent times, practitioners were faced with an embarrassing plenitude of well-proven models, being able to take their pick from a profusion of discriminatory measures that had spread the length and breadth of Christian Europe before the emancipation of the Jews: economic boycotts, prescription of compulsory residential areas (ghettoization), limitations of the freedom to move or rights of settlement, restrictions on the pursuit of certain occupations, deprivation of citizenship rights, arbitrary expulsion, forced resettlement, restriction of schooling, harassment in schools and universities ('Jew-baiting' and 'Jew-beating' often going together), special over-taxation, confiscation of property and wealth, relief from the obligation to repay loans due. These are all devices that did actually play a part both in the practice of pre-modern Christian states and in the arsenal of anti-Semitic policies, often even prior to Nazi rule in many European states.

Reference to such precedents was indeed often made in the form of a deliberately applied scheme of self-legitimation for anti-Jewish drives, since that saved their authors the bother to work out a coherent discourse to justify their procedures. Ready-made models and self-justificatory authorities for violence were easy to update, sometimes requiring only trivial adjustments. The Christian postulate of the inveterate otherness of Jews, for instance, soon appeared in the guise of assertions that Jews were incapable of subjecting themselves to common laws and were therefore unworthy of common rights (as certain ideologues of the French Revolution and in Napoleon's entourage also believed); their 'foreignness' was irrevocably at variance with the 'spirit of the people' (*Volksgeist*), and consequently they were incapable of integrating into the national community (the stance adopted by the philosophers of Romantic nationalism in Germany, Bohemia, and elsewhere); constituting an 'alien' exploitative class of 'different race,' they were extremely dangerous from an economic standpoint (in the eyes of so-called utopian socialists, following in the footsteps of Fourier, Proudhon or Toussenel); they represented a political threat to nation states (as argued by crackpot authors of allegations relative to the 'international Jewish conspiracy' and 'Jewish cosmopolitanism' (meaning: lack of patriotic attachments). Or, even more crudely, they were of racially inferior stock to 'Aryans' (following propositions of racist anti-Semitism elaborated since the latter half of the nineteenth century). Certain Christian notions about the moral depravity of Jews, including the persistent libel of ritual murders committed on young Christians, have been handed on unchanged from the late Middle Ages down to our own times, becoming widely distributed *folk* beliefs, especially in countries with Roman Catholic and Eastern Orthodox majority populations. Traces of it could still be found not so long ago in Slovak and Hungarian villages and French towns alike, as documented, for instance, in a scare-story about the disappearance of young girls in Jewish-run shops, that became widespread in Orléans during the 1960s.

However 'modern' the logic in which it may be dressed up, the old Christian roots of the anti-Semitism of the recent past and present day continually come to the surface. It seems obvious to surmise that the conditions for the emergence of the latter were created by those roots, in conjunction with the two factors mentioned above: the crystallization of notions of the radically negative otherness of Jews and the offer of historically 'proven' methods of anti-Jewish violence. Anti-Semitism in the modern era merely added 'modern' theories to these historical foundations and behavioral models, in part by means of a string of more or less new types of ideological rationalizations (as in the case of anti-Semitic anticapitalism), in part by updating the (political) arguments to re-legitimate a recourse to extreme violence (a legitimation that temporarily lost its validity during the period of emancipation). These two factors, the revival of the negative set of concepts relating to Jews (more details of which will be given further on) and the restoration of legitimacy for violence employed against them (which will be discussed mainly in connection with the rise of Fascism), are the keys to gaining any understanding of modern anti-Semitism.

Anti-Semitism as a self-inducing and self-fulfilling prophecy

Little has been said so far about how relations between Jews and non-Jews have evolved since the eighteenth century; indeed, the topic has been almost completely passed over. That is because the historical links discussed here are largely, or maybe even entirely, products of the Christian world's internal ideological workshops (or devil's kitchens). That is the meaning of the previously mentioned 'self-inducing' nature of the anti-Semitic system of justification, or in other words, of the high degree of ideological autonomy that characterizes the development of anti-Semitism.

That statement is not meant above all to acquit Jews 'of all re-sponsibility' for anti-Semitism that afflicted them, for 'Jewish sins and defects' have not been confined in any case to Judaeophobic ideolo-gies alone but feature as a recurrent subject in the self-reflections of Jewish authors as well during the nineteenth and twentieth centuries. Anyhow, it is more a matter of the obvious proposition that the 'theory' and practice of anti-Semitism have little, if indeed anything at all, to do with actual social reality invoked by anti-Semites, as can be attested by numerous empirical observations.

As has already been noted, some anti-Semitic calumnies can be easily rebutted when submitted to critical historical scrutiny or exami-nation in the courtroom, and yet they have still not lost their credence or their frightening power to stir up crowds. For all that some of them—the blood libel would be one—can be put down to a form of collective delirium and morbid vision, worthy of interest only as sub-jects of mass psychology, their influence remains demonstrable down to the present day. Recently a Hungarian publisher (who should have known better) did not shrink from affirming the legitimacy of the charge of ritual murder in putting out, just a few years ago, an auto-biographical memoir by the investigating magistrate who dreamed up and prosecuted such a case in the infamous Tiszaeszlár show trial. Others still cite alleged authorities long exposed as baseless, such as the proven forgery that the Russian secret police put out in 1905 under the title of *The Protocols of the Elders of Zion*: it is still being used after a century to whip up anti-Jewish public opinion in Arab coun-tries and elsewhere (including Croatia and Hungary).

Other direct evidence of the discontinuity between anti-Semitic as-sertions and reality is the fact that even after the Shoah the mills of anti-Semitism grind on in societies literally without any Jews. Some of these are former western colonies to which colonial powers 'exported' the anti-Jewish phantasmagoria of their staff (not infrequently through the catechizing activities of right-minded missionaries and 'Christian' schools). As we know, the fact that barely five thousand Jews were left, in a total population of forty million, in no way hindered the abil-ity of anti-Semitic figments of the imagination, or its political conse-quences, to proliferate in socialist and, indeed, post-socialist Poland. (By way of comparison, before the Shoah three million Jews lived there in a population of thirty million.) One of the most stubbornly recurring facets of obsessional anti-Semitism is, indeed, a gross over-estimation of the number of survivors (together with the not less patent underestimation of the number of victims of the Shoah)—lacking any plausible basis. Traces of that are still regularly found both within the former socialist bloc and in other countries with thriving 'anti-Semitism without Jews'.

Further proof of the high degree of autonomy typical for the intellectual and cultural 'superstructure' of anti-Semitic phantasms is the extraordinary ease with which the obsessional topics of Judaeophobia spread from one country to another, indeed encompass the entire globe, so that they may take root in societies totally dissimilar from one another with regard to the social status and numbers of local Jews. The bulk of anti-Semitic ideologies, endowed with just a shred of consistency, have long given up making believe in the existence of Jewish 'cosmopolitanism' or 'global conspiracies.' Yet anti-Jewish notions truly recognize no frontiers between regions, ethnic groups, states or continents, even if we know that the reception they encountered and the acceptance they could count on was always exceedingly variable, depending—though differently from place to place—on social stratum, class, subculture, and religious or national affiliation.

Anti-Semitic discourses generally manifest in ideological constellations so malleable, Janus-faced, ambivalent, and murky that they are applicable to practically any end. They are just as likely to target the most assimilated or 'nationalized' Jews as those remaining most distant from host civilizations, the wealthiest as the poorest, 'modern Jews' who are vehicles of cultural and social renewal or conservatives adhering to their ancient religious customs, 'plutocrats' as socialists, and so on. Under those circumstances it is hard to defend a view that anti-Semitic notions have roots in, and acquire their nature through, the soil of actual social reality. Any hypothesis linking anti-Semitism to some 'transgression' or 'faulty' social strategy on the part of Jews thereby loses all explanatory power. Anti-Jewish ideologies are, in truth, utterly indifferent to the flesh-and-blood Jews against whom they stir up crowds and, on occasion, set the wheels of autocratic or Fascist state machines in motion. Of course, that was anyway always the case with traditional Christian Judaeophobia, appearing as it did as a purely theological construct from the very outset. It is more astonishing, though, that those same abstract arguments and generalizations should also nurture the anti-Semitism of the modern age, proposing a 'solution' to what is purported to be a precisely circumscribed set of problems, the so-called 'Jewish Question,' in a given social domain at a given moment in history.

Perhaps the best evidence for the extraordinary detachment of anti-Semitic ideology from reality, its self-inducing character, is nonetheless the patently obvious fact that, from the standpoint of the collective interests of the majority societies concerned, its chief manifestations are so irrational, that is to say, socio–economically and indeed politically harmful. In all probability, modern nation states have never profited anything at all, on balance, from the exclusion or persecution of Jews, even if this does not apply to certain strata within those societies : some mostly élite sectors, as will be discussed in the next chapter, undoubtedly could derive profit from anti-Semitism. To put the problem simply and in relation to the most obvious historical example, it seems highly questionable whether the campaign of extermination that Nazi Germany conducted against the Jews really did lie in the interest of its own power ambitions. The Nazi state thereby not only tied down significant economic and even military resources, which of necessity had to be withheld, among other things, from its war efforts, but in addition denied itself considerable financial, economic, scientific, and intellectual capacities that it might otherwise have been able to mobilize amongst German (or, outside the *Reich*'s borders, Germanized) Jews. It should not be forgotten that, at its onset, more than a few Jews identified with the German national goals that the Third *Reich* was pursuing (and still more would have been open to persuasion as to their validity). The Nazi leadership was, incidentally, well aware of the costs of persecuting the Jews and the damage it was causing. In December 1941, the *Reich* civil administration for the occupied territories in the East (*Reichskommissariat für das Ostland*) set out in a directive that 'for reasons of principles, it is not permissible to take economic interests into account... in the treatment of Jews,' even though the German defense industry and other sectors of the economy were struggling from severe manpower shortages. In the midst of war, the Nazis thus regularly chose to keep shipments of munitions idling purely in order to give priority to trains carrying deported Jews to the camps. It is quite probable that this blind hatred did far more damage to the 'Thousand-year *Reich*' than all the alleged losses that were attributed to the reputedly harmful nature of the Jews.

Nevertheless, even if it must be recognized that the theory and practice of anti-Semitism can be considered as being, to a large extent, decoupled from, that is to say, not directly determined by, social circumstances, this is not to suggest that their occurrence is historically random, 'by chance' as it were. We are in no way relieved of the responsibility of providing a socio–historical analysis. Such an analysis may be embarked on from two approaches. First and foremost, one may proceed from the specific social functions that the anti-Semitic discourse fulfilled within the groups that propagated and accepted it or actively tried to implement its program. On the other hand, one may attempt to identify in that discourse the socio–historical aspects that may have served as starting-points, points of reference and justifications in its elaboration, and thereby contributed to winning society's credence for certain of its outgrowths (and not infrequently some of the most bizarre ones at that). The application of these two approaches is presented in the next two sections dedicated to some functional models of contemporary anti-Semitism.

Functional models of modern anti-Semitism: the code of negativity and symbolic violence

The 'specific functions' were materialized in the various forms of anti-Jewish violence, ranging from symbolic duress to physical aggression, state-organized persecution and, under the Nazi régime, programmatic collective eradication (*Ausrottung* in Hitler's vocabulary). I shall come later on to the nature and extent of the violence in question, but my primary aim with presenting the typology or 'ideal types' (in the Weberian sense) of anti-Semitic interventions in what follows is to throw light on the distinctive roles that anti-Semitism has played in a number of European societies since the nineteenth century. The presence of one of these models in a given milieu does not preclude the possibility that other models might assert themselves simultaneously or alternatively in that same setting. As to the violence that is actually fanned, there are good reasons to suppose that its forms and degrees also depend on the economic and political balance of forces prevalent in countries with different social set-ups, as well as the technological and sociological conditions on which the feasibility of the planned collective violence is predicated. Nazi Germany was able to become what was, unarguably, the most aggressive and destructive power in this respect because, amongst the several countries aiming at radical anti-Semitism, it alone possessed all the key conditions necessary for the execution of the genocidal program: the unambiguous political will to carry it out (in the absence of any significant overt resistance), the technical means to do this (automatic weapons, death camps, gas chambers), the geopolitical position (with the greater part of European Jewry living on territories occupied by the *Wehrmacht*), and reliable police and military forces ('willing executioners' recruited from the temporarily victorious German and other allied armies). At the same time, the Nazis added very little new to the ideological groundwork of that program (as will become clear from the discussion of the 'intellectual' history of modern anti-Judaism in later sections). In essence, then, the Nazi project of genocide was also one of the 'functional models' of modern anti-Semitism, albeit—without any question—the most horrific one.

The most common role of anti-Semitism, in the final analysis, is nothing more than that of a 'cultural code' to designate negative phenomena that may be experienced in any society.

In the first place, the anti-Jewish cultural code is embedded in communications carried out in tight circles of small, private groups, evolving within a framework of mundane exchanges of ideas or certain semi-public and ritualized relations of verbal reciprocity (in sports halls, bars, coffee-houses, or, during periods of rationing—in wartime or in the socialist states, for instance—just standing in line outside shops). The use of the term 'code' here is justified for two reasons. Firstly, in such cases Jews tend to be mentioned in a purely metaphorical sense only, as actual abstract embodiments or causes of the 'ills' to be rejected or condemned. It is characteristic of such antipathies, which may sometimes be uttered in an extremely rough-spoken manner, that they employ ready-to-hand clichés and have mostly not much to do with actual experiences with Jews or with the reality of Jewish–Gentile relations. Second, this sort of anti-Jewishness is based on common consent, its precepts are abstract and stereotyped in character, and they have no connection with the historical practice of violence directed against Jews. In extreme cases they may be spread or shared even by people who maintain good relations with Jews in their private lives or their occupations. It is therefore possible for the same 'code' to be used in another 'régime' or against other groups who are considered to be 'outside the norm.' This has occurred (and is still occurring) with Gypsies, for example, throughout Central and Eastern Europe, especially in Communist and post-Communist societies with substantial Roma populations. Under other circumstances, though, it could equally be turned against other abstract political enemies, whether that was the 'Germans' (as in Hungary during the period of patriotic arousal in 1848–49 and the ensuing absolutist reprisals by Habsburg Austria), the Russians and Ukrainians (as in Poland from the time of the 1795 partition onwards), or other neighboring nationalities regarded as hostile at some particular time (as attested by many instances in the modern history of the multinational states of Central and Eastern Europe).

In the cultural code of Judaeophobia, therefore, the characteristic form of the xenophobic verbal (symbolic) violence is clearly discernible. A whole structure of ethnic stereotypes may be involved in the code, including puns, witticisms, stock phrases, proverbs, and jokes. This oral literature of commonplace remarks, innuendo, and gossip is primarily a phenomenon of urban subculture, though its traces may also be found in traditional peasant *folk*lore. Nowadays (like earlier) this practice and 'code' offer an excellent opportunity for proclaiming loyalties or giving vent to hostilities on the terraces of sports grounds, those classic arenas of symbolic struggle between 'imagined' *ad hoc* status groups. It is no accident that some of the crudest manifestations of public anti-Semitism, in Hungary and elsewhere, during the twentieth century have occurred at sports competitions. Football matches are played in a veritable 'structural pressure situation,' depending on the structure of relations between the teams and their supporters, that forces the two sides into opposing commitments: anyone who cheers for one side automatically places himself in opposition to the other. In that case, the hurling of racial abuse ('Jews,' 'Gypsies,' 'Blacks,' etc.) against the opposing side springs directly from the 'structural pressure situation' amongst those who also resort to (or at least are aware of) the code of anti-Semitism in other situations. To outsiders, the arbitrary use of this cultural code,

with its negative significance, is equivalent to an anti-Semitic movement, even in cases where there are no real Jews implicated, or at most
only symbolically, and the person uttering the abuse is not necessarily
thinking specifically of them either. Such is the case these days for the
mostly non-Jewish players and supporters of the Hungarian football
club MTK, which was funded, before the Shoah, by members of the
Jewish bourgeoisie in Pest and actually did line up a high percentage
of Jewish players as well. Ever since Fascism started to spread, both
during the reign of Nazism, and especially under Communism and
even beyond (with public expressions of racial hatred generally being
outlawed), football matches in Austria–Hungary, Germany, and Eastern Europe have been the scenes on innumerable occasions for such
'coded,' though for all that verbally no less crude, anti-Semitic manifestations.

The second model of anti-Jewish violence differs from the foregoing inasmuch as it takes actual Jewish individuals or communities as
its targets.

This is the socially more or less 'accepted' or allowed mode of re-
buffing Jews, with some groups even explicitly holding it to be justified, indeed praiseworthy, especially in the case of mass hysteria
against Jews deliberately fomented, organized or controlled by the
ruling élite. The Russian pogroms of the nineteenth and twentieth
centuries offered good examples for such anti-Jewish verbal or behavioral excesses, which could, obviously, be often identified during the
growth of Fascism in Eastern Europe (above all between 1935 and 1944
in Romania, Hungary, and Slovakia, for instance), in Nazi Germany, or,
to take some more recent examples, in Czechoslovakia during the 1950s,
after the Slánsky trial, and in Poland during the official Jewish purges of
1968. In these situations it was officially licensed, indeed encouraged, to
give free rein to anger and resentment against Jews, who were regularly
defined in negative terms as 'aliens,' social outsiders or properly outcasts. That might cover public 'rebukes' or humiliation of Jews, but also
their suspension, and possibly physical removal from their jobs, exile, or
deportation. An anti-Semitic aggressor might well feel in a juncture of
anti-Jewish hysteria that he had become part of the cause of the war
against a 'common enemy' in the service of the 'common good.' His
acts of aggression found there legitimation and justification. They could
hence gain public approval and might even be a source of pride. Any-

how, most important of all was the license to indulge his aggressive impulses. That situation comes about when the apparatus of legal, customary, religious, family or other kinds of moral controls, set up in the given society to curb and penalize spontaneous violent impulses, is either weakened or broken down and/or when Jews are categorized by the authorities as being outside the law and thus stripped of their civil rights. Their deprivation of the entitlement to normal protection against violence also sets them up as possible targets for mass aggression, should the occasion arise.

Anti-Semitic passions were unleashed and asserted themselves all the more readily on such occasions because their targeted victims were usually considered—by force of their pacific cultural habits and frame of mind—to be unprepared or, with due regard to the unfavorable balance of forces, not daring to give a correspondingly robust response to the harassment. It was indeed characteristic of such situations that the aggressors enjoyed complete impunity (except possibly during the periods of Communist régimes that were not anti-Semitic) in regard to both their own authorities and their victims. That encouraged the degeneration of their deeds to sadism. One might define the most important social function of anti-Semitic interventions of this sort as being, in essence, the legitimate exercise of aggression for its own sake. This sadistic dimension of anti-Semitism, which by its very nature finds much more powerful expression in the lower social classes (for whom the use of aggression is usually much more commonplace) than in the upper strata (amongst whom overt or even merely verbal violence is usually an object of 'civilized' censure), has barely, if at all, been given attention by research into the topic.

Anti-Semitism as a compensatory mechanism for social disadvantage

The third in the series of functional models was likewise brought into play by the means that have just been described, but now with the goal that gentile groups 'treated like underdogs,' lacking prestige, or having experienced a loss of prestige, should gain a certain social 'distinction,' dignity, and prestige through which they can acquire more self-esteem and a measure of respect in the eyes of their associates.

Here too we have to do with anti-Semitism more likely to be found amongst the bottommost social strata or those in decline, comprising the outcasts of society (such as the urban lumpenproletariat) and others living in near-poverty (menials, janitors, postal workers, concierges, railway-men), along with economic victims of capitalism and groups that were becoming déclassé or losing power (gentry who have lost their lands, former guild craftsmen, peasants with dwarf holdings). These are groups which often stood in relations of direct dependency or clientage to those belonging to the middle and upper classes (and thus sometimes to the Jewish bourgeoisie) and were increasingly being swept aside or marginalized by the process of modernization. It is a historical fact that the bulk of these groups were not composed of Jews, even if one takes into account the social milieu of the frequently impoverished Jewish populations of Poland and Russia. Those concerned could look on themselves as 'little men,' petty people, 'sons of those below,' part of the 'masses,' who had been forced to the very bottom of the social ladder and thereby deprived of any chance to raise their voice against 'those on top' or of disturbing the prevailing order—unless, of course, that happened to be against the Jews: because the latter, however of the 'better sort,' were denied the protections due to members of their stratum.

Accordingly, the lumpenproletarian 'brown shirts' who sided with Nazism ('the revolt of the assistant caretakers') were partial to setting upon Jews. This was not only because they considered that to be especially equitable, but also because they could thus gain a feeling of getting even for their social fate, which otherwise denied them any exercise of power or the possibility of venting all their bottled-up frustrations, especially what was seen as an entirely justified rage directed at the 'well-off.' Apart from that, anti-Semitism, whether verbal or in the form of physical assault, that was sanctioned, indeed encouraged 'from the top,' assured the members of déclassé or other marginal groups of significant symbolic advantages. Thereby they were even able to identify with the ruling classes that provided the anti-Semitic ideology and authorized its application. They could thus have a part in 'their business.' This was one of those rare historical occasions when, as in wars, the lower classes were able to stand side by side with the upper classes in fighting a common enemy that, however imaginary a bugbear it may have been, was by common consent rightly being exposed to the 'verdict of the people.'

An essential feature of this type of violence consists in the fact that it does not merely apply verbal or physical means but introduces an institutionalized system of discrimination and segregation into schools, residential areas and social intercourse (in business, marriage, sport, etc.). In other words it drastically excludes Jews from the majority society, drawing an inviolable boundary between 'them' and 'us.'

The social self-revaluation that is so fervently sought is only possible with the validation of an ideology of radical discrimination, for in that way reference can be made to metaphors that engender a high emotional fervor: 'Christian values,' loyalty to the 'ancestral' culture, the 'fatherland,' 'rootedness,' the 'authentic' nature of the non-Jewish lifestyle, and all the other topics and subjects of gutter anti-Semitism. Such discourse resists any interpretation, having no substance in reality but, for precisely that reason, it appears unassailable and possesses great inflammatory power: 'blood community,' 'unity of land and character,' 'racial purity,' segregation by 'blood and soil' (*Blut und Boden*), etc. This kind of anti-Semitic 'arguments' magically gloss over social inequalities deriving from the class structure and set in their place a mythical construction, the glorified non-Jewish 'us.' At the same time it transforms that 'us' into what, from the viewpoint of the actual structure and power relations of that society, is a sort of neutralized no-man's-land. The more the negative character of Jews is emphasized, therefore, the more positive that makes 'us' appear. That non-Jewish 'us' offers an eminently cultic basis for collective narcissism, feeding on the ideology of radical otherness, for a nationalistic self-admiration that places the groups located at the very bottom of society—likewise figuratively speaking—on a common denominator with the ruling classes, thereby securing for them an unprecedented symbolic elevation in rank and social dignity that would otherwise be impossible to achieve (outside the wartime conjunction of patriotic euphoria and rallying). Anti-Semitic fundamentalism, from Richard Wagner and his French contemporary Edouard Drumont to Nazism and beyond, has always exploited self-adulating ethnocentrism to drum up the masses to its banner.

Scapegoating, occupational competition and class rivalries

A fourth functional model of anti-Semitism is represented by the set of ideas which deflects the blame for all ills in society to the Jews. In this mechanism of the scapegoat, Jews are absolutely deleterious elements in society, and therefore it is possible to project onto them everything that is not working, disagreeable or judged to be bad.

Such a monomaniac imputation of blame for social ills to a single 'cause' is an obsession accompanied by important symbolic advantages and often also political benefits for every fanatic who subscribes to it. It relieves the non-Jewish leadership of any responsibility, or at least moderates its weight, when things go wrong. This happened when the shapers of public opinion for the Central Powers, for instance, diverted the anger of the impoverished masses during the First World War against Jews, using the corrupt practices of some individual Jewish arms suppliers as an excuse. The method can be used to 'explain' any setback or misfortune that befalls the national community. According to German nationalists, the sole reason for losing the First World War was the treacherous 'stab in the back' that the German nation had received from pacifist Jews (*Dolchstosslegende*). The obsessional representation of the Jews as a general scapegoat offers an extremely simple, flexible 'practical sociology' endowed with a strong power of persuasion precisely because it may be used at any time and for any purpose. The impossibility of contesting or refuting it considerably reinforces its efficiency, as a scapegoat theory evades any attempt to empirical verification. On top of that, the theory contains a very obvious implicit suggestion for reform: all that has to be done to put an end to all of society's woes is to get rid of Jews.

A factor that contributed even more powerfully to the credence in the magical efficacy of a casting-out of the scapegoat in the modern era was the historical fact, discussed in earlier chapters, that Jews were indeed often to be found in relatively higher numbers (in many areas, very obviously over-represented statistically) amongst those actively promoting modernization. In the commonest manifestations of the scapegoat theory, then, the Jews were linked with modernism and what are deemed to be its dismal consequences. This historical interpretation blames Jews for the downsides of capitalism and of Communism alike—often in the same breath. The attack is aimed directly at the Jews, in other words, but indirectly it merges—and thereby acquires a much more general validity—with a critique of western-style democracy, economic liberalism, the Soviet system, freemasonry, feminism, the Esperanto movement, or any other modernist trend. Before the Shoah, this type of anti-Semitism often contained elements of hostility to urbanization and the bourgeoisie (cf. the concept of 'sinful Budapest' in Horthy-era Hungary or 'sinful Vienna' in interwar Austria) and a measure of cultural nostalgia for a vanished, preindustrial world. In the aesthetic field, its targets were cultural modernity, avant-garde movements or any other experimental artistic endeavors, linking them, whether justifiably or not, to the activities of Jews. As soon as they had attained power, the appointed guardians of the Nazi spirit showed how such 'destructive,' 'degenerate' art (*entartete Kunst*) was to be dealt with. The Stalinist supervisors of state expropriated culture under Zhdanov, who regularly branded Jewish and non-Jewish avant-garde creative artists as agents of 'western cosmopolitanism' (and 'handled' them accordingly), acted no differently.

With the fifth functional model we move away from the abstract, general and purely ideological concepts of Judaeophobia to get closer to reality. This model reflects the conflicting economic–occupational or other (e.g. cultural) interests between Jews and non-Jews; in other words, it concerns specific cases of social class competition for resources which may be of material nature (share in professional markets), purely symbolical (rivalry between scholarly schools of thought, lobbies) or a combination of the two. This occurs primarily in the middle classes, the intelligentsia, and ruling élite groups, having very little to do with the lower strata.

Here too, of course, the preconditions for this kind of topical elaboration of irreconcilable Jewish–non-Jewish conflicts are formed by a 'primary' anti-Semitic bias that acts as a self-fulfilling prophecy. The model is nevertheless a distinctive embodiment of that prejudice, amongst other things, because the Jews in question really do play a part in the worsening of Jewish–Gentile coexistence in form of a clash of group interests. The more the role of the dangerous or unfair rival was hung on the Jews, the more they were forced onto the defensive and likely to behave in conformity with that role (e.g. by taking counter-measures). Moreover, during the decades following emancipation, a growing disparity became apparent in the chances of social mobility of Jews and non-Jews, to some extent at the expense of Gentiles. This was particularly apparent in Eastern Europe, with countries lacking strong 'national' middle class strata but ruled by a traditional political stratum of landed and office-holding aristocracy, or their landless version, the gentry. These élites were often opposed to modernization and thus took less advantage than did upwardly mobile strata (including the Jews) of the opportunities opened up in post-feudal free market economies. Such differences in mentality, which also found expression in divergent work ethics, chances of academic success, entrepreneurial skills, cultural creativity, etc., not infrequently gave rise to a competitive situation that could, indeed, be regarded as disadvantageous to Christians in the liberal professions, the creative intelligentsia (journalism or even certain branches of the arts and literature), and the capitalist economy (e.g. between banks, industrial firms and wholesale enterprises run by Jews as opposed to others run by non-Jews).

One of the first consequences of that situation, from the beginning of emancipation, was an arbitrary partition of middle class intellectual markets and activities in Central and Eastern Europe. The more or less acknowledged aim of that was to exclude Jews from or not to let them enter with equal chances of success in careers of the civil service and the public industries under state or municipal control (railways, local mass transport, water, gas and electricity works, etc.) as well as positions of political power. It is no accident that in most German-speaking countries, from the later decades of the nineteenth century onwards, it was students, teachers, civil servants and other elements of the educated middle classes, the *Bildungsbürgertum*, who provided a majority of the adherents and activists for the movements that can be considered the harbingers of Nazism (for example, some 57 per cent of members of the Pan-German League in 1901).

Anti-Semitic repertoires of this kind were built up even more vigorously in states that rejected civic emancipation of the Jews (Russia and Romania): much wider occupational prohibitions remained in operation there, inasmuch as they also restricted the entry of Jews into certain liberal professions, to no small degree through the quota systems imposed on access to secondary schools and universities (as in Russia) or even direct obstacles (as in Romania, where such systems were implemented for most of the liberal professions, with the exception of medicine). With the spread of Fascism during the inter-war years these legal interdicts, sooner or later, became general throughout Central Europe (except Czechoslovakia), usually with the unconcealed aim of bolstering the 'Christian middle classes,' who were proclaimed to be 'constitutive of the state' or 'pillars of the state.' It deserves emphasis that this occurred in several countries during the 1930s. That is to say, legislation on the Nuremberg model to impose more general anti-Jewish occupational prohibitions was introduced even before unequivocally pro-Nazi régimes had been installed or the country had come under military occupation by the *Wehrmacht*. A '*Lex vallachicus*' was passed in Romania in 1934, for example, and the first so-called 'Jewish Law' in Hungary in 1938.

These regulations were all directed at restricting Jewish competition in markets where the middle classes were active and, through high-handed state intervention, at delivering an ever greater proportion of positions occupied by Jewish professionals (physicians, veterinary surgeons, lawyers, engineers, managers, etc.) into the hands of their non-Jewish competitors, in more than a few cases at precisely the juncture when these positions had been dwindling due to the Great Depression of the 1930s or, as was the case in Hungary after 1919, as a consequence of the resettlements, with their attendant floods of refugees of the intellectual class, prompted by major revisions of the state's borders.

Even after the Shoah, Soviet-type régimes did not shy away from promoting artificial competitive constraints, generally to the disadvantage of Jews, between Jewish and non-Jewish interest groups, cadres or 'lobbies' for purposes of more effective control of the state machinery. The methods varied, but the process was in every case grounded on anti-Semitism on the part of certain circles within the Communist leadership that, tacit though it may have been, was none the less crude. This was obvious during the latter years of Stalin's rule in the Soviet Union, in Czechoslovakia after the Slánsky trial, in Poland after 1968, and so on. This 'borrowed anti-Semitism' of sorts was sometimes expressed, as during the Rákosi era in Hungary (1948–1956), even amongst cadres of Jewish descent at the very highest levels of the leadership. It might be manifested in the manner in which the Party was purged of 'infiltrating bourgeois elements' (i.e. Jews) in favor of 'people's cadres,' but also in the way 'sensitive' posts within the state apparatus were doled out between Jews and non-Jews, sometimes in order that they might keep an eye on and hold one another in check, sometimes, by promoting or demoting Jews, as occurred in Hungary during the Kádár régime (1956–1988) on more than one occasion, in order to give a show of the government's neutrality in this domain.

Anti-Semitism and conflicting political interests

The last of these functional models of anti-Semitism is linked to the relations of ideological and political interests between Jews and non-Jews.

One is justified in separating this from the previous model because the relations come into being through other mechanisms, not according to the logic of pursuance of specific advantages by particular groups or strata. Although here we deal with real political–ideological power relations in the given societies, it should be emphasized that the phantasmagoria of projections, 'secret intentions' or clandestine 'conspiracies' are also asserted in this domain as soon as there is a need to portray the Jews or their allies as political enemies. The conflicts of allegedly political interests in question are in any case, as elsewhere, strongly permeated by an initial or primordial Judaeophobia, a supercharged negative concept of the Jews' radical 'otherness,' and the self-fulfilling prophecy that the enemies of the Jews are constantly compelled to resort to self-defense, that is to 'counter-violence.' Naturally, those who have proclaimed Jews to be their enemies from the outset can only behave hostilely towards them, and expect nothing other than similar behavior from the other side, even if this may extend far beyond their collective interests.

It is understandable, then, that Jews, irrespective of the political régime in question, should everywhere support those political forces favorable to Jewish emancipation and the equality of opportunity as implicit in policies of social mobility and economic advancement, that is, which would not discriminate on grounds of creed or race. In the process, of course, all they were doing was provoking or reinforcing the hostility of their enemies. On the other hand, Jews often found allies in movements and organizations sustained by universalistic and progressive ideologies deriving from Enlightenment principles, such as liberalism, radicalism, most (if not all) branches of freemasonry, and sometimes (though not often) national liberation movements when they were in need of the support from 'non-nationals.' (The nationalism of the liberal Hungarian nobility in the first half of the nineteenth century fell into that category.) Social democracy and certain Communist labor movements in some stages of their development also belonged to such obvious options. As a result, political anti-Semitism was regularly (though certainly not always) conservative, antimodernist, authoritarian, and generally found fertile soil within circles that rejected the ideological legacy of the Enlightenment, at least in the long nineteenth century.

It is perhaps more important, though, here than elsewhere to refrain from any generalizations. The Enlightenment programs and utopias of modernization could conceal a Judaeophobic dimension (after all, a 'liberation movement' might with equal ease also aim, as indeed the earliest of Marx's projects did, at 'freedom' from Jews), in just the same way as the converse could also occur. This is to say, depending on the structure of the local political arena, there were certain authoritarian, conservative social plans which, from a Jewish viewpoint, contained favorable elements. Nineteenth-century liberal nationalists tended to be Judaeophile in France or Hungary, but overtly anti-Semitic in Bohemia (in the Young Czechs movement). After the defeat of the 1848–49 War of Independence fought by Hungary's liberal nationalists, imperial absolutism may initially have seemed anti-Jewish, given that the autocratic repressions were also directed at those sections of the Jewish population that had identified themselves with the Hungarian national cause, but it soon became Jewry's most resolute protector in Europe. The political version of Judaeophobia that was primarily instrumentalized elsewhere, above all in Nazi Germany and Central and Eastern Europe, was absent from Fascist movements of Latin countries (Italy, Spain or Portugal), not even under their reigning Fascist dictators. The conservative and legitimist aristocracy and gentry of former Austria–Hungary, for the most part, tended often to be indifferent on the matter, if not exactly Judaeophile, whilst their Prussian equivalents, the Junkers, were inclined to support the most extreme variants of political anti-Semitism. Polish nationalism lent more towards Judaeophilia, or at least towards projects of

Jewish integration, up till the last third of the nineteenth century, before turning ever more expressly anti-Jewish. During the 1918–20 Russian civil war, the Bolsheviks received significant support from the Jewish masses (in return for protection against the pogroms of the counter-revolutionary 'White' armies), but that did not stop Stalin from introducing brutal anti-Semitic measures as early as the 1930s. Admittedly, that happened within the context of a broad degeneration of the Stalinist dictatorship, with the position of Jews in the Soviet Union declining as the dictator aged, the most lethal measures not being instituted until after the Soviet victory over the Nazis (particularly after 1948). Some Soviet satellite states, often strongly staffed by leaders of Jewish background, sometimes appeared in the forefront of the 'fight against Zionist imperialism,' which was an almost unhidden form of vicious anti-Semitism (like Czechoslovakia after 1951 or Poland in 1968), but other Communist countries (like Hungary, Yugoslavia or Bulgaria) remained almost unaffected by the anti-Jewish hysteria of the dark years of Stalinism.

Thus, political Judaeophobia was a function of the configuration of local political forces and of the historical juncture, or in other words, of the place accorded to Jews in the relations of interest between the ruling élite groups. Nothing better reflects the political exploitation of anti-Semitism (or philo-Semitism) than the way national conflicts evolved in Central and Eastern Europe during the nineteenth century, between Poles and Ukrainians in Galicia, Hungarians and Slovaks in what was then Upper Hungary, Hungarians and Romanians in Transylvania, Czechs and Germans in Bohemia and Moravia, and so on. In these internal political struggles now one side, now the other, wooed—often only transiently—the local Jewish population to their cause against their opponents, who as a result would usually resort to the weapon of anti-Semitism in defense of their presumed interests.

From this typology of the social functions that anti-Semitism has fulfilled in modern times, sketchy as it may be, one can draw the confirmation of our initial hypotheses that the 'essentialization,' or absolutization, of alleged or real differences between Jews and non-Jews, and the isolation of Jews within the social domain in accordance with that, can play a decisive role in this context in at least two senses. Firstly, it provides retrospective ideological justification for an already preexisting, primary or indeed 'atavistic' anti-Jewish attitude. Secondly, and more importantly, it justifies the not uncommonly extreme 'abuses' that go along with that exclusion. Were it not possible to portray the 'differences' in question as fundamental or primordial, then it would not be possible to ascribe to them the danger potential that they assume in the fevered imaginations of anti-Semitic fundamentalists.

The social logic of anti-Semitism is always conducive to the over-reaction against an imagined or self-constructed enemy; hence the distinctively monstrous forms in which it manifests.

Mechanisms of 'poor concertation' and 'Jewish conspiracy'

As has been seen, it is possible to find in the ideologies of modern anti-Semitism a series of old arguments, used by Christianity to justify the repudiation of Jews, but now they are dressed up in modern form to meet the requirements of the times. This is not the place to trace the genealogy of those transformations and discursive cross-references. All that will be attempted here is to recall some of the most frequently elaborated theses of Judaeophobia in the modern and present era, and to touch upon the most unrepentant of the fabricators of these singularly simplistic 'systems of ideas.' All of them have, naturally enough, links with religious-type anti-Jewish constructs, though they lack any kind of transcendental reference or theological purpose. They take over from Christian concepts of Jewry above all the dogmatism and intransigent absence of historicity: They propose a one-sided, indeed monomaniacal perception of society, and—not unlike the Churches—urge their disciples to commit themselves to tenets devoid of uncertainty or room for debate. As has proven to be the case all too often in totalitarian ideologies, the less the accusations and statements resorted to as arguments are open to proof, the greater their rabble-rousing potency. Moreover, not only are overlappings as well as themes that complement one another common in the canon of Judaeophobia, so too are contradictions, as well as logical, socio–historical or political absurdities, but they exert nonetheless their influence by posing as a coherent system, based on stereotyped fantasies that predicate and, as it were, magically confirm and reinforce one another. The incoherence of anti-Semitic doctrines derives in no small measure precisely from their being a concoction of old and new motifs of Judaeophobia.

Our concern in this section will be new *topoi*, for which references were supplied by the system of relations between Jews and non-Jews evolving in European societies in the period following the French Revolution. These notions were also fed by more traditional earlier motifs of Judaeophobia and, furthermore, they were not uncommonly interdependent, so as to appear together. Hence, any attempt to present them in separate clusters, as here, is bound to be somewhat arbitrary.

One of the oldest and most widespread motifs of modern anti-Semitism, and at the same time the most protean in its manifestations, is that of the 'Jewish conspiracy.' Its modern variants are rather original indeed and they often relate to specific events in nineteenth-century social history, so that they obviously pertain to the present discussion. The phantasms of 'conspiracy' in recent times are linked, in part, to the perception of the differential socio–economic mobility of Jews and non-Jews. As was discussed earlier, following (and sometimes preceding) emancipation a Jewish élite quickly made its appearance, and in certain areas—the stock exchange, the banking system, the textile industry, the liberal professions, the press, etc.—acquired significant economic power, intellectual recognition, and, indeed, occasionally also political influence in several Western and Eastern European countries. The sudden and seemingly spectacular growth of power by these 'foreigners' in modernizing nation states lent itself very well to reformulation of the 'conspiracy' topos. On the other hand, again simply conforming to the mechanism of the self-fulfilling prophecy, that same figment of the imagination was nothing more than a 'translation' of self-organizing and self-defensive activities of Europe's Jewish élite—that actually were taking place—into the language of primary anti-Semitism. The international network of Jewish organizations that emerged, first in Europe and later globally, towards the end of the nineteenth century, with the foundation and institutionalization of the Alliance Israélite Universelle (1860) and the World Zionist Organization (1897), was indeed initiated precisely in the face of movements of political anti-Semitism that happened to be showing their colors around that time.

Perhaps the first instance in which the ancient topos of a 'universal Jewish danger' was formulated in unvarnished form in the modern age was when it was chosen by the French Jesuit, the Abbé Augustin de Barruel, as the centerpiece of his *Memoirs to Serve for the History of*

Jacobinism (1797). Its foundation was a veritable demonology, having as its principal thematic element a secret conspiracy of Jews for the suppression of Christians or for perpetual anti-Christian action which was manifested, as the occasion arose, in betrayal, upheaval of the social order, espionage, and other subversive work carried out on behalf of 'foreign interests.' Traces of this near-superstitious belief can be found as early as the Renaissance era in Spain and elsewhere. In the eyes of many in the counter-revolutionary camp, the Grand Sanhedrin of Jewish representatives, ordered by Napoleon in 1807, was likewise an assembly that convened to further devilish plans of this kind. This conviction was bolstered by the widely held notion that Jews possessed boundless occult powers, which they had placed in the service first of the French Revolution (which squared with the stereotype—obviously not a twentieth-century invention—of the Jew as a 'disturber of the peace,' 'subversive,' and 'revolutionary'), then of Napoleon I. This in no way hindered the subsequent spread of the belief in various Eastern European countries, that Metternich, the prime mover of the anti-Napoleonic Holy Alliance, was also a Jewish hireling. The establishment of the Alliance Israélite Universelle in Paris fitted perfectly into this scheme.

The subject crops up in the bulk of the anti-Semitic literature of the nineteenth century, particularly in the disputes over the Dreyfus Affair. One important element of this topos is the condemnation of the activities of masonic lodges. From the time of the writings of the Abbé Barruel and other contemporaries onwards, Roman Catholic and antiliberal anti-Semitism in general, whether it remained merely conservative or later debouched into Fascist extremes, has heaped its curses on freemasonry for having been set up as the executive arm of a 'Jewish plot.' The *fin-de-siècle* right wing in Europe increasingly tended to treat free-masonry as a shorthand equated with the Jews. The global popularization of the motif of the 'Jewish conspiracy,' on the whole, did not come until after the First World War, through the assistance of that infamous forgery, *The Protocols of the Elders of Zion*. This had originally been cooked up by an agent of the tsarist secret police in Paris, immediately after the First Zionist Congress (1897), by tailoring the details of an earlier anticapitalist booklet to fit a Jewish context. It was put out in Russia itself in the wake of the 1905 Russian revolution as a 'preparatory measure' for the elections of representatives to the first Duma. This counterfeit amplifies the conspiracy charge with lurid insinuations and calumnies. (Just to quote one preposterous assertion in the work: Jewish bankers in the major capitals of Europe were taking part in the construction of underground railways in order to lay their hands on power, their plan being to blackmail governments by threatening to blow up the cities by placing explosives in the tunnels...) In Russia the *Protocols* inspired the instigators of the bloodiest of the pogroms during the upheavals of the civil war. They were also spread widely (in translation) in Germany, thus helping to corroborate right-wing nationalist propaganda that shifted the blame for the country's loss of the First World War onto the Jews for 'stabbing the nation in the back.' It is hardly surprising, then, that the subject-matter of the *Protocols* was a Nazi hobbyhorse throughout the campaign of annihilation that they unleashed against the Jews. Anti-Zionist agitators in non-Jewish circles similarly made frequent use of the book, even before the Shoah. It goes without saying that, from time to time, it has had a prominent place in the anti-Israeli ideological armory of Arab countries (e.g. in Nasser's Egypt).

Anti-Semitism as anticapitalism

Another major thematic strand of modern anti-Semitism blames the Jews for all of capitalism's ills. It is not hard to hit upon the premises for this thesis in the fact that, as discussed earlier, Jews were active in significant proportions in virtually every branch of the free market economy across Europe. That topic was latched onto in two different ways, one a left-wing version, the other right-wing in character, though there are identifiable overlaps between the two.

The classic formulation of the left-wing approach goes back to Marx himself. In one of his early essays (*On the Jewish Question*, 1844) he tied his solution to the 'Question' to the abolition of capitalism, or to the termination (*Aufheben*) of Jewry as a distinct social and religious unit. Socialists adopting Marxism—often themselves of Jewish ancestry, as in the case of Ferdinand Lassalle and Otto Bauer—always proclaimed that assimilation of the Jews was inevitable in the forthcoming socialist régime. That in reality was no more than a moderate reformulation of Marx's thesis. But, at the same time, they categorically rejected Judaeophobia not based on class distinctions, regarded as the '*Socialismus der dummen Kerle* /socialism for idiots/', to quote August Bebel's bon mot. Friedrich Engels cast all his authority into the scales in his book *Anti-Dühring* (1878) in order to purify German social democracy of the corrosive influence of Eugen Dühring, the racist anti-Semitic philosopher in Berlin.

Another traditional current of socialism, which struck roots mainly in France, was not free of xenophobic hatred of Jews either. Taking a lead from François Fourier, one of the forerunners of early 'utopian' socialism, Pierre-Joseph Proudhon, and even more his contemporary, Alphonse Toussenel, looked on the Jews in aggregate as a 'class enemy,' the source of all social ills, and 'enemies of humanity.' The French labor movement was unable to shake off that influence for a long time. Even during the Dreyfus Affair French socialists were incapable for some time to reject decisively the anti-Semitic temptation. At first, even a socialist leader as influential and highly respected as Jean Jaurès categorized this nation-wide socio–political crisis as mere 'in-fighting' between factions of the bourgeoisie, before later going on personally to take a firm stand in the Dreyfusist camp.

The right-wing version of identifying Jews with capitalism is similarly long-established. The German economic historian Werner Sombart provided a subsequent theoretical framework for this, in *Die Juden und das Wirtschaftsleben* (1911), by imputing the 'spirit of capitalism' to the Jews, in contrast to his academic colleague, the sociologist Max Weber, who linked it with Protestantism. This essentially anti-Jewish approach to capitalism was nevertheless adopted and further elaborated by almost every ensuing anticapitalist movement: nostalgists for the feudal system, 'syndicalist' socialists, the declining upper strata of the *ancien régime* (the landed nobility, the urban patricians), or the classes that were increasingly losing out on the fruits of capitalism (petty bourgeois handicraftsmen and shopkeepers, peasant smallholders, etc.). Romantic anticapitalism made much of the immoral business methods and corrupting influence ('the depraving role of money') allegedly characteristic of Jews. This was one of the guiding principles of right-wing anti-Semitic publicity in France during the Third Republic, when many cases of large-scale corruption came to light with the passage of time in which a number of Jewish (and other) financiers happened to be implicated. The most notorious of them were the Panama Scandal (1889–91) and the fraudulent bond issue behind the Stavisky Affair (1933). These were catalogued alike by Édouard Drumont in his highly tendentious journal *La Libre parole*, his much read book *La France juive* (1886) as well as by Charles Maurras and those who wrote for his influential daily paper *Action française* (since 1908), mouthpiece of the rightist movement of the same name.

Another well-worked mine for populistic anti-Semitism was the denunciation of 'parasitic capitalism.' According to the tenets of classical economics, further developed by Marxism, this form of capitalism does not produce value but is 'parasitical' on the results of creative capitalism lauded by Marx and Engels in the *Manifesto of the Communist Party* (1848). In the anti-Semitic versions, the economic behavior of this kind is claimed to be either exclusively or primarily typical of Jews, in that they were principally active in finance, wholesale commerce, distribution and stock-exchange transactions. The conspicuous fortunes made by some Jewish banking families— epitomized by the Rothschilds—served as an emblematic pretext to make 'parasitism' a favored topic of political anti-Semitism from the late nineteenth century onwards.

Unsurprisingly, inflaming the passions of the 'little men,' the 'exploited' or the 'ruined' against the 'upstart' nouveaux riches, having made their way in the triumphant capitalist world, proved to be an equally potent weapon for anti-Semites of both right and left, all but bringing them together in a united front. Later on, however, with the growing strength of socialist movements in the nineteenth century and the Bolshevik take-over of power in Russia, the right-wing critique of 'Jewish capitalism' was complemented by the *topoi* of the exposure of 'Jewish Communism.' The reference that these had to reality can likewise be located in political developments of the time, particularly in the oppositionist political stance of certain sections of Central and Western European Jewry who had become disenchanted with emancipation and of sections of Eastern European Jewry whom emancipation had passed by. Definitive personalities of the Jewish intelligentsia in Austria–Hungary, Germany, and elsewhere came to the fore early on in the socialist movements. For many of them this served as receptive medium for assimilation, and later on (in Bolshevik Russia and the

Soviet satellite states) also as avenues for social advancement. A similar phenomenon also occurred in tsarist Russia when a measure cultural assimilation and especially secularization got under way and led, among other things, to a separate Jewish labor movement. Estimates have suggested that around one quarter of the political prisoners languishing in tsarist gaols were Jewish around 1900.

It is not difficult to understand that the theme of 'Jewish Communism' fitted together well with earlier explorations of the 'conspiracy' topos. The anti-Semitic régimes of Germany, Hungary, and Romania did not allow themselves, before the Shoah, to be disconcerted in the least by the logical contradiction of using one and the same ground for declaring a 'war of self-defense' on both 'Jewish plutocracy' and 'Judaeo–Bolshevism.'

Judaeophobia and romantic nationalism

From the French Revolution onwards, the geopolitical rearrangement of Europe and the modernization of public institutions within post-feudal nation states raised the question of the national status of ethnic and cultural minorities, the Jews amongst them. The establishment of nation states fixed borders for close on half a century, up to the end of the First World War. The process was completed, for all practical purposes, with the Austro–Hungarian Compromise (1867), the end of the process of Italian unification (1870), the founding of the German Empire (1871), and the independence and international recognition of the new Balkan states (in 1878 or soon after).

Almost everywhere (except in Romania and Russia) this was associated with the legal emancipation of the Jewish populations, accelerating their cultural and social integration. At the same time, disparities in the progress achieved in this respect and diverging assessments of that integration, supplied a number of striking items in modern anti-Semitism's repertoire of motifs. It was easy to rebuke Jews who remained loyal to their traditions for their 'foreignness,' their 'alien' manners, their 'outsider' status, their separation from a majority civilization—henceforth designated the 'national culture'—as well as for allegedly seeking to set up a separate political organization and, as such, showing themselves to be untrustworthy in terms of the 'loyalty to the state' expected from citizens. Even before that, Jewish communities (*kehal* or *kehillah*) had provoked charges that they 'formed a state within the state.' Fear of Jewish political autonomy or self-determination, and a presumption of their doubtful national commitment (ascribed to their 'dual identity') troubled many in the political leadership of emerging nation states. This was the case even of such open-minded liberals as the Hungarian Lajos Kossuth (who certainly could not be accused of anti-Semitism). Yet during the age of assimilation that question was raised both over assimilationist as well as traditionalist Jews.

There is a far wider selection of thematic handholds if we turn to Judaeophobic animosities that hit out at assimilated, 'nationalized' Jews.

One such was the allegation of being 'devoid of national feeling.' Citing their international economic and cultural networks, those leveling this charge regularly suspected Jews of 'cosmopolitanism,' and hence of 'antinational' behavior or attitudes 'alien to the national spirit.' This might take on formulations of a political, socio–historical, or even aesthetic guise in different countries and socio–political settings. The principle of 'proletarian internationalism,' the need of 'vagrant' immigrants to fit in, or even the cultural 'rootlessness' and estrangement from tradition of the artistic avant-garde, and so on were all topics equally capable of eliciting anti-Semitic reactions. The Nazi invectives against what they regarded Jewish 'degenerate' modern art and, further to the east, the attacks of Stalinist censors, leaping to do the bidding of Zhdanov's cracks of the whip, on the 'cultural cosmopolitanism' of Jews sprang from one and the same stock.

There was also a far more general, more unbending and effective variety of the same accusation, which became an important constituent in the founding myths of Romantic nationalism that typified late-emerging nation states, especially in Germany, Romania, Bohemia, and elsewhere. The point at issue was that Jews, with their 'doubtful' origins, 'foreign' cultural background, non-Christian creed, and (partly on account of their exclusion) separate identity and self-perception, should be denied in principle the very possibility of 'nationalization.' Hence the postulate of their basic 'unassimilability.' This notion was based on the same sort of circular reasoning as other mechanisms of self-fulfilling prophecy: Jewish 'otherness' served at once both as cause and end. Since they were perceptible 'others,' they were presumably also dangerous and also incapable of merging with the nation, thus everything had to be done to keep them out. As a consequence, the marks of their 'otherness,' their 'separate identity,' could only grow stronger.

This sort of anti-Semitism, which was later to gain expression in the '*völkisch*' discourse concerning the 'basic national character' of the *Blut und Boden* kind, is grounded on a mythicization of the notion of national 'roots.' This posits an absolutely necessary link between native land, blood ancestry, and national culture, its values and the feelings it inspires. Thereby could be contested the Jews' ability and inclination, as well as right, to assume membership of the 'body of the nation.'

Towards the end of the nineteenth century, Heinrich von Treitschke, a distinguished professor of history at the Humboldt University in Berlin, was just as forthright in arguing against the idea that local Jews living in his own milieu (for example, teaching at his university), however profound their German culture or for however many generations they may have been settled there, should be regarded 'true Germans.' In just the same way the ideologues of the 'Young Czech' movement rejected any consideration of the possibility that a Bohemian Jew might become a 'true Czech.' Richard Wagner's operas offer an entire Teutonic mythology for a near-religious expression of the 'authentic German spirit,' which could not be shared by those of other race—meaning the Jews first and foremost, against whom Wagner nurtured very personal and much publicized antipathies. Wagner indeed went even further in his anti-Semitic chauvinism than other exclusionist nationalist trends with his demand that Jews had to be stripped totally of the influence they exerted on German 'national' culture. The Wagner cult (along with its anti-Semitic features) was fostered after his death by his wife, Cosima Liszt, and his son-in-law, Houston Chamberlain. One can find amongst its early active propagators, paradoxically enough (except for its anti-Jewish implications), cultivated circles of the Austro–Hungarian Jewish bourgeoisie. It was vigorously pressed by the German nationalist right wing and the Nazis into the service of their own cause. Hitler himself was a devoted fan of the master of Bayreuth. The Pan-German and Pan-Slav movements, getting established during the final decade of the nineteenth century, also adopted many elements of this culturally grounded Judaeophobia. The political role played by the Pan-Germanists made their movement one of the precursors of Nazism proper. In Russia, the wide spectrum of ideological trends that designated themselves as Slavophile, including the custodians of the idea of tsarist autocracy and the revolutionary Narodniki, could be reduced to a common denominator on one point: their vehement rejection of Jews.

Intellectual sources of the ideology of 'rootedness'

Concepts relating to 'rootedness' had at least three kinds of tributary sources: the idea of the bondage to the soil, a cult of cultural specificities, and consciousness of a common ancestry.

The first of those alone made it possible to proclaim Jews as being radically 'alien' to the community of European peoples, which, in the nineteenth century, was to be understood as the aggregate of ethnic groups destined to lead a national existence—even though it was well known that such nation-building claims might run into conflict or contradict one another. The Jews of Europe were deprived of any prospect that they might appropriate a 'national' territory consecrated as their own, on the pattern of other nation-building movements. Their 'bonds to the soil,' what is more, were regarded as conspicuously weaker than those of other ethnic groups in two respects.

For one thing, Jewish populations almost everywhere (even in the *shtetl*s of Eastern Europe) lived geographically interspersed amongst non-Jewish peoples. Only within individual settlements were they concentrated in (more or less) separate districts. They could not even claim the compulsory 'Pale of Settlement' in Russia as 'their own land', since the majority of the population there was made up of Poles, Ukrainians, Germans, etc.

For a second thing, not only did they count as historical 'immigrants' everywhere in Europe (even when their 'settlement' had happened far back in the Middle Ages), but they did, indeed, generally show much greater readiness to be geographically mobile, even disregarding the far from isolated instances, even in more recent history, when that mobility was forced on them. For example, as late as 1891, it was possible for the bulk of Jews living in Moscow to be expelled by ukase, whilst the imposition of *Numerus Clausus* restrictions from the late nineteenth century onwards turned large numbers of Russian Jewish school-leavers into migrant students at Western European universities. We have already (notably in Chapter 1) touched on the importance of an extraordinarily high degree of urbanization for Jewish strategies of social advancement, security, intellectual modernization, etc. at a time when the overwhelming majority of European populations (with the possible exception of England and a few early industrialized subregions in the West) still lived in rural blocks of ancient lineage that had been tied for many generations to single villages. The absence of such 'bonds to the soil' left palpable traces in the external image of Jews.

Whilst this might have served as a motive for their social exclusion, certain anti-Semitic movements and governments (e.g. the post–1935 Polish leadership) applied the very same concept to justify a sympathetic handling of Zionism, insofar as the project of setting up a Jewish state outside Europe would solve the local 'Jewish Question' through a voluntary withdrawal of all these undesirable 'aliens.' Jewry's recognized 'tradition of emigration' lent considerable credence to the Zionist-inspired exodus plan. And yet that plan, in its very conception, rested on the idea that the Jews, who had by then been living for more than half a millennium on Polish and Lithuanian territory, were *de facto* 'aliens.'

According to the second thematic element of this topic, the very reason why those 'aliens'—unlike certain others 'of different race'—could not be assimilated, and why they resisted integration into 'deeply rooted' majority groups, laid in their cultural difference—being 'foreign' (in essence, non-Christian), in a somewhat mythicized anthropological sense of the word. Even the mildest varieties of anti-Semitism gladly dwelt at length on the idea that it was practically impossible for Jews and non-Jews to become one 'emotionally' and in terms of values. The reverberations of the 'soul of the people' could not be picked up and entered into by such outsiders, even in the event of the most thoroughgoing linguistic and cultural assimilation. In this never more closely definable 'emotional' domain, having an identical mother tongue, common schooling, professional and economic collaboration, even baptismal water was regarded as unable to wash away that 'otherness' from Jews. The difficulties of 'national' identification with the Jews were conspicuous to ideologues of even the most liberal host milieux. (Admittedly, the Christian Churches never officially endorsed this concept, as the sanctity of baptism, from their standpoint, would transform the religious status of Jews once and for all time. Even the Churches, however, were obviously opposed to 'token conversions,' or in other words, to seeking baptism purely for reasons of convenience.)

It took just one further step to cast Jews irrevocably into the cleft of radical otherness, inasmuch as the concept of 'rootedness' could be based not merely on cultural heritage but on common ancestry. From this standpoint, Jewish 'otherness,' as indeed most ethnically based differentiation, acquired an 'objective' validation in the fact that Jewry was demographically isolated in very much the same, though not completely similar, way as other national minorities. Their 'difference' was though aggravated by the special factor (particularly significant from the standpoint of common ancestry) that during the very period when nation states were emerging, the possibility of Judaeo–Christian intermarriage still encountered institutional obstacles in many European countries, specifically where inter-denominational civil marriage was not yet introduced. This was still common enough even after the emancipation of Jews (in Hungary, for example, up till 1895, and in Austria proper even longer, beyond the end of the Monarchy). Whilst it is true that members of other ethnic groups within multinational nation states, for their part, traditionally married amongst themselves up to the threshold of recent times, there were nevertheless no institutional barriers to their demographic mixing, *connubium* being not outlawed, like for long between Jews and Gentiles.

As we shall see, the most decisive facet of political anti-Semitism in the modern era was precisely the idea—stepping beyond the old Christian anti-Judaism, which was founded on religious and cultural arguments but not, in light of the principle of Christian universalism, on common ancestry—that 'racial differences' must serve as the point of departure to absolutize the 'otherness' of Jews. By a deliberate abuse of the Darwinian evolutionary theory through its perverse application to social history ('social Darwinism'), this idea was raised to the status of a scientifically proven thesis in the form of 'race theory.' This was of huge significance. On the one hand, it allowed the difference between Jews and non-Jews to be definitively 'naturalized,' transformed into an irreversible natural endowment, whilst on the other hand, it provided a justification—as part of an operative political program—for the social exclusion of Jews in terms of the principle of the 'struggle for life' among racial groups. Already implicit in the logic of racial struggle, of course, was the 'scientific legitimation' for subjection, 'vanquishment,' physical removal and even, should the occasion arise, annihilation of the Jews.

The notion of a link between social and anthropological inequalities and differences—that is to say, investing genealogical or 'racial' divergences with cultural or political significance—was actually a very old one. It had been a long-standing practice of Spanish and Portuguese aristocrats since the Renaissance to justify their power on the grounds of their 'purity of blood' (*purezza del sangue*) and thereby exclude all outsiders from high state offices. This scheme was of course directed especially against Jewish converts to Christianity (*conversos*) or their descendants. Basque nationalism, from its antecedents in the times of the *Reconquista* of the Iberian peninsula from the Arabs onwards, has cited the allegation that the Basques alone never mixed with either Moors or Jews. This used to serve for the legitimization of their demands for political autonomy. From the time that European countries first began to expand territorially overseas (and especially from the eighteenth century onwards) and 'white' conquerors, merchants and explorers were confronted with the anthropological diversity of the world's inhabitants, numerous attempts were made to classify human races on the basis of alleged primordial and definitive intellectual or social inequalities. Thinkers as distinguished as Hume, Buffon, Linnaeus and Rousseau followed such line of thought. Some Enlightenment philosophers of history even sought to explain the conflicts of European states and social classes in terms of divergent anthropological descent. There were many Frenchmen, from the Comte de Boulainvilliers to Abbé Sièges, who, in their protests against the *ancien régime*, made use of claims that the Gauls had in the past constituted the majority population and (as the theory went) had been oppressed by a conquering Frankish minority in order to institutionalize their hold over the country through the hierarchy of estates of a feudal nobility. In this way, 'our ancestors, the Gauls' (as history textbooks in French schools were later to put it) were able to assume the form of forebears of the revolutionary *tiers état* ('Third

Estate'). Those theories, however, carried little or no practical consequences for the course of relations between Jews and non-Jews
(except on the Iberian peninsula, where the only Jews who remained
after the end of the fifteenth century were the Marranos, converts to
Christianity who secretly maintained their Judaic faith).

The 'Aryan myth' and early versions of racial doctrine

The notion that there was a link between ancestry and social differences gained a new socio–historical scope when German philologists
hit upon the relationship between the Indo-European (or Indo-
German, as German scholars termed them) languages and civilizations. The works published by Franz Bopp, from 1816 onwards,
spring first to mind in this context. Romantic historico–philosophical
elaboration of this discovery were conducive to the myth of an
'Aryan' race endowed with remarkable collective virtues, abilities,
and accomplishments.

The essence of this Aryan myth, first propounded by the German
philosopher Friedrich Schlegel in the early years of the nineteenth
century, is the scientifically totally unfounded postulate that language,
material and symbolic culture, along with 'race' (a people of common
ancestry), form an indissoluble unity. The adherents of racist theories
later in the nineteenth century took from here the idea that the
'Aryans,' descendents of the high castes of ancient India (the 'Whites'
of Indo-European culture), had created European and American civilization in its entirety, and by dint of that 'racial determinism' were
destined by definition to rule over 'inferior races.' The emphasis
placed on the Aryans' exclusive possession of creative abilities is one
of the self-justifying basic precepts of all kinds of racist (and hence anti-
Semitic) ideological currents that became fashionable in Europe during
the nineteenth century. Further philological research, building on the
work of Max Müller, the German-born Oxford philologist, from the
1870s onwards, definitively rebutted any relationship between language
and biological descent ('race'). The 'Aryan myth,' which was soon narrowed down to a declaration of the superiority of the so-called 'Nordic
races' (principally Germans and Anglo-Saxons), was only able to
achieve the political effectiveness that it sought by pairing it with a

counter-myth of negative attributes ascribed to Jews (as well as to other 'inferior races'), founded on the newly acquired authority of the then nascent science of physical anthropology. Even an early scientific falsification of those notions was no obstacle to the 'Aryan myth' and the counter-myth relating to the Jews becoming, by the end of the nineteenth century, the main point of reference for Judaeophobia and the renewed social exclusion of Jews in several countries.

Before going on to present the further development of racial doctrine and its political operationalization, it is necessary to emphasize the significance of the point in time, and more specifically the *fin-de-siècle* socio–political nexus, that marked the start of its popularization. The ideological dominance of the Judaeophobic phantasmagoria of Christian anti-Judaism and 'rootedness' seems to have been supplanted by a secular anti-Semitism based on the racial doctrine, together with the political agitation that it provoked, at precisely the very historical moment when the cultural assimilation and social integration of Jewry were accelerating with the substantial achievement of emancipation in the European powers and the ensuing secularizing legislation (civil registration of births and marriages, equality of religious denominations, disengagement of states from matters religious, etc.). The racial doctrine appeared on the scene as soon as it had become clear that, in essentially all respects (nationalist sentiment, cultural identity, political behavior, etc.), French Jews had become Frenchified, German Jews—Germanized, Hungarian Jews—Magyarized, and so on—that is, when the program of assimilation and the appropriate 'emotional identification' appeared to have been successfully accomplished. This happened all the more when, with the general advance of secularization (sometimes, as in France, through the agency of an expressly anticlerical state policy), even religious anti-Judaism had started to lose its former hold on society in many places—as a way of taking over the baton, so to say, in the relay of anti-Semitism's dominant motifs. This can be dated with some precision across Europe to the last two or three decades of the nineteenth century.

It was a French diplomat, Arthur de Gobineau, who first attempted a systematic formulation of these exceedingly murky ideas of race in his two-part work *Essai sur l'inégalité des races humaines* (1853 and 1855). Good Catholic that he was, he could not refuse to admit as his

point of departure the Biblical doctrine of man having a common ancestry. In practice, though, he put forward a polygenetic hypothesis of
the evolution of species by placing the origin of 'black' races in Africa
and that of 'yellow' races in Asia. He constructed a scale of values
amongst races that unambiguously favored 'whites' (classing Arabs
and Berbers with them, but excluding Jews), whilst recognizing some
particular abilities of Jews and also other colored races. Amongst the
Whites, the Aryans would be the true creators of high civilizations,
but only insofar as they had or would preserve their racial purity.
Gobineau had a pathological dread of 'racial intermixture,' seeing in
this the main cause of the decline of high cultures. This is wherefrom
the book drew its pessimistic vision and critique of the western world
as suffering from what it saw as an already lethal infection of miscegenation. Gobineau may not have brought in anti-Semitism as a direct
topic of his study, but his racialist doctrine, precisely because it
seemed to give intellectual respectability to the idea of racial inequality, exerted a huge influence (especially from the 1880s onwards) in
the emergence of a new wave of Judaeophobia that prided itself on its
soundly 'scientific' foundations. This was particularly true of Germany, though also of Britain and the United States. The *Bayreuther
Blätter*, the periodical put out by Richard Wagner, the *Gobineau
Vereinigung* (Gobineau Society), founded in 1891, and the *Alldeutscher Verband* (Pan-German League), founded in 1893, all helped in
giving a substantial boost to the spread of Gobineau's views in ever-
wider circles. Its tenets gained unexpected 'scientific' corroboration
through mediation by the vulgarized, ideological perversion of Darwinian evolutionary theory, which in France too provided nourish-
ment for the anti-Semitic passions of various currents within both the
conservative right wing and the socialist left wing.

It was indeed the British biologist Charles Darwin's epoch-making
*On the Origin of Species by Means of Natural Selection, or the Pres-
ervation of Favored Races in the Struggle for Life* (1859) which inad-
vertently gave a decisive impulse to the rise of social Darwinism. The
central arguments that Darwin propounded to explain the evolution of
animal species—natural selection, the survival of the fittest (those
species that were best adapted to their environment), and a continual
struggle for life between species—opened the way for the concoction,
often via deliberate distortions of the original arguments, of numerous

socio–political ideas relating to inequalities between human groups. Some of those were aimed at improving conditions of life for the working classes (for example, Bismarck's social legislation). Others were inspired by *Hereditary Genius* (1869), the pioneering work of the English physical anthropologist Francis Galton, to launch a movement of eugenic engineering, aimed at improving the biological quality of the human race by the selective breeding of attributes deemed to promote social success. There is no hint in Galton's work—any more than in that of his cousin, Darwin—to justify a racist interpretation of his scientific findings and hypotheses. Yet German eugenics very quickly became charged with anti-Semitic polemic. In this view, Jews were the economic parasites of a crisis in the industrial era, disrupting the 'racial purity' of the nation, vitiating its unity, and consequently diminishing Germany's chances of getting the upper hand over other imperial powers in the 'struggle for life.'

Chamberlain, the father and high priest of anti-Semitic racial doctrine

By the turn of the nineteenth into the twentieth century, racist anti-Semitism had already been the subject of numerous writings, but the job of welding these into an effective system was undertaken by Houston Stewart Chamberlain. Though the son of a British admiral, Chamberlain's upbringing was unusually cosmopolitan. He spent his university years in Geneva and Dresden, before taking up German citizenship and, as a son-in-law of Richard Wagner, settling at Bayreuth to become a driving force in the Wagner cult. In his *Grundlagen des neunzehnten Jahrhunderts* (1899)—translated as *The Foundations of the Nineteenth Century* (1910)—he set out a modern theory of racist anti-Semitism, which made himself a direct ideological trailblazer for Nazism.

His entire argument is built on a completely secular historico–philosophical dualism greatly indebted for its effectiveness to the author's train of thought, which rests on his energetic exposition of prejudices presented as facts, unquestionable value judgements and indeed obsessional ideas. In his construct, 'Rome' and 'Judah' stand for the negative racial forces of European social development, the

Teutons of the 'Germanic' North (which incidentally included Celts and Slavs) its positive forces. There was a dualism of good and evil, in other words, which obliged the Aryans not only to engage in battle with the forces of 'evil' but also to lay claim, as the creators of a new civilization, to the mastery of the world. This is where they came face to face with 'Judah,' which was likewise seeking world domination. Chamberlain cloaked his racial disquisition in quasi-mystic murkiness, introducing new conceptual categories, such as that of *Rassenseele* ('race soul') and *Rassenbewusstsein* ('race consciousness'). He claimed them to be unalterable endowments through which the irreconsilability of the opposed powers, the 'war of the races,' was manifested.

The anti-Semitically motivated cult of 'deep-rootedness' was a fertile soil for innumerable fantasies, each more bizarre than the last, some with philosophical pretensions, others with mystic overtones, and yet others chasing distinctly esoteric or superstitious ambitions. There is no space here to delve further into these, even though they played a major part in shaping the intellectual climate of the turn of the century, right up until the 1920s. However, to pick out a few of the more interesting topics at random, purely to give a sense of their flavor, one may mention the revival of pre-Christian German traditions, the Romantic cult of nature (and its denunciation of an urban lifestyle linked to the Jews), the rejection of modern medical procedures (blood transfusion, injection of drugs), the attribution of occult powers to Jews, etc. Nor were vestiges of similar mysticism wanting subsequently amongst the masters of the Third *Reich*: this was to be the only modern European state whose leaders would regularly consult astrologers before making political decisions.

Anti-Semitic xenophobia in German-speaking countries was often associated with flat opposition to universalistic or super-national movements, institutions or collaborations of any kind. The adherents of the Pan-German ideal, for example, loathed Catholicism and also, more generally, the Latin peoples, whom they saw as typical representatives of the latter. Chamberlain himself had an abhorrence of Mediterranean civilizations. An even more generalized antipathy was manifested towards Christianity as such, regarded as root and branch 'fettered to Judaism.' Indeed, the long-standing tension between Hitler and Mussolini was at least partially ascribable to this, with the leaders of the two 'Fascist' great powers displaying mutual contempt for one another's ideological obsessions (which in Mussolini's case extended to Nazi Judaeophobia). Nazi jurists, for example, did everything in their power to ensure that the system of Roman law which, through the spread of Christianity, had been adopted as the basic codes of jurisprudence across much of Europe, should be replaced by allegedly ancient, purely Germanic legal principles.

The glorification of 'Aryan' virtues impelled many anti-Semitic authors into casting doubt even on Jesus Christ's Jewishness, leading them to proclaim him an Indo-European, some even going so far as to locate his birthplace in Westphalia... Others in that same intellectual mood attempted to 'de-Judaise' the Jewish tradition itself. Some scribblers argued that the Old Testament Pentateuch, or *Torah*, could actually be traced back to Thor, the Norse god of thunder, whilst the Germans were one of the lost tribes of Israel. Along these lines even the *Kabbalah* could only have been the work of ancient Germans... All these figments of anti-Semitic imagination sprang from a guiding notion which denied non-Aryans any cultural creativity. Certainly the stockpile of sheer drivel produced by such anti-Semites is inexhaustible.

Chamberlain was to become the mentor of most of the influential ideologues of the entire pre–1914 German imperialist stance (including the Kaiser, William II, himself) as well of the ensuing Nazi movement. More surprisingly, his book had a not inconsiderable influence in England (though less so in France), even amongst such luminaries of left-wing liberal and socialist circles as H. G. Wells, G. B. Shaw or Sidney Webb. The socialist utopia promulgated by the Fabian Society of the time, in which all three were prominent, included tenets of 'racial hygiene' and the notion that the model of social organization developed by the 'Anglo-Saxon race' was valid for the whole developing world. The Nietzschean doctrine of the 'superman' (*Übermensch*) having special natural rights was rapidly admixed with theories about racial inequality and hostility with a potentially anti-Semitic import, which had gained widespread currency within Europe's intellectual élite prior to the First World War. Nietzsche himself though, against interested expectations, and indeed to the dismay of many, would have nothing to do with anti-Semitism, that he forthrightly dismissed and indeed despised as an utterly 'vulgar' doctrine.

The notion of Jewish 'racial inferiority' nevertheless left its mark, albeit not explicitly, on legislation to control the policing of foreigners and immigration in more than a few western countries, as in the case of Austria's 'Pan-German' law (1887), the United Kingdom's Aliens Act (1906), or the subsequent quotas that were imposed on immigration into the United States (1924). The latter proved to be particularly unfavorable for Jews, being designed among other things to keep out 'eastern' Jews' setting off from Europe. The thinking behind such measures was dominated by 'racial protectionist' considerations with the aim to preserve the demographic predominance of the Christian, the 'Nordic' or the 'Caucasian' stock in the population. After the First World War, with the growing pressure of German right-wing anti-Semitic racism, most European democracies (though not the Americans to the same extent) temporarily or permanently dropped this exclusionary approach, up till the outbreak of the Second World War. This ideological orientation lead to the increasing alignment with Fascism that occurred in most states of Central and Eastern Europe, particularly after 1933 (with the exception of the Czechoslovak Republic and, in part, Yugoslavia and Bulgaria).

Forms and historical dimensions of anti-Jewish violence in the recent past

The hotchpotch of notions encompassed by anti-Semitic ideology encouraged three main types of action.

The first of these may be referred to as ordinary, everyday anti-Semitism. This was generally (but not invariably) manifested in forms of individual behavior aimed at the exclusion of Jews from usual channels of social intercourse. Examples of that were economic boycotts ('We won't buy from Jews'), the refusal of mixed marriage and other opportunities for *connubium*, avoidance or rejection of camaraderie and any other personal (friendly, collegial, neighborly, etc.) contact, segregation of Jews in residential areas and schools, utterance of insulting remarks. This type of conduct has operated in many parts of Europe without even the slightest break in continuity from the Middle Ages down to the present day—but not, it should be emphasized, universally and to the same degree or with the same intensity.

Its strength and frequency were largely functions of the level of modernization of the given society as well as, more concretely, of the social environment (layer, class, substratum) concerned. Democracies, that statutorily enforced respect for human rights, placed legal barriers in the way of the public expression of such attitudes, especially when they comprised an encroachment on rights. The behavioral model for such ordinary anti-Semitism is not specific to social relations between Jews and non-Jews. It is a modality of more general practices to maintain social distance that may be set into operation with similarly discriminatory intent against any other ethnic, cultural or *ad hoc* minority group defined as alien or 'radically different': not local, newcomers, foreign-tongued or accented, etc.

The second type has to do with collectively exercised or mass violence, whether spontaneous in character or planned and organized (sometimes with the connivance of the authorities). It may either circumvent or directly infringe upon existing laws serving to maintain public order. Its classic manifestation was the urban pogrom, in the course of which looting, ransacking or razing of Jewish shops, workshops and dwellings were allowed free rein, and physical assault and even murder were permitted. Such outbreaks of violence were visited with considerable regularity on many Jewish communities in Russia, as in the case of Odessa and other cities throughout the nineteenth century, especially after 1881. Also of this category were the 'Hep! Hep!' riots in Germany (1819), the anti-Jewish disturbances in Pest, Pozsony (Bratislava), and other Hungarian cities during April 1848, the mass demonstrations, likewise in Hungary, that followed the acquittals of the defendants in the Tiszaeszlár blood-libel trial (1882–83), and the anti-Jewish disorders at the end of the century in Prague (1897–99), as well as in France during the Dreyfus trial (mainly in 1898). Equally, this type covers the attacks by student associations on their Jewish fellow students that became customary, indeed all but ritual, at universities in Germany and sometimes even in Austria–Hungary from the 1880s onwards. That form of 'Jew-baiting' was perpetuated between the two world wars in Hungary, Romania, and elsewhere. The system of 'Jewish benches' in Polish universities (introduced during the 1930s) represented also a more than purely symbolic pattern of anti-Jewish violence. Such actions were usually conducted with the tacit consent, and not uncommonly active collusion, of the responsible state, municipal, university, police and other authorities, with a blind eye being turned to the legislation in force, destined to protect individuals and minority groups. The common feature of that kind of collective violence, all the same, was their relative 'spontaneity,' at least in the sense that they were not backed up by precisely defined anti-Jewish goals, deriving from an overtly proclaimed, long-term political program. The precipitating causes were manifold, embracing religious animosity, the opportunity of free plunder, thanks to the passivity of responsible local authorities (in tsarist Russia even the government could occasionally resort to such handiest safety-valve for relieving social tensions), envy at the social and economic achievements of Jews, and so on. It is worth though to distinguish these incidents from programmatic political anti-Semitism, despite the fact that the outward forms they assumed were not infrequently identical.

Political anti-Semitism represents indeed the third major type of anti-Jewish violence. Its invariable concomitant was the emergence of political organizations and parties urging the state to take measures against Jews via legislative or other institutional interventions. Anti-Semitic actions in this case were part of a political program with the ultimate goal of excluding Jews from the benefit of rights normally bestowed on other citizens. Two forms of such political anti-Semitism may be distinguished, depending on whether the movements pursuing the programs in question represented a minority (i.e. they were in opposition) in the competition for power or actually held power in the state. Organized anti-Jewish actions and the repressive administration of justice that typify the latter may be identified during the nineteenth century in countries which refused to grant legal emancipation to the Jews, namely, Russia and independent Romania. Elsewhere, organized political anti-Semitism, with open government support, emerged rarely in the long nineteenth century, but some powerful movements started to be organized to this effect since the late 1870s and much more generally in the inter-war years. In other words, political anti-Semitism became widespread after the achievement of legal emancipation, when the social integration of Jews reached an advanced stage. In this new situation the aim of such movements was to undo some of the consequences of emancipation.

In almost every case, this occurred under particular socio–historical circumstances within countries concerned during the period between 1875 and 1880. This was clearly the era when large clusters of modernized and secularized Jews, with the repeal of the very last restrictions, finally gained admission into élite circles and began to take their places, in growing numbers, in the new middle classes. Hence their sudden visibility in universities, the industrial and agricultural bourgeoisie, the liberal professions, even the army or public offices in Western and parts of Central Europe, etc. This period was also marked by capitalism's first general crisis, sparked by the collapse ('*Krach*') of the Vienna stock exchange on 9 May 1873, but soon spreading across Europe and to the United States, which was to set back the dynamism of the continent's economic growth for decades. It was also the period, in the wake of the 1878 Berlin Congress, where the nation states formed in the Balkans had gained international recognition. By the same token all European states (with the exception of Russia, to be sure) had introduced some kind of representative parliamentary system of western type, though in both Austria and Germany the government was taken over by antiliberal, conservative forces. This combination of circumstances framed the political, economic and socio–historical background for the rise of political anti-Semitism which quickly became a determining factor—albeit to very different degrees from country to country—in public life throughout Europe.

The appearance of militantly anti-Semitic politics was linked even more closely to the establishment of new types of mass parties and the emergence of new forms of political action that facilitated the public airing of minority views. That process went hand in hand with the growing impact of the press, offering a platform to the free expression of opinions, an ending (or weakening) of censorship, guaranteed freedom of speech in parliament and other public forums, legal rights to demonstrate in public space, liberty to speak up at party assemblies, to hand in petitions, to organize protest movements, etc. This was most likely a big element in the transformations of Judaeophobic initiatives, as it enabled them to become visible vehicles of public opinion. In addition, one must also take into account the dual impact of the perceptible worsening of the anti-Jewish pressure exerted by tsarist autocracy from 1881, as manifested by the great wave of pogroms and the 'May Laws' of 1882. These served as a model throughout Europe for radical anti-Semites for the use of force to solve the 'Jewish Question.' Hungary, where there was barely any local tradition pogroms (if one overlooks the exceptional, albeit serious disturbances in April and May 1848, inefficiently repressed by the freshly installed government), was not long afterwards, following the Tiszaeszlár trial of 1882–83, swept by the first nation-wide wave of pogroms (or attempts at such). In conjunction with those events, the mass emigration of Jews from Eastern and Central Europe made public opinion in the 'developed' part of Europe—and that included circles of socially integrated Jewry—suddenly confront with Jewish traditionalism, the 'caftaned' Jewry of Eastern Europe, the 'assimilability' of which looked manifestly doubtful. This gave unexpected force, and a sense of wider legitimation than previously, to those who were pushing for the Jews to be 'checked.'

Overall, the inauguration and consolidation of political anti-Semitism in many countries after 1875 produced the impression of being part of some coordinated, world-wide undertaking. That view was reinforced, first, by the observable transfer and spread of anti-Semitic views between states (mostly through the press) and, second, by various forms of international cooperation between anti-Semitic movements. The first ever European congress of anti-Semitic parties took place at Dresden in September 1882, with delegates coming from all German-speaking countries and from Hungary by then convulsed by the Tiszaeszlár trial. A second gathering of this kind was held the following year at Chemnitz, by now with representatives of anti-Semitic parties from further countries (France, Romania, Russia, Serbia) also in attendance. Nevertheless, if one looks at the fate of this congregation of local initiatives, it is easy to find out that national policy withstood them in most places, albeit to variable degrees, depending on the ties of interest binding Jews to leading strata in host societies. Thus, representatives of Hungarian, French and Romanian anti-Semitic movements may have founded a Universal Anti-Semitic Alliance in Bucharest (1886), for example, but this did not survive for long. The attendance at subsequent major meetings of anti-Semites in Cassel (1886) and Bochum (1889) was, in practice, restricted to delegations from German-speaking countries only. Although organized anti-Semitic movements and parties indeed surfaced everywhere in Europe during these years after 1875, their influence was exceedingly varied and oscillating. They acquired no significant political role actually in either Great Britain, the Benelux states, Scandinavia, the

Mediterranean region or the Balkan states (Romania excepted). The overwhelming bulk of public opinion as well as the state authorities there more or less firmly distanced themselves from any attempts on the part of organized anti-Semitic movements to gain a footing. Some of these countries (Denmark and Finland can be equally quoted here, together with Fascist Italy) resolutely withstood radical anti-Jewish temptations even during Nazi German influence or occupation.

The evolution of political anti-Semitism will be outlined, country by country, in the next chapter. For all the variations, there seems to be a perceptible difference between the decades preceding and those following the First World War. The years 1918–19 represent a genuine historical watershed, marked both by a redoubling of anti-Semitic violence and the reorganization of anti-Semitic movements across Europe, with the Soviet Union, then still in the process of installing itself in power, the dominant Czech provinces of the new Czechoslovakian state as well as several Balkans states representing major exceptions.

The revival of political anti-Semitism in Eastern Europe

The administration of justice in tsarist Russia and the 'Christian Article' of Romania's constitution (which stipulated that only those of Christian faith could become Romanian citizens) excluded native Jews from the outset from many basic civil rights by denying them, among other things, freedom of choice over their place of residence and occupation. In these two countries, then, one is dealing with true state managed (and in part generated) anti-Semitism, which operated within an institutionalized framework up to the end of the First World War. Not only did its effects not diminish with the passage of time, they actually reached their fullest pitch during the early decades of the twentieth century as political movements and parliamentary parties avowing explicitly Judaeophobic programs gathered renewed strength.

In Russia the system of tsarist autocracy permitted organizations to operate only under the government's official supervision. Accordingly, the first major anti-Semitic association, the Holy League, which was credited with setting off numerous pogroms in the wake of the assassination of Alexander II (1881), remained underground, even though it had the support of many potentates within the government. Another formation of similar tenor, the Union of the Russian People, materialized in 1904, when it became obvious that the Russians were facing defeat in their war with Japan, but this time it was overtly under the patronage of the government. Its armed wing, the 'Black Hundreds,' responsible for the most dreadful pogroms in 1905, received financial support from Tsar Nicholas II in person. The Union had a significant role in the Duma right up till the February revolution of 1917, inasmuch as it was able to block the passage of any planned measures that offered to alleviate in the slightest the wretched position of Jews in Russia. Other anti-Semitic organizations came into existence subsequently, one of the most radical being the 'United Nobility,' instigator notably of the infamous Beilis trial (1913). This show trial, which sparked world-wide indignation and ended, despite the efforts of the authorities, in the defendant's acquittal, was the last major judicial case in Europe to be constructed on the Judaeophobic fantasy of ritual murder (if one discounts cases that were mounted in Nazi Germany without provoking much noticeable reaction).

In Poland anti-Semitism gradually established itself in the political arena of Congress Poland during the decades that followed the crushing of the 1863 uprising against the Russians. Its emergence in Austrian-ruled Galicia in part preceded and in part followed the successes achieved by anti-Semitic parties in Vienna around the turn of the century. Anti-Jewish demands were being voiced in the provincial diet by the 1880s, but during the 1890s it was the Polish Catholic People's Party which organized the first large-scale anti-Jewish demonstrations, initially aimed mainly at weakening the economic positions of the Jews. It first took the indirect forms of setting up cooperative societies and peasant credit banks and (more directly) organized boycotts on Jewish shops. The 1898 elections were accompanied by over thirty pogroms that were sparked off, despite determined countermeasures by the imperial authorities, by the party's head of propaganda, the Jesuit Father Ignac Stojalowski.

With the revival of Polish nationalism in Russian Poland during this same period, the National Democracy Party (the *Endecja*, or *Endeks*, as they were commonly called after the party's acronym), under their founder-leader Roman Dmowski, drifted away from liberalism towards the far right in executing a political about-turn to anti-

Semitism, in no small part with the close cooperation of the tsarist authorities. The Endeks' influence also extended to Galicia, even supplying the faction leader of the Polish delegation sitting in the *Reichsrat* in Vienna when the party won the local elections in 1907. Dmowski also controlled two seats in the Russian imperial Duma and coordinated the first large-scale campaign to boycott Jewish businesses in Warsaw, which coincided with the elections for the Fourth Duma. The executive arm for that campaign was *Rozwoj*, the Office for the Support of Polish Industry and Commerce, in essence nothing more than an agency for anti-Semitic 'agitprop.' During the First World War the party supported Russia, but it also won a decisive voice in independent Poland's first national assembly, the Sejm, thereby securing an excellent platform to sustain and add further muscle to its tradition of hardline political anti-Semitism in Polish parliamentary and political life between the two world wars.

Though Poland had signed the clause in the Versailles Treaty that referred to the protection of minority rights, attacks against Jews (at least symbolically) began on the very first day of independence. A campaign for the introduction of a *Numerus Clausus* (1922) led to more than half of Polish university faculties either refusing admission to Jewish students or drastically curtailing it. During the 1930s, the academic segregation of Jews was established overtly with the installation of 'Jewish benches' in lecture halls, a practice that was enshrined in law in 1937. At the same time, physical separation of Jews and non-Jews in some cities was also extended to market places. In the period between the wars there was no end of anti-Jewish boycotts, attacks, and even riots, engineered by the *Endeks* and the Catholic parties, which in these actions, often with the open blessing of the Catholic Church, could count on both the lower clergy and the church hierarchy.

This was the moment in Polish history when Catholicism finally laid the foundation of its nimbus, later to become legendary, as the central pillar of the nation state. Though General Piłsudsksi's *coup d'état* in 1926 deposed Dmowski and his party from their government positions, their political influence continued to grow unbroken. In 1933 the *Endeks* announced a program of rapprochement to Nazi Germany. After Piłsudski's death, political anti-Semitism in Poland came increasingly under the influence of the Catholic extreme right, turning into an unrelenting state-sponsored anti-Semitism which, within the space of a few years, promulgated a whole series of repressive measures. In 1936, Polish Jews living abroad were stripped of their Polish citizenship, leaving several tens of thousands of them stateless. In 1938, priests of Jewish descent were removed from their posts, despite the fact that this blatantly racist decision infringed canon law. In the same period the established rights relating to ritual slaughter of animals for meat were restricted, and Jews were stripped of their voting rights in chambers of commerce. The Catholic parties nevertheless continued to push for more direct steps on the lines of Hitler's 1935 Nuremberg Laws. This 'colonels' Poland' was being carried towards Nazi-style Jewish policies, the original propagators of which were, before long, to turn against them and sweep them away when, on 1st September 1939, the *Wehrmacht* launched its invasion of the country, without prior declaration of war, to defeat them militarily. The occupation of Poland was followed in short order by the direct incorporation of the western provinces into the Third *Reich*.

In Romania the French ambassador to Bucharest considered in 1900 that 'anti-Semitism ... is more than just an idea: it is the collective obsession of every party politician, of the Orthodox Church and, beyond them, of every single peasant, whether Wallachian or Moldavian.' It was no accident that the Universal Anti-Semitic Alliance should have picked Bucharest as the venue for its founding assembly in 1886 and bestowed the presidency on the infamous Jew-hating publicist Edouard Drumont. Amongst prominent Romanians, later to be found in the ranks of the World Anti-Semitic Alliance and the Universal Anti-Semitic League (1895), were Professors Alexandru C. Cuza and Nicolae Iorga. Cuza, throughout his long career, was to propagate an irrational Judaeophobia, peppered with the doctrines of Eastern Orthodox Christianity, which ultimately led to an attempt to restrict Jewish citizenship rights during the brief premiership of the violently anti-Semitic Transylvanian-born poet Octavian Goga, in whose government Cuza held a post between the late 1937 and early 1938. Iorga coupled an exceptional academic career as a leading historian of much distinction with his political activities. Having broken with Cuza around 1922, he founded a League of National Christian Defense and elaborated an ideology that melded xenophobia with a Romantic 'Romanianism,' the main basis of which was supplied by a populism based on an idealized peasant world as well as an anti-Semitism that, in the local context, could be called moderate.

The times then, however, were not favorable to temperate hatreds. Romanian popular anti-Semitism had already shown its venom with anti-Jewish atrocities perpetrated during the peasant uprising of 1907, and ever-decreasingly spontaneous cases of Judaeophobic violence proliferating in the inter-war years. The new components in the latter were complex. Just one of these was a tripling of the Jewish population in the country, due to the annexation of Bessarabia, Bukovina and Transylvania to Romania in 1918. The resultant 750,000 Jews now represented 4 per cent of the total Romanian population. Also important were the conflicts that had surrounded the granting of legal emancipation to Jews—a condition that the victorious Entente powers had only wrung from Romania at the Versailles Peace Conference by the application of acute political pressure. Another obvious factor was the country's gradual sidling up to, and eventual military alliance with, Nazi Germany during the 1930s.

During the inter-war period, all the larger parties and ideological currents in Romania had an anti-Semitic flavor, but the most violent of them—one not shrinking from murder of its opponents as a political tool—was the Archangel Michael Legion, better known as the Iron Guard. This was founded in 1927 by a law student, Corneliu Zelea Codreanu, and fellow students of the '22 generation,' who in 1922 had conducted an aggressive campaign seeking the imposition of severe quotas on Jewish university entrance. By 1937 it was the third-largest party in the country (winning 16.5 per cent of the votes cast in the elections that year). The Legionaries were typical of the conspirative type of Fascist movements, grouping in an armed, paramilitary organization and sustaining an ideology combining heavy reference to Eastern Orthodox religious mysticism ('blood brotherhood'), a veritable death cult (especially idolatry of their own 'martyrs'), and the notion of 'ethnic regeneration.' They represented the radical, revolutionary right wing, with a program including improvements in the living conditions for peasants but centered principally on virulent anti-Semitism. That fanaticism spurred the Legionaries not only into physical intimidation of Jews but also increasingly violent intervention against political movements—'traitors,' in their eyes—that defected from the cause. As a result, even successive right-wing governments treated the Iron Guard as dangerous rivals, and in the course of retaliatory actions carried out against them several hundred (including their leader, Codreanu) lost their lives. Despite that, other Legionary members continued to play a leading role in the ever more drastic forms that the state's anti-Semitic policies assumed from 1937 onwards.

For the rest of Europe the center of gravity for political anti-Semitism lay in Austria and Germany, but it also exerted a significant influence for a while in Hungary (between 1875 and 1895) and France (after 1886). As anti-Semitic parties had managed to gain a solid footing in parliament and the local administration of several large cities (e.g. Vienna) in Austria and Germany by the close of the nineteenth century, these two countries will be discussed separately.

Two 'liberal' counterexamples: France and Hungary

The birth of political anti-Semitism in France is bound up with the defeat suffered at the hands of Prussia in 1870, the ensuing Paris Commune, and the chaotic conditions that accompanied the protracted difficulties of the establishment of the Third Republic.

Having set out with a liberal, modernizing program but not consolidated politically until 1877, the new régime had to contend from the start with numerous internal enemies—Catholic conservatives, royalists, Bonapartists, to say nothing of socialists—who frequently leagued against it and even more frequently augmented the groundswell of anti-Semitic unrest. From the 1880s, the latter movements were able to mount serious political forces behind their aims, yet a good part of their actions remained extra-parliamentary, tending to find most vigorous expression in mass organizations, street campaigning, demonstrations, and in the press. It assumed variable forms in connection with a succession of scandals linked to the various political crises that the government went through, ranging from the failure of the Catholic-run *Union Générale* bank (1882), through the political campaigning of the dismissed minister of war, General Georges Boulanger, in 1889, amidst growing scandal over traffic in the decoration of the Légion d'honneur associated with Grévy's second term as president (1887), and the uncovering of the Panama Canal corruption scandal in 1892, to the world-wide stir provoked by the long-running Dreyfus Affair (1894–99).

Paul Déroulède, who had instituted a *Ligue des Patriotes* in 1882, was already overtly linking the corruption rampant in the republic to anti-Semitic slogans when he attempted to use the League to promote Boulanger's political ambitions (the latter fled France in early 1889 under accusations of having planned a *coup d'état*). On the back of the resounding success of his book, *La France juive* (1886), Édouard Drumont set up a National Anti-Semitic League (1890) to further that message, whilst the right-wing, anti-Semitic ideological sentiments behind the subsequent *Ligue de la Patrie Française* (1898) and the long-lived 'Action Française' movement, founded by Charles Maurras in 1899, were direct products of the crisis stirred up by the Dreyfus Affair. Encompassing a medley of allied organizations and movements, such as the Parisian Anti-Semitic League (refounded in 1897), the League of Anti-Semitic University Students (established in 1894), and the large membership of the National Anti-Jewish Party (inaugurated in 1901), *Action Française*, along with the newspaper of the same name (1908), exerted a peculiarly persistent and ever-growing influence on French public opinion over nearly half a century (till its outlawing in 1944, due to collaboration with Nazism). It actually ended up by providing the ideology for the Nazi-collaborationist Vichy French state, even if some of its individual members did join the resistance movement. For all that the socialists, under the leadership of Jaurès, abandoned their anti-Semitic bias inherited from their forerunners (whether Proudhon or Toussenel) over the course of the Dreyfus Affair, and most of the leading parties in the National Assembly preserved their liberal traditions in respect to the Jews, at least up till their defeat in 1940, the clerically charged anti-Semitic climate fostered by the opposition to the Republic in the press and often in the streets was to form part of French political life until the country's liberation from Nazism in 1944.

In Hungary, where most politicians who constituted the liberal noble élite and later (after the 1867 Compromise) the governing parties of the new nation state, like the republican ruling class in France, were vigorous supporters of Jewish social integration, a belligerently anti-Semitic political movement, probably the first such in Europe, was formed in 1875 under the leadership of Győző Istóczy, a dissident parliamentary representative of the governing Liberal Party. On the prompting mainly of Liberal but also, to a smaller extent, of Independence Party representatives, an Anti-Semitic Party was established in 1883, in conjunction with the nation-wide popular unrest aroused by the Tiszaeszlár ritual-murder trial. The party enjoyed a certain amount of success in subsequent elections, securing 17 parliamentary seats in 1884 (though with only a marginal 4 per cent of the total votes cast) and 11 seats in 1887 (2.5 per cent of votes). Its representatives remained a completely isolated faction in parliament, their radical platform being rejected with more or less unanimous distaste by the ruling National Liberal majority. Their strident addresses provoked either derision or indignation from most fellow deputies as well as in 'gentlemanly' public opinion. As a result, overtly anti-Semitic agitation remained fairly rare in Hungarian public life prior to the First World War, though without ever vanishing completely.

The Anti-Semitic Party itself proved ephemeral, though a part-successor, the Catholic People's Party under Count Nándor Zichy (founded in 1895), was likewise in the habit of airing anti-Jewish slogans in its representation of 'agrarian interests' (the traditional land-owning class, that is to say) against the advance of the 'agri-business bourgeoisie' (the champions of which process it discerned to be Jewish rural renters, flour-millers, bankers, and merchants). Its clamor, which was in reality restrained compared with the brutality of the earlier movements, was intended more for 'internal consumption' of the party's hard-core supporters. Thus anti-Semitic discourse did not become more widespread until the year the First World War was declared—but then a perceptible intensification was experienced—in a parliament dominated by party alliances opposed to any kind of exclusionist policy and based on an assimilationist 'social contract.' Vilmos Vázsonyi, for instance, a practicing Jew, became minister of justice in several governments that preceded the break-up of the Austro–Hungarian empire. He proved to be, though, admittedly the first and last one to reach such a government post in Hungary—as a professing Jew—under the pre–1945 old régime.

The bourgeois–democratic 'Chrysanthemum revolution' of October 1918–February 1919, the succeeding Communist Soviet Republic (March–July 1919), and the subsequent 'White Terror' brought wrenching changes to Hungarian political life. An authoritarian-conservative régime installed itself, which rested its program on the anti-Semitic demands of the Christian middle classes—civil servants, university students, and those in the liberal professions in particular—who were counted amongst the biggest losers in the truncation of the country resulting from the Trianon Treaty. A *Numerus Clausus* on university admissions, legislated for under pressure from the proto-Fascist 'Awakening Hungarians' movement and coming into force as early as the autumn of 1920, initiated a process of squeezing Jews out of job markets of the educated middle-classes. It was closely followed by a mounting number of dismissals of Jews from public service posts and the institution of a state economic policy that systematically favored Christian businesses. During the period that extended from these indirect or (in the case of the *Numerus Clausus*) slightly veiled anti-Jewish political measures up to the advent of the first legislation that directly curtailed the civil rights of Jews (1938) the stirring-up of an anti-Semitic political climate became increasingly more widespread in all public forums—parliament, the pro-government press, and even universities—especially in the 1930s. Indeed, early on it was limited to the moderately anti-Semitic 'Christian–national course' of the 'consolidative' government led by István Bethlen (1921–31), to such an extent that in 1928, on the advice of Kunó Klebelsberg, the minister of education and religious affairs, the anti-Jewish rigor of the university *Numerus Clausus* was temporarily mitigated by an amending law.

After 1932 a sharp change in political direction was staged. The power of more or less extreme right-wing forces grew under, initially, the influence of the alliance with Mussolini's Italy and, later on, the ever closer rapprochement to Nazi Germany. Nevertheless the 'Jewish Laws' were not introduced by extremists but by a conservative camp, trying to take the wind from the sails of a radical right that, by then, was flying the banner of Nazism. By adopting those bits of the Nazi program that suited their own interests, the conservatives simultaneously fended off the weak bourgeois–liberal and rather more substantial Social Democratic opposition.

Both in France and Hungary, then, a genuine alliance of interests between 'nationalized' Jews and the ruling liberal political forces did succeed for a while (albeit on decidedly shaky ground during the Dreyfus Affair in France, and only up till 1918 in Hungary) to reduce the risk of anti-Semitic movements commanding or influencing the exercise of power. That was not the case either in Austria or in Germany.

Austria from von Schönerer and Lueger to the *Anschluss*

In the Monarchy's Cisleithan provinces, which after 1918 constituted the Republic of Austria, two rival movements competed to mobilize anti-Semitic passions for political ends. One was Pan-Germanist, anticlerical, and anti-monarchist in outlook, the other conservative–Catholic, monarchist, and populist. The latter emerged as victor from this contest to unify the anti-Semitic camp of the electorate during the decades running up to the First World War. (It should be borne in mind that in this part of the Monarchy all adult males were enfranchised from 1907 onwards). These two parties may be said to have embodied two possible paradigms for modern political anti-Semitism. The first rested on the Christian–national tradition of conservative Catholicism, and thus did not resort to racist doctrines, whereas the second steered clear of, or totally ignored, Christian references, constructing its ideology on what were essentially secular grounds, such as the alleged 'racial' incompatibility of 'Aryans' and Jews. The bulk of support for both parties came from the petty bourgeoisie and various marginal groups from the primarily urban lower strata, giving political anti-Semitism a long-standing and rather stable electoral base from the 1880s onwards. The topic was thus secured a hitherto unprecedented presence in public campaigns, against which the successes gained by similarly oriented movements elsewhere, including Germany (though France during the period of the Dreyfus Affair might be regarded as an exception), paled by comparison.

The Pan-German movement, promoting a Greater Germany, was originally an offshoot of the radical–democratic and nationalist left wing, led by Georg von Schönerer, an Austrian provincial nobleman with considerable oratorical gifts. The Austrian brand of Pan-Germanism had its roots in revolutionary republican (and therefore anti-monarchist) traditions going back to 1848, with no small part having been played in its emergence by liberal, bourgeois, and intellectual circles within Austrian Jewry, seeking to achieve social integration under the aegis of German culture. This was the reason why a Heinrich Friedjung or a Viktor Adler—both future Social Democrat leaders of Jewish descent—were initially attracted to Schönerer. At Linz in 1882 they even worked together to elaborate for the Austrian Pan-German movement an 11-point program, urging radical social reforms and annexation to Bismarck's empire. Not long after that, however, Schönerer broke with his Jewish allies and added a further point to the Linz program, which called for 'the elimination of Jewish influence in every sphere of public life'. After 1882, the anti-Semitism of the Pan-Germanists switched to extreme radicalism, proclaiming the superiority of the 'Germanic race' over all the Monarchy's other minorities—Jews in particular—in line with the ideology of racial domination.

This hatred fed off two main points of reference, the one being anti-capitalism (war primarily on Jewish capital), the other anti-monarchism. The latter found part of its justification in the fact that, discounting those segments of Viennese Jewry espousing *gross-deutsch* ideals, the bulk of Jews in Austria–Hungary, having no territory of their own, had developed strong sentiments of 'imperial patriotism.' Professing to be a veritable *Staatsvolk* ('state supporting people'), they counted actually as amongst the most loyal of the Monarchy's subjects. As a result, political forces hostile to the multinational Monarchy were able to call on this as a justification, albeit not the most essential one, for their radical Judaeophobia. By the 1890s this was being coupled with an anti-Catholic stance, the Catholic Church having historically been one of the main pillars of the Monarchy, due in particular to the support it had received from the Habsburg state for the Counter-Reformation. It is therefore not as surprising as it may seem at first sight that anti-monarchist anti-Semitism in Vienna should be channeled into a mass movement demanding a break from the Church (*Los von Rom!*). At the peak of this campaign, Schönerer personally made a very public conversion to 'the true German confession' of Lutheran Protestantism, though there can be no real doubt that this dramatic change of faith had much more to do with political calculation than with religious convictions. Pan-German activists like himself were more likely to subscribe to a pagan 'Teutonic' ancestral cult, if any. As far as anti-capitalism was concerned, that could be readily reconciled even with antagonism to socialism, because leaders and supporters of both Pan-German camps, for all their apparent opposition to one another, were able to sink all differences by hitting on Jews as the arch-enemy. Austrian Pan-Germanists espoused the most extreme of the racialist versions of anti-Semitism of that time, which in the Bismarck era meant the mainstream, *völkisch* type of German Judaeophobia exemplified by Eugen Dühring, Paul de Lagarde and Richard Wagner.

Schönerer's paranoid but charismatic personality, and his vision of a radical break with the Monarchy's liberal system of government, exercised tremendous influence on the 'native Austrian' sections of Austria's student societies. These *Burschenschaften*, or fraternities, had a tradition of anti-monarchism going back to 1848, which was greatly bolstered by Prussia's victory over Austria in 1866. They tended to idealise the virtues of the Bismarckian *Reich* just as blindly as they held their own empire in contempt, especially when the Monarchy's defeat at Sadowa–Königgrätz ruled out any possibility of its joining the emergent German Confederation. Their general xenophobia had earlier been directed against Slavs, Italians, and other minorities, but at some point around 1878 it switched against Jews, even though many of the latter, up till then, shared the same *Grossdeutch* commitment. The Austrian student conference of 1896 adopted an overtly racist clause in its constitution which disqualified Jews from 'giving satisfaction' by fighting duels (*Satisfaktionsfähigkeit*), which was one of the unquestioned conventions of bourgeois students in that era. This was a key step in the process of the symbolic exclusion of Jews from the educated middle classes. However, the extravagance of Schönerer's rhetoric against the Catholic Church and the Monarchy, coupled with his proneness to acts of thuggery (for which in 1888 he was given a prison term, stripped of his title of nobility, and deprived of voting rights for five years), continued to estrange him from the Austrian masses, most of whom remained loyal to the Habsburgs. After a semi-success in the first elections it fought—winning six seats in 1887 and 21 in 1901—his Pan-German Nationalist Party progressively broke up, with many voters turning away from it to swell the ranks of the rival Christian Social camp.

This other, possibly more strongly rooted in the current of Austrian political anti-Semitism, was led by Karl Lueger. From 1889 onwards his movement managed to secure a solid base in Viennese local politics over a prolonged period, eventually becoming the major political force within the Austrian state between the two world wars, right up to the *Anschluss*. Formally established with its anti-Semitic program as the Christian Social Party in 1893, within two years it had already won a decisive majority of 66 per cent of municipal council seats in Vienna. This unparalleled success and Lueger's popular appeal as a formidable demagogue was greatly to the court's distaste. Franz Joseph at first repeatedly refused to confirm his appointment as mayor of Vienna, before finally being prevailed on to relent in 1897. Lueger was to hold this post until his death in 1910.

Anti-Jewish propaganda in Vienna can be traced back to at least 1848. Its early promoters were recruited from the conservative Catholic élite, with the work of spreading it being entrusted to journalists and the lower clergy. Its main targets were the economic success of immigrant Jews, the corruption ascribed to them, and the 'destructive' nature of modernization. This movement drew seemingly respectable intellectual support from August Rohling, a Rhinelander, who was professor of Semitic languages at the University of Prague. This mediocre but unscrupulous scholar brought together a collection of scurrilous forgeries in his book *Der Talmudjude* (1871) which succeeded in whipping up a previously unheard-of level of anti-Jewish feelings by linking the age-old accusations of Catholic anti-Judaism (e.g. with its libel of ritual murder) and the then current popular hostility to wealthy Jews. Rohling's influence was undiminished by the fact that the false allegations, contradictions, and malicious conclusions in which the book abounded were exposed and condemned in a court of law, so badly damaging his reputation that he was not only dismissed from his chair but also obliged to withdraw from public life. Nor did this deter him in the slightest from continuing to produce his anti-Semitic screeds.

Keeping aloof from this type of vulgar anti-Semitism, Baron Karl von Vogelsang projected a very different tone, albeit with the same objective, in *Der Vaterland*, the newspaper that he founded in 1875, and through its associated political organization, the Christian Social Union (*Christlich–sozialer Verein*). The baron, a German Lutheran who had Catholicized and settled in Vienna, cloaked his anti-Semitic message in a far more elevated, 'civilized' guise. His attacks were directed against the 'rapacity' and 'perniciousness' of free capitalism and, alongside that, against cosmopolitanism, modernism, and their concomitants, nihilism and atheism. He associated all of these phenomena with the Jews, and proposed the restoration of a state organization based on guild corporatism as a Romantic alternative solution, an echo of which was later to be found in the 'state of Christian estates' of pre-*Anschluss* Austria.

Feudal–Christian values of this kind also inspired Lueger, although he, like Schönerer, began his career as a radical democrat. Their ways parted early on, however, due to their differences of view over Catholicism and the Monarchy. The Christian Social Party remained loyal to the idea of a monarchical state to the very end, in 1918, and vociferously declared that the empire as a whole needed to be re-Catholicized, in the first place by debarring Jews and Social Democrats from public affairs. It was with this platform that Lueger's party, in gaining power in Vienna in 1895–96, was able to win over a large part of Catholic circles within the city's middle classes and conservative aristocracy, whilst maintaining faith with the lower-middle classes (the members of which since an 1882 electoral reform had also been given the vote, on the proviso that they paid at least 5 crowns annually in tax). He succeeded this all without losing the backing of the middle classes of German and Czech background and the many loyalist (*kaisertreu*) political forces opposed to Hungary (and to the Hungarian Independence Party). Anti-Jewish, anti-Magyar and anti-socialist professions of faith were harmoniously mingled in the Christian–Social political discourse.

Lueger thus found himself at the head of a broad-based, heterogeneous but workable coalition, the main cohesive force of which was radical anti-Semitism. Though this frequently availed itself of archaic sloganeering and sentiments, it was little tainted by the doctrines of Pan-German racism, and in any case, as soon as Lueger won power in Vienna and Lower Austria, he prudently trimmed the sharpness of his anti-Jewish rhetoric in favor of a mutually beneficial *modus vivendi* with representatives of the Jewish upper-middle class. In doing so, of course, he opened himself up to attacks from the Social Democrats, whose electoral base was considerably broadened by the introduction of general male franchise in 1907. Enjoying the support of the Vatican (in 1895 the papacy went so far as to chide Austria's prelates for their reluctance to endorse the anti-Semitic demagoguery of the Christian

Socials), the party was even able to allow itself the luxury of electing a few converted Jews to its leadership.

Throughout the German-speaking areas of the empire a host of organizations—with memberships drawn primarily from the middle classes—came into being around the turn of the century. They made little more than a show of furthering the organization's ostensible aims, their far from subsidiary purpose being much rather to demarcate themselves from Jews of the same class. The ranks of these organizations also supplied the bulk of the cadres and supporters of Austria's anti-Semitic parties. It has already been mentioned that university student bodies began excluding Jewish members in 1878, and that example was followed by organizations that safeguarded the interests of small artisans (1880), the Austrian Reform Society (*Österreicher Reformverein*, 1882), the German School Association (*Deutscher Schulverein*, 1896) and, with the approach of the First World War, the Gymnastics Association (*Turnverein*), the *Wandervögel* youth movement, and the Austro–German Alpine Association (*Deutsch–Österreicher Alpenverein*). This moderately anti-Semitic (that is to say, non-racist) compromise gave rise to a peculiar kind of political culture, found only in Austria, which united populist social Catholicism, anti-intellectualism, anti-socialism and anti-capitalism under a single banner. This ideological platform was conformed to by most of the parties in power and, indeed, opposition groupings up till the *Anschluss*. The only conspicuous exceptions were represented by the Social Democrats—a major political force in some cities, including Vienna, after 1907—and the last Mohicans of classical liberalism.

The right-wing extremists who followed in Schönerer's footsteps still carried on their anti-Semitic vituperations, but waited in the opposition for the union with Germany, which duly arrived in 1938, although their largest base of support lived on mainly amongst the geographically circumscribed *Sudeten* Germans, put under heavy pressure from ascendant Czech nationalism. In 1902, all 51 representatives elected to the provincial assembly of Lower Austria (the region including Vienna) were anti-Semites of Lueger's Christian Social Party. In the first elections for the imperial council (*Reichsrat*) following the introduction of the general male franchise, the 67 Christian Social delegates were joined by 29 other conservatives to form an anti-Semitic 'parliamentary club,' which was also the largest bloc in parliament.

With the dissolution of the empire at the end of 1918, a new division of political roles was established in Austria. The Social Democratic Party gained control of the capital's local administration, whilst between 1920 and 1932 parliament and the governments of the greatly shrunken state were now dominated, without a break, by a coalition of Christian Socials and Pan-Germanists. They were held together by their shared anti-Semitism, presenting a united front against the Jewish intelligentsia (who provided many of the Social Democrat representatives) and capitalism, which they considered to be a Jewish institution to the core. Extremist (i.e. unequivocally racist) anti-Semites set up paramilitary organizations as the successor associations of the old anti-Jewish movements, the *Heimatschutz* and *Heimwehr* amongst them, and strove to accomplish a form of 'right-wing revolution.' They were united in their hatred of the republic, 'Red Vienna,' and democracy as well as a viciously anti-Semitic resentment, vented on many occasions (for instance, in conjunction with the Zionist Congress held in Vienna in 1925). Towards the end of the 1920s, and particularly after the Great Depression, the Christian Social grouping formed an alliance with the *Heimwehr* in order to stamp out the 1927 Social Democrat rioting in Vienna. Then it proceeded to set aside the institutions of parliamentary democracy and, in 1934, proclaim a new constitution, making Austria a proto-Fascist, 'Christian–Gemanic,' corporative state.

This ushered in an era of officially sponsored, albeit erratically implemented, policy of excluding Jews from many domains of Austrian life. Declared enemy though it may have been of what it saw as the 'pagan' Nazism of the Pan-Germanists, in reality it prepared the ground for the Nazi take-over. The Austrian disciples of Nazism were, in fact, able to exploit the new régime's growing unpopularity, which sprang in part from the government's inability to mitigate the effects of the country's on-going economic slump, in the same way as it turned to good account the rising prestige of Nazi Germany (which in marked contrast had pulled off the 'economic miracle' of eliminating unemployment). They also capitalized upon the anticlericalism of a segment of the urban proletariat, as well as an anti-Semitic ideology still more radical than that of the government (the constituency for which had, in fact, always been larger in Austria than in Germany itself). Once the Social Democrats were out of the way, therefore, the Nazis were able to portray themselves as an opposition liable to offer a credible alternative to the weak and dwindling 'corporative state.'

The *Anschluss* (11th March, 1938) brought Austria's experiment with self-restrained state run anti-Semitism to a close. When German troops marched into their country, millions of Austrians fęted Hitler and participated in or attended to the shameless harassment of their Jewish fellow citizens. The union with the German *Reich* seemed like a final triumph of the 'Greater German' ideal, erstwhile the shared common ground between left and right wing, even to an Austrian public that in other respects had no great love of the Nazis. At all events, many Austrians—who will be quick enough to present themselves as the 'first victims of Nazism' after the Second World War—, made the event memorable by engaging in atrocities against Jews falling into their hands. Such behavior was still far from being an everyday occurrence in Nazi Germany itself prior to the organized *Kristallnacht* and *Kristallwoche* pogroms of later that year (8th–14th November, 1938).

German imperial anti-Semitism from court chaplain Stöcker to Hitler

The first major organized movement of political anti-Semitism in Germany bore the same name as Lueger's party, once it had changed its name from the Christian Social Workers' Party (*Christlich–soziale Arbeiterpartei*), deemed to sound too left wing, to simply the Christian Social Party (*Christlich–soziale Partei*). From the very beginning it trumpeted anti-Jewish slogans a good deal more extreme than those of Lueger's party. Its electoral base was likewise composed primarily of the malcontent elements in the urban petty bourgeoisie, who had either lost their original social standing or were in the process of losing it. The party was founded in 1878 in Berlin by Adolf Stöcker, discharging from 1874 to 1891 the function of Lutheran chaplain to the imperial court.

Historical circumstances were doubly auspicious for the emergence of such a political force. For one thing, the early 1880s in Germany, as elsewhere, were marked by widespread anti-Semitic agitation. An important episode in this was the public dispute about the 'Jewish Question' (*Antisemitismusstreit*) in which engaged the historians Heinrich von Treitschke and Theodor Mommsen, two of Berlin's respected academic luminaries. In an 1879 article that had attracted much attention, Treitschke had thrown doubt on the proposition that the Jews were capable of complete assimilation and integration into the German people. Whilst denying that he was an anti-Semite, he laced his text with a number of ill-advised remarks, including one in particular which would gain renewed currency under the Nazis: '*Die Juden sind unser Unglück*' (the Jews are our misfortune). Mommsen responded sharply to this in 1880 by, amongst other things, getting up a protest on behalf of 'distinguished public figures' to demand the enactment of a full and consistent emancipation for the Jews. It was signed by a group of famous Christian academics, such as Droysen and Virchow, and well-known industrialists, such as Siemens. The flurry stirred by this controversy gave rise to a string of longer- and shorter-lived anti-Semitic parties, including the rabidly Judaeophobic movements of Bernhard Förster, one of Nietzsche's brothers-in-law, Ernest Henrici, and Prussian Junkers such as Max von Sonnenberg. The polemics were fanned by notoriously anti-Semitic publicists like the ex-Socialist Eugen Dühring (who had been catapulted to fame mainly as the target of Engels' *Anti-Dühring*) and the journalist–philosopher Wilhelm Marr, who was credited with coining the term 'anti-Semite.' By the end of the century the German press resounded with the banal slogans of the anti-Semitic propaganda campaign.

The second occurrence was linked to Chancellor Bismarck, in the process of switching political allies. Having rejected continued support from Liberals (who had appropriated Bismarck's original *Kulturkampf* against the Catholic clergy for their own ends) in favor of the conservatives, he accepted their predisposition to anti-Semitism. Bismarck was well known to have cultivated close ties with Berlin's assimilated Jewish circles. Amongst others, his private physician, lawyer, and financial adviser were Jews. The latter, the famous banker Gerson von Bleichröder, being a particularly close intimate, Bismarck could hardly be accused of vulgar anti-Semitism. That did not stop him, however, from admitting, out of political calculation, the assistance of anti-Semites for the purpose of breaking down the mounting opposition of the Social Democrats and Liberals.

Stöcker's party was indeed originally envisaged as a machine to fight the Social Democrats and Jews, coupling extremist nationalist demagoguery with radical anti-capitalism, xenophobia, and a streak of religious fanaticism (which for a while ruled out any racist angle). For a time, especially during the 1890s, it was able to mobilize a mass base of support in the German electorate, often by declaiming the most scurrilous anti-Semitic execrations. An ephemeral, tactical alliance with rival anti-Semitic parties, under the umbrella of the so-called Berlin Movement (*Berliner Bewegung*), made it possible to organize a mass Anti-Semitic Petition, which demanded a halt to Jewish immigration, a ban on Jews holding public offices, and the establishment of a special property qualification for Jewish voters. Some quarter of a million signatures were collected for the petition, mostly in eastern and northern Prussia. It was presented to Bismarck in 1880, though it had no significant consequences. Stöcker, however, was a member of the Prussian parliament from 1879 to 1898, and of the *Reichstag* from 1881 to 1908 (with a gap of a few years), generally giving his support to the governments of Bismarck and his successors. This allowed him to work unceasingly to gain political endorsement for the Judaeophobia that he represented, and reach out to a public beyond extremist right-wing circles.

The German Reform Party (*Deutsche Reformpartei*) founded by elected *Reichstag* deputies of various anti-Semitic trends controlled 13 seats in 1898. That unity was just a pretence, however, and the party was dissolved, but only to be replaced by others under various names during the years leading up to the First World War. The total number of *Reichstag* seats they could muster overall continued to vary between 13 and 25. So they had considerably less influence than their equivalents in Cisleithan Austria during the same period. Moreover, their main stamping ground was pegged back largely to the provinces of Hesse and Saxony–Thuringia. It is clear, however, that a more moderate anti-Semitism was on the increase throughout the country amongst conservative voters as well as substantial numbers of liberals. (It should be borne in mind that Treitschke, who sparked off the 'Anti-Semitism Dispute,' was himself member of the Liberal Party). Although Stöcker's political influence seemed to be waning, this was not accompanied by any check in the spread of the 'civilized' but nonetheless resolute anti-Semitism for which he stood. A string of essentially anti-Semitically motivated political organizations, like the German National Commercial Support Association (*Deutschnationaler Handels-gehilfenverband*, 1893) and the various groupings that made up the Pan-German League (*Alldeutscher Verband*), had networks covering the entire *Reich* and even beyond (extending to Austria, Bohemia, Silesia, and other German inhabited areas). They broadened their social basis all the time with their anti-Jewish propaganda in the press, booklets and lampoons.

From the turn of the century, all of these organizations began tub-thumping about notions of 'pure bloodedness' and the nation's links with the ancestral soil (*Blut und Boden*). Amongst these, the Pan-German League under the presidency of Heinrich Class (from 1908), acquired an influential and substantial membership (including no fewer than 60 elected *Reichstag* deputies between 1894 and 1914), endorsing a political program with German imperialism, 'national regeneration' and the creation of a strong, authoritarian state founded on *völkisch* lines (that is, uniting those of 'true' German ethnicity and excluding all others), as its main tenets. It goes almost without saying that this went hand in hand with the implicit aim of winding up the system of parliamentary representation. Using a pseudonym, Class laid out his program in a widely read book, *Wenn ich der Kaiser wär* (If I Were the Emperor, 1912). This pamphlet already contained a detailed plan for stripping Jews of their civil rights, including exclusion from public offices and the army, and expropriation of the assets of Jewish newspaper proprietors, bankers, and landowners. Active Judaeophobia had already become one of the League's hobbyhorses before as well as during the First World War, to replace the glorification of German imperialism that had earlier been given more prominence. Class was subsequently to become one of the founders of the *Vaterlandspartei* (1918), which united under the same umbrella all the chief currents of political anti-Semitism throughout late imperial Germany. From this point onwards, anti-Semitism became not merely 'presentable' (*salonsfähig*) in every conservative and right-wing movement active in German politics, but a properly indispensable element in the representation of the interests of the German nation.

The unfortunate outcome of the war, the humiliating peace terms laid down in the Treaty of Versailles, serial outbursts of revolution, the installation of a Weimar Republic that relied on the support of the liberal parties and Social Democrats, hyperinflation and economic slump—all this played a part in pushing the conservative masses to realign increasingly to the more extremist political fringes. The 'Jewish threat' seemed far more direct now that German Jews, for the first time in their history, were able, under the democratic arrangements of the Weimar state, to enter posts in public administration and political power without any official ostracism or hindrance. (A total of five Jewish ministers were to serve in governments of the Weimar Republic). Deprived of its hitherto accustomed political hegemony, the right wing's fears were now given expression in extreme anti-Semitism, coupled to a radical antidemocratism, which afforded unprecedentedly fertile ground for incubating ideological chimeras. The new element in the discourse relating to Jews did not lie amongst the above-listed topics, all of which had been exhaustively trawled even before the First World War. The novelty lay, in part, in an increasingly unconditional acceptance of the perpetration of violent acts against Jews and, in part, in the shift in anti-Semitic rhetoric to the exclusion of Jews on racist principles.

The years immediately following the First World War were marked by a previously unheard-of spread of political violence in Germany. The assassination of Jewish-born Walther Rathenau was just one of its culmination (1922). Before the war Rathenau had succeeded his father as head of the huge AEG electrical works, before being made responsible for organizing Germany's war economy in 1916. He was minister of foreign affairs in the Weimar Republic at the time of his death. This led to a proliferation of open anti-Semitic incitement in the press and in the streets, exceeding anything seen before. Right-wing groups, specialized in organizing anti-Jewish operations mushroomed in the country. A contemporary estimate put their number at more than 430. One of these, the German Workers' Party (*Deutsche Arbeiterpartei*) may occasionally have stood out amongst them for its extremism, but before 1919 it had not achieved any particular status within right-wing forces, nor did it even represent any particularly original political trend. Its rise to national prominence only came much later, with the onset of the great economic slump.

The rise of Nazism and the road to the Shoah

In this study Nazism and the Shoah are both central and marginal issues. Central since they have given a new direction to Jewish history,
and marginal because they represent the devastating intervention of
unprecedented and—for many observers— much like 'irrational'
forces. Hence they could hardly be seriously accounted for in terms of
social or political history, in spite of having attracted an enormous and
ever-growing mass of scholarly attention. Given this fact I will limit
the following discussion to some basic developments and empirical
findings related to the Jewish catastrophe.

The would-be Nazi party took on its definitive name *National-
Sozialistische Deutsche Arbeiterpartei* in 1920. Its program combined
radical anti-capitalism, agrarian reform, advanced social policy, refusal of the Versailles dictate, anti-parliamentarism and anti-Semitism,
which were the common stock of right extremism of the time. The
party was organized, like some others, in militant groups prepared for
aggressive moves. A gifted but uneducated orator, Adolf Hitler, rose
soon to its leadership and made himself remark by his specially extremist statements. As early as October 1923, Hitler tried to persuade
the rightist military commander and the prime minister of Bavaria to
march on Berlin and topple the Weimar democratic state. Failing to
succeed, with the help of his SA troops (*Schutzstaffel*) ready for street
violence, he attempted a putsch which backfired. His five years prison
term (of which less than one year was accomplished) offered the
chance of drawing up his political manifesto published under the title
Mein Kampf (My Combat) and earned him the glory of a martyr of
rightist causes, together with the support of the prestigious war hero,
general von Ludendorff. In 1924 the united parties of Hitler and von
Ludendorff collected 32 seats among 472 in the parliament of the
Weimar Republic. But this remained their best electoral score up till
the 1930s, marked in Germany more than elsewhere in Europe by the
catastrophic economic consequences of the Great Depression.

The lack of parliamentary success did not discourage Hitler to reinforce his highly personalized control of his party and build it into a
quasi military machinery prepared, if necessary, for the violent seizure
and maintenance of power. Violence had been indeed inscribed into
the party's actions well before its accession to government. Its anti-

Jewish message, clearly stated in *Mein Kampf* as well as in the party press, was exemplified among other acts in 106 cases of vandalism against Jewish cemeteries between 1923 and 1931, the organization of an attempted pogrom during the Jewish high holidays in the Autumn of 1931, the assault on selected Jewish businesses and personalities. During the economic slump putting on the streets 6 million German industrial employees, the Nazi party was the only rightist movement capable of gaining influence in working-class circles. This added to the reasons why some of Germany's biggest Gentile capitalists—the Thyssens or the Stinnes—accepted to fund the Hitlerite enterprise. In the 1930 elections the Nazis won already 37 per cent of the votes and maintained their positions at the elections of November 1932 with 33 per cent of votes.

Though head of a minority party, after various manoeuvres and negotiations and thanks especially to the agreement of the conservative Catholic *Zentrum*, Hitler was appointed chancellor of the *Reich* on the 30th of January, 1933. Strong with 44 per cent of votes after the following elections, but also supported by a small rightist party, together with the tacit consent of other conservative forces—which preferred Hitler to the socialists and the Communists—, the Nazis achieved a parliamentary majority. They establish themselves immediately as exclusive masters of Germany. The Communist Party was banned after the burning of the *Reich*stag in March 1933. A month later Hitler invested himself with full powers for four years—against the unique opposition of the socialists. In May 1933 the political police (*Gestapo*) was set up and in June of the same year the one party system imposed. After the death of President Hindenburg in 1934 Hitler was proclaimed *Führer,* combining in a dictatorial manner all state powers in his person.

Though the political, ideological and technical conditions for the long-promised program of 'racial purification' were fulfilled, it is questionable whether the Nazi plans included the industrial accomplishment of the 'final solution' from the outstart. Massive collective murder of Jews did indeed not start before the opening of the eastern front against Soviet Russia. There are no written sources for the demonstration of when exactly the plans for the genocide were drawn up. They are usually associated with oral orders of the Führer dating from Spring 1941 or late 1940, during the preparations for the invasion of

Russia. Officially the organization of death camps were definitely decided upon at the Wannsee conference on the 20th of January, 1942, when the machinery of extermination was already in full operation on the eastern front. Before that, following their rhetoric, the Nazi project was merely to make Germany *judenrein* (free of Jews) and its implementation began right after the *Machtergreifung* (seizure of power).

First objective of the anti-Jewish measures consisted in the exclusion of Jews from all significant power positions in German society, depriving them progressively from earlier economic, political, cultural or other influence and power. They started with a number of intimidating and humiliating rules imposed on 'non Aryans' as early as April 1933: ruthless boycott of Jewish businesses, public burning of Jewish and other books regarded as anti-Nazi (notably those of self-exiled German authors), exclusion of Jews from civil service but also from public places (*'Juden unerwünscht'*), physical assault on Jews and their property, all this accompanied by uncouth anti-Semitic propaganda in the state-managed media. The culmination of initial anti-Jewish measures was reached by the two laws voted by the party in Nürnberg (15th of September, 1935). The first divested Jews from their German citizenship (transforming them into mere 'subjects of the *Reich*'). The second forbade 'interracial' marriages and sexual relations in order to avoid any 'racial pollution.' The thirteen odd decrees completing the Nürnberg Laws added a final stamp to the expropriation and social degradation of Jewry. The ongoing 'aryanization' process practically deprived Jews of any livelihood, leaving them no other choice than emigration in miserable conditions. Most of them did just that, but all could not comply— for various reasons. One of them was certainly the closure of the borders of most usual countries of immigration—including Palestine under British mandate since the publication of the 1939 *White Book* of his Majesty's government. In May 1939 an official census found 214 000 'non-Aryans' in the *Reich*. Two years later they were still 169 000. Most of them will perish in deportation to death camps in by then occupied Poland, starting at mid-October 1941.

However, signals about the danger of physical elimination were not lacking up till then. Much before the implementation of the 'final solution' the true nature of Nazism had been revealed by a number of murderous atrocities. These became customary especially after the *Anschluss* of Austria (13th March, 1938) and even more during the

Kristallwoche (week of 'broken glasses') starting with the *Kristallnacht* of 9th of November, 1938. On this occasion the Nazi assault troops organized bloody pogroms in the whole country, plundering some 7,500 Jewish shops and flats, burning 191 synagogues, killing not less than 91 persons and dragging off into concentration camps over 20,000 Jewish members of the middle classes. Henceforth Jews were not admitted to schooling and their economic ruin via 'Aryanization' came close to completion. In his speech in January 1939, celebrating the 6th anniversary of his accession to power, Hitler was already holding out the prospect of the 'complete extermination' of European Jewry in case of war.

The genocide was indeed closely connected to the war for several reasons. The occupation of most of continental Europe placed under Nazi rule the great majority of European Jewry from Norway to Greece and from Paris to Kiev and Odessa and this already late 1941. Such major geo–political development allowed the transformation of the anti-Jewish thrust from a mostly local, internal and political procedure into an all European program, putting on the agenda in concrete terms the hitherto mostly theoretical threats of extermination as a major Nazi project.

In all but a few occupied territories, allied countries or even those under Nazi menace, the Germans found a number of willing collaborationist to execute their plans. Some of the states concerned anticipated German demands—though not independently from Nazi influence or the fear of it—to enact severe anti-Jewish legislation. Among them must be counted Romania (with the January 1938 law under the Goga government, that followed earlier discriminatory restrictions, revising Jewish citizenship rights), Hungary (with its 'First Jewish law' in May 1938), Yugoslavia (October 1940), Bulgaria (January 1941), Vichy France (with its 'Jewish statutes' of October 1941). The *'Manifestazione della razza'* promulgated in Fascist Italy in November 1938 appears to be a clearly tactical concession of rather limited practical scope to the military alliance with Nazi Germany. Anti-Jewish policies will be adopted very fast by the German protectorates or collaborationist puppet states after their establishment (Slovakia, Croatia, Norway) and extended progressively over the newly occupied territories (Belgium, Netherlands, Greece, Serbia, Ukraine, etc). There were though significant differences in their application, as will be discussed below.

The Jews of Europe in the Modern Era

In a few countries under Nazi rule or influence, Jews hardly suffered any legal discrimination. It is true though that their numbers were insignificant as compared to those in most occupied countries. In occupied Denmark the local administration did not adopt and even less enforced anti-Jewish measures, doing its best—when the danger of forceful deportations took shape—to help those destined to persecution to flee to Sweden. In Finland, a military ally of Germany in the war against the Soviet Union, there were no anti-Jewish measures whatsoever. Native Jews remained normally integrated in Finnish society (army included), though at one time a few Jewish refugees (less than a dozen) were delivered to the Gestapo. Franco's Spain, another Nazi ally, served to a large extent, though not at all times, as a transitory refuge for persecuted Jews. More importantly, its diplomatic services protected and saved through consistent efforts a number (going into thousands) of designated victims of Nazism in various countries (like in German occupied Greece or Hungary).

Technically, the mobilization for the war brought about the military apparatus both capable and ready to execute the genocide. Some of the most ordinary army rabble—as recent research has shown—, not to mention fanatic Nazi elite troops, accepted to participate in mass murders in exchange of benefits or privileges (the worst camp guardianship equaled to vacationing, as compared to service on the eastern front, especially after Stalingrad) or, more simply, as the imperative duty to execute orders.

Finally the anti-Jewish measures—if not the mass murders implied, which were cautiously hidden to the public as much as possible—could be interpreted by the Nazi propaganda as necessary actions to curb the danger of espionage and control or eliminate those liable to counteract against German war objectives. To boot, ordinary troops could also be easily employed for bloody actions in the framework of 'normal' military operations abroad. A significant part of Jewish victims perished indeed as hostages in acts of retaliation against partisan activities or under the pretext of such. By the way, death camps proper, as they started to be organized as soon as Poland was defeated in September 1939, were mostly located outside the territories of the *Reich*.

All this is not to deny the unique nature of the Nazi war against the Jews. The machinery of extermination was based on a number of murderous programs, of which death camps proper were just one, even if they can be regarded as the most 'industrialized,' horrendous and unheard of way of collective assassination in human history. To deportations in death camps with the aim of murdering inmates by gassing must be added military mass executions—especially on the Russian front and in occupied territories in the East—by army units or specially trained death squads (the so-called *Sonderkommandos*), killing camp detainees via starvation and overcharge of work (*Vernichtung durch Arbeit*), indiscriminate slaughter of hostages, criminal experimentations with allegedly medical purposes in the camps, deprivation of means of living in closed ghettoes (like in cities of occupied Poland) or a combination of the above.

In the following let us try to present a brief account of how the Shoah was carried out or—sometimes—thwarted in various European societies with significant Jewish minorities. If the treatment of Jews proved to be ultimately rather different from country to country, the reasons of such disparities can be identified in the interplay of a number of factors as diverse as the following: local force and/or influence of Nazi Germany, the political support or toleration it could gather from established authorities (including that of the Churches) on the strength of anti-Jewish traditions and dispositions, the actual scope of popular collaborationism proper (linked to the impact of Fascist movements and parties), the economic and political stake represented by Jewish presence, degrees of social integration of Jews (as measured by indicators of assimilation or perception of Jews as aliens), the size of Jewish refugee populations, facilities of the technical identification of Jews (by names, public records, etc.), ecological circumstances (degrees of urbanization, extent of rural environments weakly exposed to administrative or police control), the attitude of local military commanders (whether German, Italian or other), etc.

The implementation of the genocide

In a tentative empirical typology one can classify in four patterns the Nazi treatment inflicted upon European Jewry: direct mass murder, deportation to death camps, 'local holocaust' in allied territories and (as the rarest species) abstention from or resistance to the physical persecution of Jews.

Mass murder was the first type of extermination practice implemented as soon as the German troops crossed the Soviet borders unexpectedly, as it appeared, on the 22nd of June, 1941. It is well known
that Stalin voluntarily neglected the defense of the western frontiers,
thus neither the Red Army nor most of the population concerned were
aware of the immediate danger of invasion. The front line was deliberately divided by the Wehrmacht in sectors. Behind each of them a
Sonderkommando or an *Einsatzgruppe* was charged—following explicit orders of the high command—to put to death arrested Soviet
political officers. Very soon though, Jews were included in the category to be liquidated without trial or much discrimination. Initially
some—like children—were spared. Afterwards no selection was
made, but the policy of killing every identified Jew does not appear to
have been a uniform one. Historians indeed could not find convincing
evidence that the liquidation of Jews in Soviet territories followed an
explicit order of the high command.

The first such mass murders by shooting were organized by German and Romanian army units in the region of Czernovitz in July
1941. But Romanian soldiers initiated murderous pogroms already in
the very first days of the war in their own country in Iasi and elsewhere (with a total of some 12,000 victims). The Lithuanian Fascists
also started a similar program immediately after the retreat of the Red
Army on the 25–26th of June, 1941. Later in November 1941 over
30,000 Jews were killed in Rumbuli, near Riga. But in Estonia or
Latvia—with much smaller Jewish populations to be sure—no similar
'spontaneous' reactions were documented. In the rest of occupied
Soviet lands the *Einsatzgruppe* actions got into swing with the prolon-
gation of military operations. Alone in the zone of *Einsatzgruppe* A 3
some 137,000 people were murdered before 25th November, 1941.
The killings could follow partisan attacks or arranged without apparent pretext. On the 29–30th of September of the same year close to
38,000 victims disappeared in a mass grave in Babij Yar near Kiev.
By Spring 1942 a number of lorries were also introduced into the
process of mass murder where victims were gassed. Till their defeat in
Stalingrad (February 1943) the Germans were not making much effort
to hide their crimes. Later a special commando was charged with
making the traces of some 1–1,5 million victims (following various
estimations) of the military extermination program disappear.

The best known and documented process of the Jewish genocide was connected to death camps and the industrial organization of gassing deported Jews. Concentration camps belonged from early on to the Nazi way of neutralizing their political enemies. But with the occupation of Poland a new project to build camps on a hitherto unprecedented scale was initiated. First Polish Jews were closed into inescapable ghettoes, then the inhabitants were sent to the camps in order to make them work to death or to kill them straightaway. This process was generalized in Nazi occupied Europe everywhere. French, Belgian, Dutch, Danish, Norwegian, Croatian, Slovakian, Serbian, Greek, Czech, Italian and Hungarian Jews were first forced into city ghettoes, then transported by train in inhuman circumstances to concentration camps, mostly located in Poland, then exterminated there in various ways, in some places by gassing.

The gassing program in hermetically sealed lorries started to be experienced in late 1941 in camp Chelmno as well as in occupied Serbia. The procedure was repeated elsewhere too. The scale of these operations of collective murder changed with the construction of the first gas chambers in the south Polish camps of Auschwitz, Birkenau and Majdanek early 1942, which were thus promoted to death camps proper. Gassing began in March of that year in Auschwitz and in September in Majdanek. At the meeting of high Nazi officials near Berlin (Wannsee conference, 20th of February, 1942) all the technical details of the 'final solution' program were adopted. Within months three new camps were equipped with gas chambers and started to operate (Sobibor, Treblinka, Belzec), all in Poland. The network of death camps was later completed by Mauthausen (in Austria) and Strutthof (Prussia). With the exception of Belzec—which remained in operation till 1945—, all were dismantled by the end of 1944 following Himmler's order, to make the traces of industrial murder disappear. Although the camps were mixed and supplied also free work-force for local industries, the definite number of Jewish victims could be reasonably estimated between a minimum of 2,8 million and a maximum of 4,7 million, though some authors have brought out higher estimates as well.

But death was a frequent visitor in other concentration camps too, which were not primarily destined to industrialized murder. Another major camp, Theresienstadt (in Bohemia) served as a model one of sorts, presentable for propaganda purposes even to representatives of the international Red Cross. This was a place of temporary internment, together with Mauthausen, of the most eminent enemies of Nazism, Jews and non-Jews, and constituted 'ante-chambers' of death camps proper. A number of other such 'ante-chambers' earned sinister reputation like Bergen-Belsen, Buchenwald, Dachau, Ravensbrück in Germany, Drancy in France, Westerbork in the Netherlands, Jasenovac in Croatia and many others. In most of the latter arbitrary assassinations, over-exhaustion in work, starvation, atrocious ill treatments, lack of medical care, poor living conditions contributed to a high mortality rate, besides the fact that some of them served for the selection of hostages in case of resistance activities, earmarked for execution. History has registered a number of attempts at revolt, notably in Treblinka and Sobibor—which were closed following the event in late 1943—as well as in Auschwitz-Birkenau, where the Jewish *Sonder-commando*, in charge of the dead in the gas chambers, themselves organized a rebellion in October 1944. None of them survived their desperate action.

The same applied to closed city ghettoes; when those interned were not simply assassinated without any particular reason by the guards, they died a slow death. The biggest ghettoes were located in Poland and some in other occupied territories in the Soviet Union. Their organization started soon after the military occupation of territories concerned. But deportation procedures to death camps started even later everywhere with the concentration of victims in local city ghettoes, wherefrom they were extracted to be directly murdered or transported in horrendous circumstances in overcrowded wagons to their final destination in the Nazi network of death machinery. Some ghettoes and camps staged resistance movements before being liquidated. This was the case of the biggest one in Warsaw on the 20th of April, 1943. The hopeless combat of the Ghetto fighters was not definitely crushed and the ghetto itself burnt to ground before the 15th of May, 1943.

As to the selection of victims feeding the extermination machinery, one has to mention above all the quasi totality of Polish Jewry. Those remaining in occupied Poland mostly perished in death camps. But the same applied to more or less large sectors of Belgian, Dutch, French, Greek, Italian and Norwegian Jewry from Western Europe, the bulk of Slovakian Jews—deported in several waves—, some of Croatian

Jewry and the majority of Hungarian Jews (especially those from the provinces), the latter representing the last big contingent of victims (some 450,000–500,000) in Auschwitz in Spring and early Summer 1944. This enumeration indicates already that most victims of the camps were gathered from territories under direct German military occupation (with the partial exception of Slovakia and Croatia—these military allies of Nazism, not occupied all the time while deportations occurred). In all the above mentioned countries the local administration participated—most often with collaborationist zeal—in the concentration procedures and in the technical organization of deportations of local Jews, Western Europeans included (with the above mentioned marginal exception of Denmark to which must be added the special case of Italy, the major military ally of Nazi Germany).

Still the Jewish genocide was also carried out locally outside the German system and inscribed in specific national political histories. They are worth to be recalled separately, above all when the genocide was organized, delayed or thwarted following local initiatives in countries where national authorities kept the upper hand in their Jewish policies in Central and Southern Europe. This proves eloquently that the Shoah was not everywhere and always a historically unavoidable necessity imposed by Nazi power. Resistance was also possible in several circumstances as well as voluntary intervention to organize a genocide of one's own—limited or large scale as it could be—within territories exclusively controlled by national armies.

The Soah. Local variants and the reaction of the allied

Let us start with the less tragic case, that of Italy. Though the Italian anti-Jewish law, dated 1938, was formally as drastic as any other similar one, it was never fully implemented in a country lacking any significant tradition of political anti-Semitism —especially not under Fascism, Jews being fully integrated in, to the extent of often supporting the Mussolinian state. The quasi-failure of anti-Jewish measures was due in practical terms to the joint disapproval of Pope Pius XI and the king, the lack of enthusiasm, inefficiency and corruption of the bureaucracy in charge of its execution, as well as—may-be above all—the veritable resistance put up by the army officer corps, largely imbued with the values of liberal (and philo-Semitic) freemasonry prevalent in modern Italian culture. Hence, in spite of the application of some legal restrictions against Jews, the latter enjoyed actually a quasi-general protection from the 'final solution' in Italy as well as in Italian occupied territories—like south-eastern France, Croatia, Greece or Albany—till the fall of the régime in late Summer 1943. Deportations started though after the German take-over and in the puppet 'Salo Republic,' but with much less victims in proportion of those threatened than anywhere else in the continent. Even in the worst days Jews could count on the active help of most of their fellow citizens, whether in the Church, the administration, the army or the general public. Army leaders in charge of Jewish affairs would declare, occasionally, that Nazi measures stood in contradiction to their officer's honor...But this was an unique exception.

Bulgaria's case was obviously different, even if its outcome can be similarly qualified. In Bulgaria a harsh anti-Semitic legislation was in force since January 1941, in view of the military alliance with the *Reich* entered into in March 1941. But here too there was no in-rooted tradition of Jew-hatred, let alone persecution. After the annexation of Greek Tracia and Macedonia in return for the military support in the invasion of Greece, the Bulgarian authorities allowed the deportation of Jews of these territories. But when the deportation of 'native' Jews started to be pressed by the Germans, it was met with stiff opposition on the side of the king, the head of the Orthodox Church and a coalition of politicians. A petition of protestation was signed by 42 members of Parliament led by vice-president Pesev. The movement proved to have full success. No Jews were deported or otherwise put danger in Bulgaria.

In the line of reluctant but finally unsuccessful resistants to the 'final solution' Hungary must also be quoted. The country was loaded with a heavy anti-Jewish past since the post-world war revolutions (initiated by a murderous White Terror proper), responsible for one of the first Nürnberg type legislation in Europe since May 1938 (which was followed by a number of other laws depriving Jews of most of their property and civil rights) and a military ally of the *Reich* in the war against the Soviet Union and also the Western Allies (without any particular claims, for that matter). One of the consequences was that the government expelled in late Summer 1941, following its entry into the war, over 18,000 Jews who could not document their citizenship.

Most were massacred by the SS in Galicia. A number of unarmed Jewish forced labor units accompanied the army on the eastern front and were exposed to murderous vexations. But Hungary refused to comply with further German demands. With the defeat of the *Reich* in perspective after Stalingrad, it also tried— unsuccessfully—to negotiate separate peace, provoking thus its occupation by the allied *Wehrmacht* on the 19th of March, 1944. Thus the road was set free for the Shoah. Ghettoization and deportation of the whole provincial Jewry was promptly organized before July 1944 with the active assistance of the Hungarian administration. But regent Horthy could halt the deportation of Jews from Budapest while he stayed formally in power. The Fascist putsch masterminded by the Germans on the 15th of October, 1944, following a failed attempt to change sides in the war, initiated a new wave of persecutions. Budapest Jews were deported, mostly rushed on foot towards the Western borders. Many fell victim of blood-thirsty Fascist vandals on the shore of river Danube. Some 70,000 were massed in the closed-in ghetto district by November 1944 or in so-called 'protected houses' under the aegis of neutral embassies (that of Sweden with the help of the heroic Raul Wallenberg, Switzerland, Spain and the Vatican). As a consequence, most of the remaining Budapest Jewry survived till the arrival of the Red Army in January 1945.

Among the aborted but often dedicated, even heroic collective rescue actions must be counted the unsuccessful Greek resistance. Greece was to be surely occupied and also divided by German, Bulgarian and Italian troops which installed a puppet government to safeguard the appearance of the maintenance of the state. Deportations were cautiously planned by the Germans, but they met simultaneously the refusal of the Italians to accept deportations and the strong opposition of local authorities, especially the leadership of the Orthodox Church. Though the Germans finally prevailed and deported the bigger part (60,000) of the largest Sephardi communities in Europe (among them the Jews of Saloniki), many of the would-be victims (some 12,000) were saved by the Greek Church, the Resistance, the rank and file population as well as foreign embassies (particularly that of Spain).

The story was utterly different in the other German satellites.

New-born Slovakia, connected to the *Reich* with a *Shutzvertag* (contract of protection), appears to be the only country where the deportation of the Jews was initiated by the local government. The nationalist movement was indeed imbued with xenophobic traditions among which anti-Magyarism and 'anti-Chechoslovakianism' competed with anti-Semitism (often confounded, by the way, for good reasons). The parliament of the one party régime voted the measure unanimously (with the exception of count Esterházy, representing the Magyar minority) as early as December 1941. Some 60,000 Jews were thus deported between March and October 1942, before the operation was halted due to protestations emanating notably from the Vatican. But the Slovakian state went as far as to offer for each Jew deported 500 marks 'in compensation for German expenses' in the affair. After the anti-Nazi 'national revolt' in October 1944 renewed deportations demanded some other 16,000 victims.

The Croatian state under Ante Pavelić stood also under the protection of the *Reich*, so much so that part of the country was occupied by German and Italian troops till 1943. Pavelic's ultra-nationalist Ustacha movement was directed more against Serbia and local Serbians than against Jews. The local tradition of anti-Semitism was indeed far from being central in the Ustacha credo. This did not hinder the nationalist extermination program to be carried out in the same savage way against those two 'alien enemies.' Most of the Jews who could not hide or take refuge (in the Italian zone or in Albania) were murdered in the infamous Jasenovac death camp. The rest was deported to Auschwitz. The Croation 'final solution' can thus be largely qualified as a 'local holocaust' of sorts.

This was obviously much more clearly the case in Romania. The Romanian nation state, as discussed above, was built on exclusivist xenophobic ideological foundations, exacerbated in the 1930s under the impact of Nazi alliance, among other things. Though the Romanian holocaust was the outcome of very complex political developments in which the competition of more or less anti-Semitic forces was a central issue, by the early 1940s a new situation emerged. The extremist Iron Guard sealed its attempted coup against the government on the 20th of January, 1941 by the massacre of over 120 Jews in Bukarest. This pogrom was followed by mass murders in Iasi and its outskirts, organized by the army in the first days of the war. Pogroms of more limited scope occurred in villages and townships occupied by Romanians in former Soviet territories in a disorganized manner. The head of state Antonescu did not plan such massacres but did nothing to prevent them. The government project concerned the deportation of Jews to newly acquired territories in Transnistria. This was already started in July 1941 but was opposed sometimes even by the Wehrmacht. In the makeshift camps set up beyond river Niester over 150,000 persons were crowded, mostly from Moldavia. Some 27,000 of them were summarily shot by their guardians by the end of Summer 1941. Later on, mass murders took as many victims as starvation, lack of hygiene, absence of medical care in the 30 odd camps under Romanian rule. The army was particularly active in the assassination of tens of thousands of Jews remaining in Odessa, a city conquered only after months of fighting from the Soviets.

In spite of all such atrocities, Romanian Jews were not affected elsewhere so harshly as in Moldavia and the new territories. Though forced labor service was organized in Transylvania and Wallachia as well, Jews were not expropriated systematically nor obliged to wear a yellow star. Even if huge sums in ransom type payments were imposed on Jewish businesses, German demands for organized deportations were not obeyed. The Hungarian and the Italian examples served as a reference for such refusal, as a question of 'national prestige.' In December 1942 Antonescu definitely cancelled the planning of deportations for reasons which have not been sufficiently clarified. Foreign protestations and the possible German defeat looming large in the eastern front, where the Romanian army had also suffered enormous losses before Stalingrad, may have played their part in the decision. From 1943 onwards anti-Jewish pressures started to be eased. Helped by corruption, many surviving Jews could wait for the end of the war in better condition than in the first war years. After April 1944 when massive deportations began in Hungarian occupied northern Transylvania, would-be victims of zealous Magyar collaborationists could find refuge in Romania. As a cruel irony of history, if the final score of the 'local holocaust' was as high as some 280,000 dead, Romania belonged to countries where the majority of Jews survived: in 1945 it hosted the biggest surviving Jewish community in Europe outside the Soviet Union.

A major historical question of the Shoah, which touches the problem of indirectly shared responsibilities of both Jews (like the so-called 'Jewish councils' in Nazi occupied territories) and Gentiles outside and inside the sphere of Nazi domination, including that of the Churches and governments of the anti-German Alliance, is related to the availability of information about the German policy of genocide. The question 'Who knew?' or 'When did they learn it?' can be safely reformulated also as 'Who wanted to know?,' or 'Who accepted to face the dire reality?.'

Convergent evidence suggests that several Western authorities were informed as early as in the first months of 1942 about the starting up of the machinery of extermination. The apostolic nuncio in Bratislava appears to have been aware of it already in March of that year. The *Bund* sent in May 1942 detailed radio reports to London in this matter, which were broadcast by the BBC in June, stating that the Germans had already killed over 700,000 Jews. (This must have been close to reality.) The *Times* and other British journals also published the declaration of the Zionist representative in the National Council attached to the Polish emigrant government announcing that the number of Jewish victims of the genocide had reached one million by late June. This was also confirmed on the 9th of July in a press conference of the Polish emigrant cabinet. After some hesitations the British and American belligerent authorities decided to give full credit to this information after November–December 1942. The relevant public statement of the allied governments was indeed published on the 17th of December, 1942. It was repeatedly broadcast by the BBC and the British MPs greeted the memory of Jewish victims of Nazism by standing in silence.

If the information was already publicly accessible at this early stage, few believed them among contemporary observers, whether among future victims or those capable to intervene. The fact is that neither the Allies nor other authorities concerned did much to stop the murderous process. When during the deportation of Hungarian Jews the regular bombing of one or two railway lines would have sufficed to paralyze the machinery of the 'final solution,' none of the Allies consented to divert the necessary (rather limited) air force for the purpose, though aircrafts were never lacking for the terror bombardment of cities in the *Reich* or in territories under German rule, even when they comprised no military targets.

Chapter 5

Epilogue: after 1945

Survivors of the Shoah, or the impossible return

It remains to recount, at least in broad outline, what happened with Europe's Jews—the survivors of the Shoah and their direct descendants in particular—after the horrendous destruction was over.

Taking the 1939 population figures as the basis for calculations, a great majority of European Jewry (more than two-thirds, according to the most reliable estimates) vanished in the course of the genocide perpetrated in the name of national socialism. In all the countries of Central and Eastern Europe (leaving aside the Soviet Union and Romania) the ratio of victims was above 70 per cent, and the same also applies to Greece (77 per cent) and the Netherlands (90 per cent). Only in France, Italy, Bulgaria, and Russia did the human loss suffered at the hands of Nazism not significantly surpass one quarter of the Jewish population—if we disregard Great Britain, the neutral states, and Scandinavia, where, (except in the case of Norway), the local Jews were either never under direct threat or else managed to escape that threat. The largest single bloc, comprising the originally or still Yiddish-speaking Ashkenazi Jews who resided in the land belt stretching over several countries from Vilna to Odessa—more than four million souls in all—ceased to exist for all practical purposes. Their compeers in Romania, Hungary, and Czechoslovakia shrank to under one-third of their former populations (in Romania not least as a result of the deportations from the region of northern Transylvania, then under Hungarian control). Not so many years previously, Jewry from these countries had served as a demographic reservoir feeding a

Jewish emigration which reached all areas of the globe. After the Shoah only fragmented communities were left. The bulk of them comprised Soviet Jewry, exposed to ever more intense assimilatory pressure, the smaller portion consisting of survivors concentrated almost exclusively in a few metropolitan or regional centers in Central and Eastern Europe (Budapest, Warsaw, Bucharest, Iasi and Prague).

From a geopolitical standpoint, this process amounted to a contraction of the settlement net of European Jewry to an essentially bipolar structure, with the Soviet Union as one agglomeration and Western Europe as the other. From now on the formerly persecuted from all over Europe tended increasingly to migrate to the latter (besides *Eretz Israel* and America) in the post-war period, as the flight of Jews from Eastern Europe gathered pace—albeit to varying degrees and proportions from country to country—during the decades after 1945. Thus, the abandonment of the old Ashkenazi centers of settlement, to the extent that these had survived at all, continued, both as a repercussion of the Shoah's devastating impact and, at the same time, under the burdens imposed by consolidating Communist régimes, which in some countries, as will be seen, fell especially heavily on Jews.

The Shoah may not have impinged directly—and if so, very unequally—on every national community. But in cold fact only a negligibly small number of Jewish families in Europe, or even overseas, remained untouched. That, it may be emphasized, goes even for countries that escaped German occupation, as most of the Jews who had recently emigrated to those places (Britain and Sweden, for example) had relatives unable to escape the depredations of the Brown Plague. For the survivors, liberation brought an interminable mourning and despair, that was not only endured personally until their own, often premature deaths but, as a rule, passed on to their offspring as well. The Shoah carried on sedulously culling its victims long after the camp gates had been opened, with a far from inconsiderable number of survivors dying of illnesses that had been acquired before liberation, sometimes even under the physical and psychic shock of the latter. The trauma of surviving was to have an impact for long after, affecting the second or even third generation of descendants, in the form of suicidal tendencies, inability to integrate or reintegrate into 'normal' life, depression of all sorts, and a host of other physical and psychosomatic sufferings.

The tragic consequences of the Shoah assumed all too concrete forms, however, even at the moment of liberation. The experience of deportation or, in the 'better' case, surviving the dangers of concealment or flight abroad (the principal destination—as to numbers concerned—for Jewish refugees being the Stalinist Soviet Union) represented such a major rupture with previous existences that those involved were often confronted with unsolvable dilemmas, once they were freed. The nature of those dilemmas, and the chances of surmounting them, was a function in part of quite accidental social and situational factors, such as the country of origin, whether liberation had been achieved by Western or Soviet troops, the extent and type of the family losses (e.g. whether parents, spouse, children etc. had survived), disposable wealth and qualifications, age and gender. Four typical eventualities can be nevertheless differentiated.

Most survivors, originally taken from western countries, returned home, having their civil rights restored and regaining their old assets and economic positions (though this was far from automatic or immediate), and thus were able to pick up their old life again or restart it anew—at least to the extent that personal circumstances (following the survival of other family members, etc.) allowed. What greatly facilitated return and a renewed integration into society in these countries was the experience of liberation itself, as a common bond between Jews and the majority of non-Jews. Jewish returnees would often be greeted with special warmth due to the main victims of a common enemy. With the restoration of peace, constitutional democracy was also re-established throughout Western Europe with all its appurtenances—security of property, freedom of occupation and enterprise, the possibility of obtaining legal redress for the wrongs endured, and the absence of institutional discrimination against Jews.

The second case is typical of survivors originating from eastern countries. They too were able to return home, but this incurred heavier costs. A twofold change in socio–economic conditions was awaiting them: first the consequences of the change in socio–political régime imposed by the Red Army, which were still hard to foresee in the immediate aftermath of 1945 (though all too evident within a few years), and second the peculiar uncertainty, or rather lack of security, that was the lot of Jews returning to countries that, in most cases, had been earlier military allies of and showing official sympathy to the Nazis.

Liberation and returning to a formerly occupied western country with democratic institutions, on the one hand, homecoming back amongst a 'Fascist population' that was in the process of 'being brought into line' by Communists, on the other hand, were entirely different life experiences.

The third variant was the lot of the large mass of Jews from Poland, the Baltic states, Bessarabia, and in some cases even Germany, who had earlier fled to Russia in various circumstances. They were a mixture of civilians and also forced laborers for the Nazis who in effect had been captured as prisoners of war (like survivors of the forced-labor brigades deployed alongside the Hungarian regular army on the Russian front). Though most of them were eventually allowed to return home (at least those who did not perish on the islands of the Gulag reserved for foreigners), this was usually only after years of further forced labor, often spent locked up with some of their former executioners also fallen prisoner to the Red Army.

Finally, the fourth major category was that of the stateless, or 'displaced persons' in the official parlance of that period. This too was a substantial class of people who, following the liberation of death camps and ghettos, had nowhere to go for a number of reasons. They might have no wish to return to their native land and mix again with those who had witnessed, carried out or were complicit in the horrors inflicted on them. They also might feel there was nowhere to go, because anything liable to be denoted 'home,' in the human and social sense of the word, had been destroyed. Many were individuals who as orphans, widows, family heads having lost their children, etc. had been robbed of all immediate family or human ties to a community.

The realities of liberation created many situations far more complex than even the above, especially in the countries of Central and Eastern Europe. After 1945, the borders of the territories under Soviet occupation could be traversed more or less easily for several years. So moving around from place to place was fairly common up to the beginnings of the Cold War during the years 1946–48. Jews, whether they had hung onto life in their own country or returned from the camps, not infrequently came into conflict with their immediate milieu and preferred to go back to a refugee camp in the hope of later moving on to the West or to Palestine. Camp survivors who reassembled in Poland had to face a civil war situation in which, willy-nilly, they were regarded as 'objective allies' or sympathizers of the Communist camp, and thus frequently under very real threat to their lives. Moving on was therefore often a straightforward escape before the Communist régime gained full command of the situation, though the establishment of the latter did not rule out the risk that Jews who did stay might later (in 1968, for example) feel constrained to flee the supposedly 'Judeophile' power that was thereby installed. Chance combinations of the specific circumstances of the return could also play a big part in prompting a decision to move on. This could depend, for instance, from the still living members of the family found on getting back home, the prospects for making a living, the nature of possible confrontations with neighboring residents, whether there was indeed a place to live. Not surprisingly, given the acute housing shortages that war had brought, most homes, left behind by those hauled off to the camps, had been taken over by new tenants, whether knowingly or unsuspectingly. The existence of Zionist recruitment or aid organizations, operating in the locality, could also be a factor.

At all events, it is bizarre that the main collecting and transit localities for survivors, whether displaced or deliberately seeking a new home, should be refugee camps set up in Germany, of all places, albeit in the zones occupied by the western Allied forces. They could be part of the relief operations mounted initially by those forces and later on organized by international Jewish agencies, such as the American Jewish Joint Distribution Committee (the 'Joint' or JDC), the United Hebrew Sheltering and Immigrant Aid Society (HIAS), and others. Some 160,000 Jews classed as displaced persons were in Germany at the end of 1946, and if the rest are added to them, the total may well have run to over 200,000. Many spent long years in the refugee camps, often shuttling from camp to camp within the territory of the old *Reich* for lack of a country willing to receive them. The destination countries of the great transatlantic migrations by then were accepting only restricted numbers of refugees. Even those admitted were strictly selected by age, health and/or qualifications, unless the immigration was for purposes of joining close family members already in the country. Zionist organizations, of course, also trawled the camps for recruits, especially amongst young men prepared to work (and fight). They had often to slip their consignments of volunteers into Palestine behind the backs of the British authorities, which banned docking of their ships in *Eretz* itself. For most of those concerned, the way out from this protracted quandary was to come only with the foundation of the state of Israel in May 1948. Yet the early years of existence of the Jewish state were themselves desperately difficult. A 'War of Independence' was still raging, and the precariousness of conditions within the country made it unsuitable for some categories of people, such as solitary elderly individuals. Besides that, many survivors still had major reservations about the idea of a 'return' to *Eretz Israel*, which in their eyes was tantamount to a new exile. As Europeans in search of new roots but, being long assimilated or left-inclined in their thinking, they often remained distrustful of such a 'colonialist enterprise.' As a net result, the refugee camps emptied slowly, the last one in Germany being closed in 1953 only.

Trauma of survival and painful 'liberation'

Jewish camp survivors from Eastern Europe returning to their original country had frequently great difficulties in reconciling themselves with their milieu. Relations between Jews and non-Jews after the Shoah were shot through with misunderstandings, ambivalent modes of behavior, and frequent clashes. This situation of potential conflict was ascribable to two sorts of litigation, one material, the other symbolic in nature.

On the crudely materialistic side, the survivors in Eastern Europe virtually never regained in entirety their assets and properties stolen or officially expropriated from them. The leaders of régimes set up on the Soviet model dismissed out of hand any idea of the sort of restitution or compensation to Jews for their losses that western democracies normally instituted by force of law, albeit in all cases with imperfect and, from one country to the other, very variable success. Many times there was no one left to reclaim robbed assets, 'Aryanized' property or those sold off forcibly under duress. In rural Hungary, in Poland or Lithuania, and many other places not only the legal owners but also all their successors had perished. Consequently, in all countries fallen under Nazi occupation, but especially in Central and Eastern Europe, millions were (and still are) living in what had formerly been Jewish dwellings. Just as many were (and still are) using 'unclaimed' Jewish assets and personal effects, making them 'objective body-looters,' as it were, even though most of them cannot be made personally responsible for that. In countries where no official efforts were made to compensate victims, as in Soviet occupied Eastern Europe, the reasons for refusal that were cited ranged from limited state budgets to difficulties in carrying out restitution, but even doubts were expressed about the legitimacy of 'Jewish' claims. More than one Communist leader held the view that awarding the Jews any special compensation would amount to 'privileging' them, which would not go down well politically with the bulk of the population and, furthermore, would be ideologically unsound, given that 'the entire working class suffered under the old régime.'

The same problem arose very differently in the West. The Federal Republic of Germany, under Chancellor Konrad Adenauer, was quick to accept (in 1953) the principle of compensating victims, and to this day continues to pay out large sums to survivors who have settled in Israel and in the West for the crimes committed in the name of the German people as a whole. The Cold War, however, provided a pretext for the German state, as a western ally, to refuse to remit similar payments, in part or whole, to victims still living in a Soviet satellite country. The freeze imposed on such compensatory payments—in any case often trivial sums—was only relaxed during the 1980s, by which time most of those entitled to receive them were either not traceable or no longer alive.

The change in régime that came with the collapse of Communism, however, created a new situation here too. Some Eastern European countries themselves followed the western example. In Hungary, for instance, a series of legal acts passed after 1989 offered symbolic and a measure of financial recompense for those who had been persecuted (though a truly slight one, as compared to the crimes for which the governments of the war time were responsible). Western countries have been following up to obtain restitution of misappropriated assets under the prevailing legislation, but many cases have dragged on for decades and, in no small number, remain unsettled to this day. Only in 1996 did international Jewish organizations succeed in their efforts to get hold of records relating to assets expropriated from Jews by Nazis and the proceeds from which had been placed in Swiss bank accounts. Austrian banks did not initiate similar steps of restitution until 1999. A similar situation pertains to Jewish-owned art objects stolen during the occupation of France, to say nothing of the 'confiscated' art treasures from Central and Eastern European Jews, no small part of which found their way to the Soviet Union as plunder of the Red Army and, to this day, grace the official collections run by the Russian successor state.

The other controversial matter was tied up with the liberation experience itself. In the Nazi occupied West, many Jews joined up with non-Jewish compatriots in united national fronts formed to throw off the German yoke. The defeat of the *Wehrmacht* in the East was likewise a great moment of liberation for surviving Jews, whatever the conduct of the new occupying force and the political line that was imposed on those countries by the Red Army. The non-Jewish majority, however, often interpreted the situation quite differently. Substantial segments, indeed in some case the overwhelming majority, of the population, not just within the German *Reich* but also in former Nazi allied states (like in Austria, Bulgaria, Croatia, Hungary, Romania or Slovakia), considered themselves to be defeated, as war losers. This was borne out, to a large degree, by the way the new occupant treated the territories that it had conquered with a brutality which it deemed to have been fully 'merited' by the 'Fascist criminals.' Indeed the Soviet leadership gave their troops temporarily a free hand to rape, pillage, and plunder at will in some areas (notably in Germany itself), in the manner of Asian despots. Many of the inhabitants of Poland and the Baltic states could justifiably feel that this 'liberation' was no better than slipping out of the frying pan and into the fire, having already gained abundant experience in their history of what accompanied occupation by the Russians.

Jewish and non-Jewish survivors were therefore radically divided from the very beginning by objective differences in their experiences of liberation.

Cases where Jews and non-Jews were rallied into a single camp by a shared Communist commitment offered by incipient Soviet-type régimes were the exception. Outside Austria, a brief period of democratic experiment, which lasted at best up to 1948—Hungary's 'year of change' or the Prague coup in late February—was succeeded throughout Eastern Europe by the establishment of Soviet-type Communist dictatorships. The same thing that had divided survivors and receiving societies over the experience of liberation was manifested in the different historical perspectives of Jews and Communists in regard to the events of the Second World War. For Jews, the Shoah could not be seen as anything but a unique criminal act in human history of which they alone (with at best the Gypsies included as an afterthought) were the openly designated victims. The Communist authorities, by contrast, did everything within their power to play down and in practice minimize the extent of Jewish sufferings. They tended either to set them at the very bottom of the list of crimes attributed to the Nazis or the old régime or else making no distinction at all from the sufferings of others. In this concept, Nazism (or collaboration with the Third *Reich*) was seen merely as the final and harshest phase of the old society—the logical end-result of the 'imperialistic era,' as it were, in terms of a 'scientific' analysis of history—which had uniformly oppressed 'the working class as a whole.' This minimization of the specific targeting of Jews in the genocidal campaign led to the major controversy over Auschwitz in Poland during the 1980s, with both sides setting huge emotional store on whether the site should remain a memorial to the uniqueness of the Jewish martyrdom, or whether Jews and Christians might make joint use of it (by erecting Christian religious symbols and a monastery) and the moral capital attaching to it.

Two very divergent developments were linked to the diversity of situations in which returnees from Nazi camps found themselves in Eastern Europe, now under Soviet control and still holding the majority of survivors of the Shoah, namely, the frictions experienced in living alongside their Gentile compatriots, and the socio–political inclination to move to outside the zone of Soviet power.

A return of Jewish survivors must have been an unwelcome prospect, from the outset, for old acquaintances in countries having voluntarily accepted a Nazi régime, the populations of which had good reason to fear reprisals or vengeance—and particularly those who had obtained (or robbed) dwellings, chattels or money from Jews destined to deportation. Equally, the returning Jews appeared to most of their compatriots as 'objective allies' of the new occupying power, the excesses of which, or the political dictatorship that it sponsored or supported, provoked the emergence of resistance (sometimes, like in Poland, even military resistance) in a number of countries. It is not surprising, then, that in the eyes of the local rank and file inhabitants, the Jews often personified the hated Communist régime, as well as—with variable implications between Poland, Romania, Hungary, and the Baltic states—a traditional national enemy that was again seen as a threatening oppressive force.

From this standpoint, the ugliest situation developed in Poland. There, the Red Army and its local allies were faced with the formerly London-based government-in-exile's internal forces—remnants of the 'Home Army' having sprang from the war-time anti-Nazi resistance movement—which saw themselves as representing 'national' continuity. Returning Jews, whether or not they were sympathetic to Communism, were caught in a cleft stick and often express targets for the civil war that, in some regions, smoldered for years. A majority of the Polish population, falling back on a combination of their long anti-Russian tradition and Jew-hatred, evolved a sense of the legitimacy of this struggle against the new (and historically ancient) enemy. As a result, they had all the pretext needed to bear down on Jews as such. With the active complicity of a Catholic leadership that was fearful, with every reason, of a Communist take-over of power, the anti-Communist extreme right, wherever it could, mounted a veritable war of terror against Jews during the first two years after the war. Jews would be thrown out of moving trains without the slightest provocation. Jewish orphanages were attacked. Murderous pogroms were sparked spontaneously by the most primitive anti-Semitic rumors (the slander of ritual murder, for instance). Even amongst these, the vicious assault launched against the Jewish community center in the town of Kielce on the 3rd of July 1946, stands out for its bloodlines. There were no less than 42 deaths and 80 wounded by lynching, without the police called to defend them, or the civil and ecclesiastical authorities on the spot lifting a finger to intervene. It is estimated that of the order of a thousand Jews fell victim to this sort of violence over the period 1945–47.

Poland represents an extreme case, but similar incidents and crimes were not at all uncommon elsewhere in the area during the early post-war years. Even in a country like Hungary, where there had been very little in the way of a historical tradition of 'spontaneous pogroms,' yet incidents of this sort in Kunmadaras and Miskolc claimed several lives in early Summer 1946. Two Jewish survivors were murdered at Zilina,

Slovakia in 1945, but anti-Semitic mass demonstrations broke out also in Bratislava in both 1946 and 1948 (as they had a hundred years previously—in the then German–Hungarian city of Pozsony/Pressburg). The total number of victims of anti-Jewish atrocities in Eastern Europe during the post-war years has been put at around 2,000.

Exodus and the questionable 'new start' in sovietized Eastern Europe

There were many reasons prompting Holocaust survivors to leave Eastern Europe and set off for other parts.

Amongst the 'repulsive' factors should be included not only the hostile reception that often awaited surviving victims, but also the wretched post-war living conditions in the ruined and ransacked countries that were the legacy of Nazism and the war, in addition to the already outlined difficulties of reintegrating into the old framework of existence, compounded by the sense of loss of so many beloved ones. Added to that was the economic threat presented by Communism. From the early years of liberation the all too real danger of social exclusion loomed large, directly affecting a substantial proportion of the returnees, being members of the former propertied bourgeoisie who were to be stripped of their assets by the régime and made déclassé. To all this must be counted the remaining consequences of the Stalinist reign of terror, which, with the renewed anti-Semitic course of Soviet policies since late 1948, could appear as peculiarly burdensome for Jews.

Besides these, a string of 'attractive' factors likewise argued in favor of emigration. Western democracies were, obviously, more highly developed, and the unprecedented economic growth that they experienced from the 1950s onwards (due partly to the much advertised Marshall Plan) promised a far better quality of life to ever broader segments of the population. At the same time, these old democracies were also the victorious opponents of Nazism, and equally, in more than a few cases, themselves its victims. All this could serve as the basis for a close emotional and political community of interest between Jewish refugees and a decisive majority in such host societies. The emergent Israeli state, on the other hand, offered a near-messianistic hope of a happy future within a Jewish national framework for those who saw no place for themselves in a Europe polluted by the Nazi plague. What is more, the transitional governments installed in Eastern Europe prior to complete sovietization were not at all ill-disposed towards the new Jewish state, and for a while (up until around 1949, thus even somewhat beyond the point of the full Communist take-over) tolerated the activities of the Zionist institutional network in organizing emigration to Palestine. Without Zionist mediation, many who wished to leave would never have arrived either to Israel or the West.

On top of those factors, at this socio–historical juncture, and given the psychological state typical of camp survivors, leaving one's native land and 'pulling up one's roots' was no more associated after the Shoah with the same emotional strain as not so long before, when those concerned had experienced a very different, far more wrenching shock to their very existence. Furthermore, Jewish emigrants of that time, as a result of earlier migratory movements, often had quite extensive kinship and other (not uncommonly business or professional) ties abroad. Furthermore, for the sufferings they had undergone, they were also entitled to a considerable fund of moral sympathy. (This could sometimes, though not invariably, be banked on when dealing with western immigration authorities.)

Taken together, all these positive and negative factors had a role in pushing a great majority of surviving Jewry in Eastern Europe to opt for emigration, whenever that opportunity arose. These, in short, were the principal circumstances that conduced to the brisk stream of Jewish emigrants who set off from Eastern Europe in the immediate aftermath of 1945. As to its numerical scale, one can only say that these cohorts of Jewish emigrants were certainly by far the most sizable in the modern history of Jewry (and in most cases of the population as a whole) in the countries in question, the major exception being the Soviet Union itself, which for several decades completely closed its borders to all nationalities living on its territory and liable seek to leave.

According to a census in June 1946, some 240,000 survivors were then to be found in Poland, a majority of whom—some 157,000—had returned from the Soviet Union. Thanks to the *Berihah*, the massive underground rescue operation organized by the Zionists at the end of the war, less than half of them remained in the country half a year following the Kielce pogrom. That shrinkage continued over the ensuing years and decades. When the Polish Zionist movements were wound up in 1949, virtually every activist—around 30,000 people in all—had already departed. By the end of the 1950s, Poland's Jewish population numbered barely more than 25,000. A renewed wave of emigration (or more accurately, expulsion) began in 1968, touching most erstwhile Jewish Communists and intellectuals. As a result, by the end of the millennium Poland was empty of Jews. A mere 5,000–6,000 of them are still recorded in a nation state whose territory prior to 1939 had been home to the second or the third largest Jewish community in the world (next to the Soviet Union of that time and the United States).

Much the greatest concentration of Jewish survivors in the whole of Europe, after the Soviet Union, was that in Romania—around 430,000 of them. Here too mass emigration followed the war, though it is hard to document its numerical scale prior to the temporary closure of the frontiers in 1947. The departures resumed immediately later on, as soon as the régime permitted, only to be suspended again in 1952. By 1956, at all events, the presence of only 146,000 Jews could be attested in Romania, and by 1966 no more than 43,000. This was barely one-tenth the immediate post-war population, especially if one takes into account the unquantifiable compensatory demographic surge that followed the Shoah.

In the case of Bulgaria, despite its being the sole Eastern European state where social solidarity was successful in saving the local Jewish community in its entirety, the establishment of the state of Israel marked the start of a veritable exodus, with the full consent of the Communist authority. Nine-tenths of the 48,000 Bulgarian Jews set sail for the Near East prior to 1951. A similar demographic loss was also exemplified in Czechoslovakia, especially after the Communist take-over: of the 44,000 Jewish residents recorded in the 1948 census, just 18,000 remained by the end of 1950, and 15,000 by 1957. Virtually all Jewish survivors left Ruthenia—before the war part of Czechoslovakia but in 1945 annexed to Soviet Ukraine. They went initially for Slovakia, but in most cases only to move on further to the West, when the erstwhile Nazi puppet state became a Soviet satellite in 1948.

Right up until the authorities imposed a final prohibition in 1949, there was a steady but altogether mitigated flow of emigration from

amongst the 191,000 survivors (probably a grossly conservative estimate) to be found in Hungary in 1946 (some 144,000 of them being
actually of Jewish faith). Even after the winding up of the Zionists and
the 'Joint,' however, a further 3,000 people were allowed to leave for
Israel under a bilateral agreement between the two states. That exiting
trickle gathered some pace in 1956 and subsequently, but even so it
was a good deal less intensive than that from other parts of the Soviet
bloc. The numbers leaving after October 1956—just like before
1951—were estimated at some 20,000–25,000 altogether. The bulk of
those who stayed were concentrated in Budapest, where from 1957
onwards their number stabilized at around 100,000. The most recent
surveys have come up with an estimated figure of the same order, with
the qualification that the on-going processes of assimilation and miscegenation (through mixed marriage, change of faith, dissimulation,
the Communists' rejection of inherited groups identities) have thoroughly muddled perceptions of identity within Hungarian Jewry. Any
estimate of numbers must be henceforth treated as increasingly doubtful. In any event, Hungary was the sole state within the Soviet system
not to lose the bulk of its surviving Jewish population in the first years
following the war, or possibly even since then either. Estimates to this
effect appear to be borne out by findings of a major sociological survey carried out in 1999.

On that point, it is perhaps hardly necessary to remark that data
relating to Jewish populations after 1945, in the West and East alike,
are ever less reliable as time goes by. Even the rare data available
from regular censuses (in Romania, for example) offer a rather poor
interpretation (usually equal to ignorance) of the multifaceted nature
of modern Jewish identity. Nowadays even a self-applied designation
of being 'Jewish' may indicate any one of a variety of actual identity
situations—referring to religion, birth, mother tongue, descent from
Jewish born parents, descent from one Jewish parent, etc. or a combination of some of these criteria. Religious affiliation could be checked
in some Eastern European countries up to the Communist take-over
only, though in Romania or the Soviet Union Jewish nationality continued to be identified regularly at population censuses. Before the
Shoah most of these countries (except the Soviet Union, obviously)
recorded Jews by religion in official birth, marriage or death certifi-
cates. Such practice even continued for some years after the Second

World War. In Hungary, for instance, birth records oddly enough maintained reference to religion in many places, Budapest amongst them, as late as April 1950. A modern definition of Jewish identity (including self-definition) may, however, disregard any such 'objective' criteria, particularly religion. It may or may not refer to them. Any kind of Jewish affiliation, however remote or not recognized by traditional Jewry, may suffice to develop an even strong sense of Jewish identity. One encounters in this matter totally subjective self-classifications on the part of individuals who would not fall under a single one of the classical categories permitting the claim for Jewish identity. Equally, others might be categorized as being Jewish by those same categories, without maintaining any links at all with the Jewish community, and would even refuse to be classed as belonging to it. (This was a typical attitude amongst Jewish–Communist cadres.)

In countries with advanced Jewish assimilation, a significant proportion of those who would later fall victims to Nazi persecution, were at least nominally Christians by faith. This was the case in Hungary, for instance, for 8 per cent in 1941 (and as many as 17 per cent in Budapest); in Bohemia and Moravia for 28 per cent in 1938; and even in Germany for 9 per cent in 1939—in other words, after the bulk of Jews affected by the Nuremberg laws had emigrated, amongst whom it is very likely that there were many more converts. Presumably those disengaged from the Judaic faith formed an even higher proportion among the Shoah survivors. That ratio would only have increased further with the passage of time, bearing in mind the active campaign of Christian proselytism for several years after 1945. (This could be even statistically demonstrated for Hungary.) All these factors serve to throw serious doubt on census or other statistical estimates of the size of Jewish populations based on confessional or ethnic criteria, especially when such information referred to on the informants' own declarations. In light of the horrific tribulations they had endured (which as a rule had begun with the registration of Jews), it is hardly surprising that many Jews had no wish to be recorded as being Jewish on any sort of list.

Apart from the direct consequences of the Shoah, European Jewry faced two types of challenge to its collective existence after 1945, both weighing more seriously in Central and Eastern Europe than in the West. The first was related to the material problems of restarting life, the other to the handling of Jewish identity, and the need for its redefinition, that was felt by virtually every survivor. Those who had been the targets of persecution were often forced to make distressingly tough choices in both respects. However many times they may already have abandoned any hope of regaining their former living conditions and self-definition, their new circumstances in any event signified a rupture, often an all too real *tabula rasa*, with what had been 'before.'

Those rescued from the Nazi camps had to begin a new life in the most literal sense of re-establishing entirely the financial, emotional, and family basis of their existence. The loss of all wealth by previously well-off survivors brought in its train involuntary switches of career, the loss of earlier professional market positions and, in many cases, a loss of social status. The sweeping land reforms, with the break-up or confiscation of larger landed estates—one of the first stages in the change of régime—applied just as much to Jewish owners as to any others. At the same time the Jews belonging to the landless peasant stratum (admittedly a small number) got very little if anything out of those reforms. The same applied more importantly to the nationalization of factories, banks and large commercial businesses (which in Hungary occurred as early as 1946), whilst liberal professionals, small traders, and artisans were placed somewhat later under comparable threat by forced collectivization policies and ideological 'class-thinking' inaugurated in the new régimes. These very occupational spheres had formerly provided a living for most Jewish survivors.

In parallel, with the ending of previous professional prohibitions and discriminations, Jews now found (for the first time in Central and Eastern European history) practically unhindered access to employment in the civil service, the armed forces and public industries. One way or another, most returnees were soon obliged to start a new occupation in the newly organized (and in Eastern Europe, collectivized) economy. Their range of choices for making their way in sovietized countries was, on one hand, narrowed by the elimination or drastic contraction of the private sector. On the other hand, their options expanded considerably, in that rapidly proliferating (sometimes earlier non-existent) positions in state bureaucracies were now open to them.

A necessity for change likewise made itself felt in the private sphere. Countless families had been dismembered by the Holocaust, and the previous frameworks of social existence were wrenched or put still further out of joint via migratory processes that ensued after the Shoah. Many survivors were therefore faced with the need to find a new spouse, start a new family, build up new circles of relatives, personal friends, neighbors and other social relations and alliances. One objective reflection of that may be observed in the growing rates of remarriage, and a correspondingly high 'compensatory' birth-rate in various Jewish populations. Those rates were particularly significant in the years immediately following the end of the war (even in German refugee camps), though given the disarray of demographic conditions that was one of the Shoah's legacies, a growing proportion of the new families were both denominationally and ethnically mixed. The imbalance of gender and age-groups contributed to the frequency of mixed marriages: the number of marriages between Jews and Christians in Hungary by the end of the 1940s had reached over one-third among Jewish males, even if only formally mixed marriages are counted and other relevant unions are disregarded, like those entered into by couples of Jewish descent, converts or else—increasingly in the early years of the Communist era—young people getting married without declaring any religion.

Easy as it may seem to the outsider to redefine one's identity, the reality was very much difficult to endure. The Shoah had blighted, discredited, or at the very least made questionable most of the identity options accepted and acceptable in the past. Many traditionalists had their faith shaken to the core by the incomprehensible atrocities that they had lived through. For others it was quite the opposite, and that applied to more than a few who had abandoned the faith or been brought up in a secularized or de-Judaized milieu: the very experience of the ordeals and humiliations brought some of them back to religious observance, or at least to a dissimilant desire to declare publicly their Jewish affiliation. For many 'de-Judaized' survivors (especially in German-speaking countries and in Hungary) the mantle of 'national' assimilation—formerly donned with such pride and regarded as an unequivocal vehicle of high values and a passport to social success— now looked like a cruel historical trap. Surrendering one's Jewish identity became, in retrospect, a senseless form of self-denial, a purposeless betrayal. A questioning of the assimilationist option was a general phenomenon after the Shoah, at least in Nazi collaborationist societies, extending as it did to survivors in western countries. (This was spared to countries where Jewry had been left largely unscathed by the Brown Plague, as in Scandinavia, Albania or Italy). Even assimilated Jews with extreme left-wing views were not completely immune to doubts as, with the best will in the world, a Jewish Communist could not extirpate all memory of the Ribbentrop–Molotov pact, which had gifted the Nazi leadership well-nigh two years of complete freedom to prepare for, and indeed launch the genocide in Poland and the Balkans with the conniving passivity of the 'mother-country of socialism.'

People of the Shoah

The immediate post-war years were a Promethean moment of history for all Jews, and not just in the sense that they were obliged to redefine their relationship to their inherited identity, but also, at the same time, that they had a freedom of choice, at least up till the consolidation of the Communist régimes, such as they had possibly never had before. Rethinking of identity options could not be carried out in this juncture without a reflection on the experience of the Shoah. Remembrance of the Shoah and the imperative 'not to forget' became a unifying factor, both internally and externally, in definitions of Jewishness. Whether or not they wished to be, European Jews—and, more broadly, any active or passive bearer of Jewish identity in the world—became, first and foremost, the people of the Shoah. The main consequences of this new situation may be summed up as follows.

To begin with, the 'traditional' factors that distinguished Jews from non-Jews were expanded by the Nazi persecutions with a new one that, through its henceforth indelible imprint in collective memory, proved far more potent than most previous ones, creating a new kind of rift between Jews and non-Jews. This rift remained an objective component of Jewish consciousness, that not even the most ardent assimilationists were able to bridge completely. The dynamism of this new kind of otherness contributed to a proliferation of choices of identity (in many cases advocating separatism and a new dissimilation). Its core elements were supplied and nourished by a collective narcissism of sorts based on the moral superiority of innocent victims, or potential victims, over those who, in one way or another, attended their ordeal. The customary forms of collective narcissism, proper to all self-conscious group, were fed in Jewry by various sources, such as the religious belief of the 'chosen people,' the Jewish contributions to high culture and civilization, etc. They were now supplemented by a distinctive new dimension bestowed by the moral capital gained via unjustifiable persecutions, the exposure to a historically unparalleled crime of collective injustice. Even in circles in the past inclined to assimilation, in the West as well as the East, post-Shoah mourning was accompanied by a vigorous and general rehabilitation of Jewish consciousness, which now imparted a positive value to an experience of being Jewish that previously had tended rather to be negative. 'Modern' Jews had been able to muster cogent arguments for denying legitimacy to traditional Jewishness, for regarding it as 'antiquated,' 'outworn,' 'obsolete.' They could not deny a fundamental solidarity with and identification to those of the people of the Shoah, whatever cultural or social differences could have been among them. A measure of dissimilation, a sense of singularity, even a strong conviction of moral distinction in an absolute sense became a structural concomitant of the consciousness of the post-Holocaust generations of Jewry.

Dissimilationist attitudes could be manifested in many different versions. The positive self-image of most Jews was enhanced, para-doxically, by at least passive identification with the role of martyr, even in the case of those, like Zionists or Communists, who publicly inveighed against such a role: morally speaking, it was incomparably better to have the role of the heir, fellow sufferer, or descendant of innocent victims than that of the executioner or an accomplice or, at the very best (as in the case of a large part of the general public of Central and Eastern Europe), one who 'looked the other way' when Jewish neighbors were hauled away for deportation.

The founders of the state of Israel, over the prolonged initial stage of nation-building, made extensive political use of this positive sense of otherness, and the moral capital with which it was invested, in two different ways. On the one hand, for 'external consumption,' the ar-gument that the Jews had 'earned' their own homeland through the blood they had spilled was extremely potent in the West, when inter-national recognition was sought to endorse the existence of a Jewish state. On the other hand though, in a rather negative sense and mainly for 'internal consumption,' they did their best to distance themselves from the role of passive martyrs surrendering themselves to their unchosen fate. Israeli patriotism set up as its paragon a self-fulfilling image of the Jew as a combative resister, so that the educational system and political discourse within the country, for a long time, played down the topic of how Jewry of the Shoah and the *Galut* ('dispersion') had lived, together with the cultural legacy of 'assimilated' Jewry, however vastly it contrasted with the original vision of early Zionists, Herzl and his associates (as was seen in the discussion of the ideological sources of Zionism).

To summarize, then, manifestations of the dissimilationist consciousness relating to memories of the Shoah revealed themselves amongst survivors in a multiplicity of ways. It can be attested even for those following a strategy of deliberate dissimulation, the conscious concealment of their Jewishness (not uncommonly through repression proper, 'keeping quiet in front of children,' etc.), as was typically the case with Jewish cadres of Communist régimes or some Jewish leftist circles in the West. Communist (and other left-wing) parties, in deference to their universalistic ideology and their own best political interests, expressly enjoined their personnel to keep a low profile about, if not properly hide their origins. That, however, not infrequently had quite the opposite effect. Public denial of inherited identity forced those concerned to hang on much more strongly to their sense of otherness. Obligatory repression does not weaken but strengthens in-bred elements of identity via the very consciousness of its public dissimulation.

Second, after the Shoah, the relationship of Jews to outside society was clouded by the shadow of suspicion. In the past there had been many neutral domains in which networks of contacts could be sustained between Jews and Gentile, especially in countries of high level assimilation. Of course, some of those domains still subsisted, or were re-established after 1945. But Jews would never be able—at least unconsciously—to get rid of a feeling (especially during the immediate post-war decades), that any social partners from 'the other side' owed them a sort of 'truth-test' in regard to their conduct during the persecutions, before there could be any question of an intimate relationship with them. That suspicion became deeply imprinted in the consciousness of Jews, whatever identity strategy they might adopt, whether dissimilant or dissimulant, proud or ashamed, active or passive as to manifestations of Jewishness. Survivors in countries that had espoused a Nazi régime or collaborated with the Nazis could not afford to let slip the need to dig, often obsessively, into the recent past of anyone with whom they planned to build up closer links. This became a touchstone of all further partnerships—business, leisure, friendly, or even sexual or amatory—between Jews and non-Jews. Contact with those infected with the Brown Plague, even if only indirect or symbolic, was morally compromising for survivors down through several generations. This is why many, most particularly those settled in Israel, would categorically avoid any contact with German territory, unless it was a matter of making a pilgrimage to the sites of their ancestors' martyrdom.

Being thus organically built into relationships between Jews and non-Jews, this suspicion naturally influenced decisively political commitments, professional and economic strategies, the choice of residence or the network of preferential or acceptable contacts. Even within circles of Communist Jews, who did everything they could to keep their party role free from 'Jewish implications' and to cultivate relations as neutral as possible with all those committed to the 'common cause' (i.e. other 'comrades'), many phenomena of the political and social scenery had a double coding. To the official angle was appended, by way of amplification, qualification or negation, a reading of 'our' standpoint in which, though the 'us' in question was usually not explicitly declared, even in private conversation, it was unequivocally a reference to Jews.

Yet 'sensitivity' to matters of any sort relating to Jews—the same as what non-Jewish public opinion has traditionally put down to 'Jewish over-sensitivity'—increased just as much among Jews in western democracies as it did throughout Eastern Europe since the collapse of Communism. Let it be added that the same now also applies to wide segments of non-Jewish but Judaeophile public opinion. Characterized briefly, in the 'age of suspicion' that has set in since the Shoah, the vigilance both of those directly affected and of a growing camp of those who avow solidarity with them has decisively increased and the threshold of reaction has been significantly lowered, in regard to manifestations of anti-Semitism. As a result, it would be fair to say that 'innocent' or 'spontaneously candid' relations between Jews and non-Jews have actually become more difficult since 1945, and for a while they could almost never be anything other than 'conditional,' often despite the carefully maintained appearances to the contrary that marked the efforts of the most highly assimilated groups of European Jewry (typically left-wingers, Communists, or Western Europeans).

Third, the obligatory alteration of Jewish identity as a result of the experience or memory of the Shoah, at some, primarily conscious level, neutralizes, renders null and void as it were, the inner contradictions of Jewish identity, the persisting cultural and religious divisions of Jewry, its tendency since the *Haskalah* to a proliferating diversity in regard to self-definition, but without the disappearance of the above divisions in social reality. Just as the Nazis, in implementing their program of genocide, treated their chosen victims impartially, making no distinction between the assimilated and traditionalists, Orthodox and Reform Jews, solid bourgeois and *Luftmenschen*, reclassifying completely 'de-Judaized,' indeed long-Christianized individuals (and sometimes even their descendants) as 'Jews,' so the recollection of the Shoah introduced a new unifying principle in the self-image of all those with any kind of link to Jewry. The consciousness of belonging to the 'people of the Shoah' became equally valid for converts, partners in mixed marriages, those dissimulating their Jewish origins; in other words, for all who would in no way have been counted as Jewish by former criteria, indeed often for their descendants as well across several generations. The homogenizing effect of remembrance of the Shoah has thus produced unexpected 'reconversions' to Judaism. Sons of converts or children from mixed marriages who previously, in all likelihood, would have lost or strategically severed all links with Judaism, may be disposed (even to the extent of finding a path to the synagogue) to rebuild and accept an identity for which their parents and other relatives were forced to undergo such immeasurable suffering.

In the 'balance of affiliations' for partners in mixed marriages of old, for instance, the sense of Jewishness was generally played down: There was even a regular temptation to revoke it altogether (via conversion to Christianity that often followed such a marriage, if indeed it had not already preceded that, simply in order to avoid the complications attendant on mixed unions). From now onwards, more commonly the Jewish partner and the Jewish identity that became dominant in the self-definition of a 'mixed' family,' so that the non-Jewish partner, in many cases, would not only perceive that transformation as a concession but would adopt it deliberately. The moral capital of the 'people of the Shoah' now, not uncommonly, proved a stronger, more attractive, or more important factor of identification than 'Christianity,' the more banal subject of that same historical reference, marred by the awareness of its having sustained the 'worse' historical role and compromised in the eyes of many. Rejection of the 'Christian' reference and a preference for the Jewish one in 'mixed families' became thus not uncommon in Hungary, for instance, where the 'Christian-national' ideology of the country's inter-war governments, regarded in retrospect—whether justifiably or not—to have ushered in Nazism, achieved a significant devaluation of 'Christianity,' especially in liberal or secular Gentile circles. Hence, no longer did intermarriage in any way lead, inevitably to a definitive estrangement of the offspring from Jewry; it might now set them off on the opposite road.

The semantic auras of 'Christian' and 'Jewish' identity were also increasingly likely to undergo a fundamental change during the decades following 1945. Prior to the Nazi persecutions, Christianity and Judaism had embodied mutually opposed, or at least exclusive, identity patterns, especially in societies with a low level of secularization. Since then (and above all in most recent times) it has become possible for someone to be Christian by creed and also Jewish, as he or she would choose. Jean-Marie Lustiger, the current Catholic archbishop of Paris, whose own family bears most cruelly the scars of the Shoah, provided a conspicuous example of that by his public declaration of his Jewishness, on being elevated to cardinalship. Remembrance of the Shoah not only pervades the consciousness of every group of Jews but contributes empirically, in a very real way, to a significant broadening of the circles of those who openly accept their affiliation to Jewry, even if, admittedly, often only in the abstract sense of the 'people of the Shoah.'

Fourth and last, the Shoah fundamentally changed the way in which the public sphere of host societies around European Jewry operate, insofar as anti-Semitic discourses of any kind have become compromised in most, if not all social circles (possibly once and for all time).

The defeat of Nazism, let it not be forgotten, also radically destroyed the social legitimacy of a secular Judaeophobic discourse that had been current for centuries (since at least the beginnings of modernization) in many European societies and was questioned only within certain sectors of public opinion (liberals, left-wingers, freemasons, etc.). Now the Shoah represents in this sense a milestone in European intellectual history, notwithstanding the fact that anti-Semitism itself has far from having ceased to exist, as it will be discussed below in a sub-chapter. Still, opportunities for it to gain public expression are now subject to drastic restrictions, censorship, and self-restraint. Above all, anti-Semitic organizations have been disbanded in most European countries, in the East as well as the West, and in many of them (notably in Great Britain as early as 1976, but later also in Finland, Italy, Poland, Switzerland) the practice of, or incitement to, racial, religious or ethnic discrimination of any sort have been made punishable by legal sanctions. From the 1980s legislation in certain western democracies (e.g. France, Belgium, Spain and West Germany) has also penalized the growing 'revisionist' literature tending to deny the historical reality of the Shoah.

The official taboo on anti-Semitism has also fundamentally altered the behavior of even inveterate anti-Semites. It is now rare for them to declare their anti-Jewish prejudices publicly. Most of them are avowedly 'not anti-Semites at all,' often make reference to 'their Jewish friends,' treat separately 'good Jews' and others. Their discourse refers often indirectly, yet 'transparently' only to Jews, with a predilection for clothing their stigmatization in the coded language of universalistic or 'national' interests. An essential component of the new situation is the abandonment of official, state run anti-Semitism in countries where it had earlier formed an organic part of government policy (as in much of Central and Eastern Europe), or at least (as in some Communist states) its concealment under the cloak of some other pretext (namely anti-Zionism). Even the most savage (and bloody) Stalinist terrors to be visited on Jews between 1948 and 1953, or later, did not overtly reference their anti-Semitism; instead, Jews would be referred to as 'cosmopolitan,' 'alien,' or 'bourgeois' elements that had 'wormed their way into the party.' This may not have altered the plight of the actual victims of persecution but did nevertheless mark a self-limiting mechanism of sorts even within the very campaign of terror: it prevented the horrors directed against specific individual Jews from completely degenerating into indiscriminate persecution of Jews in general. This statement remains historically true even if, allegedly, Stalin did nurture such a paranoid project in the last period of his life.

It is important to mention also, amongst the institutional manifestations of this *volte-face* in the history of the 'European mind,' the new kinds of messages—henceforth, as a rule, philo-Semitic—issued by the Churches. Most Protestant authorities were ahead of the Catholic Church in its *aggiornamento* (renewal) beginning with the Second Vatican Council (1962–65), which amongst other things removed from the liturgy the passages offensive to Jews. The new attitude of the Christian officialdom deepened the Judaeo–Christian dialogue in everyday religious practice, and opened the way to a fundamental revision of theological anti-Judaism. Ever since then, the Churches have regularly made placatory gestures to Judaism within the framework of numerous ecumenical initiatives. One of the most recent of these (in 1999) was Pope John Paul II's ceremonial apology for historic crimes that his Church had committed against Jews and others. It is fairly obvious that such attempts at *rapprochement*, inconceivable before 1945, were aimed primarily at the 'people of the Shoah.'

Israel and the new Jewish identity

The appearance of Israel on the stage of history has brought a widening of the range and structure of available options in the choice of Jewish identities. Officially founded on the 14th of May, 1948, the Hebrew state created a genuinely new assignment of roles for European Jewry in its attitudes to identity and equally its political and (in regard to migratory movements) geographical orientations. It is only in this specific context that Israel will be referred to here, the developments that led to or followed its establishment falling outside the strictly European framework of the present study. The significance of the Jewish state to European Jews is best summed up by two notable circumstances.

For one thing, for the first time every member of the Diaspora was now able to count on a 'homeland' that would extend a proper welcome, if necessary, in the way that the nineteenth-century prophets of Zionism had envisaged. Jews of old fleeing from danger were not uncommonly subject to protracted waits, the pestering and slights of

immigration officials, or the risk of being shuttled, at further risk, between several countries, or even (like those leaving Nazi Germany at a
late point in time) several continents, before they found a refuge
somewhere, if at all. That situation was now radically over, and the
status of Jewish emigrants instantaneously became far more propitious
than that of most others driven to seek sanctuary abroad. Every new
settler coming to Israel was assured of immediate assistance for settling down and obtaining full citizenship rights, a passport valid for all
countries and, through that, possibly a chance to move on to another
country. For those coming from an Eastern Europe, fallen first to Fascism then to Bolshevism, this amounted to a fabulous chance, a real
status mobility, most of them never having experienced a comparable
position before (at least since the collapse of the liberal Habsburg
Empire), or having any hope of achieving it in their native land or,
indeed, any other host country.

The need to have Israel as a defensive bunker after 1945 was indeed very considerable. During the decade after the Second World
War the demand for a target for emigration grew not just amongst
survivors of the Shoah, but also amongst Jewish residents in Muslim
or Arab countries of the Near and Middle East as well as North Africa.
The latter regions had hitherto counted as relatively tranquil places of
settlement. They served as a home to most of the world's Sephardic
community, now that the devastation of Nazism (in Greece, Serbia,
Bosnia, Croatia, etc.) and ensuing migratory movements had removed
the greater part of the Sephardic bloc from the Balkan countries. During the long years of the Cold War, for masses of Jews in Eastern
Europe (and especially the Soviet Union)—deprived as they remained
of contacts with world Jewry and, in many cases, even of chances to
emigrate—, Israel's existence represented a far from abstract or symbolic hope of liberation.

To that virtual, albeit very real advantage should be added the
moral cachet, the symbolic surplus, that *aliyah* (ascent) to Israel possessed over emigration to any other destination. The Jewish state, in
war to this day with some of its neighbors, might not be able to secure
for its new citizens total physical security, but it certainly could offer
the full rights that go with belonging to a nation-state and a concomitant human dignity that would not be immediately attainable anywhere
else: *olim*, newcomers to Israel, from the very outset are not treated as

second-class, tolerated immigrants but as real citizens, sharing the poignant experience of participating in a great project of nation-building.

Furthermore, during the decades succeeding its foundation Israel, almost belying the negligible size of its population, has become a significant factor in international politics, a veritable diplomatic great power. Its prestige obviously rests also upon the fact of being the only Western type democracy East of the Mediterranean. It also demonstrated by its military successes and victories in a series of wars, that it possesses the most potent armed force in the whole region. The Jewish state is thus able to intervene politically (and on occasion by armed force as well) in defense of Jews across the world. In comparison with the past, this has created a totally new situation, specifically one of a general shift in the balance of forces in favor of the Jews, from the viewpoint of the Jewish Diaspora's sense of security, collective self-assurance and relations to 'host' states. Since the Jewish state has proved that it can offer political and, in the extreme case, even military assistance against the threats of anti-Semitism, its mere existence provides a boost to self-confidence and to faith in the future for Jewish masses that, earlier, had been cruelly denied any ally in the form of a reliable state power.

Second, the settlement of the position of the Jews in Israel, an internationally recognized western-style nation state, a 'country like any other,' which moreover has been accommodating a continuously growing share of the world's Jewish population (by the 1990s it accounted for about one-third of all Jews), opened up new perspectives from the viewpoint of determining, or reformulating Jewish identity. Put simply, acceptance or rejection of the Israeli state, whether as a purely symbolic act, an expression of emotional sympathy or in form of active financial support, political lobbying, economic investment, plans to settle down there, or merely visit as a tourist, now became an inescapably integral part of the definition of what constituted 'being a good Jew' or a 'proper Jewish behavior.'

Admittedly, the Jewish state was far from having an undilutedly positive image, in this respect. It divided at least as much it united Jewish public opinion and the associated choices of affiliation. A broad cross-section of the strongly 'de-Judaized' western Jewish community, especially adherent of universalistic salvation ideologies (the various shades of left-wingers, Communists, anarchists, etc.) in the East as well as the West, continued to dismiss the ideal of a Jewish state. For this, even if unconsciously, they were often trotting out Stalinist arguments and accusations against it ('colonial creation,' 'lackey of American imperialism,' 'oppressor of the Palestinian people,' 'racial state,' etc.). Yet the dissimilationist mentality that evolved in the wake of the Shoah, as remarked earlier, in many cases was, at the same time, also based on pride in Israel's successes, which added to the growing attraction of the Zionist project. A substantial portion of western Jewry, perhaps even a majority, including many who would not seriously entertain the thought of *aliya*, gradually formed a kind of symbiotic relationship with Israel. This could be manifested by undertaking trips to *Eretz* in a genuine spirit of pilgrimage, youngsters joining *kibbutz*es to work during their summer vacations, donating money to Zionist organizations, etc. For many survivors of the persecutions, these symbolic advantages, significant as they were for sustaining a sense of Jewish identity, were factors that could tip the balance, even in the face of concerns about safety, in a decision to get settled in Israel. It is true to say that, in general, the popularity of the Zionist project (as reflected in the rising numbers of those choosing *aliya*) grew steadily over the post-war decades. This could be observed even in countries and social circles (e.g. most western countries or Hungary) where the bulk of those concerned (especially members of the middle classes and intellectual occupations) had previously, more often than not, shown undisguised hostility to the idea of a Jewish state.

Of course, the political influence, even popularity, that the Israeli state enjoyed during the decades after its foundation with the powers-that-be in Western Europe played a part in this development. In the war with Egypt that broke out in 1956, following the nationalization of the Suez Canal, Israel was allied militarily to France and Britain. The United States provided the country with financial aid from the very start. West Germany, within the framework of collective and individual reparation payments, assured Tel-Aviv of enormous financial and, besides that, unflagging political support. Though the geopolitical climate was less favorable to Israel after the Six-Day War of June 1967, and more particularly following the 1973 Yom Kippur War and the ensuing oil crisis, because the western powers began to steer a more balanced (and hence more Arab-friendly) policy course, the more restrained inter-state cooperation did not significantly undermine the dominance of pro-Israeli support amongst the western general public. Admittedly, some of what otherwise (or previously) were the most reactionary anti-Semitic forces had a part in boosting this political sympathy, such as extremist supporters of French Algeria, who were inclined to appraise the military successes of the Jewish state over 'Arabs' as triumphs for 'western' or even 'White' colonial power. A rapprochement to Israel also commenced in the countries of Eastern Europe during the 1980s, assuming more definite contours after 1989, to the extent that some of the neophyte democracies—and not necessarily those where the general public had a particularly good historical record in respect of its attitudes towards Jews (as in the case of Poland or Hungary)—instrumentalized this as proof of their 'European credentials.' This was a step that the national–Communist dictatorship of Ceausescu's Romania had already taken, having steered its own path independent of Moscow since 1967. Ambiguous and in several respects contradictory as this political sympathy towards Israel may have been, incidentally it bolstered the social position of Jewry in European societies.

Religious indifferentism and 're-Judaization'

The conditions for the regeneration of identity patterns, shaped by the Shoah and then by the appearance of Israel, led to a series of new processes. Conspicuous amongst these were a continuing spread of religious apathy, whether that was under duress (due to the atheist régimes prevailing in Eastern Europe) or spontaneous (as in the West). But the opposite trend was also typical of the period, in various—denominational, cultural or symbolic—forms of dissimilant 're-Judaization,' along with a realignment of relations between the various sectarian communities within religious Judaism. Here we must content ourselves with a sketchy presentation of the impact of these various trends in the transformations of the social and cultural complexion of European Jewry.

A growing secularization of Jewry as well as other ethnic groups and religious constituencies was obviously most typical of sovietized

Eastern Europe, where official atheism had a direct coercive role to this effect and where, in at least some countries (as demonstrably in Hungary, but probably elsewhere too), the losses in the Shoah had been most severe amongst Orthodox Jews, living as they had tended to do in greater social isolation, in more closed rural communities, with fewer Christian contacts to call on for possible protection. In Hungary reform Jewry survived in much larger proportion also because a good part of them lived in Budapest, where the majority of the persecuted escaped deportation to death camps. But the relative protection of the religiously 'modern' or indifferent pertained to a process important for native-born segments of Western European Jewry as well. Post–1945 secularization continued to be linked, in part, with other modernization processes. It can be checked by rising educational qualifications, reductions in birth rates, family planning, and efforts directed towards greater socio–economic mobility. In part, and perhaps paradoxically, Israeli statehood could lend a special legitimacy to some utterly arreligious candidates for *aliyah*, thanks to the secular (and in individual cases even anti-religious, anticlerical) commitment of some Zionist activists, given that the majority of citizens of the Jewish state were widely known to be non-observant, just as a large portion of Zionist movements were religiously indifferent, and sometimes, in the case of the most left-wing organizations (especially in socialist *kibbutze*s), held explicitly anti-religious views.

However, there also existed two trends of behavior, diametrically opposed to this, which gained expression in a new relation to religion, at times even with the very groups that had proceeded furthest down the path of de-Judaization.

First of all, abandonment of Judaism had, in the past, brought in its train a radical break with Jewry. 'Assimilees' either crossed over into another square on the denominational 'board,' and in so doing publicly espoused a 'Christian national' self-definition. They also may have set their sights on a modern and (not being predicated on practice of any religion) religiously uncommitted identity model, the ideological basis for which might be liberal humanism (e.g. under the aegis of freemasonry), socialism, Communism, anarchism, etc. Both through the memory of the Shoah and through links to Israel (with increasingly palpable bonds of family and friendship), however, many 'assimilees' accepted the burden of a dual symbolic affiliation, which might sometimes (like in Communist states) be hard to sustain, attended by public odium, or even (during Stalinism) entailed dangerous repression. The supreme tests of strength for assimilees with such dual loyalties was a positive attitude to Israel: participation in organized actions on behalf of the Jewish state, intervention against anti-Zionist campaigns, correspondence with Israeli relatives (which for some time was forbidden under Communism), etc. That same line of behavior also frequently led to cultural or even a measure of denominational 're-Judaization.' This could be expressed by merely symbolic forms of religious observance, in the American sense of 'civil religion,' by rituals destined to the demonstration of Jewish identity (on major holidays, at burials and, possibly, marriages), interest in Jewish cultural heritage, preferential option for social and professional contacts with fellow Jews.

Second, secularization and religious indifferentism after 1945 was less often a one-way process (i.e. a definitive one) than it had been before. Previously, desertion of religion was progressive and without return, as a rule. Those who passed into that camp generally left the synagogue forever, soon becoming more or less totally indifferent to their original faith, besides that, usually out of social conformism, they often got themselves baptized. After the Shoah however, at various points in the life-cycle (not necessarily just in old age) even amongst descendants of assimilees, the pull of Judaism made itself felt in the form of nostalgia for ancient ways, a wish to study like earlier or even worship on a regular basis. For many 'returnees' Judaism could again become a deliberately chosen way of life.

One of the common motivations for that change was a symbolic restoration of the unity or the continuity of families that had been destroyed or torn apart in the Shoah or by emigration. More specifically, it could be a mark of loyalty to vanished parents, grandparents, or other ancestors, many more of whom had been religiously observant. Formal acknowledgement of those sectarian links (for instance, through having sons circumcised or celebrating their *bar mitzvah*) might also prepare the ground for emigration to Israel in that this was one way that descendants of families having lost or cut their links with the faith (possibly by conversion to Christianity) could gain official confirmation of their Jewishness. Through religious observance, it would become possible to recreate, within highly rationalized living conditions of developed industrial societies, old style, traditional community's networks with all their warmth, caring relationships, etc. This was a way to recover an integrative medium perceived as 'primordial,' unconditional, 'natural'—an important need for those who, for whatever reason, became rootless or social outcasts. Understandably, that was common amongst survivors of the Shoah and not uncommon amongst all kinds of recent immigrants. Such alienated situations could be found in a multiplicity of forms amongst Jewish–Communist cadres disillusioned with the régime or fallen from grace. Mihály Farkas, one of the 'four horsemen of the Apocalypse' making up Hungary's post-war Stalinist leadership (as the first head of the secret police, then minister of defense until 1953), allegedly ended his days in Orthodox Jewish circles, since only they were prepared to open their doors to this once much dreaded (and loathed) Bolshevist potentate.

Anyhow, since 1945, the long-running historic move towards religious indifferentism has intersected, not uncommonly within the lifespan of those concerned, with a new form of re-Judaization, often not exclusively religious in function. This commenced earlier in western countries, gathering force in Eastern Europe mostly after the fall of Communism around 1989, that is, the moment that the residual Jewry who had been stranded there regained a free hand in choosing their identity.

One important component of that development was the resettlement in Western Europe of large groups of Sephardic Jews, at less advanced stages of secularization and social assimilation, from North Africa (Algeria, Tunisia, Morocco) and the Near East (Egypt, Lebanon, Syria, etc.) at various points in time (after 1954, and especially in 1962, in the case of Algeria's French–Jewish community, numerically the largest of these groups). Not only did the newcomers from the south and south–east bring with them more traditional customs and relics of their own distinctive Jewish culture and thus demand an expansion in the range of ritual, educational and cultural services offered by religious institutions, and not only was their social and economic stratification less middle class and less 'modern,' but, since no small number of families had left their native land to head for Israel, either directly or by a detour through Western Europe, they also maintained much closer links with the Jewish state. The Sephardim, then, tipped the balance of internal sectarian forces within Western European

Jewry in favor of those with a stronger sense of Jewishness and the 'Israel affirmers.' They also replenished the by then demographically thinning ranks of Jewish communities in several countries. This applied principally to France, whose Jewish population became the largest in Western Europe after 1962. The emigration to the West of a segment of the Eastern European Jews, emerging from Communist secularization, undoubtedly had largely opposite effects. This may have had a no less significant impact on the inner ideological realignment of western Jewry, contributing for instance to the delegitimization of Communism within left-wing Jewish circles and, in the wake of 1956 and the 1960s, even more widely.

Hostages of Cold War in the Soviet Union

Palestine's dramatic partition into two states by the United Nations in November 1947, preceded by violent clashes between local Arabs and Jews, dragging in the British forces mandated to administer the territory and followed by a whole series of Arab–Israeli wars, came at the very moment when the Iron Curtain was finally falling into place between the West and Soviet occupied Eastern Europe. Despite that, Stalin and his satraps gave their support to the creation of Israel (only Tito's Yugoslavia abstained from voting). This was obviously meant to stir up discord between western states and, above all, as a snub to 'British imperialism' threatening the Soviet Union's claims to extend its sphere of influence to the Near East, Greece, Persia (Iran), and elsewhere.

A paradoxical situation arose in which the United States and the Soviet Union jointly assisted in the birth of the Jewish state—even though, at the time, both were pursuing diplomatic courses that, in their different ways, could be regarded as anti-Jewish. This had many consequences, albeit strictly transient in character. The main supplier of armaments to the Jewish state, when it first came under attack from its Arab neighbors was Czechoslovakia, which had been taken over by the Communists in February 1948. Communist Poland permitted the formation of a Jewish volunteer corps, thereby assisting Israel militarily.

Still more significantly, the countries of Eastern Europe, and even (though to a much more limited extent) the Soviet Union itself, temporarily granted their own Jewish citizens a measure of freedom to emigrate up to variable points in time (1951 in Czechoslovakia and Bulgaria, 1950 in the Soviet Union, 1949 in Hungary, and 1952 in Romania). Those legal or semi-legal emigrants joined the masses of their predecessors smuggled out illegally to the Near East by Zionist organizations. When their disembarkment was thwarted by the British authorities, as was frequently the case before the United Nations resolution to partition the territory, the emigrants would be sent to British camps set up on Cyprus, and in some cases even back to refugee camps in Germany (as in the famous incident of the *Exodus* in July 1947). One way or another, with the opening of the ports of *Eretz* following the establishment of the Jewish state, a total of 687,000 people 'ascended' into Israel between May 1948 and the end of 1951, of whom 52 per cent were Ashkenazi Jews, the majority from Eastern Europe. That nearly doubled the Jewish population of the new state, which prior to the mass immigration had numbered only 750,000.

The onset of the Cold War, however, brought an immediate freeze and thereafter, until the collapse of Communism in 1989, a braking, if not a complete standstill, in the flow of Jews out of Central and Eastern Europe. The distribution of Jewish populations within Europe over the long term shifted steadily towards Israel and the West with the continuous stream of Jews out of the Soviet satellites, uneven as it may have been from one country to another, as a function primarily of the policies that each Communist country pursued, often separately, in relation to the Jews. In regard to those policies, some of the 'people's democracies' indeed displayed unexpected divergences, as compared to other areas, where it was mandatory to adopt Moscow's line. During the Cold War, Zionism, the situation of the Jews, and their freedom to emigrate emerged as one of the major bones of contention between the West and the socialist camp, in two different ways.

On the one hand, whilst western states established more or less close links with the Jewish state, not long after the foundation of Israel (1950–51) Stalin cast his vote in favor of switching political and military support to Arab countries. His successors maintained that anti-Israeli stance with minor variations right up until the collapse of the Communist régimes. On more than one occasion, the entire Muscovite camp let itself be carried away as one into melodramatic gestures, as when diplomatic links with Israel were severed on Moscow's instructions, following the Six-Day War in 1967. There were only two dissenters. One was Yugoslavia, engaged on its own foreign policy, independent of Moscow since 1948. The other was Romania, which had likewise been going its own separate way since Ceausescu's rise to power in 1965. On the other hand, that same official anti-Zionism, especially from 1948 onwards, provided an ideological cover for countries following the Soviet pattern to introduce various anti-Semitic policies, though admittedly these were implemented in a fairly haphazard, uncoordinated manner, and in sometimes unusually idiosyncratic versions, as compared with the uniformity of approach seen within the Muscovite camp on other issues.

The first 'anti-Zionist' purges in the Soviet Union date back to the years of the Great Terror, between 1935 and 1937. The Nazi-Soviet Pact of 1939 was followed by mass deportations of Jews to Siberia from the areas of eastern Poland and the Baltic states that then came under occupation by Soviet armed forces. Jews suspected of having links to Zionism and *Bund*ism and even the Social Democrats were obviously also involved. Moscow went so far in its demonstrations of good will towards its new Nazi ally as to hand over to Germany many members of the political opposition to Nazism who had fled to territories occupied by the Red Army. The lethal machinery of oppression was also extended to Jewish institutions, the rabbinate and Yiddish-speaking intellectuals. The launching of 'Operation Barbarossa,' the invasion of the Soviet Union, on the 22nd of June, 1941, naturally brought about a change in that policy. In the interests of mobilizing all possible forces to the country's defense, a Jewish Anti-Fascist Committee was established in August of that year under the chairmanship of the famous Yiddish actor Solomon Mikhoels. Soviet anti-Nazi propaganda, however, largely ignored the genocide of the Jewish people (or at best did not ascribe much significance to it). Moreover, the Jewish population living in Galicia was given no advance warning of the Nazi threat, nor was anything done to evacuate them. As a result the Jewish masses that had unsuspectingly hung on in this Russian-held territory were sitting targets to be hauled off to concentration camps and systematically exterminated by the German invaders. Soviet propaganda even failed to react to the *Reich*'s anti-Semitic provocations. The official history of that period, when it came to be rewritten in the wake of the Red Army's eventual victory, shrouded the uniqueness of the Shoah in profound silence, just to insist on the equal share in the vast sufferings endured at the hands of the Nazis amongst the whole Soviet population. This minimization or neutralization of the unique nature of the Shoah went as far as banishing the word 'Jew' from textbooks, unless it was mentioned in a pejorative sense— mostly in the context of such officially condemned phenomena as Zionism, 'cosmopolitanism,' or 'the legacy of the bourgeois past.'

The year of 1948 appears to be of cardinal importance in that respect, particularly in hindsight of earlier events. In a debate at the United Nations in May 1947, on Stalin's order, Gromyko took the side of Palestinian Jews, voting in support of the establishment of Israel. The Soviet Union went on to recognize the new state from the day following its proclamation, and not just *de facto* (like the United States at first) but *de jure*. In the West's eyes, however, that was deemed to be a political charade, if not an attempt sow discord amongst the Allies, as during the very same months Stalin was launching a drastic assault against Jewry under his rule. In January 1948, Solomon Mikhoels was officially declared to have died in an automobile accident. In plain language: he was murdered. Within a year of his death the illustrious State Jewish Theatre in Moscow had been closed. Ilya Ehrenburg, the well-known Russian-Jewish writer, was obliged to write an article against Zionism, which appeared in the 21st of September, 1948 issue of *Pravda*, the newspaper of the Communist Party's Central Committee. The disbandment of the Jewish Anti-Fascist Committee in November signaled the start of a wave of persecution by the secret police claiming the lives of a number of Jewish intellectuals, writers, and artists. That anti-Semitic campaign, waged in the columns of the press and in prison cells alike, reached fresh heights of frenzy when most of the other members of the Jewish Anti-Fascist Committee and the most popular Yiddish authors were condemned to death and executed. In January 1953, Pravda revealed the 'proofs' behind Stalin's last great stage-managed undertaking, the 'Doctors' Plot.' It was the allegation that a group of distinguished Leningrad physicians had conspired to poison Stalin. In addition to the ensuing mass deportations of Jewish intellectuals, six of the nine defendants charged and sentenced to death in the 'Doctors' Trial' were Jewish. They were subsequently rehabilitated in April, soon after the dictator's fortunately timed death on the 3rd of March, 1953.

Thanks to the closure of Stalinism and the ensuing 'thaw' in international relations, the Soviet state's anti-Semitic policy also relented somewhat, though it was not by a long way dropped altogether. The Moscow leaders known as 'liberals,' Khrushchev amongst them, refrained neither from making speeches against Jews nor from taking anti-Semitic actions. The numbers of Jewish institutions employed for religious purposes were savagely cut back and confiscated synagogues turned over to uses that were each more profane than the last. The ever more strident anti-Zionist propaganda openly brought to bear well-worn anti-Semitic arguments, especially after the Six-Day War, which touched a raw nerve for the Soviet leadership in that it represented a defeat for their closest clients (and their own weapons). The official Soviet publishing houses went as far as rushing out books critical of Judaism, often sporting the imprint of national academies of science. The 'nationalistic' programs that political leaders pursued during the 1960s were coupled with purges in which functionaries of Jewish background were removed from all positions in the state machinery where they might come before the public eye.

In 1966, however, developments took a new turn. The Soviet premier, Kosygin, raised the prospect of allowing Jewish emigration under the banner of a 'family reunification' program. Moscow was almost certainly intending to make better use of the thaw in the new international climate. In order to wring some profit, both political and (by obtaining western credits) financial, the Soviet leadership decided to let a limited number of Jews leave the country. It would, so to speak, be tossing out some ballast in order to keep the economically sinking airship of the country afloat. Though a means of implementing that option was not sought immediately, given the resurgence of anti-Zionist rhetoric following the Six-Day War, a few years later (1969) the project was resumed with exit visas being issued to thousands of applicants. True, there were always many times more applicants than those allowed to leave, as Moscow set arbitrary limits on the number of departures. On top of that, it subjected applicants who were rejected, the *refuzniks*, to any number of nuisances, which damped down the demand from the start. Still, when Moscow invented a special tax imposed on those seeking to emigrate, it soon had to withdraw the measure under a storm of international protest, especially when in March 1973 Senator Jackson tabled a bill in Congress that would have made the granting of further American credits to the Soviet Union dependent on allowing free emigration.

The signing of the 'Final Act' of the 1975 Helsinki Conference, with its agreement on reaffirming the respect for human rights and easing of contacts between peoples of different nations, likewise gave an understandable boost to the emigration process, which, at its peak in 1979, recorded no less than 51,000 Jews leaving the country. In 1981, however, the number of exit visas plummeted again to below one thousand, so the subsequent course was not unequivocally positive. The emigration process picked up again in 1985, when Gorbachev consolidated his position, and in that year the Jewish population of the Soviet Union dipped under 1.8 million. During the 18 years up to the beginning of the change in régime, an annual average of 14,700 people—in total about 265,000—were able to leave the country. Once the borders were wide open after 1990, there was naturally a further acceleration in the rate of departures. Only a portion of them was directed to Israel, with the remainder—in some years a majority—being distributed amongst European and American host countries. For a long time, especially prior to 1985–86, a great number of *refuzniks*, expecting an exit visa after years of delays only, were meanwhile deprived of any legal means of subsistence. They were the ones who paid for the fiction, asserted by the Soviet power, that those who left the 'mother-country of socialism' were traitors fully deserving the inhuman treatment meted out to them.

This outline of the anti-Semitic aspect that frequently blemished Bolshevist practice also supplies the framework for the policies towards Jews adopted by other Eastern European states under Soviet rule. Each of those countries, however, filled in that framework in line with its own political traditions and with regard to the position of Jews within local politics.

Remnant Jews and new fangled anti-Semitism in the Soviet satellites

In Czechoslovakia striking changes did not occur in the immediate aftermath of the Second World War until after the Communist *coup d'état* of February 1948, which ousted the tolerant (and essentially

Judaeophile) régime under President Benes, installing a Stalinist state apparatus in its place. The 'show trial,' in late November 1952, of Rudolf Slánsky, the country's vice-premier (and until recently Communist Party secretary), along with thirteen other officials, assumed the form of a veritable anti-Semitic witch-hunt, resuscitating all too concretely the horrors of accusations of 'Jewish conspiracy' that had been thought dead and buried in a country famed for being among the best in Europe for Jews in the pre-Nazi decades. Of the fourteen defendants in the trial, eleven were Jewish. Nine of them were executed.

The subsequent fate of Jews in Czechoslovakia took a doubly distinctive course. For one thing, the Slánsky trial was followed by systematic purges within the state administration, resulting in the arbitrary arrests of several hundred personnel of Jewish origin. This was tantamount to an 'Aryanization' of sorts of the Communist Party hierarchy and, if the effects on students enrolled at Prague University are included, to the introduction of a *de facto* anti-Semitic *Numerus Clausus*. Second, while the 'thaw' commenced elsewhere in the Soviet bloc as soon as Stalin had died and shortly brought in its train the rehabilitation of many purge victims, it did not take place in Czechoslovakia until much later, well into the 1960s. In 1956, some 300 Jews were imprisoned, and the same fate befell many others, including 27 religious leaders as alleged 'Zionist spies.' This happened after Israel's Sinai Campaign, launched in late October 1956 to coincide with the Anglo–French Suez Campaign. The repressive course of the 'normalization' that followed the end of the 'Prague Spring' in 1968 rekindled the flame of official anti-Semitism, as a result of which 3,400 of those affected fled the country during the months of uncertainty later this year.

In Poland, removal of Jews from the state apparatus was completed in several successive waves.

The first anti-Semitic purges took place around the end of 1953 and early 1954. In the course of factional in-fighting within the party hierarchy there were plenty of Jews amongst the ranks of Stalinist hardliners, but more still amongst 'revisionists,' so the Stalinists had no compunction about throwing anti-Semitic arguments into their campaign against the reformist trend represented by Gomulka. Gomulka prevailed to become the country's leader in late 1956. Though anti-Semitic propaganda did not disappear altogether, there was at least some respite for those Jews who still remained in the country. Negotiations started on the return of 25,000 Polish-born Jews held in the Soviet Union, and *Folksstimme*, a Yiddish newspaper was even allowed to refer openly to the crimes committed by Stalin against Jews. Emigration to Israel was again permitted: between 1957 and 1959, some 52,000 Jews left the country, thereby bringing the total now left in Poland to barely 30,000, living mostly in Warsaw and a few other cities. From then on, Jewish institutions (a museum, a theatre, a historical institute, publishers, retirement homes, cooperatives, etc.) could also be maintained.

A new crisis in the régime prompted the Polish authorities to try and burnish their threadbare prestige by resorting to extreme anti-Semitic sloganeering and activities. The years 1968–69 saw the disappearance, for all practical purposes, of Poland's remaining Jewish community. As part of a large-scale, at times near-hysterical anti-Semitic smear campaign, Jews were removed from any positions of power they might hold within the state apparatus, including the army, police force and universities. The vast majority were driven to emigrate, but for all that this brought an end to any notable presence of Jews in the country, the Polish public proved obdurate—as it does to this very day—in its obsession with keeping its bizarre 'Jewish Question without Jews' as a live issue. From the 1970s on, 'vulgar' manifestations of political anti-Semitism became increasingly common. Many of the remaining Jewish intellectuals became prominent supporters of KOR, the Committee for the Defense of the Workers, at the time when Solidarity, the independent, self-governing trade union, first emerged in 1980 and during the ensuing period of martial law. They also played a conspicuous role in the political movements leading to the fall of the régime in 1989, and have continued to do so as supporters of the anti-Communist—but also anticlerical—liberal camp in the post-Communist era. Even though the number of Jews left in Poland has shrunk to what is now a negligible 5,000–6,000, the fertile imagination of many Poles (fuelled by the Judaeophobic fantasies of local Catholicism) persist in envisaging the country's Jewry as running into the millions.

In Romania, the genocide was only partial, being suspended at a relatively early stage (in 1943), so that the complete rupture in the continuity of institutionalized Jewish life that occurred elsewhere did not ensue here. Thus, close to two-thirds of Romanian Jews survived this 'local Holocaust.' Therefore, after the country's liberation, they constituted the largest Jewish community in Europe outside the Soviet Union. The new régime, possibly seeking to dissociate itself from its pro-Nazi predecessor, continued to permit emigration for a long time, even after the Communists gained absolute power in 1947–48, though, admittedly, the period of unrestricted egress was interrupted by transitory bans of variable duration, as between 1952 and 1958. Even then Jewish institutions were allowed to carry on their functions undisturbed until around 1959–60. Up till then, 153 officially registered Jewish communities sustained no fewer than 841 synagogues, 67 ritual bathhouses, 86 *kosher* abattoirs, 54 courses providing *Talmud Torah* (religious study), and even a *yeshiva*, an Orthodox institute of higher education founded in Oradea (Nagyvárad) back in 1856. All Jewish schools (of which in 1946 there were still 190, teaching 41,000 pupils) were nationalized in 1948, it is true, but a number of them were still allowed to carry on teaching in Yiddish within the state school system, along with several educational establishments (students' hostels, an agricultural school, three trade schools, etc.) financed by the American Jewish Joint Distribution Committee. In Iasi they even ran a Jewish theatre between 1948 and 1968.

Romania's Communist Party hierarchy may not have taken up Stalin's brutal policy of purging all Jews from its ranks, but it agreed wholeheartedly on the need to annihilate the Zionist movement. Notwithstanding the fact that Zionist bodies had 'voluntarily' wound up their operations in December 1948, trials of several hundred Zionists were mounted in 1954, which was followed by a widespread 'Aryanization' of the power structure. The then dominant, Moscow-backed, Jewish-born foreign secretary, Ana Pauker, had been removed from office in 1952. A fresh wave of 'anti-Zionist' purges took place in 1957, in the course of which many more Jewish functionaries were stripped of their posts. The inconsistencies of Romanian policy became even more glaring during the dictatorship of Ceausescu, from 1965 onwards. The régime demonstrated its relative independence in foreign policy by maintaining good relations with Israel even after the 1967 war, but for 'internal consumption' its increasingly crude and undisguisedly nationalistic propaganda gave voice to xenophobia in general and anti-Semitism in particular.

Far from tailing off, that duality only strengthened after the dictator's fall at the end of 1989. Press freedom, the principal (and possibly only) major innovation brought by the change in régime, opened the way to the printing and distribution of innumerable publications, *România Mare* being foremost amongst them, by blatantly xenophobic and Judaeophobic parties. Those parties also formed the country's governing coalition up to 1996, when they were voted out of office.

The case of Hungary is singular for a number of reasons, although the factors involved were not unrelated to one another.

To begin with, Hungary was the only Communist country to retain a high proportion of survivors of the Shoah (perhaps even a majority, if converts or descendants of mixed marriages, etc. are included) up to the present. Second, cadres of Jewish descent probably made up a larger fraction of the top leadership in the Stalinist régime during its early years than anywhere else, headed by Rákosi, Gerő, Révai and Farkas, the notorious 'four horsemen of the Apocalypse'—to say nothing of the hated as well as feared leaders of the State Security Office (ÁVH/ÁVO). Third and last, Hungary was the only Communist state where the official anti-Semitic party line dictated by Moscow after 1948 was paid lip service but enforced at most only moderately. The number of victims of the few anti-Zionist 'show trials' that were carefully stitched together between 1950 and 1952 was insignificant in comparison to others, persecuted by the régime. The Zionist movement, which 'voluntarily' ceased its operations in March 1950, became equally *non grata* here too, but at least some of its former leaders were eventually permitted to leave the country, whereas others (the more left wing amongst them) could be absorbed without much fuss into the party apparatus. Though the anti-Zionist trials also ended with harsh prison terms (and victims continued to be held in internment camps even after serving their sentences), the movement's leaders stuck in the country were not subjected to the savage persecutions that were the lot of their colleagues in neighboring states. True, the declared goal of the purges unleashed from 1949 onwards was often little more than that of replacing 'bourgeois' (i.e. Jewish) elements who had 'infiltrated' the party with new 'cadres of the people,' but significant areas within the state apparatus (including the press, the direction of the economy, the political police, the network of academic institutions, etc.) remained largely under the supervision of Jewish-born cadres. A high percentage of erstwhile middle-class property owners, forcibly deported from Budapest to resettle in the provinces during the 1950–51 terror campaign against 'class enemies,' had belonged to the Jewish élite. This may largely be explained by the fact that they were living in the most desirable dwellings from the standpoint of Communist expropriators. In any event, the sort of barely disguised anti-Semitic rhetoric, bandied about in Czechoslovakia after the Slánsky trial, or in Poland in 1968, did not occur in Hungary. There were three Jews amongst the eight main defendants in the Rajk trial (1949), Hungary's version of the big, scripted trial, Moscow-style, but anti-Semitic undertones surfaced only negligibly in the case fabricated against them.

Equally, though, some distinguished cadres of Jewish extraction played an important part in preparing the downfall of the Stalinist régime from 1953, whether amongst Imre Nagy's intimates or in the Petőfi Circle (a good number of whose founders came from Jewish background), the press (*Irodalmi Újság*—'Literary News') or the Writers' Union. There were many disillusioned Communists amongst the Jewish intelligentsia, and a high proportion of them assumed leading positions in the intellectual leadership of the 1956 revolution. This could be borne out by their conspicuous overrepresentation amongst the victims of the ensuing reprisals, both those who were executed and sentenced to prison terms. It should be added that the uprising, which in the minds of many at the time was toppling a 'Jewish régime,' was not associated with any major anti-Semitic manifestations in Budapest or other major towns, where most of the actual revolutionary activities took place and most of the country's Jews lived. According to the *White Book*, the Kádár régime's official account of the events, there were no more than a dozen or so incidents of this kind, even in rural areas. Irrespective of that, the silent majority of Hungary's Jews must have found it hard to throw off a sense of fear in 1956, barely 11 years after the trauma of the Shoah. Yet Hungary's own 'Great October Revolution' was, at root, a united popular front across the entire population against the Stalinist repression and foreign domination, an exceptional historical moment that rallied the bulk of politically active Jews and non-Jews alike within a single camp.

A new situation pertained in that respect too after the revolution. Under Kádár's pragmatic rule, the régime likewise strove to avoid playing up the 'Jewish Question.' The initial 'clear-out' of the old apparatus certainly entailed ditching many cadres of Jewish (and other) background who had compromised themselves in the Rákosi era and were thus anyway unpopular and out of use for the régime. At the same time, however, certain portfolios that, from the standpoint of the leadership's 'national' character, could be regarded as sensitive, were entrusted to Jewish cadres known for their relatively liberal views. This was most notably the case of the cultural affairs under György Aczél, one of the longest-lived and unquestionably the most distinguished of the Jewish-born members of the Kádárist *nomenklatura*. The régime pretended that Hungary had overcome its 'Jewish Question,' choosing to ignore the persistence of anti-Semitic attitudes whilst trying to stamp out the occasional manifestations of Judaeophobia cropping up here and there both within and outside the party. This reassured the greater part of the Jewish public, though many talented young Jewish intellectuals (not uncommonly the offspring of former dignitaries) gradually became alienated from the régime, increasingly to the point of breaking connections with it or turning against it. The failure of the 'Prague Spring' and the attempt at domestic economic reform (New Economic Mechanism) launched in the same year (1968) gave the first major impetus for the still small and socially rather isolated opposition circles. They began to be organized during the 1970s as a liberal, anti-Kádárist political force, started an independent *samizdat* press, and instituted drives to collect signatures for protests which also attracted attention in the West.

Out of this emerged a liberal left-wing opposition movement which in 1989 transformed into the Alliance of Free Democrats (SzDSz) and which, after the general elections in 1994 (as well as in 2002) became the junior partner in a coalition government with the Hungarian Socialist Party (MSzP)—the reformed Communist Party. They held power first until 1998 and after the conservative interregnum since Summer 2002. Clashes between 'liberals' and an assortment of nationalist parties in parliament, the press, and other public forums were not infrequently portrayed in terms that suggested a conflict between 'Jewish' and 'Christian' parties—an antithesis invented by right-wing extremists that reminded of the old days of political anti-Semitism. The same alleged opposition, though, had a more ambivalent variant as well. It was traceable back to historical divergences between 'urbanist' and 'populist' (i.e. rural Gentile reformist) intellectuals during the 1930s over their respective visions for the planned future society, political priorities, and their 'sensitivity' to what was termed 'the fate of the nation.' Hungarian political life at present is giving every appearance of regenerating the stereotyped notion (particularly current during the Horthy era) that liberalism is some sort of a foreign import, a 'western' or indeed a 'Jewish' invention.

Anti-Semitism in the West, new and old: a changing balance of forces to fight it

Earlier in this chapter it was noted how, in the wake of the Shoah, the relationship of non-Jews changed not only towards surviving Jews but also towards the whole issue of a Jewish presence in European societies.

As a result, since 1945 public discourse in Western Europe has aired 'issues' relating to Jewry much more thoroughly and, from a Jewish standpoint, more favorably in general than in the East, where consolidating Communist régimes (from the start in the Soviet Union and since 1948 in most satellite countries) transformed it into a more or less taboo subject. The revelation of the appalling atrocities of the Shoah, to which the mass media across Europe (the East included prior to 1948, with the possible exception of the Soviet Union) ensured a wide publicity granted to the 'people of the Shoah' an unprecedented amount of moral capital. Henceforth openly avowed measures of anti-Semitism were ruled out on the part of authorities both in the East (where they were at least mostly disguised in some timely, 'respectable' phraseology) and in the West, where an agreement to fight anti-Semitism as a fundamental moral obligation, became a 'natural' political asset of governing parties and most opposition forces. The former clerically aligned dictatorships, signing up to western democracy only in the recent past (Spain and Portugal), where the historical continuity of Jewish presence had been essentially sundered since the expulsions at the end of the fifteenth century, have done everything in their power to welcome and ensure the security of the small number of Jewish 'returnees,' who have sought to settle there. Along the same line, Jewish emigrants from the Soviet Union and its successor states were accepted often without much reservations in many western democracies, above all in the Federal Germany.

Not that anti-Semitism was in any danger of disappearing. Indeed, the Arab–Israeli conflict, the survival of inherited assets of anti-Jewish phantasmagoria and the uneasy integration of larger aggregates of Jews than previously (albeit still negligible in terms of the total population) in some Western European societies, along with academic and pseudo-academic controversies (specifically the brand of Holocaust denial euphemistically termed 'revisionism') over the historical circumstances of the Shoah, at times supplied new kinds of current-political ammunition as justification for anti-Semitic bombast. European public opinion continues to be scandalized each and every time by reports of desecrated Jewish cemeteries, memorials, and synagogues, assaults (sometimes bloody) on individual Jews.

Thus public manifestations of anti-Semitism—whether in form of prejudices and *ressentiments* against Jews, anti-Jewish discourses or jokes, symbolic violence (like the desecration of cemeteries) or assaults or acts of terror on Jews and Jewish interests—, have indeed not ceased following the defeat of Nazism and the subsequently attested large scale delegitimization of customary Jew-hatred. Opinion polls found in 1991 still a significant proportion of Europeans convinced that 'Jews had too much power in their country,' notably 8 per cent in England, 11 per cent in Russia and Czechoslovakia, 17 per cent in Hungary, 20 per cent in Germany, 26 per cent in Poland and as many as 27 per cent in Austria.

Still, there have been important new developments since the Shoah. The changes can be summarized in this respect under five headings, which will all be touched upon in the following discussion.

First, western states and mainstream political forces refuse henceforth, as a rule, to lend support to anti-Semitism. On the contrary, they do their best, most of the time, to combat its manifestations. Second, dominant public opinions react systematically and often strongly against anti-Jewish occurrences. The organizational sources of such reactions will be dealt with in some detail below. Third, Jews themselves react in an incomparably better organized, consistent and resolute manner than ever before. Fourth, when anti-Semitism persists, it survives mostly under disguises, in coded language, since it is perceived even by its propagators as an odium loaded attitude, having completely lost its earlier 'innocence' of sorts. Fifth, critique of Israeli policies often serve as a convenient camouflage for Jew-hatred. Its political legitimacy or 'correctness' is indeed enhanced by the fact of being shared by many leftist or 'non-Jewish' Jews.

Instances of open political instrumentalization of anti-Semitism has indeed all but disappeared in the West, since right radicalism has been more or less efficiently isolated in the political arena, stigmatized as it has been by ruling parties and excluded from power positions (admitting some exceptions, like in Austria since 2000)—if not always from local government posts. (But this does not apply, as it has been dealt with above, to some of the new democracies of Eastern Europe.) Still, at the end of the twentieth century, many Western countries have legally operating right radical parties combining an openly xenophobic discourse with a more tacitly propagated anti-Jewish one (like the New National Front in Great Britain, *Ordine Nuovo* in Italy, *Vlaams Blok* in Belgium, *Front National, GRECE* in France, *ENEK, EPEN* in Greece, the *Freiheitliche Partei* of Haider in Austria, etc. to name only those having achieved some electoral successes). But the political meaning of such more or less political representations of anti-Semitism up till the most recent years remains ambiguous. In France for example the notoriously xenophobic *Front National* has regularly gathered some 10–15 per cent of the popular vote for the last two decades. This did not prevent the establishment of a quasi general agreement in the French population that 'Jews are real Frenchmen,' the proportion of those accepting this statement having grown from a mere 37 per cent in 1946, to 66 per cent in 1966, to 87 per cent in 1980 and to as much as 94 per cent in 1987. On the contrary, the proportion of those in France professing open antipathy to Jews fell from ten per cent in 1966 to a mere one per cent by 1987.

In the immediate aftermath of the war, anti-Semitism remained, obviously, a burning question in occupied West Germany. Opinion polls commanded by the Allies in 1946 found anti-Jewish attitudes among 40 per cent of the population. De-Nazification could not be carried out without conflicts and resistance. Still in 1952 both the restitution payments to Israel were agreed upon in Luxembourg and the neo-nazi *Sozialistische Reichspartei* outlawed by the federal constitutional tribunal which brought anti-Jewish agitation to a quasi standstill for the following decade. Officially the Federal governments have remained ever since staunchly attached to fundamentally pro-Jewish and pro-Israeli policies, unlike some other western allies. This was certainly not the case of Austria where de-Nazification was botched up or properly eschewed, while both public opinion and the governments of the 'great coalition' (till 1966) continued to keep up the myth of the country's having been 'the first victim of Hitler.'

In France both the conservative (and strongly Catholic) right and the left did their best to stress the importance of the resistance movement and minimize that of collaborationism under the German occupation. Anti-Jewish overtones could not be disregarded in the opposition to Prime Minister Mendès-France (historically the second Jew to hold this position) in 1954. In 1956 the right populist Poujade movement, openly critical of the position of Jews in the state and the economy, earned 11 per cent of votes. But anti-Semitic demagoguery was met with a powerful opposition both in conservative and leftist circles up till the 1967 Six-Day War between Israel and its neighbors. The situation was different in Britain, holding the mandate to administer Palestine. British policies against the birth of Israel were supported by large sectors of public opinion, especially when soldiers of the Royal Army fell victim of Jewish terrorism in the Near East. The dramatic bloody return of SS Exodus (1947) marked the culmination of British policies to forbid Jewish immigration to Palestine, before the proclamation of the Jewish state. But Britain soon became a major economic and political partner of Israel and there were no significant anti-Jewish endeavors or agitation in the country ever since.

A new situation was brought about by the 1967 war, when Israel emerged as the dominant military power of the Near East. The West became henceforth strongly marked by a division between pro-Israeli governments (like Federal Germany, Spain, etc.) and opinions, with demarcation lines inside the Right and the Left, due in part to the position taken by those concerned in the Cold War. General De Gaulle's statement ('The Jews are a domineering élite people') reminded elderly French Jews of nineteenth-century anti-Semitic slogans. For many, Israeli victories ('aggressions') justified or elicited anti-Jewish preconceptions, even if, for others (notably among European Jewry), they proved the 'normalization' of the 'Jewish people' among western democracies ready and capable to defend itself. Many Jews and non-Jews found in Israeli successes the working of immanent historical justice of sorts. But the same sometimes generated sympathies in xenophobic extremist circles as well—which proved to be more anti-

Arab than anti-Jewish in this particular juncture. As a contrast, anti-Zionism started to cover strong anti-Jewish *ressentiments* among leftists in various countries where the New Left had been hitherto reputed to be devoid of anti-Semitic traditions (like in France, Britain, West Germany, the Benelux or Scandinavia).

In Austria the accession of the Jewish-born socialist Bruno Kreisky to the chancellorship provoked a single political conflict, when Simon Wiesenthal, in pursuit of Nazi criminals, proved that four members of the Kreisky cabinet had a Nazi past. In the exacerbated polemics that followed, Kreisky appeared as a defendant of Austria's infamous implication in Nazism, his challengers as 'Zionist trouble-makers' (going as far as nicknaming Wiesenthal a 'Jewish Fascist') who interfered in the country's 'internal affairs.' Kreisky's stand, defending Austria against well founded accusations of Nazi collaborationism, contributed to postpone the debate on the past in the country till the 1980s. A poll of 1974 showed that 70 per cent of Austrians nurtured anti-Semitic feelings. In 1986 the direction of the 'Liberal Party' was taken over by right extremists combining in their program xenophobia and milder forms of Holocaust denial. In 1988, 'memorial year' for the *Anschluss*, the public discussion of Austrian Fascism was overshadowed by charges brought against Kurt Waldheim. The former secretary general of the United Nations and Austrian state president since 1986 was accused by the World Jewish Congress of complicity in crimes against humanity in his youth, as an intelligence officer of the *Wehrmacht* in the Balkans during the war. Some observers suggest that he was reelected president not in spite, but rather because of these compromising revelations. Indeed, if Austria was thus confronted with its historical *Lebenslügen* (existential lies), Jorg Haider's so-called Freedom Party was included for some time in the coalition government after February 2000, after having collected 27 per cent of the popular votes, that is exactly as much as the proportion of self-declared anti-Semites in the country. Austria remains one of the few European societies (together with Poland and Slovakia) where popular anti-Semitism is still widespread.

In Federal Germany an unprecedented anti-Israeli (and partly anti-Jewish) volte-face was staged among leftists who, whether independently from or influenced by the anti-Israeli attitudes of most Communist countries, started to combine their anti-capitalist demagoguery with hardly hidden anti-Jewish agitation (as exemplified in certain films by Fassbinder). A study showed that in 1974 one-fifth of West Germans harbored explicitly and one half latently anti-Jewish convictions. But the political scenery of the 1970s was occupied in Germany by Left Radical terrorism. In 1979 however, the American television film 'Holocaust' made an unprecedented emotional impact on the new generation born after the war. This gave rise to the revival of public and private discussions about the Nazi heritage, leading later, in the 1980s, to the *Historikerstreit* (debate of historians) about the German *Sonderweg* (special road of the modernization of Germany) as well as to the proliferation of scholarly works exploring the years of the Brown Plague and German social history leading to Nazism. All this could not lack to produce at least temporarily a decrease of anti-Semitic attitudes, as testified in opinion polls. But the unification after 1989 revived right extremism thanks to supporters recruited in east German youth. Xenophobic violence often turned into anti-Semitic aggressions in the early 1990s, with the multiplication of desecration of Jewish cemeteries and memorials around 1992. The Republican Party with markedly post-Fascist orientations even scored electoral successes which, to be sure, appear to have been transitory only.

Xenophobic right extremism actually occupied significant political positions in many other West European countries too, but anti-Semitism is only a marginal (France, Italy) or hardly existent element (Denmark, the Netherlands) in their programs, political messages and public proclamations. On the less political than symbolic plane though, most of the West has a hard time getting rid of the reminders of its earlier infection by the Brown Plague.

In Germany, despite—or sometimes because of—the Allied military presence, even de-Nazification of the administration was less than perfect. It is well known that Nazi experts employable in the arms industry were accorded a large measure of protection both in the West and the East, but even lower-ranking Nazi criminals (particularly army officers) were not uncommonly granted tacit immunity. Austria strove for a long time to maintain the fiction that it had been 'Hitler's first victim' in order to avoid domestic political tensions that would have been generated via thorough de-Nazification. A stretch of Vienna's inner-city *Ringstrasse*, to this day, honors the name of Dr Karl Lueger, the city's anti-Semitic mayor, just as a statue to Heinrich von

Treitschke, whose 1879 article provoked the *Antisemitismusstreit* with Mommsen, still stands undisturbed in the forecourt of the old main building of Berlin's Humboldt University. In France, until very recently the official line was to minimize or even deny the fact that the collaborationist French state had played any part in genocide, with the merits of the Gaullist-led resistance being emphasized to the exclusion of all else. Certainly, if post-war purges were massive, spontaneous and not infrequently bloody during the mob rule following liberation, not one Frenchman was brought before the courts on charges of genocide before the trial of the murderous gendarme officer Paul Touvier (1991–94), who for a long time had enjoyed secret but effective protection from Catholic prelates. Even that pales besides the case of Maurice Papon, the sub-prefect for Bordeaux in the Vichy government, who after 1945 was allowed to make an illustrious post-war ministerial career, yet recently convicted for war crimes after an investigation initiated just a few years ago (1997). It took until 1996 before President Chirac at last formally admitted the long-proven complicity of the French state in the persecution of French Jewry.

The continuation of the Near East conflict is feeding latent anti-Jewish sentiments, but also, more importantly, various forms of aggressions. The invasion of Lebanon by Israeli troops in 1982 was often commented by the media and sometimes even by politicians as a 'Jewish aggression against Arabs' even in countries with relatively weak anti-Jewish traditions (like Sweden, Switzerland, the Netherlands, France).

But Muslim or sometimes otherwise motivated (both leftist and rightist) terrorism has proved to be an efficient factor to make Jews and Western governments more concerned than ever about security problems. Jewish institutions must be and indeed are heavily guarded everywhere in Europe. France has experienced since 1978 a number of bomb attacks against synagogues and Jewish businesses. One terrorist assault ended in six dead and 22 injured in 1982. In 1990 the horrendous desecration of the Jewish cemetery in Carpentras together with not less than 372 anti-Semitic incidents in the same year provoked a nation-wide demonstration in defense of Jews. There were several victims (one dead) following the savage assault on the synagogue in Rome as well (1982). Another wave of anti-Semitic aggressions occurred in France as recently as 2002 in the wake of the exacerbation of the Israeli–Arab hostilities.

Holocaust denial (euphemistically called 'revisionism') appears since the 1970s as an international intellectual current laden with vicious anti-Jewish implications. In spite of its being outlawed and legally repressed in several countries, some established intellectuals, including Jewish ones, do not refuse to lend it their authority with various motivations. Freedom of opinion, rejection of judicial settlement of historical questions, hostility to the 'memorialization' of the Shoah, resistance to the scholarly and financial exploitation of tragic memory ('the Holocaust business') are among them. But if contemporary 'revisionism' has leftist roots as well, it mostly belongs to the ideological trading stock of right extremism and is essentially supported by those harboring nostalgia for pre-Second World War old régimes in Central Europe or for Nazi-type movements elsewhere. One of its consequences appears to be the wide-range spread of classical and new anti-Semitic literature published by specialized agencies—the infamous *Protocols* are available by now in most European languages in the East as well as in the West.

Such activities are often linked to and sometimes directly funded by Muslim fundamentalists settled in Europe or engaged in a fight for the ideological control and mobilization of Muslim immigrants in the West. The years of the millennium are overshadowed by the overwhelmingly anti-Israeli reports of the western press on the Near East conflict, which is liable to arouse anti-Jewish attitudes in many circles.

In spite of all this there is no mainstream political movement or party accepting anti-Jewish programs or indeed not ready to oppose public anti-Semitism in the West. Right extremism, anti-Israeli propaganda, public expressions of Jew-hatred are systematically kept under strict control, when possible legally repressed and politically isolated. When Le Pen came out second among all the candidates in the 2002 French presidential elections, the electorate voted overwhelmingly and in unison—whether on the left, the center or the republican right—to block his way to power. When Haider's party took governmental posts in the ruling Austrian coalition in 2000, the European Community went out of its way to disapprove publicly (if only via symbolic boycott measures) this internal development of one of its members. It is expected that political anti-Semitism will be effectively checked and dampened in former sovietized societies as well, once they have joined the Community.

The new balance of forces as to anti-Semitism, globally much more favorable to Jews as compared to the situation before the Shoah, can be explained by a number of new developments, which combined their effects to make it much more difficult than earlier for Judaeophobia to gain acceptance in the general public and state machinery.

In Western Europe a genuine process of collective education was embarked upon at various points of time, through which those societies undertook a thorough scrutiny and revision of their evaluations of the historical presence of Jewry in their midst, even if that process was not free of controversy and in no way minor contradictions.

As has already been remarked, the initiators of that enterprise of popular pedagogy were some of the Christian Churches, for the straightforward reason that they unequivocally bore a large historical responsibility in the spreading of what the French historian, Jules Isaac called in a celebrated book the 'doctrine of contempt' (*L'enseignement du mépris*). Coming to terms with the past, or achieve the indispensable *Vergangenheitsbewältigung*, to adopt the German expression used in conjunction with de-Nazification—a past that for Europe has a heavy freight of anti-Judaism, political and racial anti-Semitism—and clarifying especially its most recent past, including the blight of Nazi crimes and the collaboration with their perpetrators, all this became part of school curriculums and the political culture of every western country. In some cases—as in Germany, for understandable reasons—it became indeed a central part. This effort to 'overcome' or 'surmount' the past, of course, was not a simple process. Nor was it without its sticky patches amongst the general public in countries like Germany, Austria, France, or even Belgium or Norway, for that matter, due to the deep implication of many in those anti-Jewish crimes.

Another major factor in the change of climate is to be sought in the growing strength of, and international recognition accorded to self-organized Jewish movements. They were usually based on the full exploitation of the increased moral capital of Jewry, as well as the above-mentioned lack of confidence towards the Christian world as a whole that gained a hold within Jewry after the war. The bulk of the general public almost everywhere considered these forms of Jewish self-defense as justified. Foremost amongst these has been the Simon Wiesenthal Institute, which, although specialized in the tracking down

of Nazi war criminals, also speaks out against anti-Semitic manifestations of any kind. As a result, the balance between Jews and anti-
Semites as expressed in the mass media, has tipped mostly, when not
always and everywhere, in favor of the Jewish camp during recent
decades in Europe, like elsewhere in the western world—
independently from the controversial evaluation of the conflict in the
Near East.

Equally, though, a whole series of non-Jewish civil organizations
are now prepared to intervene actively on behalf of Jewish interests
whenever the need arises, especially in the West. The anti-Nazi general public perceives the scandal of the Shoah as reflecting a catastrophic failure of societal progress in their own countries, and in
many cases even more directly as a moral shortcoming on their own
part. Whereas prior to 1945 the public had usually reacted to anti-
Semitic provocations with equivocation, studied unconcern, or professions of moral indignation that were weak and obviously inade-
quate as to the gravity of the offences, post-war societies with democratic institutions—and, since 1989, increasingly in Eastern Europe as
well—would regularly stand side by side with local Jewish organizations and their allied international institutions in pugnaciously opposing such views and attitudes, responding to manifestations of anti-
Semitism with denunciations and, if need be, campaigns in the mass
media or, on occasion, calls for boycotts or protest marches. What
Christian (and particularly Judaeophobic) public opinion had formerly
labeled 'Jewish over-sensitivity' now has self-confident Gentile institutional spokesmen in effective, well-financed organizations with
global networks of contacts. The *Ligue des Droits de l'Homme*,
formed in Paris at the end of nineteenth century (1898) to assist in the
defense of the innocent Captain Dreyfus, with local agencies in virtually every country, has been joined by many other institutions of its
kind during the last half century. A major factor in the success of their
activities is the fact that, since December 1948, those engaged in the
fight against racism and anti-Semitism have been able to invoke the
principles of the Universal Declaration of Human Rights adopted by
an overwhelming vote in the General Assembly of the United Nations
(with abstentions only from the Soviet Union, five other Soviet-bloc
states, South Africa, and Saudi Arabia).

New conditions of social integration in the East and West

The switch in public opinion in Europe to what may be rated overall as a philo-Semitic turn of sorts has also been manifested in social relations.

Institutional walls between Jews and non-Jews tend to disappear, or to be receding, in all domains—in schooling, on sports grounds and playgrounds, in the wedding market, in professional bodies, in friendly and neighborly contacts, etc. One of the few palpable testaments to that is the hitherto unprecedented rise in the frequency of Judaeo–Christian marriages throughout Europe, both West and East, where pertinent data are collected. Even as early as in the decade from 1965 to 1975, it could be established that a majority, or a ratio very close to that, of all Jewish men and women were wedding a non-Jewish spouse, more specifically (in decreasing order): Soviet Estonia, 77 per cent; Germany, 76 per cent; Denmark, 75 per cent; the Netherlands, 61 per cent; Austria and Soviet Lithuania, 61 per cent; Italy, Soviet Latvia, and Ukraine, 52 per cent; France, 49 per cent; the Soviet Union as a whole, 48 per cent; Soviet Belorussia, 45 per cent; and Poland, 42 per cent.

These indicators are known to reflect a huge diversity of local demographic and social factors that there is no space to analyze here, but they still have enormous significance. They imply that the social integration of Jews is being much more fully accomplished henceforth than ever before in the very domain where resistance to this used to be the strongest on both sides: in the intimate sphere, the choice of kinship relations and the physical reproduction of families. This happened even in societies which previously practically ruled out similar miscegenation and integration (like Poland, for one). In some circles within these societies, opting for a Jewish partner became even a matter of straight preference. Playing a part in that was the aforementioned enhanced moral prestige of the people of the Shoah, but likewise all the processes of group psychological revaluation through which the symbolic balance of forces inherent in relations between Jews and non-Jews were revised to the benefit of Jews.

It should be remarked, moreover, that this rather positive image of Jews, as expressed in the frequency of mixed marriages, involved in most of the countries mentioned only a small fraction of the general population, given the small (and in most Eastern European countries, in historical terms, a tragically near-negligible) demographic presence of Jews. More importantly, the ever tighter integration of survivors into certain segments of the societies in question has not, however, ruled out the persistence of exclusionist tendencies, or even anti-Semitic attitudes, within other segments, as attested to above.

Projections of what applies to the distribution of marriages can also be discerned in other areas of acculturation and assimilation of Jewry: these processes, manifold in their complexity, became far-advanced throughout Europe during the decades after the Shoah. Here, just three elements, albeit significant ones, in this composite phenomenon will be touched on: linguistic and cultural integration, the improvement in school qualifications, and the expansion of social and occupational opportunities (mobility). (There is no room, however, to discuss other, no less important processes, such as the previously unequalled concentration of survivors in towns or the various demographic strategies of modernization in terms of birth control, reducing the ratio of illegitimate childbirths, the dispersion of residential options or re-clustering in new residential districts, etc.)

Linguistic and cultural assimilation of native-born Jewry into local society had been virtually completed everywhere in Western Europe much before the Shoah, with at most only recent immigrant groups (and perhaps only the more elderly amongst those at that) not as yet included. Unlike in America, it was exceptional to encounter there—in a few big cities, such as Amsterdam, Antwerp, and tightly bounded areas of London and Paris—the phenomenon of voluntary 're-ghettoization,' whereby Yiddish or, in even rarer cases, other vernaculars that had been adopted by old Jewish communities (e.g. within certain Hasidic communities of Hungarian origin in Antwerp) still lived on, for a while, in everyday use, usually alongside the national language, or that of the local majority society.

That was not the case everywhere in Eastern Europe. There, the shift from Yiddish (or Ladino in the Balkans) to the state language, or one of the majority languages, had only been accomplished in countries where assimilation had started relatively early on (Hungary, Bohemia and Moravia, Transylvania). Equally, the rapid closedown of the Jewish school system and cultural institutions in the Soviet Union after 1935 forced an ever larger proportion of

Yiddish-speaking Jewry to switch to using Russian or Ukrainian. By the 1960s, the Soviet authorities felt able to reject requests for Jewish schools to be allowed to reopen on the grounds that there was insufficient demand for them.

Romania was one of the few countries that, by the time of the Second World War, still harbored a large Yiddish-speaking population in Moldavia, Bukovina, and Bessarabia (as well as scattered Ladino-speakers in Wallachia) and for which we also have information about subsequent patterns of language use within the surviving Jewish communities. These data too indicate a rapid relegation of Yiddish, at least as the primary language. The numbers declaring Yiddish as their mother tongue dropped from 50 per cent in 1930 to 23 per cent by 1956 amongst Jewish town dwellers, and from 81 per cent to 48 per cent in rural areas. (The decrease reached 32 per cent there by 1966). By 1966, only 757 Yiddish speakers (in all likelihood elderly) were still living in Romanian villages, as compared with the 108,000 suggested by the 1930 statistics. It seems likely that the thinning (and ageing) of the ranks of those speaking Jewish dialects in Romania reflected above all the selective impact of emigration. Those leaving after 1945, mainly for Israel, tended to belong to the younger generations of the most traditionalist groups—maintaining Yiddish—, whereas the more acculturated Jews obviously had a head start when it came to fitting into the Communist apparatus (initially supplying a core of its old guard). The more elderly (who would in any event be the staunchest custodians of the traditional vernacular) would find it much harder to cut the ties with their native land and their homes.

As far as educational levels were concerned, all available indicators confirm that Jews in both Western and Eastern Europe continued to making the most of the cultural capital provided through the school system. The same shift in favor of Jews over non-Jews in the ratios of those achieving higher levels of qualifications was seen after 1945 as before. Here the completion of 13 years or more of schooling, which corresponds to the study period usually needed for an individual to be ready to commence university training, will be taken as the criterion for assessing educational disparities between Jews and non-Jews. It should be pointed out first, however, that the statistics used here do not all apply to the same point in time, nor do they make any allowance for variables of demography, social stratification, urbanization,

etc. that play an important part in determining chances of school success. Nevertheless, the data tell us that in 1970 40 per cent of Jews in
the Soviet Union had completed at least 13 years of schooling, as
compared with 6 per cent for the population as a whole; in Romania in
1966 it was 18 per cent, as against 2 per cent, in Italy in 1956, 45 per
cent, as against 11 per cent; in France between 1972 and 1976, 26 per
cent amongst Jews of European extraction and 19 per cent amongst
those of African background, as against 6 per cent in the general
population. In Hungary the comparable but not quite identical proportions (those with post-secondary schooling) were 55 per cent for Jews
and 25 per cent for the general population in Budapest in 1999. Disparities relating to national origin were, incidentally, also significant
within Israel itself, where even in 1980 as many as 30 per cent of Jews
of American or European origin had completed at least 13 years of
schooling, as compared with 10 per cent amongst those of African
origin, and 8 per cent of the Israeli non-Jewish population.

Those findings are not so surprising when the processes expressed
in the long-term overrepresentation of Jews in the school systems of
Europe, as discussed above, are borne in mind. In some countries
(including Hungary) that trend towards 'over-schooling' intensified
even further amongst survivors due, among other things, to the selective impact of losses in that the relatively more highly educated Jewish
strata living in the capital were hit relatively less hard by the Shoah
than those in the provinces.

Educational capital, however, was just one factor—albeit one of
constantly growing weight—among conditions of upward social mobility towards the educated middle classes and economic, political,
and cultural élites in the ever more speedily transforming societies and
developing economies of both Eastern and Western Europe. The specifics of the circumstances of Jewish socio–economic integration after
emancipation have already been discussed in Chapter 3. The Shoah
helped remove any last remaining obstacles (which were not large, even
before the war) that may have stood in the way of appropriately qualified Jewish groups advancing into positions of Western Europe's ruling
élites. In sovietized Eastern Europe, meanwhile, liberation in 1945 was
followed by a genuinely revolutionary transformation in regard to the
social status of surviving Jews. Here, as has been noted, the traditionally
rigid, 'bipolar' structure of the pre-war ruling strata (outside the Soviet

Union and the Republic of Czechoslovakia) had largely excluded Jews from civil service, publicly owned industries, administrative and political power positions. The change in the East was for Jews a double one. On the one hand the abolition of private enterprise made the Jewish bourgeoisie (the petty one included) properly déclassé. On the other hand it opened up all the hitherto closed doors to civil service positions to Jews regarded as 'politically reliable.'

Before looking at the main components of the changes that occurred, however, it is worth illustrating, with the help of a simple indicator, the general pace at which opportunities for greater social mobility of survivors opened up the new and old élites of a Europe divided by the Cold War. The basis of comparison is formed by the proportions within the Jewish and non-Jewish populations represented by élite categories, comprising a variety of social and professional groups with leadership functions (intellectuals, liberal professionals, managers in the economy, high-ranking political officials). In Italy between 1965 and 1971, 26 per cent of working-age Jews were in such posts, as compared with 8 per cent of non-Jews; in Switzerland in 1970, 40 per cent, as against 13 per cent; in France between 1972 and 1976, 49 per cent, as against 22 per cent; in Yugoslavia in 1971, 54 per cent, as against 15 per cent. A similarly marked overrepresentation of Jews was observable within the élite circles of other Eastern European countries as well, but very few objective data are available to demonstrate that. In Romania's centrally administered economy for example as many as 59 per cent of Jews were in 'managerial' posts or pursued intellectual or other liberal occupations in 1966, as contrasted with 12 per cent in the entire work force. A recent Hungarian survey (1999) sets at 26 per cent the proportion of leading intellectuals and executives among Jews as compared to 12 per cent of the population in Budapest (where the large majority of Hungarian Jews are residents). Differences appear to be far more limited—16 per cent among Jews and 12 per cent in the general public of the Hungarian capital city—as to entrepreneurs and independent craftsmen or shopkeepers. For the Soviet Union and its successor states the disproportionate presence of Jews among the academic personnel could be recorded since the inter-war years—with the only eclipse in the early 1950s. Up to 1975 Jewish students achieved scholarly positions in academic institutions approximately twice as often as non-Jews. Among those in research graduates with the highest degrees (academic doctors and 'candidates') represented also the double of the proportion of non-Jews with equivalent qualifications up till 1987.

In interpreting these crude, overly composite data, one has to bear in mind, alongside other factors, the occupational selection that drove the emigration of Jews from Soviet-type countries and their immigration into western democracies. It stands to reason that those who occupied the best posts, or had the most promising career prospects in socialist régimes were much more likely to stay on in their jobs than Shoah survivors from the pre-war bourgeoisie and intelligentsia, who had been robbed or stripped of their properties and were now subject to persecution. Apart from the effect of emigration, however, one also needs to recall the essentially new conditions that pertained in regard to the social advancement of Jews in Eastern Europe, which, with specific local variations in some places, reproduced the principles of a new kind of distribution of opportunities for social advancement that the Bolsheviks had already introduced a generation previously when they grabbed power in Russia.

Communism and Jewry

Communism, in effect, brought into play two kinds of diametrically opposed mechanisms—one set negative or inhibitory, the other positive or stimulatory—with respect to the occupational restratification of Jews. The set of relevant mechanisms alternated at different stages in Moscow's rule, and at various junctures in the political and economic development of countries concerned.

Leaving specifically anti-Semitic policies aside for the moment, Communist régimes, from the moment they had consolidated their hold on power, set about (or completed) the dismantling and declassing of the old régime's ruling strata *in toto* and the middle classes in part. For many Jewish survivors, therefore, heavily over-represented as 'independent' bourgeois elements (entrepreneurs, liberal professionals, artisans, and traders, even though most of them were living in rather modest circumstances), the 'construction of socialism' was often nothing short of an economic disaster. All Communists régimes very speedily, from 1948 (or earlier) onwards, implemented radical programs of expropriation and nationalization of private estates, properties, invested assets, extended even to the bulk of the smallest businesses. The breaking of the former class power of the 'bourgeoisie' not only meant financial ruin for many surviving Jews, but also saddled their children and other members of their families with a black mark in their personal files. Those affected might find that pensions or social assistance could be arbitrarily withdrawn, their family ejected from their town apartment (or at least compelled to share it), their children unable to gain admission even to secondary school, let alone university, the boys being drafted into forced labor battalions instead of called up to normal military service, etc. The relatively large middle-class stratum amongst Jewish survivors, therefore, suffered the full weight of the drawbacks and odium of the 'intensification of the class struggle,' especially under Stalin's rule in the late 1940s and the early 1950s.

On top of that, of course, official anti-Semitism often had its own additional, frequently distressing consequences inside the Soviet bloc from the standpoint of cadres of Jewish descent integrated in the *nomenklatura*. The purges of Jews (and veritable 'Aryanization' of the top political leadership) carried out in the Soviet Union after 1948, or in Czechoslovakia after 1952, accompanied sometimes by *Numerus Clausus*-type restrictive measures on university admission, were certainly in that spirit, even if they were only ever partial, ambivalent, and usually covert in character. For one thing, the purges tended to affect the highest levels of the political leadership, rather than lower cadres (with the possible exception of Poland in 1968). Second, even bodies at the highest levels of the hierarchy were not purged of all those of Jewish descent whenever the opportunity arose. Kaganovich and others kept their positions even at the height of the Stalinist terror against Jews, as did Hungary's 'four horsemen' (up to 1956), though admittedly the latter compensated by offering up numerous others as sacrificial scapegoats (for instance, Gábor Péter, head of the secret police). Thirdly, the 'Aryanization' process, as carried out in practice—for instance, when Kádár dismantled the Stalinist old guard in Hungary, or Ceausescu abandoned Romania's slavish adherence to the Soviet party line in favor of neonationalist dictatorship—had 'softer' versions. Though many officials of Jewish background may indeed have been removed from the most visible top-level positions (in the army, the party center, or the diplomatic corps), they were often transferred to other posts in the press and cultural or academic life. The Polish 'Aryanization' process, however, assumed such a massive scale, and was carried out at such a pitch of hysteria, that most Jews felt they had no option but to emigrate.

Taken together, these facts point to a conclusion that most Jewish survivors of the horrors of the Shoah and remaining in Eastern Europe faced mounting difficulties in getting along through social and occupational integration. The reality was considerably more complex than that, however, especially for those in countries that had been liberated by the Red Army. The sweeping away of the old régime's anti-Jewish laws created a new and, from the standpoint of the chances it gave Jews to assert themselves, unprecedentedly favorable situation in at least four respects.

First of all, as already noted, the ending of occupational restrictions gave Jewish survivors, for the first time in history, the opportunity to gain admission to posts in the government power structure and public services (the army, the police, high administrative offices, politics). This was indeed a new start for many, since most Eastern and Central European states almost uniformly—with the Czechoslovak Republic and possibly the Kingdom of Yugoslavia during the inter-war period as the only notable exceptions—operated a 'dual structure' arrangement for élite posts. That brought to a formal close the centuries-long process of Jewish emancipation that previously had seemed unlikely to be realized entirely in this region.

Yet this final liberation from the former obstacles to getting ahead in life occurred within a framework of Communist reform of the machinery for selection and training of the new élites, with the result that in countries that were still far from completely secularized (in other words, countries like Hungary, where the 'Jewish Question' had been one of the touchstones for the internal division of élites) the new power was widely perceived by the general public in the stereotyped image of a 'Jewish domination' or a 'Jewish régime.' To put it in more general terms, all the trumps that had previously been valid for gaining entry to positions of authority—being 'well-born' (a scion of noble or educated middle-class or liberal professional parents), having inherited wealth (especially land or property), Christian background, contacts or family relations amongst traditional élites (aristocracy, government officials, etc.), and conformism to the corresponding ideological and ethical standards—all this did not merely lose their value in the new régime but suddenly acquired a fundamentally negative signification. The erstwhile assets became seriously 'counterproductive' liabilities in regard to a person's chances of being admitted into the new élite. The selection criteria to be met for entry into the Communist power structure were mostly of the opposite color, whether in regard to class background (proletarian or peasant birth, poor parents, absence of property), or in regard to one's 'political capital' (membership of the pre-war left wing or opposition, proof of activity in the labor movement, a Communist political culture, and unconditional acceptance of 'socialist values').

The important thing here was that, in this revolutionary transformation, a Jewish origin became, at least tacitly, temporarily or conditionally, an important asset for acceding to the *nomenklatura*. For the small numbers of adult Jews, left in Central and Eastern Europe after the Shoah, their origin now assured them a distinctive political capital in the process of building up new élites, and for a variety of reasons, even if these were largely transient and tended to disappear or be neutralized later on.

To begin with, Jewish survivors could demonstrably be counted as 'natural enemies' of the overthrown régimes, and that served equally as a guarantee of their 'political reliability' for the leadership of Party-states (at least in the absence of evidence to the contrary, such as the aforementioned black mark of being from a compromisingly 'bourgeois background'). At the same time, Jews were expected, made to feel almost 'obliged' as it were, to give their support to a state whose military midwives had given them deliverance from mortal danger. Unquestionably, the anti-Semitism of the old régimes (again with due respect to the Czechoslovak and Balkan exceptions) prompted many survivors to throw heart and soul behind the new order. They were duly motivated by the fact that, in contrast even to earlier, consolidated versions of the vanished old régimes, not only did Communism formally not propagate anti-Semitic views, they actually made a stand (at least nominally) against such. Bolshevik rhetoric and to some extent even Communist politics was explicitly based on anti-Fascism, ethnic and religious equality, and eradicating social differences of every kind. Due to the murderous course of the perpetrators of the Shoah and their accomplices the telling Judaeophobic phantom of 'Judaeo-Bolshevism' really did seem to come to pass, insofar as in the early days of the new régime 'Jewishness' acted as an effective aggregator for the 'primitive accumulation' of political capital.

Second, many of those who had been persecuted by Nazism were all the more inclined to make use of that 'political capital,' sometimes even when the ideology of Communist dictatorship was totally alien to them, because it provided a means of gaining recompense, and even judicial redress, for the horrendous wrongs they had suffered. Hence the species of 'emotional Communism' felt by many who, in other respects—being subject to expropriation and loss of social status and regarded as 'class enemies,' 'nonpersons'—could have no interest in common with the régime. The trauma of Nazism at some level, even if it was not necessarily consciously admitted by those involved, placed more than a few such 'objective enemies' of Communism into the ranks of the régime's covert sympathizers. The Stalinist terror machine itself applied that abolition of inequalities of ethnic affiliation, race or creed within the ranks of its own persecutees. In prisons and in the Gulag, amongst inmates of internment camps, forced residents resettled from cities to remote villages, Jewish victims endured the tyranny of egalitarian dictatorship alongside non-Jews. Some of them, with a due sense of irony, may even have seen it as a form of symbolic elevation of status. Members of the erstwhile Jewish bourgeoisie (former entrepreneurs or renters) could now find themselves sharing the same Communist 'Jewish bench,' in an odd 'community of fate' as it were, with high officials of the old régime, divested aristocrats, and former Fascists. For that very reason, ironically enough, even under oppressions of this kind, Jewish victims of Communism may have recorded a secret satisfaction, and booked it to the régime's 'credit' column, that this time at least they were not distinguished in the persecution for being Jewish.

Third, for a portion of surviving Jews an important part in winning them over to Communism was played by the initial desperate lack of well-trained cadres, fit for leadership roles in the new régimes. Stalinist high councils, for obvious reasons, could not trust officials who had served in the old public administration. The latter were thus quickly removed, at least a portion of them, though many of them departed of their own accord anyway and left the country, whether just temporarily or for good, often enough with the columns of German forces on their retreat from the collaborationist states of Eastern Europe. Before the new régimes were able to train up their own body of cadres, then, survivors of the Shoah supplied a by no means negligible portion of the human resources indispensable to accomplishing the political about-turn. Their far higher-than-average qualifications, their management experience (which many had gained in their earlier occupations), their high political motivation (often a well-nigh religious commitment to the 'liberating' régime), and often a well-tested labor-movement discipline (loyalty to the 'party line' and willingness to follow instructions from 'above') made Jewish cadres virtually ideal candidates for Stalinist bureaucracies. Their only 'shortcoming' was one and the same as the tacit positive reason for their promotion: the fact that they were Jews might reinforce the undesirable image of the new establishment to be far too 'Jewish' in the minds of the masses. It was on this account that anti-Jewish purges (albeit officially directed against 'infiltrated bourgeois elements') commenced at a fairly early stage in the so-called people's democracies, even in cases (Hungary, for example) where leaders of Jewish extraction held supreme power, even during the first years of the thaw.

There was a price to be paid for 'entry into Communism,' however, perhaps most notably in the obligatory dissimulation of Jewish identity that it required. If a Jew had ambitions to gain a high official post, he or she had to be prepared to cover up every least sign of Jewish links, sentiments, and identification. Admittedly, that was not hard for many of them, given that they (especially those with a past in left-wing movements) had always displayed a large measure of indifference to the particularistic values of Judaism and not infrequently already long taken the path of 'national' and/or 'universalistic' (i.e. liberal or left-wing) assimilation. There were also some—the genuinely 'rootless' of the Shoah—for whom the transition from the traditional world of Jewry into the community of the party movement was equivalent to a form of 'second liberation.' The experience of severing traditional bonds ('stepping out of the ghetto') was for them the 'icing' on the cake of throwing off the Nazi yoke, so to say. In the same time the identification with Communism was necessarily accompanied by a poignant sense of achievement on finding a new community. This gave dissimulation on the part of Communist Jews an unparalleled robustness. Those who belonged to that generation often kept even their children in ignorance about their origins, not uncommonly concealing the real reason for the early disappearance of forebears and other relatives, possibly representing victims of the Shoah, in the approved Stalinist manner, as mere casualties of the anti-Fascist struggle...

Jewish cadres who felt they were compromised by the network of social contacts of their past were often obliged to adopt a strategy of twofold concealment, covering up their Jewishness on the one hand, and their 'bourgeois' background on the other. The staggering outcomes that were sometimes the product of such compulsive behavior could often only be sustained with the complicity of the powers in their milieu. In this manner, the son of a landowner might be transmogrified, on his files, into a 'peasant lad,' the offspring of a deceased entrepreneur into someone 'of working-class origin.' These pressures began to recede during the 1960s only.

Concluding remarks

The social history of European Jewry has not come to an end with the close of the last century. Notwithstanding the frightful destruction wrought by the Nazis, the forced assimilation pursued in the Soviet bloc, the assimilatory potency of western democracies, and the neutralizing impact of globalization on historical particularism of any kind, that process has acquired additional new dimensions ever since in the post-Shoah era, as well as it continues to form a playing field for near-atavistic, centuries-old challenges that were long (at least since the Shoah) thought to have been surmounted. A number of those new dimensions have already been mentioned in earlier discussions about the appearance of Israel, the trauma of survival (and avoidance of its resurfacing amongst descendants), and the new opportunities for reformulating identity options.

In this context reference could equally have made to the singular chances to evolve that a multiculturally conceived Europe opens up for the experience of Jewishness and, more generally, for group identities based on this type of 'obligation to remember.' In that perspective the homogenizing norms of identity of national statehood, set in stone back in the nineteenth century, are condemned to weaken and, perhaps, at some point to become obsolescent. Drawing the contradictory consequences of all that, certain commentators have talked about the disappearance of the historical sense of Jewish identity in recent decades. This could occur either through those concerned attaining the ultimate stage of assimilation, which—specifically with mixed marriages becoming the rule—may lead to a rapid extinction of a sense of Jewish 'otherness,' or by their professing a militant dissimilation (for instance, demanding the status of an ethnic minority, or perhaps emigrating to Israel), and thereby tearing up the social contract that binds them to majority societies. Yet even so, primitive anti-Semitic passions, and sometimes their political instrumentalization as well (and not necessarily just in former Communist states either), will still be prominent amongst the challenges, new and old.

The future is thus still an open question, but only as a continuation of the past. From many points of view, though, the events that I have attempted to sum up and analyze here cannot be considered merely as belonging to the past. The narrator steps outside the role of scientific detachment that he has imposed upon himself up to now, when he recalls that the past continues to live, not only in our memories and dreams, but also in our thinking, our reflexes, our gestures, out habits, our tastes and our postures. If the body of facts disclosed in this book has any function beyond its narration, it must primarily be that of serving a warning.

Certain aspects of the historical reality of Jewry are still shrouded by profound suspicion, distorted by myths and fixed ideas carried over from the past. Many even now, for instance, in this day and age, take such figments of the imagination as beliefs in a Jewish world conspiracy. Some still consider seriously the blood libel of ritual murder calumnies. There are politicians, publishers, and those responsible for other mass media products who do not shrink from spreading those beliefs. Equally, they often have a false picture about Zionism, the coercive conditions of a commitment to Communism, the nature of religious traditionalism or assimilation, depending on what particular political culture, tradition of self-identity, and choice of historical identity they have inherited. And then there is the constant presence, once and for all time, of that 'passion' of European Jewry, as pictured by a Hungarian poet, the Catholic János Pilinszky: 'the butcher-boys may wash themselves down, though somehow what happened still cannot come to an end.'

As we have seen, the ethical and political balance of forces throughout Europe since the Shoah has evolved more favorably for Jews than ever before. Despite that, one cannot, and therefore should not, suppose that all danger of a destructive reaction to Jewish 'otherness' has passed. Even if the poison-fangs of the 'Christian Question,' which has historically exerted such a baleful influence, have essentially been drawn by the Catholic Church's *aggiornamento*, the headway being made by the ecumenical movement, and the gradual secularization of European societies, some of the functional models of anti-Semitism outlined above still continue to operate. Although the norms of constitutionality are asserted ever more vigorously, at least in the western parts of our continent, providing a degree of security and freedom probably greater than ever before for carriers of particularistic group identities, like Jews, that does not apply everywhere by any means.

Is there any need for me to emphasize that not only does the past projected ahead into the future exist inside us, but each and every one of us, day by day, constitutes, constructs and, in cases, reproduces the components of that past? Hence our historical responsibility in Jewish matters—and that concern obviously first and foremost non-Jews—to our fellow contemporaries, to future generations and also to the victims of the Shoah to whom this book has striven to do justice in its own way, thanks to objectivist tools of social history.

Selected Bibliography for Further Reading

Specialized journals on problems of Jewish social history

American Jewish Yearbook.
Studies in Contemporary Jewry. An Annual. (New York, Oxford, since 1985)
The Jewish Journal of Sociology (London)
Jewish Social Studies (Indiana, new series since 1994)
East European Jewish Affairs (London, since 1970, continuation of *Soviet Jewish Affairs*)
Jews in Eastern Europe (Jerusalem, new series since 2000)
Jewish Culture and History (University of Southampton, since 1998)
Patterns of Prejudice (London)

Basic sources, compendia and comprehensive surveys

BARON, Salo Wittmayer, *A Social and Religious History of the Jews*, 17 vols. New York, 1952.
BENBASSA, Esther, ATTIAS Jean-Christophe, *Les Juifs ont-ils un avenir?* Paris, 2001.
BEN SASSOON, Haim, (ed.), *A History of the Jewish People.* Cambridge, 1976.
DUBNOW, Simon, *An Outline of Jewish History*, 3 vols. 1925.
Encyclopedia Judaica, 16 vols. Jerusalem, 1971. (Now available in reprint edition and as CD.)

FINKELSTEIN, L. (ed.), *The Jews, Their History, Culture and Religion*, 2 vols. New York, 1960.

JOHNSON, Paul, *A History of the Jews*, London, 1987.

TRIGANO, Shmuel, (ed.), *La société juive à travers l'histoire*, 4 vols. Paris, 1993.

KOTOWSKI, Elke-Vera, SCHOEPS, Julius, WALLENBORD, Hiltrud, (ed.), *Handbuch zur Geschichte der Juden in Europa*, I.–II. Darmstadt, 2001.

Surveys of regions, particular periods and topics

DELLA PERGOLA, Sergio, *La trasformazione demographica della diaspora ebraica*. Turin, 1983.

DON, Yehuda, KARADY, Victor, (eds.), *A Social and Economic History of Central European Jewry*, New Brunswick, NJ., 1990.

ENDELMAN, Todd M., (ed.), *Jewish Apostasy in the Modern World*, New York, London, 1987.

KATZ, Jacob, (ed.), *Towards Modernity*. New Brunswick, 1987.

MENDELSOHN, Ezra, *The Jews of East Central Europe between the World Wars*. Bloomington, 1983.

RUPPIN, Arthur, *Soziologe der Juden*. 2 vols. Berlin, 1930.

SACHAR, Howard M., *The Course of Modern Jewish History*. New York, 1990.

VITAL, David, *A People Apart. The Jews in Europe, 1789–1939*. New York, 1999.

Anti-Semitism

BERDING, Helmut, *Moderner Antisemitismus in Deutschland*. Frankfurt am Main, 1988.

BERMANN, Werner, ERB, Rainer, (ed.), *Antisemitismus in der politischen Kultur nach 1945*, Opladen, 1990.

BUNZL, Jon and MARIN, Bernd, *Antisemitismus in Österreich. Sozialhistorische und soziologischer Studien*. Innsbruck, 1983.

FISCHER, Rolf, *Entwicklungsstufen des Antisemitismus in Ungarn, 1867–1939*. Munich, 1988.

POLIAKOV, Léon, *The History of Anti-Semitism*, 8 vols. New York & Oxford, 1979.

PULZER, Peter, *The Rise of Political Anti-Semitism in Germany and Austria*. Cambridge, Mass., 1988.

STRAUSS, Herbert A., KAMPE, Norbert, (ed.), *Antisemitismus. Von der Judenfeindschaft zum Holocaust*. Bonn, 1984.

STERNHELL, Zeev, *La droite révolutionnaire, 1885–1914. Les origines françaises du fascisme*. Paris, 1979.

Nazism and the Shoah

BRAHAM, Randolph L., *The Destruction of Hungarian Jewry: a Documentary Account*, 2 vols. New York, 1963.

GOLDHAGEN, Daniel Jonah, *Hitler's Willing Executioners: Ordinary Germans and the Holocaust*. New York, 1996.

HILBERG, Raul, *The Destruction of the European Jews*, revised ed., 3 vols. New York, 1985.

LAQUEUR, Walter, (ed.), *The Holocaust Encyclopaedia*, New Haven, 2001.

POLLACK, Michael, *L'expérience concentrationnaire. Essais sur le maintien de l'identité sociale*. Paris, 1990.

YAHIL, Leni, *The Holocaust, the Fate of European Jewry, 1932–1945*. New York & Oxford, 1990.

Zionism

AVINERI, Shlomo, *The Making of Modern Zionism*. London, 1981.

HAUMANN, Heiko, (ed.), *Der Traum von Israel. Die Ursprünge des modernen Zionis*mus. Weinheim, 1998.

LAQUEUR, Walter, *A History of Zionism*. New York, 1989.

VITAL, David, *The Origins of Zionism*. 1975.

Austria

BELLER, Steven, *Vienna and the Jews, 1867–1938: A cultural history*. Cambridge, 1989.

BOTZ, Gerhart, OXAAL, Ivar and POLLACK, Michael, (eds.), *Jews, Anti-Semitism and Culture in Vienna*, London and New York, 1987.

FREIDENREICH, Pass, *Jewish Politics in Vienna 1918–1938*, Bloomington, 1991.

HÖDL, Klaus, *Als Bettler in die Leopoldstadt. Galizische Juden auf dem Weg nach Wien*. Wien, 1994.

McCAGG, William O., *A History of Habsburg Jews, 1670–1918*. Bloomington, 1989.

ROZENBLIT, Marsha L., *The Jews of Vienna 1867–1914: Assimilation and Identity*. Albany, 1983.

WISTRICH, Robert S., *The Jews of Vienna in the Age of Franz Joseph*. Oxford, 1989.

Balkans

BENBASSA, Esther, RODRIGUE, Aron, *The Jews of the Balkans : the Judeo–Spanish Community, 15th–20th Centuries*. Oxford, 1995.

BAROUH, Emmy, (ed.), *Jews in the Bulgarian Lands. Ancestral Memory and Historical Destiny*. Sofia, 2001.

ESKENAZI, Jacques, KRISPIN, Alfred, (eds.), *Jews in the Bulgarian Hinterland. An Annotated Bibliography*. Sofia, 2002.

FREIDENREICH, H. Pass, *The Jews of Yugoslavia, a Quest for Community*. Philadelphia, 1979.

LOKER, Zwi, *History of the Jews of Yugoslavia*, I–II. Jerusalem, 1991.

TAMIR, Vicki, *Bulgaria and her Jews : the History of a Dubious Symbiosis*. New York, 1979.

VEINSTEIN, Gilles, *Salonique 1850–1918. La "Ville des Juifs" et le réveil des Balkans*. Paris, 1992.

Benelux

Studia Rosenthaliana (since 1967)

SCHREIBER, Jean-Philippe, *L'immigration juive en Belgique du moyen âge à la première guerre mondiale*. Bruxelles, 1996.

MISCHMAN, Joseph, BEEM, Hartog, MICHMAN, Dan, *Pinkas. Geschiedenis van de joodse gemeenschap in Nederland*. Antwerpen, 1992.

Czechoslovakia

The Jews in Czechoslovakia. Historical Studies and Surveys, 3 vols. Philadelphia, 1968–1984.

COHEN, Gary, *The Politics of Ethnic Survival: Germans in Prague, 1861–1914*. Princeton, 1981.

IGGERS, Wilma, (ed.), *Die Juden in Böhmen und Mähren. Ein historisches Lesebuch*. Munich, 1986.

KIEVAL, Hillel J., *The Making of Czech Jewry: National Conflict and Jewish Society in Bohemia, 1870–1918*. Oxford, 1988.

SEIBT, Ferdinand, (ed.), *Die Juden in den Böhmischen Ländern*. München, 1983.

WLASCHEK, Rudolph M., *Juden in Böhmen*. Munich, 1990.

France

BECKER, Jean-Jacques, WIEVIORKA, Annette, (eds.), *Histoire des Juifs de France de la Révolution francaise à nos jours*. Paris, 1998.

BENBASSA, Esther, *Histoire des Juifs de France*. Paris, 1997.

BENSIMON, Doris, DELLA PERGOLA, Sergio, *La population juive de France : Socio–démographie et identité*. Jerusalem, 1984.

BLUMENKRANZ, Bernard, *Histoire des Juifs en France*. Toulouse, 1972.

HYMAN, Paula, *The Jews of Modern France*. Berkeley, 1998.

MARRUS, Michael, *The Politics of Assimilation: a Study of the French Jewish Community at the Time of the Dreyfus Affair*. Oxford, 1971.

PHILIPPE, Béatrice, *Être juif dans la société française du Moyen Age à nos jours*. Paris, 1979.

SCHWARZFUSS, Simon, *Du juif á l'israélite. Histoire d'une mutation, 1770–1870*. Paris, 1989.

Germany

Leo Baeck Institute, Year Book. (London, since 1955.)

GILCHRIST, Sylvia, PAUKER, Arnold, SUCHY, Barbara, (ed.), *Die Juden im Nazionalsozialistischen Deutschland, 1933–1943*. Tübingen, 1986.

KATZ, Jacob, *Out of the Ghetto*: *the Social Background of Jewish Emancipation, 1770–1870*. Cambridge, Mass., 1973.

LOEWENSTEIN, Steven M., *The Berlin Jewish Community. Enlightenment, Family and Crisis, 1770–1830*. Cambridge, Mass. 1973.

MEYER, Michael A., (Ed.), *Deutsch–Jüdische Geschichte der Neuzeit*. I–IV., München, 1996–1997.

MOSSE, George L., *German Jews beyond Judaism*. Bloomington, 1985.

MOSSE, Werner E. and Arnold PAUCKER (eds.), *Juden im Wilhelminischen Deutschland*. Tübingen, 1976.

PULZER, Peter, *Jews and the German State: The Political History of a Minority, 1848–1933*. Oxford, 1992.

RICHARZ, Monika, (Ed.), *Jüdisches Leben in Deutschland*, 3 vols. Stuttgart, 1967–1982.

SORKIN, David, *The Transformation of German Jewry 1780–1840*. New York 1987.

VOLKOV, Shulamit, "Die Juden in Deutschland 1780–1918", in *Enzyklopädie deutscher Geschichte,* vol. 16. München, 1994.

ZIMMERMANN, Moshe, "Die deutschen Juden 1914–1945", in *Enzyklopädie deutscher Geschichte,* vol. 43. München, 1997.

Great Britain

ENDELMAN, Todd M., *Radical Assimilation in English Jewish History, 1656–1945*. Bloomington, Ind., 1990.

FELDMAN, David, *Enlightenment and the Jews. Social Relations and Political Culture, 1840–1914*. New Haven, Conn., 1994.

FINESTEIN, Israel, *Anglo–Jewry in Changing Times : Studies in Diversity, 1840–1914*. London, 1999.

HOLMES, Collin, *Anti-Semitism in British Society, 1876–1939*. London, 1979.

POLLINS, Arnold, *Economic History of the Jews in England*. East Brunswick, NJ, 1982.

RUBINSTEIN, William D., *A History of the Jews in the English Speaking World : Great Britain*. Houndmills, 1996.

WASSERSTEIN, Bernard, *Britain and the Jews of Europe, 1939–1945*. London, 1979.

Hungary

BIBÓ, István, "La question juive en Hongrie après 1944" in id. *Misère des petits états d'Europe de l'est*, Paris, 1986, pp. 211–392.

BRAHAM, Randolph L. (ed.), *Hungarian–Jewish Studies*, 2 vols. New York, 1969.

BRAHAM, Randolph L., Bela, VAGO (eds.), *The Holocaust in Hungary. Forty Years later*. New York, 1985.

FEJTŐ, Francois, *Hongrois et Juifs. Histoire d'un couple singulier (1000–1997)*. Paris, 1997.

FROJIMOVICS, Kinga, Géza, KOMORÓCZY, Viktória PUSZTAI, Andrea STRIBIK, *Jewish Budapest*. 2 vols. Budapest, 1998.

GYURGYÁK, János, *A zsidókérdés Magyarországon. Politikai eszmetörténet*. [The Jewish question in Hungary. A political–intellectual history.] Budapest, 2001.

KARADY, Victor, *Juden in Ungarn : Identitätsmuster und Identitätsstrategien*, Leipzig, 1998.

KATZBURG, Nathaniel, *Hungary and the Jews: Policy and Legislation, 1920–1943*. Jerusalem, 1981.

McCAGG, William O., *Jewish Nobles and Geniuses in Modern Hungary*. New York, 1972.

PIETSCH, Walter, *Zwischen Reform und Orthodoxie. Der Eintritt des ungarischen Judentums in die moderne Welt*. Berlin,1999.

SILBER, Michael, (ed.), *Jews in the Hungarian Economy, 1760–1945*. Jerusalem, 1992.

ÚJVÁRI, Péter, *Magyar–zsidó lexikon* [Hungarian–Jewish Encyclopaedia]. Budapest, 1929.

Italy

Zakhor. Rivista di storia degli ebrei d'Italia. (Since 1997).

SIMONSOHN, Shlomo, (ed.), *Biblioteca italo–ebreica. Bibliografia par la storia degli ebrei in Italia, 1986–1995*. Roma, 1997.

Poland

Polin. (Since 1986)

ABRAMSZKY, C., JACHIMCZYK, M., POLONSKY, Anthony, (eds.), *The Jews in Poland*. Oxford, 1986.

EISENBACH, Artur, *The Emancipation of the Jews in Poland, 1780–1870*. Oxford, 1991.

GOLCZEWSKI, Frank, *Polnisch–Jüdische Beziehungen 1881–1922. Eine Studie zur Geschichte des Antisemitismus in Osteuropa*. Wiesbaden, 1981.

GUTMAN, Israel, Ezra, MENDELSOHN, Jehuda REINHARZ and Chone, SHMERUK (eds.), *The Jews of Poland between the Two World Wars*. Hannover & London, 1989.

HAUMANN, Heiko, *A History of East European Jews*, Budapest, 2002.

HELLER, Celia, *On the Edge of Destruction: Jews of Poland between the Two World Wars*. New York, 1977.

JELEN, Christian, *La purge. Chasse au Juif en Polgne populaire*. Paris, 1975.

KORZEC, Pawel, *Juifs en Pologne. La question juive entre les deux guerres*. Paris, 1980.

MARCUS, Joseph, *Social and Political History of the Jews in Poland, 1919–1939*. Amsterdam, 1983.

OPALSKI, Magdalena, BARTAL, Israel, *Poles and Jews. A Failed Brotherhood*. Hannover, London, 1992.

PALUCH, Andrzej J., KAPRALSKI, Slawomir, (ed.). *The Jews in Poland. Dedicated to Jozef A. Gierowski*. I–II. Krakow, 1999.

Romania

BRAHAM, Randolph L., (ed.), *The Destruction of Romanian and Ukrainian Jews during the Antonescu Era*. Boulder, 1997.

BUTNARU, Ion C., *The Silent Holocaust. Romania and its Jews*. New York, 1992.

IANCU, Carol, *Les Juifs de Roumanie, 1866–1919. De l'exclusion à l'émancipation*. Aix-en-Provence, 1978.

NASTASA, Lucian, (ed.), *Minoritati etnoculturale. Marturii Documentare. Evrei din Romania (1945–1965)*. Cluj–Napoca, 2003. (A rich documentation on Communist Jewish policies, mostly in Romanian, partly in Hungarian.)

VOLOVICI, Léon, *National Ideology and Anti-Semitism: the Case of Romanian Intellectuals in the 1930s*. Oxford, 1992.

WELTER, Beate, *Die Judenpolitik der rumänischen Regierung, 1866–1888*. Frankfurt am Main, 1989.

Russia and the Soviet Union

BARON, Salo Wittmayer, *A History of Jews in Russia and Poland*. Beigenfield, NJ, 2000.

BARON, Salo Wittmayer, *The Russian Jews under Tsar and Soviets*. New York, 1964. 2nd edition 1976.

DAVIES, Norman, POLONSKY, Anthony, (eds.), *Jews in Eastern Poland and the USSR, 1936–1946*. London, 1991.

DUBNOW, Simon, *History of the Jews in Russia and Poland, from the Earliest Times until the Present Day*, 3 vols. Philadelphia, 1916–1920.

FRANKEL, Jonathan, *Prophecy and Politics: Socialism, Nationalism and the Russian Jews, 1862–1917*. Cambridge, 1981.

FRUMKIN, Jacob, Gregor, ARONSON and Alexis, GOLDEN-WEISER, *Russian Jewry (1860–1917)*. New York, 1966.

KLIER, John, *Russia Gathers Her Jews: The Origin of the 'Jewish Question' in Russia, 1772–1825*, 2 vols. Illinois, 1986.

KLIER, John, *Imperial Russia's Jewish Question, 1855–1881*. Cambridge, 1995.

LÖWE, Hans-Dietrich, *The Tsar and the Jews. Reform, Reaction and Anti-Semitism in Imperial Russia, 1772–1917*. Chur, 1993.

LUCKERT, Yelena, *Soviet–Jewish History, 1917–1991. An Annotated Bibliography*. New York, 1992.

PINCUS, Benjamin, *The Jews of the Soviet Union. The History of a National Minority*. Cambridge, 1988.

Scandinavia

Nordisk Judaistik. Scandinavian Jewish Journal. (Since 1975)

ELEZAR, Daniel, ADINA, W., WERNER, Simcha, *The Jewish Communities of Scandinavia. Sweden, Denmark, Norway, Finland*. Lanham, 1984.

Biographical Index

The characterizations are only intended to provide a succinct reference to individuals who may not be immediately familiar.